SHOWDOWN AT GUCCI GULCH

Lawmakers, Lobbyists, and the

Unlikely Triumph of Tax Reform

JEFFREY H. BIRNBAUM

ALAN S. MURRAY

With an Introduction by

Albert R. Hunt

Vintage Books
A Division of Random House
New York

First Vintage Books Edition, April 1988

Library of Congress Cataloging-in-Publication Data

Birnbaum, Jeffrey H., 1956–
Showdown at Gucci Gulch.
Includes index.
1. Taxation—Law and legislation—United States.
2. Income tax—Law and legislation—United States.
I. Murray, Alan S., 1954–   . II. Title.
[KF6289.B57   1988]   343.7304   87-45971
ISBN 0-394-75811-0 (pbk.)   347.3034

Manufactured in the United States of America

3579C8642

To our beloved personal exemptions:

DEBORAH AND MICHAEL;

AND LORI

Acknowledgments

This book was made possible by the generous and unfailing support of Albert R. Hunt, the Washington bureau chief of *The Wall Street Journal*. He guided the *Journal*'s day-to-day coverage of the legislation itself and remained, through to the completion of the book, the best-informed tax reporter in Washington. As the manuscript's first editor, he saved the authors from making some embarrassing mistakes and allowed them to take credit for his insights.

The authors also would like to thank the senior editors of *The Wall Street Journal*, particularly Norman Pearlstine, the managing editor, for encouraging comprehensive coverage of the tax bill, for permitting the leave of absence during which this book was written, and for making the *Journal*'s resources available during that period.

Throughout the writing of this book, we received invaluable help from Terence Patrick Moran, who provided crucial research and editing assistance, and who was always able to find the answers to the questions that stumped us. We also owe a debt of gratitude to Linda Himelstein, who gave up her summer weeks at the beach to contribute to the research effort. And our lives were made much easier by our speedy transcriber, Jamie Richardson. We also thank our attorney, Robert Barnett, of Williams and Connolly.

Like all reporters, we are indebted to our editors. Peter Osnos of Random House deserves special thanks for coming to us with the idea for this book and for taking the lead in keeping our effort on track and turning two daily journalists into book writers. But we must also thank those who guided us in our work at the *Journal:* Paul Steiger, Ken Bacon, Bob McGilvray, Walter Mossberg, and Henry Oden and his skilled editors.

We owe a great deal, of course, to our sources. Since most of the tax story took place behind closed doors, they became our eyes and ears in reporting this story. Many prefer to remain anonymous, but we give them all our heartfelt gratitude. This is their book. And special thanks to those on congressional staffs, at the Joint Tax Committee, and at the Treasury Department, who took time out of their busy days to explain complicated tax matters to two green reporters.

Special thanks to the readers of our manuscript: Richard Fenno and James Wetzler. Thanks also to Willis Gradison, Catherine Porter, William Wilkins, and John Wilkins.

Writing a book is no easy task, and it would not have been possible without the support of our families. We are grateful to our parents, who deserve credit for the best we have achieved, but no blame for the rest: Esther Birnbaum, Earl Birnbaum, Catherine Murray, and John Murray. We also thank other members of our families, including Ezra Franks, Rhoda and Norman Galembo, Lucy Mele, and Erich Alan Murray.

Most important, we thank our wonderful wives, who supported us throughout this project and who contributed many suggestions that led to the improvement of the book: Deborah Birnbaum and Lori Esposito Murray.

Contents

Acknowledgments vii

Introduction by Albert R. Hunt xi

Note on Sources xix

Chronology xxi

1. Showdown 3

2. The Beginnings 23

3. The Horse You Rode in On 42

4. A Politician Comes to the Treasury 65

5. "Write Rosty" 96

6. The Phoenix Project 126

7. The Bear Takes One in the Back 152

8. The Gucci Boys' Revenge 176

9. The Two-Pitcher Lunch 204

10. Politics Is Local 234

11. The Running Shoes and the Sledgehammer 253

Epilogue 284

*Appendix A: The Evolution of Major Provisions
Affecting Individuals* 294

*Appendix B: The Evolution of Major Provisions
Affecting Businesses* 296

Index 297

Introduction

by Albert R. Hunt

The Tax Reform Act of 1986 was the best political story of its time, full of suspense, and with a vivid cast of characters. It marked the most significant achievement of the second Reagan administration. Indeed, in the history of the Republic, very few pieces of legislation have more profoundly affected so many Americans.

This saga was all the more dramatic because it was so unlikely. When the Ninety-ninth Congress convened, tax reform barely was on the agenda. Ronald Reagan, of course, won a resounding reelection victory in 1984, but so did 95 percent of incumbent congressional Democrats, many of whom had spent the previous four years challenging the president. The only tax message in that campaign was a rejection of Walter F. Mondale's call for a tax increase. The issue of tax reform never was joined in that campaign; so clearly no consensus on what to do could be formed.

Further, most political scientists, lawmakers, and informed analysts were convinced that radical or fundamental change was impossible. Even the first Reagan term produced only a modest amount of really significant change, and second terms traditionally are less productive. Above all, any fundamental change that affected the powerful, growing special interests seemed a political pipe dream. The importance of special-interest campaign contributions caused many to suggest that this was the "best Congress money could buy."

The 1986 tax bill endured a roller-coaster existence for almost two years. Tax reform never has been easy, and its rare successes have been aberrational. In 1969 Congress cracked down on abuses by foundations and initiated a minimum tax for the wealthy, but only after outgoing Treasury Secretary Joseph Barr caused a national uproar when he revealed that hundreds of millionaires didn't pay any income taxes. In 1975, the oil depletion allowance was repealed for major oil companies, but only after long gas lines and soaring prices made the oil industry public enemy number one.

That this measure even was considered defied the conventional wisdom. No modern president has so opposed the concept of corporate taxes or had as many rich friends who benefited from tax loopholes as Ronald Reagan. Yet the Reagan tax-reform initiative involved the largest corporate tax increase in history and the most drastic crackdown on loopholes for the affluent.

On Capitol Hill, there was never much enthusiasm for the measure, reflecting, in part, what the lawmakers were hearing at home. Most of their constituents viewed the current tax system as a disgraceful sop to the privileged, but this never translated into public support for any tax-reform proposal. A skeptical public generally felt that as bad as the current tax system was, any changes probably would compound the inequities and increase taxes for the average citizen.

And there were powerful economic and political interests arrayed against any sweeping changes in the tax law. While the public opposed special tax breaks for the other guy, attitudes changed when it came to provisions that might benefit them: home-mortgage deductions, write-offs for charitable contributions, or union dues.

Even when it came to the hundreds of loopholes benefiting only the narrower and wealthier interests, the politics were difficult. Many Americans resent these special tax breaks, but their elimination is not a top priority for them. The intensity of the beneficiaries of such favors, however, is overwhelming. They marshall sophisticated economic arguments on the economic cataclysms that would result in changing the tax code; some of these claims are even legitimate. If those arguments fail, many of these interests are able to muster something even more persuasive to certain lawmakers: money in the form of campaign contributions.

Money is the engine that fuels much of our politics. A few simple facts: From 1974 to 1984 the money spent on House general elections soared to $182.9 million from $45.1 million, more than a fourfold increase; in the Senate it skyrocketed in the same period to $146.7 million from $28.9 million. The average winner in 1974 House contests spent about $75,000; in 1984, that same typical victor spent almost $300,000. In 1984, Senate winners averaged almost $3 million per race, with North Carolinian Jesse Helms alone spending $17 million. Most politicians spend enormous time raising these funds; rarely does a night go by in Washington without a political fundraiser populated chiefly by special interests.

Nowhere are vested interests, through their political action committees, more omnipresent than in tax writing. The possibility of a sweeping tax bill that would touch virtually all these interests brought the campaign money merchants out in droves. In 1985, when the tax-writing panels were considering tax reform, political action committees gave $6.7 million to fifty-six members of the House Ways and Means and Senate Finance committees, according to a reliable survey by the self-styled citizens lobby Common Cause. This was two and a half times more money than was given to members of the same committees two years earlier. Where did the money come from? Insurance companies, banks, oil-and-gas interests, real estate, big Wall Street investment concerns, and labor unions, to name a few— all the groups that would be affected by the tax-reform initiative.

But as Alan Murray and Jeffrey Birnbaum demonstrate, these obstacles were overcome by some very forceful political personalities and a very powerful idea. One of the more unusual heroes stands as the very antithesis of the fat cats who so often dominate Washington: Bob McIntyre, the young Ralph Nader–trained, labor union–backed tax-reform advocate whose studies showing corporate nonpayment of taxes were a catalyst for this entire endeavor.

Then there were the political heavyweights: On Capitol Hill, there was Dan Rostenkowski, a longtime Chicago machine politician who learned the legislative process at the knee of Wilbur Mills, the legendary chairman of the Ways and Means Committee and the bane of most tax reformers. In the Senate, there was Bob Packwood, the smart Finance Committee chairman whose brand of Republican moderation—conservative on business issues, liberal on social issues—saw the tax code as a critical vehicle for economic and social goals.

These two veteran lawmakers were unlikely heroes of tax reform, but ultimately their political prowess and reputation rested on its success; in a political institution, that counts far more than philosophy. Yet both Rostenkowski and Packwood almost blew their opportunities on several occasions.

In the House, Rostenkowski's vaunted toughness started to crumble as even some of his closest allies began to desert him. In the end, the veteran lawmaker pulled it off with a deal that infuriated the Reagan administration but enabled him to get a bill sufficiently attractive that the White House couldn't disown it.

In the Senate, the political venality of the Finance Committee surfaced as the panel dismembered every remnant of tax reform and actually began approving new loopholes. Packwood almost beat a strategic retreat at a critical moment, but with the encouragement of a couple of pitchers of beer, he and his top aide decided to gamble instead on a bold but highly risky approach.

In the Reagan administration, the cast of characters was as improbable. Few of the rich Wall Street set suspected that Donald Regan, one of their own, would propose killing most of the tax breaks that enabled some of them to avoid paying taxes. Later the initiative would be shepherded by Treasury Secretary James Baker, a man whose political professionalism was antithetical to "reform" efforts and whose main interest in taxes had been to protect the Texas oil-and-gas interests that would surely be clipped by any tax-reform measure. The guiding strategic thinker was Deputy Treasury Secretary Richard Darman, a man with New England blue-blooded roots who could see the populist appeal of this undertaking, and a political intellectual whose public-policy insights were rivaled only by an ego that was large even by Washington standards.

These top principals all had their shortcomings and made their share of mistakes. Don Regan's political handling of the measure was inept from the inception; nevertheless, without his steadfast determination, the bill would have died several times along the way to passage. Jim Baker's loyalty to his Texas oil-and-gas buddies made some enemies and rarely picked up any converts to the tax-reform banner, but without Baker's political instincts and skills, which were second to none, there would have been no bill. Dick Darman's intellectual arrogance sometimes threatened the fragile support for this measure, but his rare appreciation of both the politics and the substance of this undertaking provided indispensable assistance to key lawmakers at critical moments.

Finally, there were two pivotal figures, both of whom made lots of money at a young age in the entertainment field and paid what they thought were confiscatory tax rates. This would motivate these two very disparate men to push tax reform with a resoluteness and intensity without which the measure clearly would have died.

The first was Bill Bradley: Rhodes scholar, former star forward for the New York Knickerbockers professional basketball team, and the U.S. senator from New Jersey. In 1982 Bradley proposed a sharp reduction in tax rates accompanied by a dramatic broadening of the base by eliminating many tax preferences. The idea received scant attention at first, but Bradley, with the same dedication and determination that made him a basketball legend, persevered, even though in a major blunder, the 1984 Democratic presidential nominee, Walter Mondale, rejected the Bradley approach. Like many of his liberal soulmates, Bradley believed the tax code was unfair and full of loopholes that made the economy less efficient, but he also appreciated the need for a tax system that encouraged entrepreneurialism and economic growth. He won the confidence of skeptics ranging from Don Regan to Jack Kemp to Dan Rostenkowski to Bob Packwood. At every critical juncture Bradley stepped in to provide an important push; rarely has a legislator with no formal leadership role or committee chairmanship played such an instrumental role in a major piece of legislation.

The other pivotal figure was Ronald Wilson Reagan, who abhorred high tax rates even back when he was a Democrat. The president's ignorance of the specifics of his own proposal was startling; throughout, he misrepresented or misunderstood the measure's tax increase on business. But President Reagan's attachment to lower rates was real and his commitment to the concept of this tax reform was even more powerful than his ignorance of the details. He never quite convinced the public, but his political persona and communicative skills commanded such respect that they scared off a lot of potential opponents. Only a few years ago, intelligent men and women were lamenting that our political system doesn't work, that presidents can't govern in a first term because they're fixated on reelection and can't govern in the second term because they become almost-instant lame ducks. Reagan refuted the former contention in his first term, and the passage of the sweeping tax bill in 1986 refuted the latter.

The coalition put together to support this measure borrowed from two important, but quite different, movements. The first was that of the tax reformers of the 1960s and 1970s, mainly liberal Democrats, guided by the late Stanley Surrey of the Harvard Law School and Joseph Pechman of the Brookings Institution. These liberals made compelling cases against an inequitable and inefficient tax code ridden by special-interest loopholes. But, more often than not, they wanted to close these loopholes to raise taxes, a losing political proposition.

The other group was the supply-siders, launched by economist Arthur Laffer and popularized by Congressman Jack Kemp in the late 1970s. They convincingly argued that cutting marginal tax rates would significantly enhance incentives and productivity; an important convert was Ronald Reagan. But they rarely talked about closing any existing tax preferences in the process; thus the rate cuts would inevitably lose revenue at a time of huge budget deficits, also an unacceptable political proposition.

Merging the lower rates of the supply-siders with the base broadening of the liberal tax reformers was the glue that held the 1986 tax bill together. Neither the supply-siders nor the liberals trusted one another, and each periodically examined the bill with an eye to understanding why their ideological adversary supported it. But both agreed it was preferable to the existing situation.

The ability of this unholy alliance to stick together throughout an arduous process—ironically with two former professional athletes, Democrat Bill Bradley and Republican Jack Kemp, as the political point men—was the key to success.

What emerges in this story, and in this book, is a fascinating human dynamic. Readers learn a lot about complicated aspects of the tax code, some of which are surprisingly interesting. They also see important institutions—Congress, the Treasury, the business lobbying forces, even the outgunned public-policy advocates—at work. And there are the human dimensions—the Bob McIntyres, the Dick Darmans, the Jim Bakers, the Dan Rostenkowskis, the Bob Packwoods, the Jack Kemps, the Bill Bradleys, and above all, the Ronald Reagans—that provide the real sustenance of this story.

Above all, this is a drama about a powerful idea whose time arrived to the surprise of many so-called insiders.

In our system, Congress, especially the House, with little party discipline or ideological rigidity, is often like a seamless web of floating coalitions. This was vividly present in the making of the tax bill; the conservative president's initiative was supported by some liberal Democrats and opposed by some conservative Republicans. The way the leading opponents and proponents tried to piece together a winning coalition, with help from the narrow-interest groups, made this an exciting saga.

To be sure, the way this legislation was fashioned, careening between extinction and dramatic revival, wasn't a very neat or efficient process; the dance of legislation rarely is. In the last century Bismarck observed that two things one never should watch being made are sausage and legislation. Compared to the Tax Reform Act of 1986, a sausage factory is tidy and orderly.

Moreover, the ultimate impact remains uncertain. Prominent economists like Alan Greenspan remain ambivalent as to how it will affect the economy; the initial consensus is it will be a small negative in the short run and a slight plus over the longer haul. It is, however, easy to find distinguished economists who disagree with both those scenarios. Political analyst Kevin Phillips is convinced the bill ultimately will prove a political loser; in the 1986 Congressional elections the most sweeping tax legislation ever passed by Congress was barely mentioned.

Whatever the economic and political effects, the tax-reform bill is a monumental piece of social legislation. It takes more than four million poor people off the federal income tax rolls, the most important antipoverty measure enacted over the past decade. And the attack on individual and corporate tax shelters makes it unlikely that wealthy individuals or businesses will be able to escape paying any taxes and thus might restore some of the eroding confidence Americans feel in the tax system.

In economic, political, social, and human terms, this bill touches most Americans in a significant way. This legislation and its impact will be debated for years; it may even become one of those rare defining issues in the American political system.

In this book Jeffrey Birnbaum and Alan Murray give us a factual and fascinating blueprint for appreciating and understanding how and why this historic measure became the law of the land, the same sort of insights they displayed in *The Wall Street Journal* for two years. I am the *Journal*'s Washington bureau chief, but other more detached observers credit Birnbaum and Murray with very special reporting that enabled the entire range of interests—rich and poor, business and labor, consumer and investor, scholar and practitioner—to follow, in vivid detail, one of the most remarkable legislative feats in years.

The authors brought different perspectives to this task. Birnbaum covered the Congress, spending most of his waking—and a few sleeping—hours in the corridors of the tax-writing committees, alternating between Gucci-clad lobbyists, earnest and sometimes naïve young staff assistants, and the elected politicians who so closely mirror this heterogeneous melting pot of a nation. Murray viewed it from downtown Washington: the executive branch with top political appointees exercising more influence and impact than they ever dreamed, the still-entrenched bureaucracies, and the business interests that were so affected by any major change in the tax system.

These two bright, industrious young journalists genuinely appreciate and believe in the political process and politicians, as well as understand that an informed public is the centerpiece of democratic government.

Note on Sources

This narrative reflects the fruit of the nearly three years we both spent covering the tax bill for *The Wall Street Journal,* from the time the Treasury began its work in early 1984 until the bill was signed in October 1986. In addition to our reporting for the paper, we spent nearly 150 hours in the summer and fall of 1986 interviewing those who were responsible for this legislative achievement. All of the principal actors in the drama—including James Baker, Bill Bradley, Richard Darman, Bob Packwood, Donald Regan, and Dan Rostenkowski—were generous in giving their time to ensure that our story was complete and accurate. We interviewed at length all of the major participants in the reform effort except President Reagan, who in late 1986 was preoccupied with the Iranian arms crisis.

Some of the dialogue in the book is taken from transcripts of proceedings; other dialogue is based on the recollections of people interviewed or on the notes of people present at the meetings. Wherever possible, the dialogue has been confirmed by more than one source. In cases where the accuracy of the dialogue is open to question, we have explicitly identified the source. Whenever people are said in the text to have "thought" something, the source for that information is the person who was doing the thinking. Nothing in the book has been invented; it is a carefully documented story.

In addition to our own reporting, we have relied heavily on the work of our many colleagues at the *Journal* who had a hand in the tax coverage. Especially helpful were Paul Blustein, who led the coverage during the inception of the tax plan in the Treasury Department; Brooks Jackson, who provided invaluable stories on the role of campaign contributions in the tax debate; Monica Langley, whose work on tax lobbying was especially useful; and also David Rogers, David Shribman, John Yang, Laurie McGinley, Rose Gutfeld, Jane Mayer, and many others.

We also owe a debt to reporters at other publications whose excellent reporting enriched our efforts. These include Pamela Fessler and Eileen Shanahan of *Congressional Quarterly;* Dale Russakoff and Anne Swardson of *The Washington Post;* Gary Klott and David Rosenbaum of *The New York Times;* Mark Kirchmeier, a Washington writer; and Jeffrey Levey of the Bureau of National Affairs. On matters of tax history, we have relied greatly on the work of John Witte at the University of Wisconsin and Joseph Pechman at the Brookings Institution. For historical information on members of Congress, we have made use of *Politics in America*, edited by Alan Ehrenhalt, and *The Almanac of American Politics*, by Michael Barone and Grant Ujifusa.

Chronology

1982

August 5: Senator Bill Bradley and Representative Richard Gephardt introduce their Fair Tax Act, the Democratic version of tax reform.

1984

January 25: President Ronald Reagan calls for a Treasury study of tax reform in his State of the Union address.

April 26: Representative Jack Kemp and Senator Robert Kasten introduce the Republican version of tax reform.

November 27: Treasury Secretary Donald Regan unveils Treasury I.

1985

January 8: Secretary Regan and White House Chief of Staff James Baker swap jobs.

May 28: President Reagan and Chairman Dan Rostenkowski of the House Ways and Means Committee appear on national television to endorse tax reform.

May 29: President Reagan unveils his own plan, which is the handiwork of Secretary Baker and Deputy Treasury Secretary Richard Darman.

October 1: After a summer's worth of hearings, the House Ways and Means Committee begins serious drafting sessions, using a plan devised by its staff as the starting point.

October 15: The committee nearly kills reform by voting to expand a tax break for commercial banks.

October 23: The bank vote is reversed after Rostenkowski agrees to retain the deduction for state and local taxes.

November 23: The Ways and Means Committee approves its version of tax reform without the endorsement of President Reagan.

December 11: House Republicans stage a rebellion that defeats the "rule" on the House floor, preventing the tax-reform bill from being considered.

December 16: President Reagan comes to Capitol Hill to make a personal plea to the GOP to keep tax reform alive.

December 17: The House passes the Tax Reform Act by voice vote.

1986

March 19: The Senate Finance Committee begins drafting a tax-reform bill, using a plan devised by its chairman, Bob Packwood, as the starting point.

April 18: Packwood withdraws his tax plan, battered by special-interest amendments, and goes to lunch with his aide Bill Diefenderfer to consider the alternatives.

April 24: Packwood unveils a new, low-tax-rate plan to his members.

April 25: Packwood disowns the new plan and blames it on David Brockway, the director of the Joint Committee on Taxation.

April 29: Packwood unveils revised approaches with a top individual tax rate of no more than 27 percent.

May 7: The Finance Committee approves its tax plan by a unanimous 20–0 vote.

June 4: The Senate begins to debate tax reform.

June 24: The Senate passes tax reform by a vote of 97–3.

July 17: The House-Senate conference begins with Rostenkowski as chairman.

August 12: With the conferees at an impasse, Senator Russell Long suggests the two chairmen go off by themselves to draft the legislation.

August 16: The conference report, the final version of tax reform, is approved.

September 25: The House affirms the bill by a vote of 292–136.

September 27: The Senate passes the bill and sends it to President Reagan by a vote of 74–23.

October 22: President Reagan signs the Tax Reform Act of 1986 in a ceremony on the South Lawn of the White House.

SHOWDOWN
AT GUCCI GULCH

Chapter 1

Showdown

The clerk will call the roll for final passage . . .

It is twenty minutes past midnight on the morning of Wednesday, May 7, 1986, and the Senate Finance Committee has been working almost nonstop since early the previous morning. Under the glare of television lights, the twenty powerful senators seated around the semicircular hearing table show signs of fatigue. Some droop back in their chairs, others lean forward, propping their heads in their hands. Committee Chairman Bob Packwood's high forehead glistens with sweat, and his eyes are dark and sunken. Next to Packwood, the committee's ranking Democrat, Senator Russell Long—son of legendary Louisiana populist Huey Long and a Washington legend himself—wears dark glasses to protect his eyes from the lights.

Despite the late hour, the marble-lined committee room is packed to the doors with people, and guards are stationed at the entrance to stop more from pushing in. Deputy Treasury Secretary Richard Darman sits near the front of the room, facing the senators, his brown hair combed straight back and his face stone-serious. Surrounding him are the staffs of the Treasury Department, the congressional Joint Committee on Taxation, and the Finance Committee. Reporters sit cheek-by-jowl around two tables not far from the door, and the remainder of the room is filled with lobbyists—lots of lobbyists.

There is a sort of hierarchy to the tax lobbyists who swarm about the

Dirksen Senate Office Building on this spring night. Those with seats in the committee room tend to be mostly notetakers. They are the lobbyists' front guard, the younger lawyers and legal assistants whose job it is to get up at sunrise and stand in long lines to make certain they secure seats in the crowded committee room. Other less eager and more highly paid note-takers fill a large auditorium two floors below. The auditorium is wired for sound, and the lobbyists listen to the proceedings while munching on take-out pizza and Dunkin' Donuts. The room has been occupied by too many people for too long, and it smells faintly like a gymnasium. A few of the lobbyists smoke and play poker at a table on the auditorium stage; others doze in the back. The room is at once raucous and somber; it has the strange aura of a wake.

In the hallway outside the committee room, more lobbyists stand ner-vously, like so many expectant fathers crowded into the waiting room of a maternity ward. These hallway loiterers include the top ranks of Wash-ington's tax lobbying world—men and women who are paid $200, $300, even $400 an hour to influence legislators and preserve tax benefits worth millions of dollars to their anxious clients. They lean against the walls and talk among themselves, trading bits of gossip. "Did you hear?" says one. "They changed the effective date for the investment credit." The whispered message travels quickly down one side of the long hallway and echoes back up the other. A few of the lobbyists huddle around the back door of the committee room, hoping to catch a senator coming in or going out, hoping for one last chance to make a pitch before the vote. The desperation in their voices makes it clear that *big* money is at stake. Their expensive suits and shiny Italian shoes give this hallway its nickname: Gucci Gulch.

Until two weeks ago, most of these lobbyists were still betting that tax reform would never happen. It was too bold, they thought, too radical. It proposed wiping out a multitude of special-interest tax breaks in return for sharp cuts in tax rates. That would be a boon to the great mass of people who pay their taxes each year without taking advantage of these deductions, exclusions, and credits. But it would be a disaster for the many business interests and high-income individuals who have come to depend on tax favors from Congress. It is those groups, the lobbyists thought, who control Washington. They have the power, the money, and the influence. They are the ones who hire lobbyists.

Then again, the lobbyists were wrong about President Reagan. They thought he would never back a tax-overhaul effort that stepped on the toes of countless Republican business constituents. But he did. And they were wrong about the Democratic House: Defying everyone's predictions, the House too approved a sweeping tax-reform bill shortly before Christmas the year before. Nevertheless, until just two weeks ago, the lobbyists were still betting that the Finance Committee would bury the effort. The com-mittee, after all, was the lobbyists' best friend. Its members were the authors of countless tax breaks that aided favored constituents; they were the recipients of millions of dollars in campaign contributions from groups determined to defeat reform. The conventional wisdom in Washington was that this Senate committee would certainly send tax reform to its grave.

But in the early morning hours of May 7, all bets are off. Something strange has been happening in the back rooms of the Dirksen Building over the past two weeks. Working privately, out of the public eye, Chairman Packwood and a handful of his committee members have undergone a remarkable conversion. They have prepared a reform plan even more radical than the one passed by the Democratic House: a plan that cuts back a wide swath of special-interest tax breaks and lowers the top statutory tax rate to 27 percent, the lowest of any major industrialized nation. It is without a doubt the most significant reform in the history of the income tax. It removes millions of low-income workers from the income-tax rolls, eliminates most tax shelters and ensures that profitable corporations and wealthy people pay at least some tax. If enacted, it would affect the lives and pocketbooks of virtually every American.

The clerk slowly calls out the names of the senators:

Senator Dole.

The dark-eyed legislator from Kansas is the majority leader of the Senate, and his vote strongly influences other Republicans on the committee. He has been critical of tax reform in the past, arguing that it does nothing to help ease the nation's biggest problem—a huge budget deficit—but he is caught up in the momentum of the past two weeks. "I want to thank the chairman for this historic effort," he says, "and I vote aye."

Senator Roth.

Senator Danforth.

As the clerk calls out the names of the Republicans, moving along the table from the most senior to the most junior member, it gradually becomes clear that all of them, even those who have been hostile to the bill all along, are voting aye.

"There, that's good work," whispers Dole to the chairman, as all eleven Republicans vote for the unprecedented tax measure.

Then come the Democrats:

Senator Long.

The Louisiana lawmaker, his sunglasses now laid aside, also gives a nod to Chairman Packwood, who is sitting to his right. Long chaired the committee for fifteen years before the Republicans took control of the Senate in 1981, and he labored hard to enact many of the tax incentives that the tax-reform bill now threatens to eliminate. But he too has become a reformer. "Like Senator Dole, I want to congratulate the chairman for the fantastic work he's done on this bill, and I vote aye," he says.

The clerk calls the names of the Democratic senators in order of seniority, and again only ayes are heard. By the time the voting gets to Senator Bill

Bradley of New Jersey, one of the most junior members of the committee, there still has not been a single dissent. The former basketball player has a proud, almost smug look on his face when his name is called. He authored a version of tax reform four years ago; he is, as Senator Packwood will later say, the "godfather" of reform. He pauses a moment and nods his head approvingly before answering aye.

The last two Democrats cast their votes, and a flush comes over Chairman Packwood's face. His dramatic proposal is not only going to win, it is going to win unanimously. No one expected that. No one thought that his committee—of all committees—could muster even a majority for such a radical bill, much less unanimous support. The chairman is the last to vote, and as he does, tears begin to well up in his eyes. He gives a slow, solemn aye.

Senator Chafee rises quickly to his feet and begins to applaud the chairman. Other senators and staff aides follow suit. Even the lobbyists in the back of the room, unable to avoid the sweep of sentiment, join in the applause. Packwood grabs the hands of Dole and Long and thrusts them into the air in a show of victory. Then he looks down at his desk, choked with emotion.

In the hallway outside, and in the auditorium two floors below, there is mostly silence. A few groans are heard. Many of the lobbyists have clients who will lose hundreds of thousands, millions, even billions of dollars as a result of that 20–0 vote. The same questions buzz through their heads: How did it happen? Why did so many special interests go down in flaming defeat? How could the usual ways of Washington be turned on their head?

As they listen to the applause, many of the lobbyists are still confused by the remarkable turn of events. But one thing is clear to all of them: In the early hours of the morning of May 7, tax reform completed its transformation from the impossible to the inevitable.

The income tax was enacted three quarters of a century ago in an attempt to bring fairness to the tax system. At the close of the nineteenth century, the government raised all of its revenue from tariffs and excise taxes, which placed a heavy burden on low-income Americans. "If taxation is a badge of freedom," stormed income tax advocate William Jennings Bryan in a fiery 1894 House debate, "let me assure my friend that the poor people of this country are covered all over with the insignia of freedom."

Bryan fought for an income tax, but was thwarted in 1895, when the Supreme Court ruled that the levy was unconstitutional. The debate raged for nearly two decades, but in 1913 the Sixteenth Amendment to the Constitution was ratified and the income tax became law.

The idea was to tax people according to their ability to pay, and income was considered the best measure of that ability. From the start, however, Congress made exceptions to that basic principle, allowing special treatment for income that was used for certain purposes or that came from certain sources.

Payments for mortgage interest and state and local taxes, for instance, were made deductible by the 1913 law. Farmers were allowed immediate write-offs for their equipment investments in 1916. Charitable contributions were made deductible in 1917. Military benefits were excluded in 1918. The special tax treatment of capital-gains income earned from the sale of assets, such as securities or real estate, was enacted by Congress in 1921. Employers' contributions to pension funds were excluded from taxable income in 1926. The list of special deductions, exclusions, and credits grew and grew, as Congress, acting at the behest of various interest groups, found more and more reasons to make exceptions to the original principle of the income tax.

Tax rates were boosted to help finance World War I and again to finance World War II. After the wars, Congress was slow to lower the rates, choosing instead to give back money through ever more tax breaks. The steady erosion of the income tax base became a landslide in the late 1970s and early 1980s. High rates of inflation increased the tax burden on individuals and businesses in various subtle ways, and as a result, the clamor for special tax breaks reached a furious pitch. In 1981, the Reagan administration and Congress bowed to these pressures and enacted a tax bill that not only cut tax rates, but also included the biggest package of tax breaks for business in history. By 1984, even Trappist monks were petitioning Congress for special treatment, asking that they be allowed to use the lucrative investment credit. "We'd like to have it," said Father John Baptist, bookkeeper of the Trappist Abbey in Lafayette, Oregon, "because everyone else has it."

Many of these tax preferences were enacted with the best of intentions. They were supposed to provide "incentives," promoting laudable social or economic goals, but the sheer volume of the breaks became a menace. As the list expanded, the code became like a giant Swiss cheese with too many holes. It was on the verge of collapse.

The astonishing dimensions of the problem were illustrated in a pamphlet published each year by the Joint Committee on Taxation. It listed federal "tax expenditures"—a term devised to show that tax breaks were really no different than direct government spending. In page after page of small type, the pamphlet showed the many ways in which the code deviated from the principle of taxing all income equally, the many ways in which the government "spent" its revenue through tax breaks.

The list included tax credits for people who paid for child care or made contributions to political candidates. There were deductions that allowed people to escape taxes on the portions of their income that went to pay medical bills, adoption expenses, or losses from theft. And there were various types of income that were simply excluded from taxation altogether, such as employer-paid fringe benefits, interest earned on life insurance, military disability payments, interest on municipal bonds, and ministers' housing allowances.

For businesses, the tax breaks were more complex. Tax experts agreed that a firm's legitimate business expenses should be subtracted from its revenues before arriving at the income subject to tax. But the definition of legitimate business expenses could be bent and twisted, and with the assistance of armies of tax lobbyists, Congress had found countless ways over the years to do just that. Oil and gas companies, for example, were able to write off certain costs of drilling successful wells in one year, even though the wells would produce oil or gas for many years—a ploy that saved the industry more than $14 billion a year in taxes. As an additional incentive, the law also allowed oil and gas firms to deduct a percentage of their gross income. Manufacturers, similarly, were able to save taxes by writing off investments in heavy equipment over five years, even though the equipment might last fifteen years or longer. Banks were allowed to deduct the money they put into "bad-debt reserves," even though those reserves were far larger than the amounts of money the banks actually lost to bad debts.

Dozens of other methods, all perfectly legal, were used to keep from paying taxes on business income. There was no end to the diversity of tax-avoidance schemes that Congress, with the help of clever lobbyists and tax lawyers, could devise.

The accumulated effect of all these tax breaks was breathtaking. The Joint Committee on Taxation concluded that by 1987, tax expenditures would cost the government $450 billion a year in lost revenue—more than the total amount the government would collect that year in individual income taxes!

The tax system became dangerously unbalanced. Some activities were taxed at extremely high rates; others faced no tax at all. Economic decisions by people and businesses were distorted by these variations in tax, and the result was to create enormous inefficiencies in the economy. Money poured into those businesses and investments that were favored by the tax system, and avoided those that were not. The tax system became an impediment in the workings of the market.

At the same time, the uneven tax system created significant disparities among taxpayers. Those who were fortunate or clever enough to benefit from the many loopholes reaped large benefits; those who were not paid a stiff penalty. Roscoe Egger, the commissioner of the Internal Revenue Service during the first five years of the Reagan administration, summed it up this way:

People were rapidly becoming disenchanted with the whole system. We began to see the emergence of tax protesters. Groups refused to file, backyard churches began to claim income as charitable contributions, tax shelters reached entirely different proportions. One couldn't fail to recognize that this was a reflection of deep-seated unhappiness with the entire tax system. By 1983 we even began to see people in the lower income levels, with incomes of only $18,000 or $20,000 a year, buying into phony tax shelters, private churches, master recordings, that sort of thing. They listened to this siren song and said, "Gee, everybody else is doing it. Why not me?"

Opinion polls showed that public dissatisfaction with the tax system was rising sharply and steadily. Horror stories about millionaires and large corporations that managed to pay no income taxes at all were common-place. Many Americans began to perceive that the U.S. income tax was not very "progressive." It seemed that the average man on the street paid a higher portion of his income in taxes than the typical millionaire paid, rather than the other way around.

Public perceptions of the income tax changed drastically. A 1972 poll by the Advisory Commission on Intergovernmental Relations showed that Americans generally viewed the federal income tax as fairer than state income taxes, state sales taxes, or local property taxes. But by 1985, the federal tax was judged in the same poll to be the least fair, by a long shot.

In part, this dissatisfaction with the tax system had its roots in the inflation of the 1970s: As wages and salaries rose to keep pace with prices, middle-income Americans found themselves pushed into higher and higher tax brackets, even though their new, inflated incomes bought no more at the grocery store than their old ones did. But mostly, the dissatisfaction re-flected a recognition of the proliferation of tax breaks.

Gary Hecht, an assistant school principal in New York City, expressed the sentiments of millions of taxpayers in a December 1984 discussion group conducted by *The Wall Street Journal*. "My feeling with the federal tax goes back to the same old story: The rich get richer, the poor stay poor, and the middle class gets poor too," he complained. "Because of the loopholes, this is going to constantly occur."

On tax day, April 15, 1985, Deputy Treasury Secretary Richard Darman gave a speech that highlighted the extent of the problem. Darman was the administration's top reform strategist, and he had a sharp mind that grasped both the politics and the substance of the issue.

The overwhelming majority of taxpayers eat lunch without being able to deduct their meals as business expenses. They buy baseball or hockey tickets without being able to enjoy the luxury of business-related skyboxes. They talk on fishing boats, but don't take the tax deduction for ocean-cruise seminars. They strain to pay interest on their home mortgages and may take the tax deduction for their pay-ments, but they can't quite figure out how others can invest in real estate shelters and get more back in tax benefits than is put at risk. They read that of those with gross income of over $250,000 before "losses," more than a fifth pay less than 10 percent in taxes; and of those with gross incomes over $1 million before "losses," a quarter pay 10 percent or less in taxes.

The phenomenal rise in tax shelters was a central part of the problem. These investments were structured to bunch several different tax incentives—interest deductions, rapid depreciation write-offs, low capital-gains rates, credits for rehabilitating buildings, credits for research and development—in ways that enabled investors to get several dollars in tax savings for every dollar they invested. Although precise figures are difficult to come by, tax-shelter sales are believed to have jumped from less than $2 billion in 1976 to over $20 billion in 1983.

Real estate partnerships were the most popular shelters. Under these schemes, investors made relatively modest contributions to a building project, and the tax-shelter partnership borrowed the rest of the money it needed. By deducting the interest and taking rapid depreciation write-offs, the partnership was able to show huge paper losses, which the investors divided among themselves and wrote off on their income tax returns. Thus, for an investment of only $10,000, a person in the 50-percent bracket might buy "losses" of $20,000 or more, saving $10,000 or more in taxes; and when the building was finally sold, the income would be taxed at the low capital-gains rate. It was an unbeatable deal—and perfectly legal.

These new tax schemes drastically altered the economics of the real estate business, making it possible for developers to build new office buildings even if the demand for office space was not strong. So-called see-through office buildings—structures with few tenants—became commonplace in cities like Houston, where the real estate market was driven by the desire for tax-sheltered investments rather than by the need for office space.

Oil and gas partnerships also attracted investors seeking to hide from the tax collector, and there were other, more exotic, tax shelters as well: cattle-feeding shelters, equipment-leasing shelters, boxcar shelters, billboard shelters, videotape shelters, even llama-breeding shelters. In Girdletree, Maryland, Bill Lilliston set up the Chincoteague Bay penny-oyster shelter, a scheme that he promised would reduce taxes, prevent prostate problems, and improve potency all at the same time. In California, a group of dentists invested thousands of dollars in jojoba beans, hoping to take large deductions during the three years it takes to determine whether a plant is female and could therefore bear more beans. The jojoba scam prompted an angry complaint from California Representative Fortney "Pete" Stark: "We shouldn't be giving tax breaks to anything that takes three years to figure out its sex."

The ultimate effects of this tax-shelter mania were dramatically illustrated in a 1985 study prepared by the Treasury Department for House Ways and Means Democrat J. J. "Jake" Pickle of Texas. The study showed that in 1983 alone, about thirty thousand taxpayers with earnings exceeding $250,000—including three thousand millionaires—paid less than 5 percent of their income in taxes. Little wonder that people felt the progressive tax was a fraud.

Expense-account living also irked the average taxpayer. People saw that their neighbors with well-paid accountants could find dozens of creative ways to beat the system. These clever taxpayers would deduct their Mercedes, their expensive meals, their country club dues, even their vacations. Ski resorts in places such as Vail, Colorado, offered "investment seminars." After a long day on the slopes, skiers could drop by the seminars, fix a cocktail, and watch a videotape telling them how to make tax-shelter investments; they could then deduct the trip as an investment expense. The average taxpayer was, in effect, subsidizing ski trips for investors who wanted to learn more about escaping taxes!

Confidence in the tax system was further undermined by the fact that U.S. corporations were paying an ever-smaller share of the nation's tax burden. Over three decades, the corporate contribution to government revenues had plummeted from 25 percent in the 1950s to just over 6 percent in 1983; the 1981 tax bill brought the corporate tax near extinction. "It's like Alice's Cheshire Cat," joked Van Doorn Ooms, chief economist for the House Budget Committee. "Everything's gone but the grin."

The decline in corporate taxes was highlighted in 1982 when a controversy broke out over the so-called lease-a-tax-break law, a provision in the 1981 tax bill. The scheme had been hatched by the Treasury Department, working in conjunction with a group of business lobbyists, and was designed to ensure that the generous new business breaks in the 1981 bill would help those companies that most needed them—companies suffering losses and therefore not paying any taxes. The provision allowed profitless companies to sell their tax breaks to profitable companies in a transaction known as a "safe-harbor lease."

Although it may have been sound in theory, the safe-harbor-leasing arrangement proved to be a political disaster in practice. The new law led to a frenzy of strange tax deals that outraged the public and their representatives in Congress: Global Marine reportedly sold tax benefits on oil rigs worth $135 million to Hilton Hotels. Ford Motor sold IBM the tax breaks on its entire $1 billion 1981 investment program, reportedly for a price of between $100 million and $200 million. Occidental Petroleum sold benefits on $94.8 million in investments, LTV sold breaks on $100 million in equipment, and Chicago & North Western sold tax benefits on $53 million worth of locomotives, freight cars, and other property. In each case, both the buyer and the seller benefited, and all at the taxpayers' expense.

The furor in Congress over the tax-break sales was swift and sharp. The safe-harbor-leasing provision was repealed, but not until after the affair had burned itself well into the public psyche.

An even bigger flap over corporate taxes was sparked in early October 1984, when a little-known public-interest lawyer named Robert McIntyre dropped a bombshell. Sitting at his computer in a cluttered little office in Washington, the scruffy McIntyre spent endless hours combing through the annual reports of the largest corporations of America. He calculated each company's domestic profit and how much federal income tax each actually paid. His result: 128 out of 250 large and profitable companies paid *no federal income taxes* in at least one year between 1981 and 1983. Seventeen of the companies paid no taxes in all three years.

The McIntyre list included the best-known names in corporate America: General Electric, Boeing, Dow Chemical, Lockheed, and others. In a particularly embarrassing revelation, the study showed that among the corporate freeloaders was W. R. Grace & Company, whose chairman, J. Peter Grace, had headed a commission for President Reagan that concluded that wasteful government spending was "sending the country down the tubes for future generations of Americans."

"Americans are wondering why the federal government is incurring the largest deficits in history even while they are paying the highest taxes ever," said McIntyre when his report was released. "This study documents one important answer: the demise of the corporate income tax."

The study made instant news. In Los Angeles, the *Herald Examiner* overlooked the American League play-offs to make this its banner headline: 128 BIG FIRMS PAID NO FEDERAL INCOME TAXES. A story in *Rolling Stone* magazine shouted in big bold letters: EARN A BILLION! PAY NO TAXES! Conservative columnist James J. Kilpatrick complained of "corporate welfare" and "AFDC: aid for dependent corporations." A labor leader at a rally in New Jersey held up a package of General Electric lightbulbs and said they had cost him more money than GE's entire contribution to the cost of government. And on national television, Democratic Senator Robert Byrd of West Virginia told of a woman in Milwaukee, "the mother of three children, who in 1983 earned $12,000. On that income she paid more in taxes than Boeing, GE, DuPont, and Texaco, all put together."

Other analysts had documented the decline in corporate taxes before, but never before had anyone named names. In the public mind, it became a powerful indictment of the income tax. "It's a scandal when members of the Fortune 500 pay less in taxes than the people who wax their floors or type their letters," McIntyre said.

Needless to say, McIntyre generated considerable irritation in corporate America. "His whole study is a pile of bunk," groused John R. Mendenhall, vice president for taxes at Union Pacific, which showed a slim 3.5-percent effective tax rate in the study. And even Whirlpool, which had the highest effective tax rate on McIntyre's list at 45.6 percent, was not particularly happy about the publicity. "It's a double-edged sword," explained Robert Kenney, the company's tax counsel. "We owe it to our shareholders to take legitimate and legal means to keep down taxes."

For McIntyre, who was trained by consumer advocate Ralph Nader, the publicity was ample return for the hours he spent deciphering corporate reports. He too was a lobbyist of sorts, working for a labor-funded group called Citizens for Tax Justice, which promoted the closing of corporate loopholes. Unlike the lobbyists who represented big business and other wealthy interests, he did not dine at plush, expense-account restaurants, nor did he spend much time buttonholing members of Congress. His $38,000 salary was a mere fraction of the much larger sums earned by his corporate lobbying foes.

No matter. In the tax debates ahead, Bob McIntyre's one-man report would turn out to be more influential than all the firepower the corporate lobbyists could muster.

The goal of tax reform was to eliminate or curtail as many tax expenditures as possible. To be sure, not all tax breaks could be eradicated: Some were politically immovable; others served critical social functions. But the tax code was badly in need of a housecleaning, and tax reform was intended to give it just that. Reform also promised a trade-off: Tax breaks for the few would be replaced with lower tax rates for everyone.

As appealing as the concept sounded, however, few in Washington thought it could be done. The groups with an interest in the existing tax system were well-organized and ready to defend their breaks at a moment's notice; the populace who stood to benefit from lower rates was unorganized and diffuse. Furthermore, Congress was a slow and cumbersome institution that usually made only piecemeal, incremental changes. Tax reform proposed something very different: a radical revamping of the entire tax structure. There was a tremendous inertia in Congress that resisted any such sweeping change. As a result, the conventional wisdom in Washington held that tax reform was destined to lose, and the conventional wisdom had plenty of history to back it up.

Tax breaks, after all, had always been part of the currency of Congress. Politicians liked to give them out; they did not like to take them back. The seventy-three-year history of the income tax had been a story of steady erosion in the tax base, with more and more loopholes being added and few being taken away. Indeed, the very structure of American government, with its checks and balances, argued against the success of such a bold plan. The American revolution had been fought largely over the question of who should have the power to tax: the King's appointed governors or the popularly elected legislatures. By putting the authority to tax into the hands of the legislature, the Constitution ensured that our tax system would become and remain a political potpourri. A parliamentary government might be able to fashion radical tax-reform legislation in the executive branch and be assured of its success in the loyal parliament, but the American system subjected such bills to the tugs and twists of 535 members of Congress, each with strong political interests to protect.

Idealists had tried with little success to eliminate loopholes almost from the day the income tax was enacted. One man even died trying: In 1956 Randolph Paul, a former Treasury tax expert, collapsed in the midst of telling a congressional hearing that the Eisenhower administration was using the tax code to stimulate business rather than just to collect revenue.

President John F. Kennedy also tried to launch an attack on the tax code and appointed Harvard law professor Stanley Surrey, an outspoken critic of tax breaks and incentives, to the Treasury's top tax post. Congressional opposition to Surrey's appointment was intense. The oil and gas industry, the mining industry, the savings-and-loan associations, and an army of others who benefited from the nation's cheesecloth tax system raised a storm of protest. Surrey's reception before the Senate Finance Committee was particularly hostile, with Chairman Harry Byrd of Virginia indignantly accusing him of harboring a low opinion of the nation's legislators. "You think that some of these tax laws were sneaked through Congress without the knowledge of a great many congressmen," Byrd charged. The senator assured Surrey that they were not.

In the face of such opposition, Kennedy's reform efforts wilted. His first tax bill, signed in October 1962, was designed to jump-start the economy rather than reform taxes. It included a huge new investment credit that subsidized the purchase of business equipment and became one of the biggest tax expenditures in the code, resulting in billions of dollars of lost revenue to the Treasury each year. The bill also contained a new provision, added by Congress, that created a deduction for lobbying expenses. Kennedy's second tax bill, introduced in early 1963, attempted to combine sharp cuts in tax rates with an array of Surrey's loophole-closing measures. Virtually all the loophole-closing provisions were abandoned or gutted, either by the Ways and Means Committee in the House or by the Finance Committee in the Senate.

The closest Congress ever came to enacting a broad reform of the income tax was in 1969. The measure got its start in early January of that year, thanks to Treasury Secretary Joseph Barr, who held the top Treasury post for only twenty-seven and a half days at the end of the Johnson administration. Shortly before leaving office, Barr testified on Capitol Hill of an impending "taxpayers' revolt," spurred on by increased public awareness of tax inequities. To ensure the fulfillment of his prophecy, he unveiled alarming Internal Revenue Service figures showing that 155 people with incomes over $200,000 had managed to pay no income taxes at all in 1967. The list, he said, included twenty-one millionaires.

That disclosure prompted a torrent of press coverage and a blizzard of indignant mail to members of Congress. The new president, Richard Nixon, was no friend of reform, but he immediately came under heavy pressure to embrace tax overhaul. After a long debate, a bill was crafted that repealed the investment credit, ended or curtailed a number of other tax breaks, and cracked down on tax-exempt foundations.

But the reforms of the 1969 bill were short-lived; subsequent legislation reopened most of the closed loopholes. In 1971, for instance, Congress voted to reinstate the investment credit and also approved new and more generous business investment write-offs, as well as a new tax break for export companies.

Congressional resistance to tax reform was symbolized by Senator Russell Long, who chaired the Finance Committee from January 1966 to December 1980. Scion of one of the nation's most colorful political dynasties, Long saw the tax code as his tool for changing society. He had no interest in reform. A wise student of human behavior, Long realized the losers from tax overhaul would make far more noise than the winners. "When we proceed to shift the taxes around so that one set of taxpayers pays a lot more taxes and somebody else pays a lot less taxes, the people who benefit from it do not remember it very long," Chairman Long said in 1976. "They tend to feel that it should have been that way all the time, and the people who are paying the additional taxes resent it very bitterly." On another occasion, the wily Louisiana Democrat gave an even more cynical assessment of reform. "I have always felt," he said, "that tax reform is a change in the tax law that I favor, or if it is the other man defining tax reform, it is a change in the tax law that he favors."

Reform-minded legislators attempted an end run past Long in 1975 and enacted legislation that cut back the oil depletion allowance, one of the largest and least-justified breaks in the tax code. But even then, Long succeeded in undermining the reformers' victory, restricting the change to the major oil companies and leaving the generous break intact for the prosperous independent producers in his state and elsewhere. Another failed attempt at reform was made in 1976, when the House passed a bill with a tough anti–tax-shelter provision, only to have it dropped by the Senate. (Ironically, the attempt to shut down tax shelters was stopped partly through the efforts of Senator Packwood of Oregon, who ten years later made a similar provision the foundation of his own tax-reform bill.)

Tax reformers breathed one last gasp in 1977 and 1978, during the presidency of Jimmy Carter. Carter made tax reform a cornerstone of his election campaign, calling the existing tax system "a disgrace to the human race" and "a welfare program for the rich." In an interview with *Fortune* magazine, the president said he thought the nation was "ready for comprehensive, total tax reform." While not divulging details, he said his plan would "eliminate hundreds of tax breaks and greatly reduce the tax rate." After taking office, Carter's treasury secretary, Michael Blumenthal, began publicly discussing some of the provisions under consideration, and they did indeed sound bold and sweeping. He floated the idea of eliminating the preferential treatment of capital gains, for example.

The response of interest groups to Carter's trial balloons was fierce and swift, and the administration's resolve was indeterminate. In the fall of 1977, Carter aides said they were "reshaping" the tax proposal to reflect changing budgetary, economic and political realities. When the plan was finally unveiled in January 1978, Carter's grand rhetoric boiled down to a few exceedingly modest reforms, such as cutting back on the "three-martini-lunch" deductions for business meals and entertainment. Even those modest measures were quickly ripped apart by Congress.

The bill finally enacted in 1978 was a complete renunciation of the Carter proposals and of any notion of tax reform. It included a host of new tax benefits. The Senate proved to be particularly generous, voting to expand many existing tax breaks and adding numerous new provisions targeted to help farmers, teachers, Alaskan natives, railroads, record manufacturers, the Gallo winery of California, and two Arkansas chicken farmers.

The defeat of President Carter's tax-reform efforts signaled a new era in tax policy, the triumph of a broad coalition of business lobbyists who came together under the rubric of "capital formation." These lobbyists argued that the best medicine for the faltering U.S. economy was to create new tax breaks for businesses and investors. They championed a provision in the 1978 law that enhanced the preferential treatment of capital-gains income, bringing the top tax rate on gains income down to 28 percent from the existing rate of 35 percent or more. Reformers complained that the special treatment for capital gains was unfair and fueled the growth of tax shelters, but the capital-formation coalition said the tax break would encourage investment and promote economic growth. The economy was in trouble, they argued, and lower capital-gains taxes were a solution. Tax reform was clearly out; "capital formation" was in. The influence of special interests in Congress had reached new heights.

The symbol of this new era was an elite group of Washington business lobbyists who in 1978 began meeting each Tuesday morning for breakfast at the Sheraton-Carlton Hotel in downtown Washington. Known among themselves as the "Carlton group," they were the cream of Washington tax lobbyists—highly paid representatives of the largest corporations and the most influential business organizations in America. They developed into a virtual fourth branch of government, devising new tax schemes that would eventually become the law of the land.

It was this pinstriped-suited group that gave birth to the biggest business tax break ever adopted—the accelerated cost recovery system, a loophole so large that it allowed many big, profitable corporations to slip through without paying a penny in corporate tax.

The reputed father of the Carlton group was a man named Charls E. Walker, an expatriate Texan who pronounced "corporate" like "carpet," and who became the slow-walking, smooth-talking embodiment of the capital-formation crowd. Walker, who was deputy treasury secretary under Nixon, ran a lobbying firm that represented dozens of major industrial clients, from the Aluminum Company of America to the Weyerhaeuser Company. All of them invested heavily in equipment, and all sought ways to reduce the tax burden on their investments. To provide research to back up his efforts, Walker also ran an organization known as the American Council for Capital Formation.

In Walker's view, encouraging business investment in equipment was the most important goal of tax policy. He told acquaintances that he viewed capital investment the way Mark Twain viewed good bourbon: "Too much is barely enough." He felt there should be no tax on corporate investment; indeed, he apparently had no qualms about outright tax subsidies for investment, and that is what his generous tax write-off scheme amounted to for some. His clients were the heart of smokestack America, and their power in the economy was declining rapidly, as foreign manufacturers grew more competitive and as the U.S. economy turned more toward services. His job was to get government to help halt that decline.

For Walker, promoting investment tax breaks was also good business. As a child in tiny Graham, Texas, he had sometimes slept on the porch when the family was able to rent out his room in their hotel for a night. But as a Washington lobbyist, he learned to live luxuriously. He was, in his own words, "a very diminutive millionaire," who could garner as much as $7,500 a speech, and who served on four corporate boards. He traveled in a large black limousine and smoked cigars nearly as large, called "Ultimates."

In 1980, Walker initially threw his support to fellow Texan John Connally, who was making a futile attempt for the Republican nomination for the presidency. But when Ronald Reagan won the nomination, Walker joined his team. He was asked to become Reagan's adviser on tax policy, and he jumped at the chance.

At the time Walker joined the campaign, Reagan's tax policy was the brainchild of two congressional Republicans who were leaders in the so-called supply-side movement, Representative Jack Kemp of New York and Senator William Roth of Delaware. The Kemp-Roth proposal was a tax cut for individuals known as "10-10-10"—a 10-percent tax reduction across the board in each of the next three years. Walker helped convince candidate Reagan to embrace another set of numbers: 10-5-3. Those figures represented the accelerated write-off scheme fashioned by the Carlton group. The plan would enable businesses to "depreciate," or write off, the entire cost of a building in only ten years—compared with thirty years under existing law; to write-off investments in equipment and machinery in five years—compared with ten under existing law; and to write off cars and trucks in just three years, compared with three and a half under existing law. It was an extraordinarily rich tax break, worth hundreds of billions of dollars to business.

Why did Reagan accept such a costly scheme on top of his own tax cuts for individuals? "He didn't know what he was doing," Walker later speculated; but Walker certainly knew, and the payoff for his clients was enormous.

Once elected, the president kept his campaign promise to corporate America. He continued to push for Walker's 10-5-3 plan, as well as for Kemp-Roth's 10-10-10. Only once did the administration show signs of wavering on the massive business tax break: In June of 1981, the Treasury Department began to worry that the tax cuts were too big and would exacerbate the budget deficit. In response, the White House considered cutting back the proposed depreciation schedules, but Walker and company showed they could still flex their muscles. In an event later dubbed the "Learjet weekend," corporate chieftains from across the country raced into Washington to protest any diminution in the 10-5-3 plan. The Treasury quickly backed away from its concerns and even added a few new sweeteners to keep business on board.

In the end, the 1981 tax bill, called the Economic Recovery Tax Act (ERTA), served as proof of the new power of the advocates of business loopholes. It not only included a revised version of 10-5-3, it also lowered the top tax rate on capital gains yet again to 20 percent from 28 percent. A congressional "bidding war" between Democrats and Republicans to see who could be more generous to whom added even more special giveaways. The Carlton group had triumphed.

In the 1980s, tax reform seemed even more unlikely than it had in earlier decades. Accompanying the rising influence of business lobbyists was the proliferation of political action committees (PACs), which dispensed campaign contributions. From 1974 to 1984, PAC spending on congressional campaigns increased nearly tenfold. PAC giving to congressional candidates totaled $12.5 million in 1974 and soared to $104 million in 1984. Some of the biggest beneficiaries of this largesse were members of the tax-writing committees. Nearly $3.5 million of PAC money flowed into the coffers of fifty-six tax-committee members in the first half of 1985 alone. With so much money going into their campaign chests, members of Congress became more beholden than ever to narrow interests.

Changes in the way Congress operated also stood in the way of tax reform. A decade and a half before, Congress was controlled by committee chairmen and a few leaders in both parties. Wilbur Mills, for example, held the pen for all legislation that was written by the Ways and Means Committee during his fifteen-year reign as chairman. In the 1980s, however, Congress was more democratic, and members were more independent of their leaders. Congressional subcommittees had proliferated. There were no longer just a few key power centers; power was spread throughout both chambers. The administration could not simply cut a deal in a back room with a handful of important members; it had to negotiate with a Congress full of independent thinkers and minor potentates.

The yawning budget deficit also appeared to work against reform. Supply-side guru Arthur Laffer, a California professor, had convinced President Reagan and others that the 1981 tax cuts would cause a surge in economic growth strong enough to eliminate the deficit. Instead, the economy slid into recession and the huge tax cuts helped create the biggest peacetime budget deficits the United States had ever known. Republicans had complained about $60 billion deficits in the Carter administration; but under the Reagan administration those deficits soared to more than $200 billion a year, and they showed no sign of coming down. The deficits were clearly the nation's number-one economic problem, and tax reform, as envisioned by Senator Bradley in 1982, offered nothing to reduce them. It was to be "revenue neutral," raising neither more nor less revenue than the current tax system. Tax reform seemed to be a sideshow, a distraction from the real problem. Furthermore, the small reform successes of the past had occurred in bills that cut taxes. Barber Conable, a long-time Republican member of the Ways and Means Committee and a keen observer of Congress, predicted reform could only occur when overall taxes were being lowered. "Tax reform must be bought," he insisted. But with burgeoning budget deficits, the idea of "buying" reform by cutting revenues was unthinkable.

Moreover, the men who had their hands on the levers of the tax-writing system in Washington—Finance Chairman Bob Packwood, Ways and Means Committee Chairman Dan Rostenkowski, Treasury Secretary Donald Regan, and later, Treasury Secretary James Baker—were scarcely reformers. They all helped fashion the 1981 tax bill, and they all had done their part to create and preserve the tax breaks that riddled the existing system. They could hardly be expected to champion an effort to rid the code of special-interest tax breaks.

Bob Packwood was the unlikeliest reformer of the group. Again and again during his nearly two decades in the Senate, Packwood had proved his commitment to maintaining and expanding the vast web of social and economic incentives in the tax code. He was the author of countless provisions benefiting special interests, a man whom lobbyists felt they could count on to defend their tax breaks against the threat of a sweeping reform.

"On taxes, I'm as predictable as the sun rising," Packwood told *The New York Times* before taking over the Senate Finance Committee in early 1985. His statement was irrefutable. He had always been, in his own words, "a big credit man." He had peddled tax credits for parents who sent their children to private schools; tax credits for child-care expenses; tax credits for solar energy, wind energy, ocean energy, even biological-waste energy. "I sort of like the tax code the way it is," Packwood admitted shortly after the Treasury Department unveiled a plan for a comprehensive overhaul of the tax system.

Packwood's words were sweet music to those lobbyists battling to keep tax benefits, and they paid the piper generously. During his first year and a half as Finance Committee chairman, the senator received nearly $1 million in campaign contributions from PACs—far more than any other member of Congress. The money poured in from investment banks, insurance companies, auto companies, real estate companies, drug companies, steel companies, the carpenters' union, the food workers' union, the bricklayers' union, airlines, law firms, the American Hospital Association, the American Dental Association, liquor associations—in short, from almost every organization with an interest in preserving the existing tax system.

If Packwood seemed an unlikely champion of tax reform, so too did Treasury Secretary Donald Regan. The silver-haired former chairman of Merrill Lynch was the very picture of corporate America. He was one of the many executives who chanted the mantra of "capital formation." During his years on Wall Street, Regan frequently jetted to Washington to push for big-business tax benefits. His firm also aggressively marketed a type of tax shelter known as "straddles," even though the IRS had raised questions about their legality. When Jimmy Carter was considering his own ill-fated tax-reform plan, Regan was quick to criticize. He was particularly contemptuous of reports that the president was planning to limit the special break for capital-gains income. "The market is going down," he said in 1977, "and the administration is trying to kill off one of the few tax preferences coming to the individual investor, so why should he bother to take risks?"

When Regan became Treasury secretary in 1981, his tax philosophy seemed clear. He remained true to that philosophy, serving as the point man in the administration's efforts to enact the biggest corporate handout in history.

James A. Baker III, the White House chief of staff who later swapped jobs with Regan, was also an unlikely reformer. A Texas lawyer, he became Treasury secretary in 1985 largely because the job of secretary of State—his top choice—was not available. Despite his training as a lawyer, Baker had no abiding interest in tax policy and at times seemed to have no interest in policy at all. His first love was politics, and he viewed everything through that prism. He encouraged the president to call for a tax-reform "study" in early 1984, largely because he feared the Democrats might make reform an issue in the presidential campaign. But he also listened closely to the advice of Republican pollster Richard Wirthlin, who said the public would be skeptical of any effort to "reform" the tax system and would probably view it as a tax increase in disguise.

The largest gulf between Baker and tax reform was filled with oil. Baker was a Texas aristocrat, and like many wealthy natives of the Lone Star state, his roots ran deep into the reservoirs beneath the tumbleweed plains. His interest in oil was not only financial; it was cultural, societal—oil ran in his blood.

The problem was that oil and tax reform were like oil and water. The oil industry had been a major beneficiary of tax loopholes since 1918, when generous depletion allowances were first enacted to help drillers. Any legislation that did not cut back on the generous oil and gas tax breaks could hardly be called reform, but any legislation that did cut back those cherished breaks would be inimical to Baker.

Dan Rostenkowski, the big, blustery Democratic chairman of the House Ways and Means Committee, shared the Treasury secretary's preference for politics. Raised under the tutelage of Chicago machine-boss Mayor Richard Daley, he too was no reformer. He joined the Ways and Means Committee in 1964 not because of a deep interest in taxes, but because the panel at the time had the power to determine which committees Democratic House members would be allowed to sit on. With his training in ward politics, Rostenkowski knew that the power of patronage reigned supreme.

Rostenkowski became chairman of the tax-writing committee in 1981, and his first year in the job was a trial by fire that marked him as anything but a reformer. Confronted with President Reagan's effort to force a Republican tax bill through the House, Rostenkowski responded by "sweetening" his version of the bill with even more tax preferences in order to buy support. In the bidding war that followed, Democrats and Republicans both handed out tax breaks in a desperate grab for votes. The Democrats—and Rostenkowski—lost, but in the process, Rostenkowski found himself backing a tax bill with business tax breaks so generous that even business lobbyists were stunned. "This is nothing short of astounding," said a surprised Richard Rahn, chief economist for the Chamber of Commerce of the U.S.A. "If you'd told me a few years ago that the Democrats would propose this, I would have said you were out of your mind."

President Reagan also was, in many ways, an unlikely tax reformer. He had always thought the reformers' notion of tax expenditures was a "liberal myth." The government had no inherent right to a taxpayer's money, he reasoned; therefore, forgoing taxes on any portion of that money could hardly be considered the same as government spending.

The president also had a natural antipathy for the corporate income tax. Speaking to a group of businessmen in Bedford, Massachusetts, during January of 1983, he shocked his political advisers by saying that "there really isn't a justification" for taxing corporations at all. "The elimination of the corporate tax," he said, was "something we ought to look at." The incident sparked immediate retractions from his aides in Washington, but the inadvertent comments were a clear reflection of the president's feelings. They certainly did not suggest that, nearly three years later, he would triumphantly sign a tax bill that closed dozens of loopholes and raised corporate taxes by $120 billion over five years—the biggest corporate tax increase in history.

But in one very fundamental way President Reagan was a natural advocate of tax reform; he had a passionate desire for lower individual tax rates. He had vivid memories of his days as a young Hollywood actor, when he was reluctant to make too many movies in one year because more than 90 percent of his pay would go to the government. All other concerns paled in the presence of this obsession; on his list of domestic priorities, cutting personal tax rates ranked first, second, and third. If closing loopholes and raising corporate taxes was the only way to pay for lower rates, then so be it.

It was that unswerving dedication to lower rates that compelled the president eventually to embrace reform. And it was his staunch support for the bill, despite his sometimes surprising ignorance of its details, that enabled tax reform to overcome countless obstacles and become the law of the land.

Chapter 2

The Beginnings

In the spring of 1982, a young senator from the industrial Northeast met with a ragtag group of reporters to discuss an unusual idea. The meeting took place in the Black Horse Tavern, a dimly lighted restaurant on the edge of downtown Washington. The lawmaker was former basketball great Bill Bradley of New Jersey. His idea was to overhaul the federal income tax by shearing away the most coveted tax breaks enjoyed by the nation's industrial giants and its influential well-to-do.

Politicians had suggested reforming the tax system before, to be sure, but Bradley had a new twist. He proposed a marriage of two ideologies, one traditionally Democratic, the other Republican. His plan would not only close loopholes, it would also provide a dramatic drop in the top tax rate. It melded his party's concern for fairness with the new drive among Republicans to promote economic opportunity. It offered a rare chance for the goals of social equity and economic efficiency, which usually were in conflict, to work hand in hand.

"We should have a tax code in which all citizens with equal incomes are treated essentially the same way," he said in his plodding monotone.

We should have a tax code that is simple enough for all citizens to have at least a basic understanding of how the system works and how their own tax obligations are determined. We should have a tax code which allows taxpayers to make their economic decisions on the basis of real value in the marketplace—with little, if any, regard for tax implications.

The lighting was so poor in the back-street eatery that the towering Democrat had to strain to read his speech. He vaguely remembers that a dog wandered aimlessly through the crowd as he delivered it, and that a man and woman sat quietly near the front without taking notes.

"The couple over to the left of me were there for lunch; they weren't there to hear my speech," Bradley remembers. "They kept looking up and wondering, 'What is this guy?' "

After Bradley finished, the lone television reporter in the group walked up to the senator, stuck a microphone in his face and said: "Now senator, we're both grown men. We know politicians are always talking about tax reform and never doing anything about it. Why should we think you're any different?" The public and Bradley's fellow politicians were equally unimpressed. The story was ignored by *The New York Times, The Washington Post,* and the three major networks.

It was an unaccustomed situation for the neophyte senator. Though he was not yet forty years old, he had been a national idol for nearly two decades. As an undergraduate at Princeton University, he was acclaimed as one of the greatest college basketball players of all time. But he was more than that. He was an athlete-scholar, the classic profile of a leader of men. He graduated from the Ivy League school with honors and went on to study at Worcester College at Oxford University, as a winner of the prestigious Rhodes scholarship.

He was, in short, a model youth. He was religious, claiming that much of his strength of heart and mind came from his belief in God; he taught Sunday school at the First Presbyterian Church even after the sleepless nights that followed big Saturday night games.The time between the game and Sunday classes was often spent in the library, where he would cloister himself for study. He was the picture of determined intelligence, with luminescent green eyes and wing-tipped eyebrows, the left of which arched upward on his forehead like that of *Star Trek*'s Mr. Spock.

Even his modesty was legendary. He liked to say he lacked natural athletic ability, that he was too short, not very fast, and not much of a leaper; yet, he was the most-storied amateur athlete of his time. He also was fond of saying he was not as bright as his Princeton classmates and had to work twice as hard to keep pace, but those who know him well are convinced that he remembers everything he reads.

Great things were always expected of Bradley, and he almost always delivered. In 1964 he was a member of the United States Olympic basketball team that won the gold medal in Tokyo. As a senior in college the next year, he led his team to the "final four" by winning the eastern regional championship in the National Collegiate Athletic Association tournament, a feat that Princeton had not accomplished previously and has not repeated since. Although the team lost its bid to become national champion, Bradley was elected the tournament's most valuable player.

After his stint at Oxford, he became one of the most touted players in the National Basketball Association. He helped to bring the New York Knickerbockers to two national championships over a decade-long career. Once again, he proved himself to be more than just an athlete. In the midst of his pro-ball years, he wrote the highly regarded *Life on the Run,* a thoughtful autobiography about the itinerant life of a professional basketball star. A year after he retired from the Knicks, he was elected to the Senate as its youngest member.

Everyone who had contact with the talented and driven Bradley believed there was no limit to his attainments. For his memorable book about the college-aged Bradley, *A Sense of Where You Are,* published in 1965, John McPhee asked several people where they thought Bradley would be when he turned forty. "With the help of his friends, Bill could very well be president of the United States," answered his high school principal, Edward Rapp. "And without the help of his friends, he might make it anyway."

In 1982, however, at the age of thirty-nine, it looked as though Bradley would need a lot of help just to stay where he was. Political sentiment had turned away from him and away from his Democratic party. Bradley was elected to the Basketball Hall of Fame that year—but at the same time, he found himself locked in a losing battle against the rising tide of the Reagan revolution. It seemed possible that the New Jersey senator might be remembered best for his former life as a basketball star, not for his new life as a politician.

The year before, Bradley had been the sole member of the Finance Committee to vote against the deep business and individual tax cuts that were the centerpiece of Reaganomics. He took the view that the president's program of tax cuts, combined with increases in military spending, would lead to burgeoning budget deficits. He was also convinced that cutting rates without closing loopholes compounded the unfairness already in the code. Bradley took to the Senate floor in 1981 to offer a long series of amendments to limit the tax cuts and to reshape them to help middle- and lower-income families more than high-income individuals, but the amendments all went down in flames.

When the smoke from the 1981 battle cleared, Bradley was undaunted. He did not want to remain on the defensive; he wanted to play offense, make a positive statement. He needed a new approach, a new idea that he could stand behind, both politically and substantively, an idea that did not deal with the symptoms of the problem, but with its root causes. He decided to pursue a subject that he had been examining since his days as one of the highest-paid players in the NBA: a top-to-bottom revision of the federal income tax.

As a professional basketball player, Bradley had developed a healthy disdain for the U.S. tax code. He made big money, and that forced him to wrestle with the complexities of taxation. During his first contract negotiations at the age of twenty-three, Bradley was asked by his attorney a question that startled him: "How much do you want to pay in taxes?" The attorney went on to explain that Bradley could take his pay as property, as a long-term consulting contract, as employer-paid life insurance and pension plans, or even as payment to his own corporation.

"I just want to play basketball and be paid well," the young Bradley said.

"It's not so simple," the attorney replied.

Bradley never lost his distaste for the complicated tax system and was appalled by the economic contortions it forced his teammates to endure. In *Life on the Run,* Bradley records the inordinate amount of time and energy he and his teammates spent trying to avoid the tax man and their unalloyed contempt for the Internal Revenue Service. "I don't pay taxes, period," crowed Jerry Lucas, a teammate with a penchant for mental games and high-stakes business dealings. "But I do it legally. I'm not stupid."

(Years later, Bradley found kinship on such matters with another formerly highly paid professional—ex–Hollywood actor Ronald Reagan. During a meeting in the cabinet room between the president and the Finance Committee, Bradley said, "Mr. President, you came to this [tax reform] because you were an actor who paid at the 90-percent rate; that's why you want a lower rate. I came to this because I was a depreciable asset.")

On the long road trips during his pro-basketball career, Bradley had plenty of time to think things over, and he spent many off-court hours visiting local politicians and reading widely. He read Milton Friedman, the University of Chicago economist, and was fascinated to learn that a flat-tax system with a rate of just over 20 percent would raise as much money as the existing high-rate system. He also read about the largely fruitless efforts of Stanley Surrey, the Harvard Law School academic who worked to reform the income tax during the 1960s.

Bradley brought these ideas with him when he ran for the Senate. During his 1978 campaign, he wanted to advocate a broad-based, low-rate tax as one of his campaign stands, but he lacked the sophisticated tools to put the idea into practice and abandoned the effort. Instead, he suggested a targeted, one-year tax cut to counter the three-year cuts recommended by his Republican opponent, Jeff Bell. When the campaign was over, and Bradley was safely in the Senate, he looked back and marveled at how well his conservative opponent had exploited the voters' intense dislike of the federal income tax. He saw that he was not alone in thinking the tax code was unfair. "This is an issue the voters care about," he thought.

In 1979, Bradley met with his senatorial staff and said he wanted to draft a major tax-reform bill that eliminated loopholes and imposed a lower, flatter tax-rate system. They poured cold water on the plan. It was too ambitious, they chided him. But after the debacle in 1981, when his efforts to trim back the oversized tax cuts were thwarted, Bradley renewed his pursuit of tax reform. He was searching for a politically palatable alternative to the Republican tax cuts. So he plowed ahead to devise a wholly restructured tax system.

True to his nature, Bradley did not take the enterprise lightly. He applied to his legislative endeavors the same dedication to detail and devotion to fundamentals that were the hallmarks of his success in basketball. During his teen years in Crystal City, Missouri, not far from St. Louis, Bradley, the only child of a banker, maintained a maniacal practice schedule. According to McPhee, Bradley would work out on the court for

three and a half hours every day after school, nine to five on Saturday, one-thirty to five on Sunday, and, in the summer, about three hours a day. He put ten pounds of lead slivers in his sneakers, set up chairs as opponents and dribbled in slalom fashion around them, and wore eyeglass frames that had a piece of cardboard taped to them so that he could not see the floor, for a good dribbler never looks at the ball.

In college, he could analyze every shot and every move down to its smallest components. A hook shot, he would explain, has five distinct parts: the crouch, the turn of the head toward the basket, the step, the kick, and the follow-through with the arms. He also would not quit until he got things right. He would never complete his daily practice routine until he had made at least ten out of thirteen of each of his shots from every location on the court.

In 1981 and 1982, his drive for tax reform reflected all of the traits of his basketball days: discipline, painstaking analysis, and patience.

During this period, Bradley could be seen loping wide-eyed through the halls of Congress, laden with books and briefing papers. He would breeze through volumes of tax tracts and reach out to a brain trust of tax experts both inside and outside of government. While other senators left details to their staffs, Bradley remained intimately involved in the minutiae of his income-tax proposal. He demanded explanations and would not relent until he understood. He wanted to know which tax breaks he was eliminating, how they got there to begin with, and why they should go. He took careful notes in spiral-bound notebooks. He sometimes spent eighteen-hour days at his task, studying and refining the proposal for a year and a half.

The Bradley brain trust was led by Gina Despres, Bradley's own hard-nosed legislative counsel, who would continue for years as a guiding force behind the scenes. She was assisted by a lanky, bearded economist named Joe Minarik, who worked for one of Congress's information-resource agencies, the Congressional Budget Office. James Wetzler and Randy Weiss, two top-flight economists from the Joint Committee on Taxation, and Tom Troyer and Bob Klayman, two tax lawyers from Despres's old law firm Caplin and Drysdale were also part of the team. Despres called these and other tax experts together for long lunches in Bradley's office. They adhered to an agenda devised by Wetzler. During these gatherings, Bradley, in effect, was treated to a comprehensive course in federal taxation, in which he learned the most basic and arcane facets of the existing code, as well as the most widely discussed alternatives.

Bradley used these ideas to compose his plan, but he did not rely on them exclusively. He drew his own judgments and rejected some of the common academic wisdom that declared the income tax obsolete. He also talked about his plan to anyone who would listen: farm groups, Wall Street moguls, town-hall meetings back home in New Jersey. He tested people's reactions to the idea of trading off deductions that help the few in order to provide lower tax rates for the many. Slowly, and from these grass-roots encounters, he learned arguments to beat back attacks, and he came to believe that his plan would sell.

Bradley's colleagues in the Senate saw little of his touch for the common man. Many considered him aloof and dogmatic. To them, he came off more like a professor of political history than a politician. They would say they liked him, thought him quite able, and admired his hard work; but some also resented his wunderkind reputation, his rapid rise to their exclusive debating society. His dry, cerebral wit was not funny to them, and at times he seemed condescending and arrogant. He was often moody, and not quite a member of the club.

At home and on the road, Bradley conveyed a very different persona. Though he was a dull, even pedantic, speaker, he was warm and engaging one-on-one. When giving a greeting, he would wrap his long fingers around the hand of the greeted, bring down his face from its six-foot five-inch height, and look the person in the eye. This sudden attention was both a treat and a shock. Here was Bill Bradley, the legend—and a nice guy, too.

Bradley was searching for something elemental in the American psyche, a message that struck a chord. He thought his tax bill would help achieve the American dream. When a taxpayer got a raise in salary, moved up the ladder of success, Bradley's bill would allow him to keep more of the extra cash in his pocket. The top tax rate would be lower than it had been in half a century and far lower than proposed in any previous Democratic tax-reform effort—that was the opportunity it promised. In addition, when a taxpayer looked around at friends and neighbors, he could feel certain that they too were paying their share of taxes, unable to hide behind loopholes or shelters—that was the Bradley plan's essential fairness.

Like a growing number of young Democrats, Bradley was skeptical of the traditional big-government doctrine of his party. Instead, he laced his rhetoric with "Republican" talk about "free markets" as the "most efficient allocator of capital." Lower rates and fewer distorting tax incentives would allow those markets to work, he reasoned, and lead to unfettered economic growth. He hoped to call the bluff of Republicans who spouted similar free-market rhetoric, while jealously guarding tax breaks that tilted the playing field toward their friends and constituents.

At the same time, Bradley saw the populist attraction of tax reform. The fight would pit the special interests, who would struggle to keep their loopholes, against the general interest—lower rates for everyone. A central goal of tax reform must be to give the lowest possible rate to the greatest number of Americans, he said.

At the start, Bradley made three key political decisions that determined the character of his plan and that distinguished it from previous tax reform efforts:

First, he decided that his plan should not be used as a solution to the growing deficit problem. It must be "revenue neutral," raising neither more nor less revenue than the current tax system. Previous tax bills had always either raised revenue or cut it, but Bradley wanted to avoid the harsh ideological battles that would undoubtedly follow if he pushed his measure in either direction.

Second, Bradley decided not to change the distribution of the tax burden among income groups, except to provide some relief to the working poor. He believed that earlier reform plans had been dismissed out of hand by Republicans and moderate Democrats because they were Robin Hood–like redistribution schemes, taking more money away from those at the top of the income scale and giving more to those in the middle and at the bottom. He meant to avoid that pitfall.

Third, Bradley decided not to raise taxes on corporations to pay for tax cuts for individuals. Such a shift, he feared, would label the plan as anti-business and help ensure its defeat.

A key challenge for Bradley's plan—and for all the plans that followed—was how to sharply reduce the top tax rate without providing a windfall to the wealthy. Bradley sought a top tax rate as low as 30 percent—a twenty-percentage-point drop in the tax rate for high-income taxpayers. He had to find some way to guarantee that those at the top did not reap excessive benefits from the change.

The solution to Bradley's problem came from Joe Minarik, the Congressional Budget Office economist. In 1981, Minarik had done some work for Representative Stewart McKinney, Republican of Connecticut, who like Bradley was interested in an alternative to the supply-side tax cuts. Minarik drafted a plan with a bottom rate of 14 percent and a top rate of 28 percent, but the originality of the plan was the way it treated deductions and exclusions. Under existing law, a deduction is worth more as a tax-payer moves into higher tax brackets. A $100 deduction for someone in the 11-percent bracket, for instance, saves only eleven dollars in taxes; but a $100 deduction for a person in the 50-percent bracket saves a full fifty dollars in taxes. Minarik's idea was that deductions should have equal value to all taxpayers, regardless of the person's bracket. He rigged his two-rate scheme so that a $100 deduction could only be taken against the bottom rate, thus saving only fourteen dollars in taxes, regardless of a person's income. High-income taxpayers, who would enjoy big tax rate cuts under the plan, would also lose much of the value of their deductions.

Minarik was excited by his research. "I was surprised how low you could get the rate" by using this device, he recalls. But McKinney lost interest. Over lunch sometime later, Gina Despres enlisted Minarik and the McKinney plan as part of the senator's quest for tax reform.

Doubts ran high about the prospects for the effort, even among those working on the plan. "I remember it as an interesting exercise, and wishing them all godspeed and all that," said the Joint Tax Committee's Randy Weiss, who made important refinements in the Minarik scheme. "But I thought it was mostly pie in the sky."

At the conclusion of the plan's laborious preparation, Bradley chose Democratic Representative Richard Gephardt of Missouri to cosponsor the bill in the House. Gephardt was a fair-haired, serious, and inscrutable young legislator who had ambitions of rising rapidly in the House hierarchy and of perhaps running for president. He served on the House Ways and Means Committee, the sister panel to Bradley's Finance Committee in the Senate. If Bradley's Fair Tax Plan had any chance of becoming law, it would first have to win the approval of these two tax-writing committees. Indeed, since under the Constitution, revenue measures must originate in the House, a foothold in Ways and Means was especially important.

Bradley had known Gephardt casually since the early 1970s, when the then professional basketball player was flirting with the idea of running for treasurer of Missouri, his native state. Gephardt was a young alderman in St. Louis at the time, and Bradley sought his advice. Gephardt remembers that Bradley wanted to talk to a local politician near his own age. Bradley remembers Gephardt as clean-cut and hard working—not unlike himself.

Their paths crossed again in Congress at the end of the decade. Gephardt was elected in 1976 from a district that, ironically, would later include Bradley's hometown of Crystal City, along the Mississippi River. Bradley came to the Senate from New Jersey, his new home, in 1978. Both became part of a group of up-and-coming Democrats, who were being flagged as the vanguard of the party. They occasionally would go out together to make speeches intended to display the Democrats' new face. They also both had an interest in new styles of taxation. Gephardt says he was studying income-tax revision independently of Bradley, but when told of the senator's plan, he was glad to join the enterprise and lend it his name. Bradley was trying to do a favor for his House colleague, but events would later show that Gephardt was, in the end, only a fair-weather friend of tax reform.

The final version of the proposal had a simple, progressive rate structure with three rates: 14 percent, 26 percent, and 30 percent. About 80 percent of all taxpayers would pay at the lowest rate. The plan would increase the personal exemption and the standard deduction in order to remove many low-income families from the income-tax rolls. To pay for this, the plan would repeal many deductions, exclusions, and credits. It would keep a few preferences that Bradley judged to be too politically sensitive to remove: deductions for home-mortgage-interest payments, charitable contributions, payments to individual retirement accounts and payments of state and local income and property taxes. These, however, would be limited as Minarik had envisioned: they would be deductible but only against the 14-percent rate, making their value the same for taxpayers in all income brackets. For corporations, the top rate was dropped to 30 percent from 46 percent.

The Bradley-Gephardt bill contained the basic principles that would later become the Tax Reform Act of 1986, but when Bradley and Gephardt introduced their bill on August 5, 1982 (a second and final version was introduced the next year), most of Washington paid little heed. It was one of 2,151 bills introduced in the House during that session and 1,119 introduced in the Senate. At best, only a few hundred of those bills would ever become law. The Fair Tax Act of 1982 seemed to be one of the forgotten proposals, a noble but unrealistic idea.

While Bradley studied tax reform, many of his colleagues in Washington focused on the deficit. Within a few months after the 1981 tax cuts were passed, the prospect of skyrocketing budget deficits was readily apparent. Projections showed that if left untouched, the nation's fiscal shortfall would soon approach $250 billion a year—*four times* the largest deficit in the Carter years. President Reagan had promised to eradicate deficits, but now it looked like he might quadruple them. The situation was serious, and a profound embarrassment. It led to a series of tax-increase bills that were the precursors of tax reform, but also proved how tough it was to close even a limited number of loopholes in the face of interest-group opposition.

Although the U.S. economy was mired in a recession in 1982, the president was compelled to accept and eventually work for the passage of the biggest tax increase in peacetime history. The measure, known in the argot of Washington as the Tax Equity and Fiscal Responsibility Act (TEFRA), raised $98 billion in revenue over three years, half of it from corporations.

The legislation was largely the handiwork of Senator Dole, the chairman of the Finance Committee. Dole was a respected legislator with a reputation for a quick wit. A traditional Republican, Dole had little patience for the supply-siders who dominated the agenda in 1981 with their Kemp-Roth tax cut. Joking in early 1982, Dole told a group that he had good news and bad news: "The good news is that a bus full of supply-siders went off a cliff. The bad news is that two seats were empty."

Dole wanted to be president, and he was eager to demonstrate his leadership abilities in the Senate to help his cause. The deficit problem offered him th.:t opportunity. The White House was reluctant to push for tax increases, and the Democrats were reluctant to cross the White House on such a controversial issue. So Dole stepped in and took the lead. Although the Constitution said that tax bills must originate in the House, Dole put together a package of miscellaneous revenue-raisers and "loophole closings" in his Finance Committee. He then tacked them onto a minor House-passed tax bill that had been stripped of all its original provisions, passed it through the Senate, and sent it to the House.

The 1982 tax bill kept the hallway outside the Finance Committee room filled with lobbyists, who feared they would lose some of the generous tax breaks that they had been given in 1981. It was then that the hallways first took the name of the expensive Italian shoes that were worn by lobbyists. Toward the end of the committee's drafting sessions, someone commented to Dole, "There's wall-to-wall Guccis out there," to which the chairman retorted, "Well, a lot of them are going to be barefoot after this is done."

In the House, special interests rose up to stifle action. Ways and Means Chairman Rostenkowski was unable to get his committee members to agree on a formula for a tax increase, because of resistance by the formidable oil-and-gas interests on his panel. It was a source of resistance he would never forget. In the end, he was compelled to go to conference committee—the forum where differences between House and Senate measures are resolved—without a bill of his own. It was a rare and humiliating position for the reputedly powerful chairman.

Dole claimed that the bill finally signed by the president in 1982 was tax reform of a sort, but it was only a small step toward reform. It eliminated or curtailed a number of major tax breaks, but it did not offer lower tax rates in return. Supply-side Republicans like Representative Newt Gingrich of Georgia complained that Dole was merely serving as "tax collector for the welfare state." Nevertheless, Dole clung to his abhorrence of the deficit. He was also convinced that small or "incremental" efforts to close loopholes were the only way to go about reform. Broad, sweeping measures like that advocated by Bradley, he believed, would never work.

Dole's bill was a defeat for many powerful interests, but it was not long before they rallied again. Infuriated by the bill's plan to require banks to withhold taxes from the dividends and interest they paid to customers, banks and other financial institutions launched a massive grass-roots lobbying campaign in 1983 that flooded the Capitol with postcards demanding repeal of the offending provision. Republican Senator Robert Kasten of Wisconsin led the successful campaign for the banks, and Dole was forced to accept repeal.

As the budget deficit continued to rise, Dole and Senate Budget Committee Chairman Pete Domenici persuaded President Reagan in 1984 to ask for yet another tax increase, which they soft-pedaled as a "down payment" on the budget deficit. The three-year, $50 billion tax hike, much like the 1982 bill, was a collection of odds and ends. But again, the debate over the bill demonstrated the impressive power of the interests who backed certain tax breaks. Dole originally hoped to cut back the tax benefits of the real estate industry, which had benefited enormously from the 1981 bill and was responsible for most of the growth in tax shelters. The realtors' lobbyists filled the hallways outside the hearing room as Dole completed his bill, and when the chairman stepped outside, he faced a phalanx of them clustered around their leader, Al Abrahams of the National Association of Realtors. "We weren't treated fairly," Abrahams complained, twitching nervously but speaking with conviction. Dole shook his head in disagreement. On the Senate floor, the Kansan continued to battle the realtors, but he was eventually overwhelmed by their lobbying power and forced to accept a compromise. Angry and vengeful, Dole complained: "They have been camping on our doorstep. They have been in the gallery. They have been in the lobbies. They have been in the elevators. . . . I know the precise office this storm has been created by. There will be another day." (Indeed, there was to be another day, just two years later, but neither Dole nor the realtors imagined in 1984 how severe the retribution would be.)

Even after the 1984 bill, large deficits remained. The deficit in each of the following three years was expected to hover in the $170 billion range. Deficit reduction was still the top issue; tax reform was widely considered to be a luxury that the nation could not afford. Senator Long, for example, derided the Bradley bill as little more than "an attractive conversation piece."

"Most of us realize that Bradley-Gephardt conceptually is good, but it will never become law," said Representative Robert Matsui of California, a Democratic member of the Ways and Means Committee. "You will never eliminate all those deductions you have to eliminate. It would be like pulling teeth out of a lion. Bradley-Gephardt isn't doable."

As the 1984 election campaign approached, several advisers to the Democratic front-runner, former Vice President Walter Mondale, argued that the Bradley-Gephardt plan provided a much-needed solution to his party's problems. Whatever its practical failings, the Bradley-Gephardt bill had a certain political appeal. Polls showed that the Democrats were still viewed favorably by the American people as the party of fairness and compassion, attributes that held together the party's foundation among poor people, city dwellers, and the labor movement. But they had allowed Ronald Reagan's Republicans to become the standard-bearers for opportunity and growth—terms that appealed to the postwar baby-boom generation just coming of age. The trick for the Democrats in 1984 was to try to claim the mantle of growth and opportunity without abandoning the high ground as the party of fairness and the friend of the disenfranchised.

Bradley-Gephardt offered a rare chance to do that: It promised that no one would escape carrying his or her share of the tax burden, but it also offered sharply lower tax rates. What better promise, what better incentive to give a young middle-class American, with eyes looking eagerly up the economic ladder, than to say that no matter how far up that ladder you climb, the federal government will take no more than thirty cents out of any dollar you earn?

In a speech in May of 1983, Mondale told a group of businessmen meeting in Washington that he liked the general outlines of the Bradley-Gephardt plan. The speech was reported in *The Wall Street Journal* the next day. It was the candidate's first public flirtation with reform during the campaign, and the results were scarcely encouraging. The phones in the candidate's headquarters rang ceaselessly, as Mondale supporters with tax breaks to defend called and registered their complaints. "The next forty-eight hours were hectic ones in the Mondale camp," recalls Bill Galston, the candidate's issues adviser. "The list of people we heard from was a long one." Campaign workers insisted the *Journal* story had exaggerated Mondale's comments, and tax reform quickly disappeared from the candidate's rhetoric.

Bradley, eager to sell his plan to Mondale, tried for months to arrange a meeting with campaign chairman James Johnson to reignite interest in his plan, but his entreaties were ignored. He finally managed to schedule a breakfast with Johnson in his Senate office in early 1984 and spent an hour there, waiting over coffee and doughnuts for Johnson to arrive. In a gesture that seemed to illustrate the campaign's regard for the Bradley-Gephardt plan, Johnson never showed. He never even called to say he could not make it.

"The meeting was shortly after our defeat in the New Hampshire primary by Gary Hart," explains Johnson. "I've known Bradley for years, I felt badly about it, but I wasn't thinking of seminars on tax policy at the time. I was in Georgia or Alabama or somewhere trying to keep us alive."

Bradley never really got a chance to make his case to Mondale until August of 1984, when much to his surprise, he and Gephardt were asked to meet with the candidate in the living room of the Mondale home in North Oaks, Minnesota. They talked about taxes with Mondale and a few of his campaign advisers for nearly two hours. (One of these aides, ironically, was Dick Leone, the man Bradley had beaten in a Democratic primary in 1978.) Bradley made an impassioned plea for his proposal, saying that he had traveled around the country talking to groups of voters and that the idea appealed to many of them, but his arguments never sank in. Mondale offered a few throwaway lines about the virtues of Bradley-Gephardt to reporters waiting at the base of his wooded driveway, and that was the end of it.

By the time of that meeting in North Oaks, the tone of the Mondale campaign was set in concrete. The candidate had already delivered his infamous speech at the Democratic convention that resonated through the final three months of the campaign and sealed his fate:

Let's tell the truth. It must be done, it must be done. Mr. Reagan will raise taxes, and so will I. He won't tell you. I just did.

Dan Rostenkowski, standing next to the candidate in front of the cameras and the cheering crowd at the convention after the fateful speech, whispered to Mondale, "You've got a lot of balls, pal." According to Rostenkowski, Mondale whispered back, "Look at 'em, we're going to tax their ass off."

Mondale's bold step to back tax increases rather than tax reform turned out to be the biggest blunder of his campaign. The statement, for all its honesty, reinforced the voters' worst fears about Democrats. The candidate's lame retort that Reagan had a "secret plan" to raise taxes never made a dent in the president's support. Mondale lost the election by a landslide, winning only 13 electoral votes to Reagan's 538. Whether an endorsement of tax reform would have helped Mondale's cause is unclear. But the truth is that other than the brief flirtation in May of 1983, tax reform never came close to being adopted by Mondale. At the highest levels of his campaign, where the political advisers and fundraisers held sway, it never even got serious consideration. It just did not fit into the Mondale game plan, for a number of reasons.

First, although Mondale had fought to close loopholes as a member of the Finance Committee in the 1970s, he had met with little success. The Democratic chairman of the panel, Russell Long, was uninterested in such efforts, and Mondale had learned that it did not pay to cross Chairman Long. "I'd go up that hill and get knocked back down," Mondale recalls. "It was a dispiriting environment." As Jimmy Carter's vice president, Mondale once again watched reform fail utterly and was not eager to repeat the performance.

Second, as a politician with roots in Minnesota's progressive Democratic-Farmer-Labor Party, Mondale was clearly uncomfortable with the sharp cut in the top tax rate proposed by Bradley-Gephardt. "I thought there ought to be an additional bracket for high-income taxpayers," he said later. Lowering the top rate so drastically, he and other liberals believed, would give the wealthiest Americans an undue break.

Third, Mondale was convinced that the budget deficit was the "central problem in the American economy." Bradley-Gephardt was not a solution to that problem; indeed, Bradley, unlike Gephardt, believed any effort to turn the proposal into a revenue-raiser would spell its doom. Thus for Mondale, tax reform was a sideshow, an attempt to distract voters from the real economic problem that faced them.

A fourth reason that Mondale avoided tax reform, according to some in his camp, was campaign contributions. Although Democrats considered themselves the party of the little man, they had been far less successful in building a base of small contributors than their Republican counterparts had. They depended on a relatively small group of large contributors, and among those, real estate developers loomed large. Real estate magnates like Nathan Landow of Bethesda and Thomas Rosenberg of Chicago were kingpins in the Mondale fundraising apparatus. Any version of tax reform would undoubtedly take a swipe at the generous tax breaks for real estate, and a move to embrace reform could have thwarted the campaign's fundraising efforts.

Mondale vigorously denies that campaign contributors had anything to do with his decision to steer clear of tax reform. "There's absolutely no basis to that at all," he says. He even recalls that Landow once told him he liked the Bradley-Gephardt bill because it would drive the get-rich-quick charlatans out of real estate and leave more room for serious developers like himself.

The ultimate reason that Mondale avoided tax reform, a reason that was rooted in the nature of the campaign itself and that overshadowed all other reasons, was this: Mondale's was a campaign of the special interests. Its goal was to build a coalition by attracting organized groups one at a time. Tax reform was the antithesis of that strategy: It tossed out special interests in favor of the general interest. The legislation offended groups that ranged from real estate to labor to heavy industry. It would have hurt his efforts to build a coalition of special interests in a dozen different ways.

"Mondale had served on the Senate Finance Committee, and he knew that losers in tax changes are intense and aware, while the winners are for the most part not intense and unaware," says campaign chairman James Johnson. "That meant . . . you potentially pay a high price with the people who are hurt." It was a price Walter Mondale was not willing to pay.

In retrospect, Mondale has few regrets. "I made a decision which in hindsight may not have been correct, but I still think I would have done the same thing at the same time again, which was to emphasize the budget deficit," he says. "I thought Bradley-Gephardt was a good idea. It made sense to me. But I didn't emphasize it in the campaign because it was a revenue-neutral objective.

"What might have been done, what should have been emphasized more, was the record of outrageous loophole benefiters during the Reagan administration," he adds. Why didn't he do at least that? "I don't know," he says with a touch of wistfulness. "You get into these things, and you get awfully tired, and your mind doesn't work."

While Bradley's tax-reform ideas were ignored by the Democrats in the Mondale campaign, they found growing acceptance at the opposite end of the ideological spectrum, among Republican supply-siders.

In August of 1983, a group of about twenty supply-side journalists, politicians, and intellectuals gathered on the slate patio next to the swimming pool in the rear of the suburban Washington home of Jack Kemp.

It was a sparkling evening, and the group conversed in animated fashion as Kemp's wife Joanne served them food and beer. They were a small band of fellow travelers, conspiratorial in nature, and often split by factional disputes. Their differences were at times so severe that they refused to speak with each other, and this evening was no exception. But they had gained inordinate influence in the Republican Party and within the Reagan administration. They were the moving force behind the Kemp-Roth tax cuts of 1981, and they were looking for new policies to push during the second Reagan term.

The purpose of the poolside meeting, in the words of one of the group, was "to plot how to dominate the Republican platform" in 1984. Among those attending, in addition to Kemp, were the leading lights of the supply-side movement: Irving Kristol, the neoconservative New York University professor who was publisher of a journal called *The Public Interest;* Lewis E. Lehrman, who had launched and lost a supply-side bid for the New York governorship in 1982; Paul Craig Roberts, who had served as Reagan's assistant Treasury secretary for economic policy during the first year of the administration; Richard Rahn, chief economist for the Chamber of Commerce of the U.S.A.; Jeff Bell, who had run against Bradley in the 1978 New Jersey senatorial race on a supply-side platform; Jude Wanniski, an economic consultant who was forced to leave his job as an editorial writer at *The Wall Street Journal* because of his active campaigning for Bell; and Alan Reynolds, Wanniski's partner in his consulting business.

For the supply-siders, tax cuts always ranked at the top of the list of preferred policies. The problem with the American economy, they believed, was that tax rates were too high and were suffocating incentives to work, save, and invest. But since their surprising success in 1981, the supply-siders had been forced to lay low. The tax cuts enacted that year had not led to an economic boom, as they had predicted, but to a bust. Budget deficits had not disappeared, but had skyrocketed. For the supply-siders to simply endorse further tax cuts in the face of such problems would have been viewed by the public as highly irresponsible (although many in the camp would have favored just that course).

During the poolside meeting, Kristol made an unusual proposal: Why not endorse Bradley-Gephardt as stage two of supply-side efforts to get tax rates down? Sure, the plan would hit some important big-business constituents of conventional Republicans, but it offered the only chance, in the face of prolonged budget deficits, of getting tax rates down further.

The idea was appealing to many in the group. Endorsing a Democratic tax bill would certainly attract attention, which the supply-siders always craved, and it would undermine efforts by the Democrats to make tax reform an election issue. Wanniski was intrigued by the proposal, as was Bell, who had become an admirer of the former basketball player who had trounced him in his Senate bid. "We came to the conclusion," Kemp said later, "that Kristol was right, that Reagan and Kemp should endorse Bradley-Gephardt. That would have thrown the Democratic party into a state of real confusion."

Others in the group expressed their opposition to the Bradley bill. In particular, Rahn and Roberts, who both had close ties to the corporate community, were disturbed by Bradley's proposal to trim back investment incentives for business. Lehrman argued that for political reasons, it would be wiser for the group to have its own bill, rather than simply embrace the Bradley measure. The discussion continued for some time, and twilight fell over the patio. In the end, Lehrman won out: The group agreed that Kemp should draft a new version of tax reform that Republicans could rally behind.

Thus began one of the most unusual, and most important, alliances fostered by tax reform. Bradley had argued fiercely against the supply-side agenda in his 1978 campaign against Bell, and his interest in tax reform had been born out of his strong opposition to the 1981 supply-side cut. But now, as his own party was deserting him, Bradley found supply-siders turning to adopt his concept, and he welcomed them.

Shortly after that meeting in Kemp's backyard, Bell telephoned Bradley, to whom he had not spoken since their heated debates during the campaign of 1978. Bell requested an audience, and Bradley consented. The two met in September at Bradley's Union, New Jersey, office. It was a busy time for Bell, who was to be married within the week, but he was glad for the opportunity to talk to Bradley. "Bradley was very friendly and very gratified," says Bell, and out of the meeting grew a new partnership. Bradley says he was happy for the vote of confidence and was equally glad to have Bell as a resource for him in the supply-side camp. Bell kept Bradley apprised of what Kemp and company were up to; and Bradley used Bell to send messages to the supply-siders and their friends in the Reagan administration.

Kemp, in the meantime, went to work developing a Republican version of Bradley-Gephardt. Unlike Bradley's plan, the Kemp proposal sought to enhance business investment incentives by allowing rapid write-offs for equipment purchases. The Kemp plan also contained a $2,000 personal exemption to help families; it retained the full deduction for mortgage interest, maintained the full deduction for charitable contributions, and kept low capital-gains tax rates. As his Senate cosponsor, Kemp chose Robert Kasten of Wisconsin, whose successful effort in 1983 to defeat Dole and repeal the interest-withholding provision attracted Kemp's attention. Kemp and Kasten introduced their version of tax reform in April 1984.

Because of the Kemp plan's generosity in retaining tax breaks that were curbed by Bradley, Kemp-Kasten faced a serious shortcoming from the start. The original version was not revenue neutral by the calculations of either the Treasury Department or the congressional Joint Committee on Taxation. Had it been enacted into law, it would have added tens of billions to the nation's budget deficits. Nevertheless, the Kemp-Kasten tax bill helped make the quest for tax reform bipartisan, and only as a bipartisan effort did reform stand a chance. Tax reform was too big, too complex, and too controversial to be pushed through Congress by one party alone. With the power in Washington clearly split between the Democrats, who had consolidated their control of the House in the 1982 elections, and the Republicans, who still controlled the Senate and the White House, support from both sides was needed to provide even a small chance for success.

The Reagan administration focused its sights on tax reform in late 1983, as work got under way to prepare for the president's 1984 State of the Union address. White House aides were coming under pressure from the supply-siders to advocate reform, and they were also convinced—wrongly—that Walter Mondale was about to make Bradley-Gephardt the centerpiece of his election campaign.

Still, Chief of Staff James Baker was reluctant to support reform. He had heeded the advice of pollster Richard Wirthlin, who warned that "tax reform" would mean "tax increase" to many voters. He felt it would be a dangerous policy to push during an election year.

Tax reform had been discussed in the White House before. In September of 1982, Treasury officials met with the president on three occasions to review their upcoming testimony on reform at a hearing before the Finance Committee. That same year, Secretary of State George Shultz, a former Chicago economist who was intrigued by the "flat-tax" proposals of economists Robert Hall and Alvin Rabushka, tried to interest the president in the idea. In a golf match described by former Budget Director David Stockman in his book *The Triumph of Politics,* Shultz told the president that a low-rate tax system would end the inefficiency caused by tax loopholes and cause the economy to grow faster. By the eighteenth hole, the president was convinced, Stockman writes, and soon, "everyone around the White House was talking flat tax." After the golf match, then–Treasury Secretary Regan received a short note from the president extolling the idea, scrawled in the margin of an article on the issue.

But the pragmatists in the White House—including Baker, then–presidential assistant Darman, Stockman, and Economic Adviser Martin Feldstein—thought talk about the benefits of tax reform sounded like more of the supply-siders "voodoo economics," to use a phrase coined by George Bush before he became Reagan's running mate. The real problem, in their view, was the deficit, and tax reform offered no solution to that.

Before the 1983 State of the Union address, Stockman and Darman worked on a scheme that would combine long-term tax reform with a "temporary" short-term tax increase. The tax increase, they thought, could then be sold to the public and to Congress as merely a "bridge" to raise revenue until the new tax plan took effect. In Stockman's words, it was "a perfectly disingenuous plan" to convince the president to back a tax increase.

But the Stockman-Darman compromise never got off the ground. White House officials disagreed about what tax reform should look like and feared that the idea might not sell well to the public. Out of this confusion came the vague, two-pronged plan that the president pushed in his 1983 State of the Union address. He called for a "standby" tax that would be triggered only if Congress first approved the administration's budget—an unlikely condition. After that, he said, the administration would "continue to study ways to simplify the tax code and make it more fair for all Americans." The standby tax was quickly forgotten, and discussions of tax reform did not surface again in the White House until the end of that year.

As the 1984 State of the Union address approached, Baker finally decided that the best strategy was to defuse the tax issue by having the president call for a "study" of reform, without delineating any specifics. This would take the wind out of any Democratic plans to endorse the Bradley-Gephardt bill and avoid the risks of angering specific voters by putting out details of a plan. The promise of a "study" also would help the president duck the question of raising revenue to reduce deficits. The move was political, as most election-year White House decisions are, and it was based largely on a mistaken judgment about the Mondale campaign.

Treasury Secretary Regan, spurred by the handwritten note from the president, had by that time grown fond of reform, seeing it as a way to regain center stage in the Reagan administration. But his entreaties were rebuffed by White House aides. "I insisted that we had to have tax reform, that the system was crazy," he recalls. "They agreed to let me study it. Like a pat on the head for a little child, they sent me off to go and play."

On January 25, 1984, the president appeared before a joint session of Congress to deliver his annual State of the Union address. He stood on the speaker's podium, with Vice President George Bush and House Speaker Thomas P. "Tip" O'Neill seated behind him, the House members and senators spread out in the audience before him. The House chamber was a majestic room, with a stained-glass eagle on the skylight soaring overhead and symbols of each state emblazoned on the ceiling. As he spoke from the high, altarlike podium, the president was flanked by giant portraits of George Washington and the Marquis de Lafayette, a French general and early friend of the Republic. The legislators sat quietly as he spoke the following words:

Let us go forward with an historic reform for fairness, simplicity and incentives for growth. I am asking Secretary Don Regan for a plan for action to simplify the entire tax code, so all taxpayers, big and small, are treated more fairly. And I believe such a plan could result in that "underground economy" being brought into the sunlight of honest tax compliance; and it could make the tax base broader, so personal tax rates could come down, not go up.

It was an impressive performance, and those watching the president might have been convinced by the president's sincerity, had it not been for the very next line: "I have asked that specific recommendations, consistent with those objectives, be presented to me by December 1984."

December 1984: To the members of Congress seated in the House chamber, the date conveyed tremendous irony. The presidential election was in November, and the president's promise seemed no more than a cynical ploy to deflect the issue until the election had passed. Given the date, few of those who heard the speech believed the president was serious; few thought that the same president who had filled the tax code with huge new loopholes in 1981 was now ready to turn around and rid the code of those same preferences.

In a rare display of disrespect, the Democrats in the solemn chamber erupted into derisive laughter. "Did I say something funny?" Reagan asked with a smile.

Tax reform seemed no more than a joke.

Chapter 3

<hr/>

The Horse You Rode in On

November 5, 1984—the day before Ronald Reagan's reelection—Treasury Secretary Donald T. Regan walked into the conference room that adjoined his office, where a small group of his closest advisers waited for him. A distinguished-looking man, with his silvery hair combed straight back from his forehead, Regan carried himself with a patrician air that belied his blue-collar Boston accent and upbringing. He took a seat, as always, at the head of the conference table, his back to a window that looked out across East Executive Avenue to the South Lawn of the White House. On the wall was a giant portrait of Andrew Mellon, the treasury secretary during three Republican administrations in the 1920s. This was the nerve center of the U.S. Treasury Department: President Reagan had asked the Treasury to come up with a plan for overhauling the nation's tax laws, and it was here that Regan and his ten advisers were carrying out that task.

Only a few weeks remained before the tax plan would have to be delivered to the White House, and all of the men were beginning to worry that it would not be well received. They had fashioned a proposal more radical than any ever contemplated at such a high level of government. It swept away hundreds of special-interest tax breaks, and was sure to offend countless Republican constituencies. It totally eliminated the investment incentives that were championed by President Reagan in 1981. The plan was a political bombshell, and it was about to explode upon the nation. Regan's eyes twinkled mischievously as he surveyed the group, and asked: "All of you have your résumés ready, don't you?"

Few people in Washington had taken President Reagan seriously in January of that year when he called for a historic reform of the federal income tax. Treasury Secretary Regan was one of those few. He saw tax reform as his opportunity to regain prominence in the Reagan administration, and he went at the task with relish. For months, he worked diligently with this small group of men, combing through complex tax law, section by section. He kept the group isolated from the political storms of the election campaign; indeed, he kept them isolated from all the pressures that usually play upon people in power. The meetings were supersecret; the secretary ordered members of the group not to talk about their work to anyone outside of the conference room. Papers presented at the gatherings were passed out just two days before each session, in sealed envelopes marked *Eyes Only,* with explicit instructions that the contents were to be viewed only by the ten policymakers, and not by their deputies. After each session ended, the papers were collected again. Week after week, the group debated proposals that promised to shake the financial foundations of virtually every American family and business. Week after week, they made multibillion-dollar decisions that struck not only at taxpayers' pocketbooks, but at the very structure of American society. Their actions would affect the home, the family, the church, everything considered most sacred.

The men sitting around the table were an eclectic group, which included the department's two top tax experts: Ronald Pearlman, a lawyer who served as assistant secretary for tax policy, and Charles McLure, an economist and Pearlman's deputy. In addition, there were two other economists who held strong views about the tax system: Manuel Johnson, the young assistant secretary for economic policy, and Beryl Sprinkel, the department's undersecretary. Roscoe Egger, the commissioner of the Internal Revenue Service, was there as well, along with Deputy Secretary Tim McNamar, a former management consultant from California. At the far end of the table sat Bruce Thompson, in charge of legislative relations; Alfred Kingon, a former Wall Street money manager and magazine editor who was assistant secretary for planning and public relations; Thomas Dawson, a former management consultant who served as Regan's liaison with the business community; and Chris Hicks, whose job was to coordinate the activities of the sprawling department.

Until this November day, the members of the elite group had enjoyed the luxury of thinking their actions did not amount to more than reshuffling toy dollars in a giant board game, but now, they realized, the game was over. President Reagan's reelection was a near certainty, and soon they would have to complete their work. Their plan would be made public, carrying the weighty imprimatur of the secretary of the Treasury, and possibly the president of the United States.

"We didn't kid ourselves," recalls Thompson, the most politically savvy member of the group. "We knew it would be controversial. But we kept thinking that as long as we get the rates down low enough, people won't mind."

As chief executive of Merrill Lynch, Regan had been an avid backer of investment tax breaks. During his first year at the Treasury, he led the battle for the rapid depreciation write-offs in the 1981 tax bill. But in the privacy of his conference room in 1984, the secretary shed his image of a promoter of business incentives and became instead an ardent tax reformer. One after the other, he accepted proposals to do away with long-standing tax preferences. It was a remarkable transformation.

Although a bright man with a quick mind, Regan had no firm economic or political philosophy, outside of a businessman's basic conservatism. He was not introspective, not given to theorizing, and never worried much about the consistency of his positions. As a result, he was often open to persuasion by others who did have firm and unequivocal beliefs. In his first two years as Treasury secretary, he presided over a staff split oddly between committed supply-siders, who believed that low tax rates made the world go round, and doctrinaire monetarists, who thought the growth of the money supply determined all. Regan's own pronouncements were at times an awkward reflection of that split; he was unpredictable. Once, when asked whether he agreed with Regan's statements on the budget deficit, Exxon Chairman Clifton Garvin quipped, "It depends on what hour of the day he said it."

But the idea of a radical tax plan had an instinctive appeal to Regan. He relished the prospect of unveiling a proposal that slaughtered whole herds of sacred cows. At heart, he was a contrarian. The son of a railroad security guard and a former marine, Regan had worked hard to make himself into a multimillionaire. He had struggled to get where he was, and the experience had made him pugnacious and defiant. He liked to take on the establishment, even though he had labored feverishly to become a member of it. He took an almost-perverse pleasure in a good fight. One aide recalls that Regan's eyes would light up when he was preparing to testify before a particularly hostile congressional committee; the sparring enlivened him.

A symbol of Regan's defiance, well-known among his aides but seldom heard outside of Treasury, was an old saying he picked up from John "Buck" Chapoton, Pearlman's predecessor and the first supervisor of the tax-overhaul project. Chapoton told the story of a foul-mouthed, poker-playing friend of his in Texas, who once blurted out in the middle of a card game, "Fuck you, and the horse you rode in on." Regan was tickled by the saying, and adopted the last half of the phrase as his own. When an aide made a point he disagreed with, Regan would interject, "And the horse you rode in on," causing the room to break up in laughter. The phrase became a repeated source of amusement to the tax-writing group and eventually earned itself a place in history. In the large, official portrait of Regan, which hangs in the hall on the third floor of the Treasury and will continue to hang there long after Regan dies and his tax proposal has been forgotten, there is only one book that can be seen clearly on the shelves over his right shoulder; its title, *The Horse You Rode in On.*

Regan's feistiness was legendary on Wall Street as well. He shook the financial establishment in the 1970s by supporting an end to fixed commissions for brokers. Merrill Lynch under Regan became one of the first Wall Street firms to go public, and it pursued an almost-reckless acquisition strategy. Once, it even considered acquiring the Chicago White Sox.

With Regan at the helm, the firm also conducted what some Wall Streeters termed a "ruthless" campaign to bring in new clients by hiring away top securities analysts from other firms. And in the late 1970s, Regan's Merrill Lynch came up with an innovation that changed the nature of the business forever: the cash management account, which allowed clients to write checks against their brokerage accounts. Regan's revolution at the investment house was so complete that when Citicorp Chairman Walter Wriston was asked at a 1980 bankers' meeting in Boca Raton what his dream bank might look like, he replied bitterly that it already existed: "Don Regan runs it, and it's called Merrill Lynch Pierce Fenner & Smith."

"Do you know why I'm hated?" Regan said once to a *Washington Post* reporter. "I broke up their cozy little club. Wall Street was a cartel. They proclaimed capitalism—but practiced cartelism."

Tax reform offered Regan a similar opportunity to rattle the business community. It would put free-market rhetoric to the test by taking away business-tax subsidies and making everyone compete on a level playing field. Regan cherished the thought of how his proposal would stick it to the wealthy special-interest lobbyists that he and his aides referred to as the "Gucci boys." "He has these populist tendencies, that's why he took on Wall Street the way he did," said Manuel Johnson, the assistant secretary. "That's why he always liked to buck the establishment. Tax reform was a natural for him."

Regan also had a fabled ego, and he craved the public spotlight. He bridled when other economic policymakers in the Reagan administration, such as Budget Director Dave Stockman or Economic Adviser Martin Feldstein, received more news coverage than he did. "I'm the president's chief economic spokesman," he said with almost comic regularity. Despite such protests, he never felt he got the attention he deserved.

A revolutionary tax-reform bill, Regan believed, would surely put him back at the center of things. The more radical the plan, the better. As a result, the secretary never shied away from the tough decisions. He strode into the conference room one day when some particularly touchy issues were under scrutiny and declared with a smile, "This is the day we do away with Santa Claus." On occasion, he even urged his reform-minded tax experts to take more hardheaded positions than they were inclined to on their own. For instance, when Pearlman proposed putting a limit, or a "cap" on the amount of employer-provided health insurance a person could receive tax-free, Regan's response was: "Why cap it? Why not tax all health insurance?"

During his first three years as Treasury secretary, Regan had developed a reputation as the president's yes-man. "He would try to guess where the president was going to come down on an issue," complained one unadmiring administration official, "and then get there before him." Although his Wall Street background led him to fear the effects of giant deficits, Regan was nevertheless unstinting in his defense of the president's huge 1981 tax cuts. When the massive budget deficits surfaced in 1982, he insisted repeatedly in public that deficits did not really matter—a position that was anathema to most serious economists, but one that endeared Regan to the president, who was eager to avoid a tax increase. In White House meetings, Regan was "determined to prevail for the sake of prevailing—even if it meant advocating nonsense," wrote Stockman. His method of determining his position on any given issue, detractors said, was to lick his finger, hold it up, and sense which way the White House political winds were blowing.

But in that small conference room at the Treasury in 1984, there were no winds from the White House. President Reagan had expressed a general interest in tax reform, but provided virtually no guidance on what shape reform should take. White House Chief of Staff James Baker wanted nothing to do with Regan's plan, in large part because he did not want details to leak out and create controversy during the reelection campaign, but also because neither he nor others on the White House staff took the effort too seriously. "I don't think people over there realized what we were doing," says Regan, who had grown resentful and jealous of the powerful White House staff during his time in Washington. "They thought yeah, all these guys at Treasury, Christ, they're dreaming. It'll never come about."

As a result, the sixty-five-year-old Treasury secretary was rewriting the nation's tax laws in a complete political vacuum. Under strict instructions to keep details from leaking out of Treasury, Regan could not even float the proposals with key members of Congress or with people or groups likely to be affected. He had to rely on his own instincts and the advice of ten other men.

Two men, in particular, had the secretary's ear: Ronald Pearlman and Charles McLure. They invariably dominated the discussions in the conference room, and the tax plan that emerged was, in the final analysis, their tax plan. Pearlman was a short, balding Missouri lawyer with a thorough knowledge of the tax code and a theoretical bent. McLure was a soft-spoken Texas economist who had written numerous books on the economics of taxes. IRS Commissioner Egger occasionally talked about the difficulty of administering certain portions of the tax code, and Manuel Johnson frequently argued with McLure about the economic effects of business tax breaks. But for the most part, the views of the department's two top tax experts, Pearlman and McLure, went unchallenged. Backed by a talented staff of about eighty lawyers and economists, the two men set the agenda for each meeting and prepared the papers to be discussed.

They made proposals to Regan, and with surprisingly few exceptions, those proposals were adopted unchanged.

For Pearlman and McLure, it was a rare and heady experience. Pearlman had just moved into the top tax-policy-making position that summer, after serving as deputy to Buck Chapoton. McLure, a conservative economist affiliated with the Hoover Institution at Stanford University, came to the department a year earlier thinking his principal task was to head the department's effort to stop states from using an arcane taxing device known as the "unitary tax." Now, with little direction from above, the two men were being allowed to design what they thought was a perfect tax system. Indeed, Regan specifically instructed them to ignore political concerns. Occasionally, Bruce Thompson or some other member of the group would mention that a particular proposal suggested by Pearlman and McLure was going to cause howls among some powerful interest groups, but Regan was always quick to cut off such discussions. "We'll deal with the politics of it later," he said. Pearlman called the effort "the most stimulating experience I've ever had. It's the way government at some level should always work."

The theory behind the tax plan prepared by Pearlman and McLure was this: All income should be treated equally by the tax system, regardless of where it comes from, what form it takes, or what it is used for. It was a simple idea; but its ramifications were enormous. The existing tax code reflected seventy-one years of history. It represented an intricate web of social, economic, and political goals and aspirations, as complex and contradictory as America itself. The plan at Treasury would clear away that web and replace it with an academician's tax system, elegant and clean.

Pearlman and McLure guided Regan and the other members of the group through the tax code, explaining the radical changes they wished to make. They felt strongly and sincerely that their vision of tax reform was the only way to go, and they argued their case with conviction. They called for a "neutral" tax system, a system that does not influence private decisions. They chose their words carefully to appeal to Regan's conservatism. McLure railed against "tax-code socialism," arguing that the tax system should not be used as an "industrial policy." With the help of the bespectacled Egger, the two tax aides regaled Regan with stories of proliferating tax shelters and companies that paid no taxes. The time had come for a break with the past, they said. The tax code should be returned to its original purpose, which was to raise revenue for the government, not to engineer the economy or promote social change.

In the secluded conference room, those stories hit home with the Treasury chief. He listened carefully to the arguments and read the papers for each meeting from start to finish, even though they often descended into almost unintelligible technical jargon. He surprised his advisers by discovering inconsistencies in the dense arguments made to defend the proposals. But in the end, he swallowed those arguments, hook, line, and sinker. He adopted nearly every proposal his tax experts cast up, no matter how sharp a break with the past it was, no matter how certain to create a public or political furor.

"We knew we were stepping on a lot of toes," Regan recalled later. "We knew we were slaying a lot of dragons."

The dragon carcasses piled up at frightening pace. Employee fringe benefits? Tax them, Regan said; never mind that they were the bread and butter of every labor union in America. Unemployment insurance and disability payments? Tax them too; they're no different from other income. Deductions for state and local taxes? Eliminate them; they are merely a subsidy for services provided by state and local governments. Deductions for charitable contributions? Cut them back. Extra personal exemptions for the blind and the elderly? Change them; they provide the greatest benefits to those in the least financial need. Tax-free allowances for ministers' housing? "We've already stuck it to the blind, elderly, and cripples," joked one member of the group. "We might as well get the preachers too."

The harshest test of Regan's resolve as a loophole-slaying Saint George emerged on the business side of the tax code. There, he encountered the huge business-investment incentives that President Reagan himself signed into law in 1981—the crown jewels of Charls Walker and the Carlton group, the result of a legislative effort that Regan himself spearheaded. Pearlman and McLure were determined that their plan repeal both the generous investment tax credit and the accelerated depreciation write-offs. They believed that those business giveaways were a major cause of the proliferation of tax shelters, and that they enabled many large companies to "zero out"—pay nothing or even get refunds—on their federal income tax forms.

But the two tax experts also knew that these provisions lay very near the heart of the 1981 Reagan revolution and could not easily be eliminated. They knew that Regan, even before joining the administration, was a fierce advocate of such investment incentives. How could anyone expect him, or President Reagan, to embrace a tax plan that did an abrupt about-face on these once-cherished policies? "How could we," thought Pearlman, "go in and say, 'Let's abrogate 1981?' "

The investment credit, a brainchild of the Kennedy administration, was one of the biggest loopholes in the code. It provided a tax credit to businesses equal to 6 percent to 10 percent of the purchase price of new equipment. Ironically, many businesses had opposed the investment credit when it was enacted in 1962, but over the years they had learned to love this Democratic creation. It was repealed twice, but put back soon after each repeal. Now the Treasury was proposing to get rid of it for good, arguing that it distorted investment decisions. It gave huge tax advantages to businesses that invested heavily in equipment, Pearlman and McLure said, but did nothing for service and high-tech firms that did not.

The two Treasury officials also wanted to make drastic changes in depreciation write-offs. Tax experts agreed that businesses should be allowed to take deductions each year to account for the wear and tear of their buildings and equipment, but over the years, those deductions had become inordinately generous. Prior to 1954, the tax law required that depreciation write-offs be spread evenly over the "service life" of an asset. If a company bought a machine for $1,000 that was expected to last ten years, for instance, it could deduct $100 each year. Starting in 1954, however, Congress began to accelerate the deductions, shortening the write-off period and allowing larger amounts to be deducted in the first years after an asset is purchased. The 1981 bill included a sharp acceleration, providing a huge tax subsidy that far exceeded any reasonable calculation of wear and tear. Pearlman and McLure wanted to end this subsidy and return to depreciation write-offs based roughly on the expected life of an investment.

Pearlman and McClure found a tough opponent in Manuel Johnson, the assistant secretary for economic affairs. Brought to the Treasury by supply-sider Paul Craig Roberts, Johnson was committed to using the tax code to spur business investment. "This isn't an academic exercise," Johnson complained. "The question is, how can we best achieve long-term economic growth?" In his view, that was no question at all. Tax incentives had helped boost the economy, he believed. To repeal them at a time when American industry was struggling to keep up with overseas competition seemed pure folly.

Johnson proposed instead a powerful new system of investment incentives called "expensing," which would allow the entire cost of an equipment purchase by a business to be written off in a single year. The scheme was even more generous to business than the existing accelerated-depreciation allowances were, and it was, Johnson argued, a logical extension of the policies launched in 1981.

Both McLure and Johnson were soft-spoken Southerners; McLure so much so that the others sitting around the conference table had to strain to hear his words. Although a modest and even shy man, McLure, forty-four years old, had strong views about how the tax code should be shaped, and he shared every theorist's desire to impose those views on the world. Johnson, a thirty-five-year-old former economics professor at George Mason University in Fairfax, Virginia, was well-liked at Treasury for his friendly demeanor. The Alabaman was also a former Army Ranger and a Green Beret, who had learned the importance of determination as well as equanimity while training in the north Georgia mountains and the Florida cypress swamps. The purpose of that training, which was legendary for its rigor, was "to force people to their physical and mental limits," Johnson said in 1984. "It made me very disciplined." He was a formidable adversary.

For months, McLure and Johnson carried on a quiet but fierce debate in the confines of the conference room. Both men were determined in their views. McLure thought his plan was the only one that made sense. Johnson's expensing plan would tilt the tax code unfairly in favor of heavy industry and away from service and high-tech firms, he said. It would also aggravate the nation's tax-shelter problems. Johnson was equally convinced that McLure's plan could cause serious damage to the economy by discouraging equipment investment. He presented figures showing that the McLure proposal would tax investment even more heavily than the Democrats' Bradley-Gephardt proposal. He insisted the result would be slower economic growth and fewer jobs.

The two went back and forth, repeating the same arguments in seemingly endless repetition. The debate dragged on intermittently for five months. "It became like the old story of the procession of jokes in a prison," recalls McLure, "where someone says, 'Joke 91,' and everyone laughs because they know the joke and the punchline." At times the discussions slipped into technical economic language, causing others at the table to lose interest. At one point, Regan interrupted the duo in exasperation, and shouted: "Can't you guys work something out? I'm going under for the third time!"

The more the decision was delayed, the more it became clear that McLure would ultimately prevail, if only by default. Johnson's expensing proposal was expensive; it would cost the government hundreds of billions of dollars in forgone tax revenues. If Regan adopted the Johnson plan, he would have to find a way to raise other revenue in order to pay for lower rates and ensure the tax plan met the president's requirement of "revenue neutrality."

As the deadline for completing the plan approached, Regan realized he had to make a decision. The tax group was called together in the conference room to hear the debate one last time. The choice that faced them was an unpleasant one: If they accepted McLure's proposal, they would be adopting a complete reversal of the administration's position in 1981. It would be a retreat of tremendous proportions, and one that would outrage Charls Walker and his business-lobbyist friends. If they adopted Johnson's proposal, on the other hand, they would be continuing the policies of 1981, but they would be abandoning a key component of tax reform.

Still troubled by the split among his advisers, Regan called for a vote. As he went around the table, one after another tipped his support to McLure. Egger, who worried about the proliferation of tax shelters, felt McLure's proposal would help slow the growth of such schemes. Thompson, who was a former aide to Senator William Roth of Delaware, one of the fathers of the Kemp-Roth tax cut of 1981, voted with McLure, because he favored getting tax rates as low as possible, and he knew that McLure's depreciation scheme would raise far more revenue to pay for lower rates. Only Alfred Kingon, the last person to vote, gave his vote to Johnson. He worried that McLure's depreciation scheme might harm the economy.

With the druthers of his advisers clear, Regan made his own decision. He agreed to lead the Treasury in an abrupt about-face, a 180-degree reversal from four years earlier. He agreed to propose to the White House that they repudiate their own policies and throw out the investment tax breaks. It was a remarkable flip-flop. Outside the Treasury Department, none of the Washington lobbyists who worked on the 1981 bill would ever have guessed that Regan would be such a traitor to their cause. But inside the conference room, he and the others who had spent months listening to the arguments of Pearlman and McLure were convinced that the investment incentives had to go. Tax reform had found a fervent advocate in the unlikeliest of places.

Kingon says the Treasury chief was sensitive to the arguments made by Egger: "Regan felt very strongly about tax-shelter abuses. He felt strongly about corporations that didn't pay any taxes and a law that allows them to have huge cash flow, great revenues, and still escape taxation. You should have heard him. He was a solid citizen when it came to that. He despised, and I don't think I'm overstating the case, he despised those who avoided paying their own fair share of taxes."

Regan himself makes a similar argument: "Some companies were paying no taxes at all as a result" of the incentives, he said. "We'd swung too far one way rather than the other and we had to bring the pendulum back."

In part, the decision to abandon investment incentives reflected the fact that Regan, sealed in the conference room away from the outside world, had become a captive of his bureaucracy. Pearlman and McLure kept tight control of the tax-writing process, and kept Johnson constantly on the defensive. Had the circumstances been different, had other administration officials and outside interests been given the opportunity to whisper in Regan's ear, the outcome might have been very different.

But the radical proposal also reflected Regan's taste for the dramatic. He didn't want his plan to elicit a yawn from Washington politicians and pundits; he wanted it to shock them as something bold.

"He knew we were swinging for the fences," recalls McLure, "and if we got there, he knew that he'd be the one to go into the baseball hall of fame."

In his State of the Union address at the beginning of the year, the president had asked for a tax plan that was simple, fair, and good for the economy. He had insisted that it not be a tax increase in disguise, that it raise the same amount of tax revenue as current law. Beyond that, however, the Treasury Department was free to design a tax system as it saw fit.

Early on, Regan and his aides toyed with the idea of scrapping the income-tax system and switching to a tax plan based on consumption. It was an option suggested in a pamphlet issued by outgoing Treasury Secretary William Simon in 1977, called *Blueprints for Basic Tax Reform*, and it appealed to many academic economists who argued that an income tax by its very nature is biased against savings and investment.

Under an income tax, if you use your earnings to buy a pleasure boat, proponents of the consumption-based tax said, you are taxed only once, and then you may enjoy the benefits of that boat tax-free as long as it lasts. If instead you use the same income to invest in a savings bond, however, you are taxed twice: once on the income used to purchase the bond and again on the income earned by the bond. The result is a tax system that encourages people to spend more and save less, resulting in less investment and slower economic growth. The so-called consumed-income tax, on the other hand, would only tax income that is used for consumption, not income that is saved or invested.

The consumed-income tax was also popular among Charls Walker and his fellow lobbyists, who saw it as a way to free business investment from all taxation. But the mechanics of taxing consumption were hopelessly complex, and Treasury officials knew such a tax would probably be perceived as unfair by the American people. All savings would be tax-free, allowing the wealthy to bring in vast amounts of income without paying any tax. Borrowings, on the other hand, would be taxed if they were used to pay for consumption, causing heavy borrowers to face tax bills completely out of proportion to their incomes. During one meeting at which the consumption approach was discussed, Regan turned to Pearlman and said: "I'll tell you what. The next time you go to a cocktail party, you ask people what they think of a tax system in which borrowings are treated like income. They're going to tell you you're crazy." Talk of a consumed-income tax soon died out.

The group also discussed the virtues of using a value-added tax (VAT), which is a sort of sales tax imposed at the national level, to supplement the income tax. The VAT had been turned to by many European countries and had the same sort of appeal to business as a consumed-income tax. McLure was an expert on the economics and structure of VATs, but Egger made it clear to the group that a VAT would be hugely expensive to administer. Such an extensive new tax system would only be worth doing if it were big—raising $100 billion a year or more. Because the tax bill was not supposed to raise revenue, a large VAT seemed out of the question, and the idea was dropped. The secretary allowed his tax experts to prepare a book on the pros and cons of a VAT, which they thought might be useful in future budget debates, but he rejected the idea of making a VAT part of tax overhaul.

With the consumed-income tax and the VAT ruled out, a total revamping of the income tax seemed the only possible route for the Treasury's tax plan to take. "It wasn't by design," Pearlman says. "It just sort of happened."

The initial spadework on the tax plan got a big boost in early April, when Eugene Steuerle, a tax economist, returned from a year's leave at the prestigious Brookings Institution, a Washington think tank. The Treasury veteran had been schooled in Harvard Professor Stanley Surrey's theories of how to construct an ideal income tax. "When I came back to Treasury, there was nothing given to me in the way of directions," Steuerle recalls. "There were no instructions coming down from the top, and that paralyzed people."

Without direction from above, the Treasury discussions became a sort of bottom-up process. Steuerle and his colleagues would prepare proposals for McLure and Pearlman, which in turn were taken to Regan and the tax group. The Treasury tax bureaucracy felt ignored during the first years of the Reagan administration. It was forced to support a 1981 tax bill that was a vestige of the election campaign, and it had watched Senator Dole, the Finance Committee chairman, usurp all control of the tax-writing process in 1982. Now, suddenly, in 1984, the tax experts in the bowels of Treasury found themselves in a position of power.

The bookish Steuerle organized the issues to be addressed: It was important, he thought, to be comprehensive; the Carter reforms had failed because they were piecemeal. It was important also to have details, prepared by Treasury lawyers, on how to implement the changes. The *Blueprints for Basic Tax Reform* proposal of the Ford administration had gone nowhere in part because no one knew how to put its changes into place.

"It was a strange experience," says Steuerle. "As I was working on it, I began to realize it was a serious effort. I don't know what Secretary Regan expected initially. But what is clear is that as the secretary got more and more into the process, he got more and more committed to it."

A cornerstone of the Treasury's ambitious plan was to adjust, or "index," various portions of the tax code to take account of inflation. The rapid inflation of the 1970s had distorted the tax system tremendously. The average taxpayer had felt the consequences through "bracket creep," which pushed taxpayers into higher tax brackets even though their incomes, adjusted for inflation, were unchanged. Inflation wrought other, more subtle, damage to the tax system as well. If a man paid $30,000 for a house in 1970 and then sold it for $50,000 a decade later, he had to pay taxes on a "gain" of $20,000, even though $50,000 in 1980 was actually worth less than the $30,000 in 1970 after adjustment for inflation. Similarly, if a woman placed her money in a savings account earning 5 percent a year, she had to pay taxes on the annual interest even though in the late 1970s, when inflation raged at over 10 percent a year, the value of her money was actually deteriorating; she was losing money, not making it.

The 1981 tax bill had required that tax brackets be "indexed" to take account of inflation, starting in 1985. But Treasury tax experts wanted to go far beyond that. They wanted to adjust everything for inflation: capital gains, depreciation, even interest payments and interest deductions. Under their plan, a lender would be taxed on interest income only to the extent that the interest rate exceeded the inflation rate. Likewise, a borrower would be able to deduct interest payments only to the extent the interest rate exceeded the inflation rate. Such comprehensive indexing was a bold and ambitious effort, and also a complex and confusing one. It was an essential element in the ideal tax system, but one unlikely to win support among practical politicians.

Nevertheless, Regan went along with it. He was particularly intrigued by the idea of "indexing" capital gains. In fact, it was because of inflation indexing that the Treasury chief was willing to adopt one of the most controversial proposals that his tax aides suggested: the complete elimination of the special tax break for capital-gains income.

As the former head of a brokerage house, Regan had always been a fan of the special low tax rate on capital-gains income earned from the sale of assets. The capital-gains tax break had been a feature of the tax code since 1921; since 1978, efforts to push the gains tax even lower had found tremendous support in Congress and in the country at large. The top tax rate on capital gains dropped from 35 percent or more to 28 percent in 1978, and again to 20 percent in 1981, far below the top 50-percent rate on ordinary income.

But the capital-gains tax break added significantly to the complexity of the tax code, and it encouraged game-playing by taxpayers eager to convert ordinary income into capital gains income. Cattle-breeding tax shelters, for instance, allowed taxpayers to invest in cows one year, then get back income two years later that would be taxed at the low capital-gains rate.

McLure and Pearlman argued that the capital-gains break should be eliminated. Income from the sale of assets, they said, should be treated just like any other income. Egger provided powerful support for that view, saying that a third of the tax code was devoted to problems caused by allowing the preferential rate for capital gains.

Regan at first resisted, but he became a convert after discovering the powerful effects of indexing capital gains for inflation. The Treasury secretary worked out examples showing that the tax owed on a blue-chip stock purchased in the 1970s and sold in 1984 would actually be lower under his staff's proposal than under existing law. That was because most of the gain in that period was due to inflation, and under the proposed plan, that part of the gain would not be taxed at all. Armed with such examples, he decided to reverse his oft-repeated endorsement of cutting capital-gains taxes, instead supporting his tax aides' radical proposal to eliminate the special gains rate altogether.

The inflation of the 1970s had created extra problems for the poor, and the Treasury policymakers were well aware of the fact. Throughout the 1960s and 1970s, Congress tried to assure that no family with an income below the federally designated poverty level would pay income taxes. But rampant inflation in the late 1970s pushed the poor back onto the income-tax rolls, and the Reagan tax bill in 1981 only exacerbated that situation. The huge Reagan tax cuts for the middle class and the wealthy masked enormous tax *increases* for those at the bottom of the scale. By 1982, almost half of the individuals and families living in poverty were burdened with federal taxes. In 1984, a family of four had to begin paying income taxes at $8,700 in income, even though the poverty level was more than $10,600.

The condition became an embarrassment for the Reagan administration. Conservatives could argue with straight faces that welfare programs for the poor needed to be cut back to eliminate waste, but they could scarcely defend imposing big tax increases on the poor. Ways and Means Democrat Charles Rangel from New York held hearings that took the Reagan administration to task for its insensitivity, and the lambasting had an impact. By the summer of 1984, even the president realized something had to be done. "Because of the tax laws we inherited," he said at the Republican convention, trying to blame the Carter administration for the failings of his own policies, "the number of households at or below the poverty level paying federal income tax more than doubled between 1980 and 1982."

To correct this, the tax experts proposed large increases in the so-called standard deduction used by those taxpayers who do not itemize their deductions. They also proposed to expand the earned-income credit, which gave some working poor a tax refund, and to increase the personal exemption for each family member. The personal-exemption increase was being pushed by several "pro-family" organizations, and White House aide Bruce Chapman even visited Treasury to promote the cause. The failure of the personal exemption to keep up with inflation, Chapman contended, led to homicides, suicides, and virtually every other imaginable social ill. "We subsidize family failure and punish people trying to hold their families together," he argued. Increasing the personal exemption, he said, would "take some of the sting out of having families." Although such pro-family arguments later assumed a big role in the tax-reform campaign, they were never discussed in meetings of the Treasury's tax group. The personal exemption was increased to $2,000 from $1,080 largely to help ensure that poor families came off the tax rolls.

Another key element of the Treasury's ideal plan was an effort to reduce the "double taxation" of corporate income. Tax experts had long acknowledged that some corporate income was subject to tax twice: once when earned by the corporation and again when distributed to shareholders. That problem could not be solved (as President Reagan had suggested less than two years earlier) by simply eliminating the corporate tax—corporations would then become giant tax shelters in which the wealthy could hide their income—but double taxation might be alleviated by allowing companies that pay dividends to take a deduction for the payouts. The Treasury tax experts decided to propose a tax deduction to corporations for 50 percent of the dividends they paid out.

Like interest indexing, the dividend deduction had tremendous attractiveness to academics and little appeal elsewhere. Ironically, the managers of corporations that stood to benefit from such a proposal had the least interest in it; they feared it would force them to pay out more of their profits each year in dividends. Nevertheless, Regan, still swinging for the fences, put his stamp of approval on the controversial notion.

Tax-free employee fringe benefits—health care, life insurance, child care, and education aid—were also important targets of Regan's plan. Over the years, the list of benefits that employees could receive from their employers without paying tax had grown steadily. The cost to the Treasury in lost revenue from such tax-free fringes totaled $80 billion a year or more. Reformers viewed the alarming growth as unfair. Some employees received as much as a third of their income in tax-free benefits, while others received no such benefits and had to pay tax on the money they used to buy health insurance or life insurance.

The tax-free treatment of fringe benefits began as far back as 1921, when the income from pension trusts was exempted from taxes. Health-care costs were first excluded from taxation in 1939. But the real explosion in fringe benefits occurred after World War II, with such benefits jumping from 15 percent of average personnel costs in 1951 to 32.5 percent in 1981. The 1970s brought the addition of such new fringes as employee stock-ownership programs, employer-paid legal assistance, van pooling, educational assistance, and child care.

The Treasury plan proposed wiping out all of those. Companies could still provide such benefits to their employees, but under the proposal, the benefits would be taxed as income. A partial exception would be allowed for health insurance, which the Treasury Department said would be taxed to the extent the cost of a health plan exceeded $175 per month for a family.

Business-expense deductions, long a target of reformers, also were hit hard by the Treasury Department. Presidents Kennedy and Carter had both failed in attempts to curb these deductions. In Kennedy's day, the proposal to cut back expense write-offs caused such an uproar among hotel and restaurant workers that a waiter at Duke Zeibert's restaurant in Washington dumped a plate filled with a hamburger, french fries, and green peas onto the lap of IRS Commissioner Mortimer Caplin. By 1984, the deductions had become the stuff of satire. Humorist Art Buchwald, a frequent patron at Washington's posh expense-account restaurants, told the story of one man who leaned over to another in a restaurant and asked, "Do you want to buy this restaurant?" When the startled diner said "No," the man asked: "Well then, may I have your name so I can say we discussed business?"

The Treasury plan proposed to wipe out entertainment-expense deductions entirely for such things as basketball and theater tickets. For meals, it limited the deduction to $10 per person for breakfast, $15 for lunch and $25 for dinner. (When congressional staffers were later briefed on the proposal, several shouted out, "What about brunch?")

As for the numerous provisions in the tax code benefiting specific industries, the Treasury plan slated most for termination, including the rehabilitation credits used by real estate developers, energy credits, bad-debt-reserve deductions, oil-and-gas benefits, timber benefits, and others. In a move that would later spark one of the most vicious lobbying efforts of the entire tax-reform debate, the Treasury even proposed taxing the interest or "inside buildup" earned on life insurance policies. After all, Treasury officials reasoned, the insurance income is really no different than that earned on savings accounts.

There seemed to be no limits to the Treasury's desire to eliminate tax breaks. McLure even gave serious thought to going after the most popular tax break in the code—the deduction for home-mortgage-interest payments.

Home ownership was the American dream, and the interest deduction was the government's way of encouraging that dream. Millions of Americans owned their own homes, and the rest worked for the day when they could do the same. Any attempt to trim back the home-mortgage deduction would surely bring a cry of outrage from across the country. But in McLure's view, the home-mortgage deduction channeled into housing billions of dollars that might be better used elsewhere. It was, in effect, a massive tax shelter for middle-class America, and he wanted to eliminate it.

"I was pondering what we might do, knowing the political problems and the sanctity of this provision," recalls McLure. "Left to my own devices, I might have proposed that we try to phase the deduction out."

While McLure was mulling over this idea, however, President Reagan pulled the rug out from under him. On May 10 Reagan made a speech before more than four thousand members of the National Association of Realtors in Washington. He had been hounded for several days by real estate lobbyists who feared that his tax-reform effort might attack the mortgage-interest deduction. With the election approaching, the president and his advisers decided to ease the realtors' minds. "In case there's still any doubt," he said, "I want you to know we will preserve the part of the American dream which the home-mortgage-interest deduction symbolizes." The statement attracted little interest outside the Treasury, since few people had even imagined that the administration would tamper with such a popular deduction. Inside the Treasury, where the home-mortgage deduction was on the chopping block, the president's speech caused a storm. Political reality had suddenly intruded into the dreamworld of Treasury experts. The policymakers not only had to put the home-mortgage deduction off limits, they also had to fear the possibility that other interest groups might use the pressure of the election campaign to get the president to declare their tax breaks off limits.

The pressure built up at Treasury again during the summer, due to continuing misapprehension that Walter Mondale was on the verge of releasing details of a tax-reform plan of his own. White House aides asked Regan if he could have a plan ready quickly under such circumstances, and Regan replied yes, without asking his own people first. In fact, Treasury officials did not know how they could possibly complete even the rough outlines of a plan prior to November. More important, they feared that if their proposal became part of the election campaign, it would be doomed.

"It was scaring us to death," says Pearlman. "I believe that would have been the end of tax reform. That would have put all the issues out in the political arena and they would have just gotten knocked down, one after the other."

In midsummer, Senator Bradley called Treasury to ask if the department had run revenue estimates on his plan. The call was immediately interpreted as a sign that Mondale was going to embrace the Bradley plan. The tax experts waited in suspense, fearing each day they would read about the candidate's announcement in the morning newspaper. In fact, Bradley was calling for other reasons. He was worried that his own campaign opponent might use Treasury estimates of either his bill or Kemp-Kasten as an issue. Fears that Mondale would endorse any sort of tax overhaul effort were entirely misplaced.

The coarse light of politics did shine on the tax group's discussions on a few other occasions. When Pearlman sheepishly brought in a proposal to require people who inherit property to pay a capital-gains tax on their inheritance, for example, the idea was quickly thrown back in his face. Congress had fought long and hard over that issue in the 1970s and the reformers had lost; Regan did not want to fight that battle again. Existing law enabled people to pass on stock and property to their heirs without paying any tax, thus allowing huge accumulations of untaxed wealth. Efforts to change that law invariably brought a raft of complaints from family farmers, small businessmen, and a host of others who hoped to pass on their estates to their families. "I was on the Hill when they tried that before, and I remember the uproar," said Thompson, who vigorously opposed Pearlman's proposal. "There's a difference between being a tax-cutting populist and being a Jimmy Carter liberal. This is what real liberal tax reformers want to do." Sobered by the strong reaction, Pearlman quickly withdrew the proposal.

Individual Retirement Accounts (IRAs) were another break that escaped the Treasury's scorched-earth plan, in part because officials feared the popular tax-free savings accounts were politically untouchable. Indeed, the Treasury's proposal actually expanded the annual contribution to IRAs to $2,500 per worker, up from $2,000 under current law; and to $2,500 for a nonworking spouse, up from $250. The Treasury group would never have guessed that while most of their sweeping proposals would be ignored, IRAs would end up being sacrificed in the bill that finally became law two years later.

It was October 31—Halloween—when the tax-reform group met in the conference room to get its first look at possible tax rates for the plan. The group had worked throughout the year, making tough decisions to eliminate loopholes, but they had not calculated how far their plan would allow tax rates to fall. This was to be the day of the payoff. The men arrived in good spirits, expecting the plan would allow the top rate to fall as low as 25 percent—half the 50-percent rate under existing law.

But Pearlman brought bad news. The department's number-crunchers had fed all the details of the plan into a computer and had asked the computer to design a three-rate structure that met two main requirements: the plan must be *revenue neutral*—raising neither more nor less money than the existing tax system—and *distributionally neutral*—causing no major changes in the distribution of the tax burden among income classes. The computer's response: for corporations, a rate of 28 percent; for individuals, three rates of 16 percent, 28 percent, and 37 percent.

The numbers shocked the group. They had courageously attacked even the most politically sensitive tax breaks and still the top rate was no lower than 37 percent. It hardly seemed worth the effort. "We've gone through all this, and this is the best we can get?" said Kingon. Johnson said that with those kinds of rates, the plan should be called "ZAP."

Pearlman and McLure were bothered by the rates as well, although for another reason. A top individual rate of 37 percent combined with a top corporate rate of 28 percent would create problems, they believed. Individuals would form corporations to shelter their income and escape the higher personal tax rate. The opportunities would be immense for the very kind of game-playing that they were trying to end. The top personal rate and the top corporate rate needed to be closer together.

The group discussed the rates at great length, with disappointment expressed all around the table. Pearlman and McLure went over their computer runs and tried to come up with more satisfactory numbers, but to no avail. No one was happy with the way things were turning out.

Secretary Regan was particularly disturbed. The rates 16-28-37 sounded "like a football call," he complained. Others in the group erupted in laughter at the secretary's quip, but he was serious. He wanted something more symmetrical, like the 10-10-10 proposal of Kemp and Roth, or the 10-5-3 plan of the Carlton group. Thompson suggested that 15 percent, 25 percent, and 35 percent would be better rates, and Regan agreed. He instructed Pearlman to make the rates 15-25-35.

The change seemed like a small one, but its effects were profound. While pleasing to the ear, the 15-25-35 rates would raise far less revenue than 16-28-37. Pearlman and McLure went back to their computers and found that to make the plan work, the corporate tax rate would have to be pegged at 33 percent, rather than 28 percent. That eliminated their concern about the wide spread between the top corporate and individual rates. But it also meant corporate taxes would increase by an astounding *$150 billion* over five years—the largest corporate tax increase ever proposed.

None of the Treasury officials had expected their tax reform plan to be a corporate-tax increase. From the start, members of the group had assumed their plan, like Bradley's, would not alter the split in the tax burden between corporations and individuals.

But in his desire to set easy-to-remember rates, Regan agreed to accept the $150 billion tax hike, with little further discussion. It was an astonishing development. Just two years earlier, Ronald Reagan said "there is no justification" for taxing corporate income. Now, his own Treasury Department was proposing to boost corporate taxes by 36 percent. For three decades, the burden on corporations had been declining; now Regan was proposing to abruptly reverse that slide for the sake of aesthetics!

Almost as an afterthought, Secretary Regan drastically changed the nature of the tax-overhaul effort. By raising corporate taxes, Regan was able to cut not only individual tax *rates,* but also individual tax *bills.* The plan offered taxpayers an average cut of 8.5 percent in their annual payments to Uncle Sam.

Later, after the plan came out, Regan and his advisers were accused of being politically naïve, but in the end, the large rise in corporate taxes turned out to be a political godsend. Without it, tax reform might never have made it through Congress. Only a conservative Republican administration could get away with proposing such a drastic hike in corporate taxes. Once the administration led the way, other politicians were glad to jump on board. Tax reform turned into old-fashioned tax cutting, with corporations picking up the tab. "Tax reform must be bought," Barber Conable had said. Donald Regan accidentally discovered a way to buy it.

Throughout most of 1984, Regan was successful in keeping his tax plan from leaking out into the press; seldom in Washington has such a major policy initiative been kept so quiet for so long. But as the political season came to an end, reporters began to pay more attention to what was happening in that small conference room at the Treasury Department. Attention turned to tax reform and what it might hold in store for the American people.

Regan himself was the source of the first information to leak about the plan. He agreed on October 3 to attend a "Sperling breakfast" for an on-the-record discussion with reporters. A principal topic was tax reform.

Washington reporters belong to various breakfast groups, lunch groups, and dinner groups. Much of the news gathering in the nation's capital is done over meals. But the granddaddy of all these meal-meetings, and the one which regularly produces major news, is hosted by Godfrey Sperling, Jr., a long-time reporter for the *Christian Science Monitor,* who goes by the name of "Budge."

Sperling started his breakfast group in 1966, and it has since grown into a Washington institution. The breakfasts feature a major political or government figure and are attended only by newspaper and magazine reporters. Television and radio reporters are excluded, as are the news wire services. The breakfasts are always "on the record"—Sperling early on decided to eschew the common practice in Washington of allowing his guests to speak "on background" or "off the record." Usually held in the Sheraton Carlton Hotel—also home to the Carlton group's Tuesday morning breakfasts—the Sperling breakfasts provide eggs, bacon, and viscous black coffee to countless droopy-eyed reporters, invited by Sperling to come in search of an early-morning story. Washington's most famous and powerful people, as well as many of its less famous and powerful, have spent an hour with this group. Sperling now averages about one hundred of these breakfasts each year, and has hosted nearly two thousand since he began. The group has eaten breakfast with Presidents Reagan, Carter, and Ford; it has, over the years, by one calculation, downed 468,000 oranges, 187,200 eggs, 17,531 pounds of bacon, and 234,000 pounds of sautéed potatoes. If the guests say something worthwhile, their words will appear in newspapers all across the country the next day. Usually, there's no mention of Sperling; the comments are said to have been made "at a breakfast meeting with reporters." In the nation's capital, everyone knows that means breakfast with Budge.

On the morning of October 3, Regan was in a talkative mood, and in answers to questions from the twenty or so reporters, he gave some important hints about the direction his revolutionary tax plan was taking. It would be a "modified flat tax" (an income-tax system with fewer and lower tax rates), he said, rather than a consumption-based tax. He also suggested vaguely that the investment incentives of 1981 might be repealed. Echoing the rhetoric of Pearlman and McLure, he said: "We have to decide whether we want our corporate tax policy to be an industrial policy. Accelerated depreciation and the investment tax credit have definitely favored manufacturing over services. We are considering whether we should continue these."

The comments whetted the press's appetite for reform stories. Later that month, *The Wall Street Journal* published a story about Treasury's plans to curb tax deductions for mortgage-interest payments on second homes. Then *The Washington Post* reported that the Treasury proposal would tax unemployment compensation and eliminate the deduction for state and local taxes. The state-and-local story elicited a response from President Reagan, who was still on the campaign trail. "It would have to be proven to me that there's a valid excuse" for eliminating the state and local deduction, he said. "I don't believe there is."

In mid-November the *Journal* published another story about the debate over whether to eliminate the 1981 investment incentives. Regan cavalierly referred to these reports as "not leaks, but drippings"; nonetheless, they put tremendous pressure on the Treasury group. The politically controversial parts of the plan were coming out a piece at a time, and the plan faced the possibility of being leaked to death. White House officials were angry at the Treasury for allowing the piecemeal revelations; they feared that the plan Regan was putting together would become an albatross for the administration. Tempers at Treasury flared, as fingers pointed and accusations flew wildly as to who was responsible for leaking the information.

At Kingon's urging, Regan finally decided the plan had to be released ahead of schedule to stop leaks. During a meeting in his office with Pearlman, he impatiently picked up the telephone and called Chief of Staff Baker at the White House. "What's the president's schedule for the next couple of weeks?" Regan asked. "When can we schedule a meeting on this? When can we see him?" He then looked over the phone at Pearlman and asked, "Can you have it done in a week?" Pearlman hesitated, knowing there was about a month's worth of work left, but he replied, "Yes." The meeting was arranged, and Pearlman limped back to his office to spread the news.

The next week at Treasury was filled with long days and sleepless nights. Everyone involved was scurrying about, trying to put the final touches on the plan in preparation for its release.

One issue that had to be resolved quickly was a title, which became a source of considerable amusement. McLure, who by this time was convinced that the plan would be a historic endeavor, played with various possible titles. A sentimental man, he wanted to pay private tribute to his mother, who was called "Baby" by her grandchildren. After trying various alternatives, he came up with the title *Broad-Based, Simple, and Fair Tax,* which in shortened form—*BBS Fair Tax*—would, at least to him, sound like "Baby's fair tax." Without mentioning the motive behind the name, he took it to Regan and asked what he thought.

"Broad-based, simple, and fair; broad-based, simple, and fair," muttered Regan, with a frown on his face. "We can't use that, it sounds like a girl I used to date!" In its stead, Regan decided to take the title from the president's words in the State of the Union address: *Tax Reform for Fairness, Simplicity, and Economic Growth.*

On Sunday, November 25, there was a final meeting of the group to review the plan, one day before it was to be taken to the president. Regan brought jelly donuts. The group discussed the controversial changes in capital-gains taxes and investment incentives one more time. They now knew for certain the proposal would cause a political uproar. But Regan was ready; he told the White House that he would release it as his own plan, not the president's. That would protect the president from the fallout, and at the same time allow Regan himself to take the spotlight.

On November 26 Regan and Pearlman walked across East Executive

Avenue to the White House for the briefing with the president. The meeting took place in the Cabinet Room, just a few steps away from the Oval Office, where the president held most of his meetings with cabinet members and other advisers. It was a rectangular room, with large French doors facing out into the Rose Garden. On the walls were portraits of three former presidents Reagan particularly admired: Eisenhower, Coolidge, and Taft. The president sat at the center of the long, oval table, with his back to the Rose Garden. Regan and Pearlman sat across from him, while others at the meeting scattered themselves around the table. The presentation lasted nearly two hours. The Treasury officials feared the president would object to their proposal to end the deduction for state and local taxes, but he did not. His comments a month earlier about eliminating the deduction apparently had been mere campaign rhetoric. The only serious objection the president raised to the massive plan was its proposal to end the deduction for country-club dues!

The president's eyes grew hazy as Regan explained the changes in corporate taxation, and he didn't seem to grasp the significance of the proposal. But other White House officials in the room immediately realized they were being handed political dynamite. The president's own Treasury Department was proposing a monumental corporate tax increase. The proposal, they thought, bordered on treason, spitting in the face of a whole host of Republican constituencies. It was a complete denunciation of the president's policies in 1981. It was, in the view of most of those gathered about the cabinet table, an outrage.

When Regan's presentation was through, there was an awkward silence. Most of the men in the room were reluctant to embarrass the Treasury secretary in front of the president and said nothing. The only exception was the president's acting chief economic adviser, William Niskanen, a man who throughout his career had had a habit of stating his views without hesitation. He had been fired from the Ford Motor Company for denouncing that firm's policy of advocating barriers to Japanese car imports, and now he was about to make another comment that would wipe out any chance he might ever have had of eliminating the word "acting" from his title.

The president turned to Niskanen and asked his evaluation of the plan. Niskanen replied, "Walter Mondale would have been proud." It was the ultimate insult, an idea that had entered the heads of others, but one which no one else dared to utter.

The next morning, Regan briefed key members of Congress on the plan, and they too raised their eyebrows in disbelief. At 11:20 A.M. he called Dan Rostenkowski in Chicago and gave him the basic details, but was quick to add "this plan's not set in cement." At 2:00 P.M. he held a press conference in the "Cash Room" of the Treasury, a grand, marble-walled room that got its name because it once was a disbursing office for Treasury funds. After describing the controversial proposal, Regan, already beginning to question the soundness of his own work, said these fateful words: "This thing is written on a word processor. It can be changed."

At the White House, most of the president's aides were anxious to push the "delete" key. While it may have been a policymaker's dream, the tax plan was a politician's nightmare. It stung a multitude of powerful pressure groups. In background conversations with reporters, aides were quick to declare the controversial package dead-on-arrival and to distance President Reagan from it. A statement issued by the White House said the president would not embrace a tax plan until he had the opportunity "personally to review the Treasury's recommendations carefully." Secretary Regan had worked hard to put this tax reform package together, but everyone in Washington seemed convinced that his efforts were in vain. Tax reform once again seemed to be stopped in its tracks.

Chapter 4

A Politician Comes
to the Treasury

Chris Hicks, Secretary Regan's young executive assistant, was sitting in his Treasury Department office on the morning of January 8, 1985, looking over some papers, when the telephone rang. David Chew, the deputy comptroller of the currency and a friend of Hicks, was on the other end of the line. "Have you heard the news?" Chew exclaimed. "Regan's going to the White House."

Hicks glanced out the window. The sky was slightly overcast, but from his desk, Hicks could still look across the street and see the windows of the president's Oval Office. He knew that his boss had been mysteriously summoned to the president's office earlier that morning, but he did not know why. "Regan's already *at* the White House," he told Chew.

"No, I mean Regan's becoming chief of staff. He and Jim Baker are switching jobs. They're announcing it right now in the press room!"

The news stunned Hicks, and the rest of Washington as well. The capital is in many ways a small town, and secrets are seldom hidden for long. The rumor mills usually get word of major administration personnel shake-ups days or even weeks before they happen. But no one, not even the Treasury secretary's closest aides, had foreseen this. Regan, after all, was trained on Wall Street and seemed ill-suited for a White House post. The job he was getting, White House chief of staff, required a keen political mind, something Regan demonstrably lacked. Jim Baker, on the other hand, was a consummate politician, but he had little expertise in the tax and financial affairs that are overseen by the Treasury Department.

While the job swap shocked official Washington, it offered the moribund tax proposal new hope. Before the announcement of the change, Regan's tax plan seemed to be sinking rapidly into oblivion. The White House showed no clear sign of interest in the proposal, and the chorus of complaints from special interest groups discouraged even the Treasury secretary.

With Regan and Baker switching jobs, however, the outlook changed dramatically. As chief of staff, Regan would be better situated to secure the president's blessing for reform. "At least now you can be sure you'll have White House support," Regan joked with reporters later that day, after the switch was announced. At the same time, Baker's reputation for accomplishing near-impossible legislative feats improved the odds for winning congressional approval of some sort of tax reform. Baker had no abiding interest in reform, to be sure, but he was loyal. He would push for tax reform if that was what the president wanted. Wyoming Representative Dick Cheney, a chief of staff in President Ford's White House, put it this way: "The tax policy has been developed. What's needed now is a fine political hand to move it, and that's Jim Baker's meat."

It was Regan who first suggested the job switch, even before his tax plan was unveiled. As a former corporate chief executive, Regan was accustomed to having total control, and he had always bridled under the reins of the White House. He longed for the power that accompanied the chief of staff's job, a power that often eclipsed cabinet posts, and he suspected Baker might be willing to go along with the swap. Watching Baker during the fall of 1984, in the midst of a whirlwind of legislative and campaign issues, Regan had seen the chief of staff grow fatigued and restless. In a private meeting in Baker's office right before the election, Regan broached the issue:

"You know, Baker, your trouble is you're tired of this job, you're weary," Regan said.

"You're right," Baker replied.

"You know the best thing that could happen to you? You and I should swap jobs."

"You're kidding."

"No, I'm not."

Baker was indeed weary. The tough task of running Ronald Reagan's White House showed in his face and in his demeanor. He had aged noticeably during his four years in the demanding job. The chief of staff had to broker the many interests that vied for the president's attention, and work on dozens of different issues of national and international importance, all at the same time. Baker was ready to move on to the less hectic life of a cabinet post. His first choice was to become secretary of State, and his second was probably secretary of Defense, but neither job was open. At one point, Baker even considered giving up his White House job to succeed Bowie Kuhn as commissioner of baseball. By the fall of 1984, with no major cabinet shake-ups on the horizon, Baker was thinking of packing up his things and returning to his native Texas.

Baker mulled over Regan's surprise offer for days and discussed it in detail with his White House protégé, Richard Darman. As was his habit, Darman drew up long lists of the pluses and minuses of the Treasury job, analyzing the possibilities and problems to the last detail. On Friday, November 30, Baker walked across the street to the Treasury building to have a private lunch with Regan and to explore the issue further. It was clear that Regan's offer was serious; Baker indicated he was interested as well. The two men then discussed the swap with Michael Deaver, a longtime aide and friend of the president who was the only other obvious candidate for the White House post. Deaver was getting ready to leave the White House himself and move to a more lucrative job as a lobbyist in the private sector, so he readily gave his assent. On Monday, January 7, Baker, Deaver, and Regan approached the president and told him their idea. "Let me sleep on it," the president replied. Nancy Reagan had reservations: She feared Regan's brusque personality was not right for the chief of staff's job. But early the next morning, the president called Baker and Regan to his office and gave them his blessing.

James Addison Baker III had come to politics late in life. A smooth and affable man, he was a direct descendant of one of the founding fathers of Houston and was reared in the comfortable surroundings that his family's widespread legal, banking, and corporate enterprises provided. He was sent off to prep school at the Hill School in Pennsylvania, then attended Princeton University. After Princeton, he returned home to study law at the University of Texas and to become—like his father, grandfather, and great-grandfather before him—a Texas lawyer.

Barred by an antinepotism rule from joining the family firm—Baker & Botts—the young Baker became a partner in a closely related law firm— Andrews, Kurth, Campbell & Jones. He spent nearly two decades there, working as a well-regarded corporate lawyer, enjoying his position in the top strata of Houston society, hunting turkey and geese, and not thinking a whit about politics. He was nominally a Democrat, but until the age of forty, he stayed true to the dictum his grandfather had once given to a newspaperman who had asked the secret to a lawyer's success: "Study hard. Work hard. And stay out of politics."

In 1970, George Bush, a Republican congressman from Texas and a friend of Baker's, convinced him to become a county manager for Bush's Senate campaign. Bush lost with a disappointing 46 percent of the vote statewide, but in Houston, where Baker was in charge, he garnered a hefty 61 percent of the vote. The experience convinced Baker that he should become the first in his family to switch to the Republican party. It also showed him that his grandfather had been wrong; he was cut out for politics.

In 1971 and 1972, Baker served as the finance chairman for Texas Republican candidates, and during the 1972 presidential campaign he directed the effort to reelect President Nixon in fourteen Texas counties along the Gulf Coast. In the Ford administration, Baker served nine months as undersecretary of Commerce and then joined the Ford reelection campaign as a delegate hunter. Baker's success in working for Ford helped stem the rising tide of Ronald Reagan supporters at the 1976 GOP convention and convinced Ford to make Baker his national campaign manager for the rest of the campaign. Although Ford lost the election to Jimmy Carter, Baker's political reputation was boosted.

In 1978, Baker made his one and only try for elective office. He ran for Texas attorney general against Democrat Mark White, who later went on to become governor. Despite the star-studded cast that came to Texas to campaign for him—including Bush, Ford, Jack Kemp, John Connally, and Ronald Reagan—Baker lost with 46 percent of the vote. Texas was still, by and large, a Democratic state.

A year later, Baker agreed to manage Bush's campaign for president. Baker fought hard for Bush, but he also kept in the back of his mind the possibility that his candidate might end up in the number-two spot. With characteristic caution, he avoided needlessly antagonizing front-runner Reagan. After Bush was soundly beaten and accepted the vice-presidential slot, Baker took a position in the Reagan-Bush campaign and helped Reagan prepare for his televised debates with President Carter. Two days after the election, Reagan called Baker to ask him to serve as White House chief of staff. It was a surprise to the Texas lawyer, who was not part of the "California Mafia," those close advisers who had been with Reagan since his days in the Sacramento governor's mansion. But the Texan's skills had impressed the new president, and Baker gladly accepted.

Baker's enemies on the political right never forgot that he was George Bush's man before he was Ronald Reagan's, and that Bush had run in 1981 as a moderate Republican. Conservatives sniped at Baker during his four years in the White House, accusing him of being a "pragmatist," of not being a true believer in Reagan's cause. But Baker served the president well, winning battles that others in the White House could not.

By the end of 1984, Baker's authority was unchallenged. The two men who were closest to the passionate ideology of the right—Ed Meese and William Clark—had both left the White House, Clark to be secretary of the Interior, Meese to be attorney general. Baker was in command and had the complete confidence of the president. He was at the height of his power.

But he was tired, and he was not at all optimistic about the prospects for his own success in the second term. He had engineered many tough compromises in the first term, and in the process had made many enemies. In addition, he knew that Reagan's election vow not to raise taxes would make it impossible for him to deal with what he considered the nation's most pressing domestic problem—the budget deficit. Better to get off the White House hot seat for a couple of years, he thought, and let somebody else take the heat. As he told a reporter for *The Washington Post*, "The higher the monkey climbs, the more you can see of his behind." The time had come to let someone else go up the tree.

In moving to the Treasury, Baker brought with him a handful of his closest aides. Margaret Tutwiler, his trusted executive assistant, became Treasury assistant secretary for public affairs and public liaison. John Rogers, White House director of administration, became assistant secretary for management. Most important, Baker brought along Richard Darman.

In a city full of clever people with large egos, Darman was an extreme. His titles were not awe-inspiring—assistant to the president, deputy Treasury secretary—but he turned each position into an office of power and notoriety. "Brilliant" and "brash" were the words most frequently used to describe him; he was one of the most fascinating figures in the Reagan administration. A consummate Washington insider, he reveled in the twists and turns of government policy-making. Those who worked with him called him an "outstanding intellect," a "bully," a "first-rate strategic thinker," and a "royal pain in the ass." His clever ploys became so well known that Senate Majority Leader Howard Baker created a new word—*Darmanesque*—to describe any maneuver that is too clever by half.

Darman became such a celebrity in the nation's capital that his last-minute failure to attend a dinner party prompted a major diplomatic row. The party was hosted by Sondra Gotlieb, the wife of the Canadian ambassador. When the hostess learned that Darman was not going to attend, she slapped her social secretary in the face—a slap that was written about for days in both the U.S. and the Canadian press.

Darman was born into a family of quiet, prosperous Yankee textile manufacturers who had amassed a comfortable estate and plenty of New England rectitude over three generations in the business. "We were big fish in small ponds," Darman said. At Rivers Country Day School, he was captain of the varsity football, lacrosse, and wrestling teams. He excelled in his classes; he can still remember the names of the few teachers who gave him grades lower than an A. He was admitted to Harvard after making near-perfect scores on his Scholastic Aptitude Tests; he still frets about scoring 793 on his high school math SAT exam after having made a perfect 800 the year before.

At Harvard, Darman again stood out. There, he met his wife, Kathleen Emmet, a Radcliffe beauty who graced the cover of *Life* magazine in a 1963 feature called "New Women and Radcliffe." And there, he first saw the glory of government service when alumnus and President-elect John F. Kennedy visited the campus and his image was seared in the mind of young Darman as the model of success.

After Harvard College came Harvard Business School and then the start of his own government career. Darman joined the Department of Health, Education, and Welfare, where he became a protégé of then-Secretary Elliot Richardson. He followed Richardson to the Defense Department and then to the Justice Department. While at Justice, Darman demonstrated his problem-solving skills by helping to negotiate the agreement that resulted in the resignation of Vice President Spiro T. Agnew in 1973. It was a tense time for the nation. The Watergate scandal was dogging President Nixon, and the investigation of Agnew for multiple charges of conspiracy, extortion, and bribery threatened to cause a constitutional crisis. The Justice Department worked out a careful compromise under which Agnew agreed to resign and avoided imprisonment by pleading no contest to a single charge of income tax evasion. It was the sort of complex maneuvering at which Darman excelled. When Richardson resigned in protest, after refusing to fire Watergate prosecutor Archibald Cox, in the infamous "Saturday night massacre," Darman resigned with him.

Darman met Baker during the Ford administration, when they both did short stints at the Commerce Department. Although he played virtually no role in the election of Ronald Reagan, Darman, who was then teaching at the John F. Kennedy School of Government at Harvard, contacted Baker immediately after the election and offered his help in organizing the Reagan White House. Well aware of Darman's talents, Baker accepted the offer. Darman carved a place for himself in the White House as the man in charge of documents, the "paper czar"; he knew that controlling the flow of paper was critical in managing the government bureaucracy. He decided which pieces of paper reached the president's Oval Office, and he reviewed and edited the pieces that left. He made himself indispensable to the White House operation, and his stature in the administration grew accordingly.

His reputation for prickliness also grew. Darman was full of scorn for lesser intellects and full of concern that his own intellect should be adequately recognized and appreciated. At age forty-two, he still had a bit of the overanxious schoolboy in him. As political scientist Richard Neustadt, his former colleague at the Kennedy School, put it,"Dick is about as sharp a strategic thinker as I've seen, but he can't resist the temptation to say, 'Look Ma, no hands.' "

That quality grated on some of his colleagues and acquaintances, making him an inviting target for criticism. He became a whipping boy both within the administration and on Capitol Hill. While many in Washington were reluctant to criticize Baker, because of his position of power and his gentlemanly demeanor, they would freely lash out at Darman.

One senior Republican aide in the House of Representatives described Darman this way:

Every sort of conniving thing that came out of [the Treasury] they assumed Darman was part of, whether it was true or not. I mean, *Darmanesque* is a term that goes beyond whatever he does; it describes anything that is sneaky and conniving and not terribly good tax policy, and, I'm sure he got both credit and blame for things he had nothing to do with.

While Baker was clearly his mentor in the Reagan administration, Darman bristled at being referred to as Baker's "staff." His sensitivity to being dubbed an aide to Baker was so well known that Deaver and another White House colleague tweaked him by having license plates put on his car that read BAKER AIDE. After Darman took his job at Treasury, Republican Representative John Duncan questioned Darman's presence at a meeting that included no staff. Darman angrily retorted: "I am not staff. I don't think I should have had to go through the confirmation hearings and other things in order to have people come along and suggest that the deputy secretary of the Treasury is staff."

Nevertheless, Baker and Darman complemented each other so neatly that it was difficult to think of one without the other. Baker was the politician and the diplomat; he was a master at dealing with people and at orchestrating compromises. But he had little time for, or interest in, complex issues of government policy. Darman, on the other hand, liked to toy with policy ideas and was the perfect back-room strategist. Like Baker, he was a savvy political operator, but he also had an extraordinary grasp of the substance of issues—a rare and valuable combination of skills. He could quickly analyze complicated topics, and he knew how to turn and twist them to gain tactical political advantages. His problems came, however, in dealing with people. Baker cared a great deal about being liked; Darman was fully accustomed to being disliked. The two men fit together so well that their names were frequently linked as if hyphenated; in Washington it was the "Baker-Darman Treasury," an honor granted to no previous deputy secretary.

The task of shepherding a radical tax-overhaul bill through Congress would require considerable political and intellectual acumen. Most people in Washington still doubted it could be done. If anyone could succeed at the task, if anyone could strike the compromises needed to disarm some of reform's most powerful opponents, it was probably these two men. If tax reform was at the top of their agenda, its chances of success would be markedly improved.

In January of 1985, however, there was still no clear sign that tax reform was at the top of anyone's agenda. As well-known White House "pragmatists," Baker and Darman specialized in solving problems. But tax reform did not appear to address any of the pressing economic problems that faced the administration: It did nothing to reduce the soaring budget deficit that promised to be Reagan's most startling legacy; and it did nothing to alleviate the nation's trade problems that threatened to undermine the Republican party in future elections.

Furthermore, Baker and Darman both reacted with scorn when Secretary Regan brought his "ideal" tax plan to the White House in November of 1984. They thought it was a political minefield, and the events of the following weeks confirmed that judgment. The White House was flooded with complaints from constituents of various stripes, who were pleading to retain their favored tax breaks. Businessmen were outraged by the $150 billion increase in corporate taxes. Oil and gas drillers, heavy contributors to the Reagan campaign, angrily sent back the "Eagle pins" they had earned for annual contributions of $10,000 to the GOP. The Knights of Columbus launched a telephone blitz to protest the taxation of their insurance plans. Veterans paraded in protest of the taxation of their disability benefits. There seemed no end to the outcry. Treasury official McLure, who had to field many of the complaints, recalls: "I went from being a nobody to being the most disliked nobody in the country."

All of this noise badly battered Baker's sensitive political antennae. Pearlman recalls going to brief the Treasury secretary-designate before his Senate confirmation: "He was very negative about the proposal, that was apparent. Much of that negativism seemed to be because he too had been deluged by these outside complainers." The public reaction had confirmed Baker's initial political judgment: Those who are hurt by tax reform will always scream louder than those who are helped.

That impression deepened when Baker went to Capitol Hill for his confirmation hearing. Seated at a table, with the members of the Finance Committee spread out before him at the semicircular podium, Baker listened politely as one senator after another listed his reservations about the Treasury plan. Senator Steve Symms, Republican of Idaho, fretted about the effects on the life insurance industry; Senator David Boren, Democrat of Oklahoma, voiced concern about its effect on oil and gas exploration; Senator John Danforth, Republican of Missouri, raised questions about charitable contributions; Senator Daniel Patrick Moynihan, Democrat of New York, urged retention of the state and local deduction; and committee Chairman Bob Packwood voiced opposition to the proposed taxation of employee fringe benefits.

The strongly pro–tax-break sentiment of the committee was summed up in a long and bizarre discourse by Democratic Senator Spark Matsunaga of Hawaii about the importance of tax preferences in promoting his state's macadamia nut industry. An amiable Japanese-American known mostly for promoting his state's parochial interests, Matsunaga repeated a story about his days as majority leader of the Hawaii House of Representatives:

I was approached by a group of businessmen who wanted a special tax moratorium of eight years, in order to enable them to start a new industry—the macadamia nut industry. There was no macadamia nut industry at the time, so we went along with the businessmen and gave them a tax moratorium for eight years. That is the period required for the trees to bear fruit. Today the industry is up to $55 million and is projected to reach $240 million by 1990. . . . That is only at the small state level—the small state of Hawaii. Just imagine what could happen nationwide!

It was clear that members of the Finance Committee saw the tax code as their tool for molding the economy and the society to their liking. Their philosophy of government had no room in it for a radical tax reform that would wipe away all the loopholes and incentives they had struggled to put in place. The complaints hit home with Baker and did little to bolster his desire to press for reform.

Baker, of course, would fight for tax overhaul if the president wanted him to, but at the beginning of 1985, it was not even clear that President Reagan was anxious for reform.

The president gave reform a boost in his 1985 State of the Union address, making it a pillar of his plan for a "second American revolution." "The Treasury Department has produced an excellent reform plan whose principles will guide the final proposal that we will ask you to enact," he told the lawmakers gathered in the House chamber. "Tonight I am instructing Treasury Secretary James Baker . . . to begin working with congressional authors and committees for bipartisan legislation conforming to these principles."

But the next day, the president's astonishing comments in an interview with *The Wall Street Journal* blew a huge hole in the previous night's optimistic assessment. Asked about the 36-percent increase in corporate taxes in what had become known as the "Treasury I" proposal, the president professed shock and surprise. He first denied that the plan included such a boost in corporate taxes, then said that if it did, he doubted he could support such a move. "I would have to be convinced of the need" to increase corporate taxes, he said, suggesting that taxes on corporations are merely passed on to individuals anyway. "Someday, I would hope that we could arrive at a tax structure that would recognize that you can't tax things, you only tax people." The president seemed to misunderstand the very heart of the "excellent reform plan" he had praised the night before.

Along the corridors of K Street, where many of Washington's highest-paid corporate lobbyists keep their offices, news of President Reagan's comments to the *Journal* was greeted with cheers. Charls Walker was away at Harvard's Kennedy School of Government, attending a conference on corporate taxation, when the interview was published. He was up at 6:45 A.M., got a copy of the *Journal* in the hotel lobby, saw the story about the president's comments, walked into the dining room, and exclaimed: "Look! Look! Look what the president said! We may as well call off the conference." The story, he recalls, "made my day."

Despite his comments, Reagan's interest in tax reform did not wane.

Chief of Staff Regan quashed his boss's concerns about corporate taxes by arguing that only *some* corporations—those that had escaped taxes entirely in recent years—faced a tax increase. It was a less-than-candid explanation, but it was enough. Reagan's feelings about corporate taxes faded quickly when confronted with his desire to lower individual tax rates. If a tax reform that boosted corporate taxes was the only way to get rates down, then he was for it.

Once the president decided he wanted tax reform, Baker and Darman had to deliver. Their reputations were at stake.

For Baker, the role of a tax reformer was one he assumed with some reluctance. Ron Pearlman assessed the secretary's feelings this way: "I think Baker's philosophy through this whole process was: (a) I wish tax reform had never come up; (b) I wish the Treasury package had never come out; (c) we can't drop it so let's make the best of it; and (d) what we really want out of it is reduced rates, and we'll do anything we can within reason to get those."

For Darman, tax reform had a more fundamental goal—it addressed a deep and abiding problem in the American political and social psyche. The disintegration of the tax code over the past few decades had undermined people's faith not only in the tax system, but in government itself, he believed. Although he served in an administration that portrayed government as a parasite, Darman was, at heart, a true believer in government. He held a deep-seated conviction that the government can and should be a positive force in society. Perhaps it was the triumphant visit by President Kennedy to Harvard two decades earlier, perhaps it was that his own career was tied up so closely with government service, but the cynical Darman became something of a romantic when conversation turned to the importance of federal government in American society. People's faith in government had been battered by two decades of tragedies: the Vietnam War, Watergate, the Iranian hostage crisis. Darman felt tax reform was one of the ways in which the Reagan administration might help restore that faith.

"Kennedy was shot and died," he told a reporter for *The New York Times.* "Reagan was shot and survived. He personifies the restoration of this notion of the possible."

Treasury I clearly had to be changed before it could be either embraced fully by the president or enacted by Congress. It had too many problems; it stepped on too many toes. Baker's job was to do what Regan had avoided; to bring politics fully into the process. He had to walk a very narrow and treacherous line: restoring enough tax breaks to keep a coalition of powerful special interests from killing the entire effort, while at the same time repealing enough preferences to make meaningful tax reform possible. It was no easy task.

Baker and Darman were encouraged by one aspect of the reaction to the Treasury proposal. For the first time, a Reagan administration initiative was winning kudos from the political left. Many liberal reformers were heaping praise upon the plan, calling it a tremendous step in the right direction. Secretary Regan even received a warm and encouraging hand-written note from George McGovern, the liberal Democrat who had led his party's ticket in the 1972 election. "I hope it won't hurt your tax proposal to have my support," McGovern wrote. "It is a fair, common-sense reform." Regan's aides were embarrassed by the letter and tried to hide it from the press, but Baker and Darman saw in such reactions an opportunity. They knew tax reform could only be achieved as part of a bipartisan effort; partisan squabbling would surely doom such a complex and controversial bill. If they could calm some of their GOP supporters without losing the left, tax reform might actually have a chance. They had an opportunity to enhance their own reputations by accomplishing the legislative feat of the decade.

In fact, Darman eventually came around to the view that Treasury I was a brilliant, if inadvertent, strategic move: It convinced liberal Democratic reformers that they should support the administration's effort. At the same time, it put the gold-cufflinked lobbyists on the defensive; special interests would have to fight the tough proposals threatened by the Treasury plan. In order to avoid the worst, they might be willing to settle for something less onerous. For all their supposed political ineptitude, the framers of Treasury I might not have had such a bad idea. "I sometimes wish I had thought of it myself," Darman said.

In devising their strategy to get tax reform through Congress, Baker and Darman hailed back to one of their greatest successes in the White House: the 1983 rescue of the Social Security system. Like tax reform, Social Security seemed an impossible issue for the political process to deal with. The Social Security system at the time was on the verge of insolvency, yet no one dared offer a solution. When the Republicans proposed even modest cuts in Social Security benefits, the Democrats immediately piled on, whipping up fear in the minds of senior citizens that the GOP was going to destroy their economic lifeline. When Democrats proposed boosting payroll taxes to pay for continued benefits, the GOP was quick to shout its favorite refrain: Democrats are the party of "tax and spend." Mutual fear resulted in a dangerous stalemate.

To defuse the issue in the 1982 midterm elections, President Reagan appointed a commission, headed by economist Alan Greenspan, to study the issue and make recommendations after the November elections. The ploy worked temporarily, but even after the election the commission remained deadlocked.

Aware that failure to deal with the Social Security issue could cause irreparable damage to the Republican party, Baker launched a rescue mission. Huddling in private with small groups of key legislators and commission members, Baker, Darman, White House Budget Director David Stockman, and chief White House Congressional Lobbyist Kenneth Duberstein hammered out the needed compromises. It was a classic Baker operation: The meetings were held in secret, at the elegant Blair House mansion across the street from the White House. Baker and Darman went to incredible lengths to avoid reporters, using back driveways and rear doors at every opportunity. At first they met with legislators and commission members one or two at a time. Gradually they built up a small "core" group of power brokers and worked out an acceptable compromise. The group included Senate Majority Leader Howard Baker and Senate Finance Chairman Bob Dole on the Republican side, and Senator Daniel Patrick Moynihan and a representative of House Speaker Tip O'Neill on the Democratic side. With such powerful support, the final compromise was pushed through Congress in less than three months with few major changes.

Baker and Darman envisioned a similar course for tax reform. They feared that if dealt with in the normal, wide-open legislative process, the tax bill would be picked apart by legions of lobbyists. Their best chance of success was to negotiate a "precooked" deal in private with a few key members of Congress. Then after the plan became public, it could be rushed through the legislature, just like the Social Security plan, before the lobbyists had an opportunity to pounce.

It was a bold scheme—and probably a naïve one. Rewriting the nation's tax code was far more complex than propping up a single program like Social Security. The tentacles of the tax system reached into every area of American life; lawmakers were not likely to rubber stamp such a far-reaching set of proposals. Nevertheless, Baker and Darman thought their strategy was tax reform's best shot.

As the two Treasury officials saw it, the negotiations had to include the four congressional tax reformers—Senator Bradley, Representative Gephardt, Representative Kemp, and Senator Kasten—as well as the four chief tax writers—Chairman Rostenkowski of the Ways and Means Committee; John Duncan, the Republican who was the ranking minority member of the committee; Chairman Packwood of the Finance Committee; and Russell Long, the senior Democrat on the Senate panel. If a secret agreement could be reached among all eight of these men, Baker and Darman thought, it could move rapidly through Congress. Recalls Darman:

We had to make sure that the next document we came out with did not get declared dead on arrival as Treasury I had. . . . What we hoped for was a kind of joint announcement of Rostenkowski and Packwood and the president and a few others, arm in arm, announcing, not a Reagan I, but some sort of Consensus I.

The two Treasury officials began holding secret meetings with the legislators, trying to gauge where the political center might lie. Some of the meetings were held on Capitol Hill, in the offices of the lawmakers. Others were held in Baker's home on fashionable Foxhall Road. The participants met in the Treasury secretary's den on the bottom floor, which had a large picture window looking out onto the back lawn and the woods beyond. The walls in the den were decorated with stuffed ducks and big-game trophies bagged by the Treasury secretary on an African safari. A zebra skin was layed out on the floor. In these surroundings, Baker, Darman, and the various legislators compared Treasury I, Bradley-Gephardt, Kemp-Kasten, and the existing law, trying to find an acceptable middle ground. Of the four reformers, Bradley, Gephardt, and Kemp all showed a strong knowledge of their plans, and a willingness to deal. Kasten was another case. The baby-faced Wisconsin senator had clearly not taken the time to study his own complex proposal. In a discussion about taxing a multifaceted fringe-benefit package known as a "cafeteria plan," Kasten commented, "We can't tax those lunches." At a later breakfast meeting, he failed to show.

Chairman Packwood indicated a grudging willingness to play along, provided the plan did not tax fringe benefits. Senator Long seemed willing to participate as well, despite his doubts about the value of such an exercise. Duncan attended the meetings, but showed no interest in reform. A conventional Republican with an undistinguished legislative record, Duncan worried about the businesses in his Tennessee district that would be hurt by such a proposal.

But a big kink blocked the Baker-Darman strategy: Dan Rostenkowski. The proud Chicago politician did not think it was proper for him, as chairman of the House Ways and Means Committee, to negotiate with junior members of Congress like Bradley, Gephardt, Kemp, or Kasten. More important, he viewed the entire administration effort as a Republican trap. If he agreed to be part of Baker's "consensus" negotiations, the Democrats might be tricked into accepting tax reform without ever having an opportunity to put their own stamp on it or to claim credit for it, and putting Democrats back on the map with tax reform was what Rostenkowski was all about. Recalls Rostenkowski:

Baker said to me, "Danny, we can do it." We can do it? What's this "we" crap? He said, "Danny, my God, do you realize what'll happen? Do you know what we could do?" And I said, "Jimmy boy, you're massaging me. I have been handled by better than you, and your hands are cold."

Baker and Darman insisted that they wanted to complete the bill in 1985; Rostenkowski resisted that as well. That was just impossible, he said. Legislation of this magnitude would take time—lots of it. He complained privately that the new Treasury officials were just political hotshots on the make. He thought of the duo as "young analytical geniuses" who had "just left the White House thinking all they had to do was say this is dictatorial policy from the White House."

With Rostenkowski resisting, the Social Security strategy was doomed. Baker and Darman considered alternative versions of the strategy that would exclude Rostenkowski. The administration had managed to work around the stubborn Ways and Means chairman in enacting the tax plans of 1981 and 1982, as well as the Social Security plan of 1983. Tax reform, however, was different. It was a fragile undertaking and could quickly fall apart if the powerful chairman worked against it. The House, after all, was designated under the Constitution as the place where all tax bills must originate, and Rostenkowski was the chief tax writer there. Baker and Darman decided they had no choice but to put together a tax package of their own, send it to Rostenkowski, and allow him to work his will. It was a dangerous strategy, they knew, but in the face of Rostenkowski's intransigence, it was the only way.

Within the Treasury Department, a new tax-writing group was formed to craft a revised plan. On the surface, the group bore a resemblance to the team that wrote the first Treasury proposal. It met in the Secretary's conference room, with the windows overlooking the White House. Pearlman was still there, and so were McLure, Johnson, Thompson, and Egger.

But the new Secretary and the two aides who accompanied him in the meetings—Darman and Margaret Tutwiler—set a very different tone. The meetings were frequently held on Saturdays, a practice that Regan nearly always avoided. Baker would show up in casual corduroys and pick a seat on the side of the table (unlike Regan, he seldom sat at the head). He propped his cowboy boots on the table, crammed a wad of Red Man chewing tobacco in his mouth, and placed a large plastic cup in front of him to use as a spittoon ("That's disgusting," said Tutwiler, a former Alabama debutante). Where Regan avoided all talk of politics, Baker talked about little else. He had scant patience for the theoretical presentations of Pearlman and McLure. He would lean back and spit in his cup or scratch his nose and then demand, "What are we hearing on that one?" or "Who's working against it?"

For Pearlman and McLure, it was a demoralizing period. All the elaborate and elegant rationale for their original plan was simply ignored. Neither Baker nor Darman showed any tendency to defer to the two tax experts. Indeed, Darman felt that lawyers like Pearlman were poorly equipped to make judgments about economic policy and that economists like McLure knew nothing of the motivations of ordinary businessmen. The tax experts had enjoyed remarkable influence and power in the drafting of Treasury I; now that influence was being undercut as their plan was recast to reflect political realities.

Relations between Pearlman and Darman grew particularly tense. Traditionally, the assistant Treasury secretary for tax policy maintained a high profile on issues of tax policy. Pearlman's predecessor, Buck Chapoton, had been an independent force, handling all the department's tax negotiations with Congress. But after Darman arrived, it quickly became clear that *he* planned to take charge of reform. Says Pearlman:

I viewed my role as the historical role of the assistant secretary for tax policy, as the principal liaison between the secretary and Congress. I wasn't about to give that role up. Dick came in with the idea that he was going to take over tax reform, and I just wasn't going to let that happen. There was continuous tension because I didn't view myself as working for Dick Darman. I viewed myself as working for the secretary.

Baker and Darman would go up to the Hill and see a member and I would never know they'd gone and the next thing I'd know, I'd get a call from the Hill staff saying there was a meeting, and they'd start talking to me about the meeting and I wouldn't know what the hell was going on. It wasn't just embarrassing, I couldn't function that way. I discussed it with the secretary, but he didn't do anything.

For Manuel Johnson, the new Treasury team was a welcome change. Suddenly, he found the table tilting toward him. Baker and Darman agreed to repeal the investment tax credit, but they were not willing to go so far as to repeal the rapid depreciation write-offs that they had labored to enact as White House strategists in 1981. They wanted to retain some incentives to encourage investment in equipment, and they worked with Johnson to keep those incentives.

Johnson had always complained that Pearlman and McLure resisted his suggestions, but with Baker backing him up, that quickly ended. One day, after Pearlman reported that he still did not have a revenue estimate ready on Johnson's proposals, Johnson went to the secretary to protest Pearlman's foot-dragging. Baker, completely sympathetic, launched into a folksy reminiscence, comparing Johnson's problems with Pearlman to the plight of his youngest son, Dougie, on Easter:

One Easter we decided to buy little Easter ducks for all my kids. We bought them, had them ready the night before, so they could come downstairs and look at them. So they all got up the next morning, ran down, and found one of the ducks had died. My oldest son said: "Aw, look, Dougie's duck died!" And what was worse, Dougie said: "Aw yeah, my duck died."

"Now, isn't that the way you feel, Manley?" Baker asked.

"That's exactly how I feel," Johnson replied.

"Well from now on, you're going to get your revenue estimates on time."

Afterward, Johnson virtually took over the job of fashioning a revised system of depreciation write-offs, with Pearlman and McLure providing the technical expertise needed to make the plan work.

Practical politics was a new and shocking change for the veterans of Treasury I. The transformation was typified by an encounter between Pearlman and a group of angry war veterans. The veterans were deeply disturbed about the Treasury I proposal to tax veterans' disability payments, which for years had enjoyed tax-free status. Representatives of various veterans' groups demanded a meeting with Pearlman, and he agreed. A small army of them stormed into his Treasury office, led by Chad Colley, national commander of the Disabled American Veterans, who had lost both legs and one arm while fighting in Vietnam.

Pearlman, still ensconced in the theoretical tower of Treasury I, started the meeting by asking the triple amputee in Socratic fashion, "Why should veterans disability payments be treated differently than any other income?" The meeting went downhill from there. It was a natural question for Pearlman, who knew that some disabled veterans with jobs that paid over $100,000 a year were still getting tax-free benefits from Uncle Sam, but to the veterans in his office, Pearlman's comment was heresy. They were accustomed to being catered to in the nation's capital, and they had never heard anything like this. Recognizing his error, a red-faced Pearlman desperately tried to dig his way out of the hole, but to no avail. The veterans left his office and went on the warpath, calling all their allies in the White House and on Capitol Hill. They even convinced Senator Alan Cranston of California to introduce a resolution urging that the Treasury not tax their disability benefits.

The disabled veterans demanded a second meeting at the Treasury, this time with Baker. They showed the secretary a full-page advertisement that they were planning to run in *The New York Times, The Washington Post,* and *U.S.A. Today.* It had a huge picture of Commander Colley in a wheelchair, his missing appendages painfully evident. At the top of the page, in large bold letters, the copy read: WHAT'S SO SPECIAL ABOUT DISABLED VETERANS? In smaller type below, it continued: "That's what a top Treasury official said to Chad Colley . . ."

As soon as the veterans departed, Baker called Pearlman down to his office. He showed him the advertisement and said bluntly, "I think we'll have to drop this one."

Many other provisions of Treasury I were similarly cast off during the first few months of 1985, as Baker listened to various complainants. The new secretary's job during this period was to decide which tax breaks he could afford to preserve without seriously undermining tax reform and which breaks he could repeal without bringing on the opposition of overwhelmingly powerful interest groups. He kept an arduous schedule. The leaders of corporate America streamed through his door. In February alone, he met with the chairman of Texaco, who was concerned about oil-and-gas tax breaks; the chairman of the Ford Motor Company, who worried about the end of investment incentives; the president of the National Federation of Independent Business, who was disturbed by the elimination of lower tax rates for small businesses; an official from the Securities Industry Association, opposed to the elimination of the preferential treatment of capital gains, and the president of the Chamber of Commerce, who complained about plans to eliminate a host of tax benefits. In March, the pleaders included representatives of nonprofit organizations worried about losing deductions for charitable contributions, and the chairmen of E. I. du Pont de Nemours, the National Association of Manufacturers, the American Iron and Steel Institute, the Mid-Continent Oil and Gas Association, and the National Association of Home Builders. There seemed to be no end to the rich and powerful people who wanted to see the secretary, and virtually all of them demanded that their favored tax breaks be retained.

But not everyone complained. On March 28, Baker, Darman, Tutwiler, and Pearlman met with a group of seven corporate executives who supported tax reform. They included John Richman of Dart & Kraft, James Ferguson of General Foods, Roger Smith of General Motors, Allen Jacobson of 3M, William Howell of J. C. Penney, John Smale of Procter & Gamble, and Alton Whitehouse of Standard Oil of Ohio. The meeting made clear that there was a split in the business community on tax reform. Many companies, particularly those that paid high tax rates and made only modest use of investment incentives, favored eliminating tax preferences in return for lower rates. A small group of others—like Roger Smith of GM—thought tax reform would be good for their customers and encourage sales.

The fabled unity of the business community that had triumphed during the 1981 tax bill was now gone. If Baker and Darman could fashion a tax-reform plan that pried that crack in the business community a bit wider, they might at least weaken the business opposition to their bill. A strategy of divide-and-conquer could allow tax reform to succeed.

One group that the Treasury team worked hard to woo was high-tech firms, especially the small entrepreneurial start-up companies that had become the symbols of hope and promise for a changing American economy. Computer companies, software firms, biotechnology firms—these were the cutting edge of the nation's industry, developing new technologies that many hoped would reinvigorate the economy. Secretary Regan's tax team had thought these high-tech types would be natural supporters of their proposal. Unlike smokestack industries, they did not invest heavily in equipment and gained little benefit from investment tax breaks; their efforts instead relied on knowledge and research. For such companies, the trade off of lower tax rates for fewer tax preferences was an attractive one.

The Treasury I team had forgotten, however, that the lifeblood for many small companies is venture capital and that the low tax rate for capital gains encouraged venture investment. By eliminating the low gains rate, venture-capital experts complained, the Treasury tax plan would "dry up" the money available for start-up operations.

Baker and Darman were sympathetic to these high-tech arguments. Darman, in particular, felt American businessmen were too cautious and would avoid risk unless given an incentive. For weeks, he struggled with ways to develop a special capital-gains "carve-out" that would only benefit investors in risky entrepreneurial enterprises, but in the end, he failed. He found it impossible to draw a meaningful line between entrepreneurial investments and other investments. Convinced that political pressures for a low capital-gains rate would be too great to withstand, he and Baker agreed to retain the gains preference—another big loss for Treasury's tax reformers.

The new Treasury team also realized that Regan's proposal to tax most fringe benefits would have to be severely modified. Packwood made it clear from the start that his top goal was to save the tax-free status of employee fringes, especially health insurance. He told Baker point-blank that he would "kill the bill if I have to," unless employee benefits were protected. He threatened to extend Senate hearings indefinitely or form coalitions with oil-state lawmakers to block the proposal. He even threatened to take his position public and go "toe-to-toe" with President Reagan to preserve the tax-free status of benefits.

Tax-free fringes were dear to one of the Democratic party's chief backers, organized labor, which liked to bargain for hefty benefits for its members. Ironically the unions found their fiercest defender in Republican Packwood, not Democrat Rostenkowski. Rostenkowski urged the Treasury to "hang tough" with the Treasury I fringe-benefit proposal. The Ways and Means chairman knew that if the House passed a bill that taxed fringes, he would have a powerful bargaining chip when he faced Packwood in the House-Senate conference committee, where the measures passed by each chamber would be reconciled into a final bill. Packwood would accept almost anything Rostenkowski served up in order to preserve the benefits, Rostenkowski thought. The Ways and Means chairman even told AFL-CIO president Lane Kirkland, during a testy meeting, that he would not protect labor's fringe benefits and that the AFL-CIO would have to send its lobbyists to the Hill to defend them.

Baker, Darman, and Pearlman met with Packwood on several occasions in his office to discuss the fringe-benefit problem. The Treasury officials argued that they could not afford to give up the taxation of all fringes. Treasury I raised almost $50 billion over five years by taxing the benefits, and the Treasury needed some of that money to help pay the cost of lower tax rates. After several discussions, Packwood offered a compromise: Health insurance was the biggest fringe, and Packwood suggested taxing just the first few dollars' worth of employer-provided health insurance, instead of taxing the amount of insurance that exceeded a set cap, as Treasury I proposed. Treasury reformers preferred the cap approach because it would end the incentive for excessively large health plans, which some economists claimed contributed to the skyrocketing cost of health care. Packwood, however, opposed the cap because its burden fell hardest on union members with hefty benefits. His proposal, which would tax the first twenty-five dollars a month in health benefits received by every worker, would do nothing to reduce the incentive for excessive health benefits, but it would raise money and be relatively less painful to labor groups. Packwood tried to distance himself from the idea by saying that it was given to him informally by Lane Kirkland.

Treasury officials immediately recognized the Packwood plan as bad tax policy, because it hit those workers with only modest health benefits just as hard as those with excessively large ones. "The proposal was absolutely crazy," says Pearlman. "It was 180 degrees from where we should be." But Baker and Darman believed they had no choice; they could not afford to alienate the Finance chairman.

In April, Pearlman and Darman paid a visit to Packwood's office to seal the deal. Packwood indicated to the Treasury officials that he had talked with union representatives and that they supported his compromise proposal. Darman said the Treasury was willing to accept it. Then Pearlman spoke up. Knowing that the Oregon senator cared deeply about timber tax benefits as well as fringes, Pearlman said, "Mr. Chairman, are you okay on timber capital gains?" Darman put his hand on Pearlman's arm hoping to quiet him, but Packwood broke in, "That's okay, I can answer that." As long as there is "equal treatment" for all industries, he said, he would be willing to see the special capital-gains benefit for timber producers eliminated.

Darman and Pearlman left the meeting with a sense of relief. The fringe-benefit proposal made little sense, to be sure, but at least, they thought, Packwood and the unions were on board.

That relief, however, was premature. In the end, the unions were not satisfied with the Packwood compromise. They were determined to preserve the tax-free status of all fringe benefits, and they turned their backs on the Treasury plan. Kirkland's AFL-CIO, in particular, never backed the proposal. Rostenkowski later heaped criticism on the Treasury team for the deal: They had given away half the store to Packwood, but they had gotten nothing in return. The Treasury officials did get one thing they needed, however: the promise of Packwood not to torpedo reform.

As political deals were struck at Treasury, Rostenkowski urged Baker and Darman not to give away too much. He told the two administration officials that any tax breaks they gave away probably would not be taken back, that their plan would be the "high-water mark" of reform. Privately, Rostenkowski also feared the Treasury would make so many concessions that his committee would be unable to make concessions of its own to favorite interests.

The chairman also warned the Treasury secretary that there was one issue that would be his "litmus test" of real reform. If Baker failed to handle it correctly, he argued, it would be clear that the administration was not sincerely interested in reforming the tax code. That issue was oil and gas.

Oil and gas drillers had received favored tax treatment for almost as long as the income tax had existed. The generous percentage depletion allowance—a huge tax break allowing companies to deduct a percentage of their income as an incentive for pulling oil out of the ground—was enacted in 1926. The immediate write-off for certain "intangible" drilling costs came into the tax code through a series of administrative rulings by the Treasury and won full congressional approval in the Revenue Act of 1954. Treasury Secretary Henry Morgenthau railed against percentage depletion in 1937, calling it the tax code's "most glaring loophole." In 1950 and 1951 President Harry Truman took on the oil-and-gas tax breaks, arguing that a "forward-looking resources program does not require that we give hundreds of millions of dollars annually in tax exemptions to a favored few at the expense of the many." But proposals to repeal the oil and gas tax breaks were repeatedly trounced in Congress.

The oil industry owed its tax successes to a long string of oil-state legislators who managed to accumulate remarkable power in Congress. In the 1950s and early 1960s, Senator Robert Kerr of Oklahoma, the "uncrowned king of the Senate," was a powerful protector of the industry and managed to easily rebuff any attempts to eliminate or reduce the depletion tax break. Representative Sam Rayburn of Texas, speaker of the House in the 1940s and 1950s, wouldn't even consider allowing a member of the House to have a cherished seat on the Ways and Means committee unless he was committed to the depletion tax break. Senator Russell Long of Louisiana, chairman of the Finance Committee throughout the 1970s, was equally committed to preserving the oil industry's favorite tax advantages. With such powerful friends, oil couldn't lose.

Ignoring this long history, Treasury Secretary Regan had proposed taking on the oil industry once again. But this time congressional protectors of the oil and gas industry had little reason to worry. New Treasury Secretary Baker was not about to forget his Texas friends. Pearlman argued strongly that tax reform would seem an empty shell if it did not tackle oil and gas. Darman argued that Baker would weaken his position in future negotiations if he caved on oil-and-gas issues and pointed out that any oil-and-gas preferences slated for repeal by the Treasury plan would probably be restored anyway by the Finance Committee, which was packed with oil-state senators. But there was no use trying to pry Baker away from his favorite tax preferences. Protecting the oil industry clearly meant more to him than promoting reform. He agreed to a slight trimming of oil tax breaks, but no more. Instead of allowing drillers to deduct all their drilling costs in a single year, he proposed allowing them to deduct 60 percent of those costs in the first year and the rest the second year. It was a very mild swipe, designed only to enable Baker to say publicly that no special interest was spared the tax-reform knife.

To be sure, not every special interest got such generous treatment at the Baker Treasury. For example, Baker and Darman kept a modified version of Secretary Regan's plan to tax annual increases in the cash value of life insurance policies, known as inside buildup. Regan had proposed taxing all policies; the new plan only applied to new policies. Still, it created an uproar among the more than a million employees and agents of the nation's enormous life insurance industry.

Treasury tax experts argued that the cash buildup on insurance policies was no different than interest paid on savings accounts and should therefore be taxed as interest. Treasury I proposed the change, prompting the insurance industry to launch a massive lobbying campaign against the plan soon after it was unveiled. The industry hired a consulting firm to engineer a postcard assault on Congress. Full-page advertisements in *Time, Newsweek, People, U.S. News & World Report,* and *Sports Illustrated* carried sets of three postcards intended for mailing to each reader's senators and representatives. Insurance agents were given similar postcard sets, which they passed out to their clients. A videotape, entitled *David and Goliath, Round Two,* was used to whip up opposition to the tax plan among the life insurance industry's many minions, and offered step-by-step instructions on how to personally lobby members of Congress. Even in faraway places like Fairmont, Minnesota (population 13,000), the insurance industry managed to run advertisements in the local papers, the *Fairmont Sentinel* and the *Blue Earth* (Minn.) *Town Crier.* As a result, Congress was deluged by postcards from voters, with members receiving more than a million pieces of mail on the arcane subject during the first half of 1985.

The insurance industry's political action committees (PACs) also arranged massive campaign contributions to House and Senate tax writers. Early in the year, Ways and Means member Henson Moore, Republican of Louisiana, was able to attract thirty insurance lobbyists to a $1,000 a plate fundraising dinner. Alignpac, the insurance agents' fundraising group, exceeded PAC spending limits by bundling up contributions from individual members and sending them to key tax writers.

Recognizing the mounting strength of the opposition to the proposal, Baker and Darman decided that they should negotiate with the insurance executives. They planned to give in, and in return, they hoped to win the insurance industry's support for reform. But while Baker and Darman were still negotiating with industry officials, the American Council of Life Insurance, headed by former Republican Senator and Health and Human Services Secretary Richard Schweiker, launched a series of television ads criticizing the tax plan. The fierce ads included staged man-on-the-street interviews, in which the interviewees complained bitterly not only about the inside-buildup proposal, but about reform itself. The ads ran on prime-time television in sixty-two major cities across the nation.

It was a big and expensive mistake by the insurance industry. Rather than drop the insurance tax proposal, as they had planned, Baker and Darman did an about-face. Angered by the TV ads, they decided to propose to tax the inside-buildup of new policies, which threatened to cripple the industry's sales of cash-value life insurance. The insurers' TV advertisements backfired, and as a result, the insurance industry had to carry on its costly battle for many more months, until finally the Ways and Means Committee, battered by postcards and complaints from constituents, agreed to drop the provision.

As the list of givebacks to special interests lengthened, the Treasury Department ran up against its most persistent problem: revenue shortages. The president demanded that his tax plan have a top rate of 35 percent or lower, but that was an awfully expensive demand—costing more than $250 billion over five years, by one estimate. Enough tax preferences had to be curbed to raise that money. As Treasury officials tossed out the loophole-closing provisions from Treasury I, they soon found themselves deeply in the red. The new tax system had to raise as much money as the existing system, and it became increasingly difficult to make the numbers balance.

Estimating the revenue effects of tax changes is a tricky business. Sometimes, the estimates are a matter of simple arithmetic. Other times they require intricate mathematical calculations, based on large amounts of detailed tax data spun through long and elaborate econometric computer models. More often than not, the estimates also require some very sophisticated assumptions about the complex set of interrelationships that make up the U.S. economy. Who can know, for instance, how a change in the treatment of horse-breeding tax shelters will alter reproduction on stud farms? Who can guess the extent to which limits on consumer-interest deductions will cause people to refinance their homes to circumvent the limits?

Those tough questions are the domain of a small band of professional economists who toil in anonymity in the back rooms of the Treasury Department and the congressional Joint Tax Committee. Theirs is a thankless job. Unlike lawyers in both organizations, who look forward to lucrative work in the private sector once they leave government, revenue estimators are practitioners of an arcane art for which there is little demand outside of the Washington tax-writing world. When a tax bill is under way—and seldom is a tax bill *not* under way in Washington—they work long hours and unbroken weekends under intense pressure, trying to tag numbers onto an endless string of proposals dreamed up by Treasury officials and by Congress's 535 lawmakers.

Although their estimates carry an air of precision, estimators readily admit that they lean heavily on guesswork. Sometimes that guesswork is wrong, *very* wrong. In 1981, when asked to estimate the revenue effects of a proposal to expand IRAs, the Treasury estimators projected the measure would lose $5.5 billion over a three-year period. Instead, it lost $32 billion, six times what was estimated. Says Thomas Vasquez, who headed the Treasury's revenue estimating staff at the time, "banks started advertising all over the place, offering things like toasters to people who opened new IRAs." The result of that marketing effort was a flood of money into the tax-sheltered accounts.

Such enormous errors are uncommon, but they have nevertheless opened the estimators up to criticism. Supply-siders like Jack Kemp are particularly harsh in their criticism; they argue that the estimators are biased, that they understate the revenues gained from tax changes in order to thwart tax cuts. The criticisms are frequently aired as well by the editorial writers of *The Wall Street Journal,* who complain that the "static revenooers" fail to look at changes in behavior caused by tax changes.

These supply-side criticisms are off the mark. Estimators do in fact take into account a wide array of behavioral changes in making their estimates; but whether they do so accurately is hard to gauge. "The estimates are not static, they incorporate behavioral responses," says former Treasury economist J. Gregory Ballentine, but "no one knows if the behavioral responses used are too large or too small."

Whatever their flaws, the revenue estimates provide a critical discipline to the tax-writing process. Politicians would always rather cut taxes than raise them. Estimates of the effects their actions have on the budget are needed to prevent excesses. Traditionally, both the Treasury and the Joint Tax Committee have worked hard to protect those estimates from political tinkering.

In Treasury's effort to draft a tax-reform bill, the revenue estimates became shakier than ever, but they also became more important than ever. Calculating the effects of a total overhaul of the system proved far tougher than calculating the effects of an isolated tax change. More important, previous tax bills had either raised taxes overall or lowered them. Never before had the president insisted that a tax bill be revenue neutral. It was a harsh discipline: Every proposal that lost money had to be matched by one that raised an equal amount; the tax changes had to add to zero. As the scorekeepers for this exercise, the revenue estimators wielded tremendous power and influence—and bore an inordinate burden.

In agreeing to Packwood's fringe-benefit proposal, the department lost more than $35 billion in new revenue over five years compared to Treasury I. In modifying Treasury I's oil-and-gas provisions, it threw out another $50 billion. Manley Johnson's generous new system of depreciation write-offs lost an eye-popping $200 billion in comparison to the original Treasury I plan. All those losses had to be made up by raising revenue elsewhere to pay for lower rates.

The first sacrifices to the hungry revenue god were the Treasury I proposals to "index" interest payments for inflation and to allow companies to deduct half the dividends they pay out. Those two proposals, unlike most of the other reforms, actually lost revenue for the Treasury rather than raised it. Indexing interest cost the Treasury more than $40 billion over five years; the dividend deduction cost more than $100 billion. Both provisions were dear to Treasury tax reformers, but did not find supporters in the real world of business and finance. The interest indexing provision was dropped entirely, while the dividend deduction was cut back to only 10 percent.

Baker and Darman developed a tough new "minimum tax" to help stem the drain of revenue. Minimum taxes were viewed by the Treasury's tax purists as a sort of Band-Aid approach to tax reform; if the tax net was woven tightly enough to catch all income in the first place, there would be no need for minimum taxes. But once Baker and Darman began tearing the tax net apart, the minimum tax became necessary to ensure that no one slipped through entirely. Baker and Darman wanted to make certain those stories about millionaires and corporations escaping all taxes never surfaced again. Baker even suggested an unusual proposal requiring large companies with no other tax liabilities to pay one dollar in tax, a plan that would put a conclusive, if meaningless, end to Bob McIntyre's inflammatory reports of profitable Fortune 500 firms that paid no taxes at all. That idea was wisely rejected, but a tough minimum tax became a critical component of the new Treasury proposal.

With revenue problems hounding them, Treasury tax writers agreed they could not afford to compromise on one of the most controversial provisions of Treasury I: elimination of the deduction for state and local taxes. Everyone understood that the provision would cause a tremendous uproar. They knew the defenders of the state and local deduction could make a much stronger philosophical argument than the defenders of most other tax preferences. Allowing people to take a deduction for the amount they paid to state and local governments hardly seemed an egregious abuse of the tax system. Nevertheless, repealing the deduction raised an enormous $150 billion over five years. If Baker and Darman gave in on that one, they felt certain their plan would fall apart. The deduction had to be repealed, they thought, in order to make the numbers add up. Forget the argument over the merits, they decided: This one was for the money.

A political calculation also lurked behind the repeal of the state and local deduction. The deduction mostly benefited residents of high-tax states like New York and did far less for residents of states with lower taxes. Baker and Darman calculated that pitting New York against the rest of the nation might be good politics and help win the tax plan's approval. It was a risky bet, but it was a bet they felt they had to make.

Another problem facing the Treasury, along with revenue, was the distribution of the tax burden. Treasury I tried to guarantee that taxpayers of all income levels received roughly equal percentage tax cuts. The policymakers did not want to soak the rich, nor did they want to tilt the tax system further in favor of high-income taxpayers, but as Baker and Darman made their political compromises to restore some deductions, exclusions, and credits, they discovered that most of the benefits were falling to those at the top of the income scale. Many low- and lower-middle-income taxpayers, after all, did not even use deductions. The revised plan began to lean dangerously in favor of the highest-income taxpayers, a result that promised political trouble.

The distribution problem became especially acute as Darman tried behind the scenes to develop a plan with a top rate of only 30 percent. He hoped to win the support of tax-overhaul sponsor Kemp and his fellow supply-siders. Kemp insisted that Treasury I's 35-percent top rate was too high; he felt 30 percent should be the maximum. Darman directed the Treasury staff to try to accommodate that request. Such a sharp drop in the top rate, down from 50 percent under existing law, seemed inevitably to make the plan overly generous to high-income taxpayers. While that did not bother Kemp, who was perfectly willing to allow his plan to give big cuts to those at the top, Treasury officials knew that tipping the plan toward the top of the income scale would create serious political problems.

In an attempt to avoid those problems, Darman experimented with plans that appeared to have a top rate of 30 percent, but that also placed a 5-percent surtax on some higher-income taxpayers. The Kemp-Kasten proposal used a similar tactic, enabling the authors to claim a flat rate of 24 percent when in fact many upper-income taxpayers faced a 28-percent marginal rate. Darman's ploy was to claim a top rate of 30 percent, while having a hidden top rate of 35 percent. The scheme was typical of the sleight of hand that Darman enjoyed, but it was a nightmare to the tax-policy experts at Treasury. They were appalled that they had to spend time studying the idea. The Treasury was usually the protector of the integrity of the tax code; now with Darman on the job, it was becoming an originator of gimmicks. If the top rate was going to be 35 percent, Pearlman and his staff thought, just make it 35 percent outright; don't use a bizarre scheme to hide the top rate. "We wanted to be spending our time pulling things together that worked," recalls Eugene Steuerle, "and instead we were working on these crazy ideas."

Despite the complaints from the Treasury staff, Darman continued to pursue the plan, searching for a way to satisfy Kemp's demand for a 30-percent top rate, at least in appearance, if not in fact. He even presented a version of his 30-percent plan to President Reagan. But the White House ruled out the idea as fraudulent, never guessing the strange ploy would later be picked up, dusted off, and made the law of the land.

On April 23, Baker, Darman, and Pearlman made the familiar trip across East Executive Avenue to begin briefing the president on the new tax plan. It was a strange reversal of roles from five months earlier. Regan was now sitting on the president's side of the conference table, along with aides Kingon and Dawson, who also had moved to the White House from Treasury. Baker and Darman, on the other hand, were in the hot seat across from the president.

There was clear tension across the table between Regan and Baker, and between their aides. When they were in the White House, Baker and Darman had felt a certain amount of contempt for Regan, who often spoke before thinking. Regan, for his part, had resented the haughty White House officials who frequently managed to scuttle his efforts. Since the job switch, the animosity had only increased. Baker had been praised in the press for his pragmatic approach to the Treasury job; Regan had been pounded for some slip-ups as chief of staff. At the time of the meeting, the new White House team was under attack for its decision to have President Reagan, as part of his upcoming trip to Europe, visit a cemetery at Bitburg where members of the SS—the deadly Nazi elite guard during World War II— were buried. Now Regan and his aides had to watch Baker take responsibility for reviving Treasury I from the dead. They believed that they were the true fathers of tax reform; they had plunged ahead when Baker still thought the effort was foolish. Now they had to take a back seat to Baker, the born-again reformer.

During the first day's discussion, the president agreed to Baker's recommendation to reverse some of the most controversial provisions of Treasury I. The exemption for ministers' housing allowances was reinstated, as well as the exemption for veterans' disability benefits. The unusual, Packwood-proposed compromise on fringe benefits was discussed and accepted by the president. Baker also proposed easing Treasury I's tough restrictions on the deduction of business meals. The original plan limited the deduction to $10 for breakfast, $15 for lunch, and $25 for dinner. Baker's plan put a $25 limit on full deductibility for all meals, prompting Regan to quip, "There'll be a lot of expensive breakfasts going on."

The Treasury officials also told the president they wanted to stick with the original proposal to end the deduction for state and local taxes, and the president agreed.

Not until the subject of charitable deductions arose did the president balk. Treasury I allowed those deductions only to the extent that the contributions exceeded 2 percent of a person's income; Baker proposed lowering that to 1 percent. But in cutting back government spending, the president had frequently emphasized the importance of private giving. He overturned the Treasury recommendation and asked that the full charitable deduction for those who itemize be left intact.

The Treasury team returned to the White House on the twenty-fourth and again on the thirtieth of April, briefing the president on the most controversial elements of the plan. The president agreed to drop interest indexing and dividend relief and to keep generous depreciation write-offs. He accepted most of the details of the plan, and by the time he left for his trip to Europe, the Treasury team felt they had won his approval for their proposal.

While the president was gone, however, a new problem arose, the first and largest of many revenue estimating errors that would dog the tax-writing process. Treasury's tax experts discovered they had made a mistake, and it was a whopper. The plan they briefed the president on, it turned out, was not revenue neutral at all. In fact, corrected estimates showed the plan would add $150 billion to the nation's budget deficit over the next five years!

Shock waves from the mistake reverberated around the Treasury Department. Estimates of the revenues raised or lost by tax changes are always subject to error; but this was far bigger than any previous error. It was a hole so large that it threatened to sink the entire tax-reform vessel. The president had signed on to a tax plan that did not work.

The mistake and its aftereffects sparked new antipathy between Pearlman and his tax staff on the one side, and Baker, Darman, and Johnson on the other. Both Darman and Johnson suspected the tax staff might have come up with the error in an effort to force a move back to tough, Treasury I–style depreciation write-offs. "You would think if you were going to brief the president, you would take the time to check and recheck the numbers before you let it get over there," Johnson said. The atmosphere at Treasury grew tense and frantic.

Eager to solve the problem neatly and quietly before the president returned, Treasury officials scrambled to find new and unobtrusive sources of revenue. Their first move was to eliminate some key rules meant to ease the transition to the new tax system. The tax writers originally had planned to phase out the repeal of the state and local tax deduction and the repeal of the investment tax credit over a few years to soften the impact on the economy. In the desperate search for revenue, they changed course and decided to repeal both of them as of January 1, 1986. The department also intended to include a rule that protected investments already under contract from the cutbacks in investment incentives. That rule was scrapped as well. It was a cynical move, since the officials knew Congress would insist upon such a "binding contract" rule, but they needed revenue badly, and were in a hurry to patch things up.

Those changes still brought in only a third of the revenue needed to fill the gaping hole. They still had to have more money—a *lot* more.

It was Johnson who offered the solution—a proposal he had been thinking about for some time. He worried that lowering the corporate tax rate would provide an unnecessary "windfall" to people who owned old equipment and had already used up their depreciation write-offs. That was a perverse incentive, he argued; the tax code ought to encourage new investment, not the retention of old, outmoded equipment.

To fix the incentive, Johnson proposed a totally new tax called a "windfall recapture tax" to take back some of the windfall that would be reaped by owners of old capital. It was a reasonable idea in theory, but in the face of the desperate desire for money it was turned into a behemoth. The proposal was fashioned to raise roughly $56 billion over five years—far more revenue, Treasury officials later admitted, than such a provision should actually have raised if done as dictated by theory. It called for a significant increase in the taxes of many corporations and was viewed by businessmen as a "retroactive" levy, because it was based on the depreciation write-offs they had taken in previous years. "We all knew that no one was going to understand it, and we were going to be accused of having a retroactive tax," Pearlman said. Nevertheless, it was put into the plan. It was needed as a plug, a placeholder—something the Treasury could use in order to claim its plan was revenue neutral, even thought it did not have the slightest chance of being accepted by Congress.

When the president returned from Europe, the group gathered again at the White House on May 14. The memorandum for the meeting noted that "because of a computer programming error, the revenue was substantially understated in a memorandum on April 24." On the president's side of the table, jaws dropped. "I was disgusted," says Regan, whose anger was clearly mixed with glee at the new Treasury team's embarrassment. "I couldn't figure out how they could possibly have made such a mistake and why they hadn't double-checked it before they brought it over here. I had worked with those numbers for four years and we never came anywhere near a mistake like that. It was a shock!"

Confused by the turn of events, the president asked for an explanation. Baker turned to Pearlman and said sharply, "You explain it Ron, it's *your* mistake." Red-faced, Pearlman tried to say it was a computer error, but the explanation did not sit well.

The Treasury team offered White House officials two ways to deal with the huge problem. One was to increase the personal exemption to only $1,500 in 1986 and then raise it gradually to $2,000 over a few years. The White House group summarily rejected that; the $2,000 exemption had become an important pro-family symbol for the New Right Republicans. That left the other choice as the only alternative: windfall recapture. The president signed on.

The Treasury officials scheduled another meeting with the president on May 21. It was to be the last. Congressional tax writers were already beginning to complain about White House delays in releasing its plan. At the first of the year, Darman had talked of releasing the new plan on April 15, tax day, but the timetable kept slipping. Baker and Darman felt the plan had to be pushed through Congress in 1985. If it was still around in 1986 it would suffer under the strains of an election year, they feared. Rostenkowski, on the other hand, had always thought that the timetable was unrealistic; when Baker and Darman first proposed it, he and his aides had laughed at them. Now Rostenkowski's laughter was changing to irritation as the Treasury slipped past its own deadlines. "Delay saps the cause of tax reform and raises doubts about the president's nerve," he complained.

The day before the final meeting, Pearlman's staff brought him more bad news. There was another revenue error—not as big as the last one, but big enough to cause serious problems. It appeared that the revenue estimators had overcounted and that the plan was short by about another $10 billion.

Pearlman was flabbergasted. Going back to the White House and having to explain yet another error would be too much to bear. "They'll kill me," he told his staff, raising his hand to his forehead, "they really will." Some of his aides said he should just ignore it, but the conscientious tax official felt obliged to shuffle down to Secretary Baker's office and tell all. Baker took the disturbing news calmly and told Pearlman to have his people check the numbers and get back to him in the morning.

That night, Pearlman dined with Rostenkowski and some of his aides. It was a social dinner that had been arranged a few days earlier. Pearlman was in a dejected mood, but he did not mention the troublesome new development to Rostenkowski. After dinner, he went home to get some sleep and prepare for dealing with the disaster the following day.

The next morning, Pearlman was up early and on his way to work well before six o'clock. Besides his all-important meeting with the president, he also was scheduled to testify before a committee in Congress. As he approached the Treasury gates, however, he felt a sharp pain in his stomach and a flash of heat through his body. He threw off his tie, turned his car around and drove past the Treasury building to nearby George Washington University Hospital. He was feeling so ill, he simply left his car out front and rushed into the emergency ward.

The Treasury official was in the hospital for almost three hours and treated for what doctors finally decided was a bad case of food poisoning from the previous night. When he was released, he discovered his car had been towed to make way for rush-hour traffic. Sick, exhausted, tie-less, and car-less, Pearlman hailed a cab back to his office.

As he trudged in, his staff gave him a tie and some good news. The previous night's revenue problem, they said, was a mathematical error that had been found and corrected. There was no new revenue crisis. Nevertheless, the experience of the previous twenty-four hours seemed to symbolize the new Treasury plan for Pearlman. It was scarcely an exhilarating experience.

The final meeting with the president that afternoon held even more defeats for the beleaguered Pearlman. The meeting was to deal with the few major issues that remained. Among those: capital gains. Baker had proposed simply leaving the top capital-gains rate at the same level as under existing law: 20 percent. Pearlman wanted to boost it to at least 22 percent to help solve the plan's "distribution" problem. As it was, the plan was far too generous to the rich, and a higher capital-gains rate would cut back the benefits to those in the upper-income category. But the president had often expressed his view that lower capital-gains rates are good for the economy, and he did so again in this meeting. Regan quickly joined the bandwagon, and the irony could hardly have been heavier. As Treasury secretary, the chief of staff had approved *raising* the top gains rate to 35 percent only five months earlier; now he did yet another backflip and proposed lowering the rate to 17.5 percent. The reason for the reversal? Aesthetics, the chief of staff argued. A rate of 17.5 percent would be an even half of the proposed top rate on ordinary income of 35 percent. It would be a nice, neat exclusion of 50 percent of all long-term capital-gains income.

Regan's capital-gains proposal came as a blow to the Treasury team. Lowering the gains rate only exacerbated the plan's distributional problem. It meant the president's proposal would cut the tax bills of those earning more than $200,000 a year by nearly 11 percent, while cutting the bills of those earning $20,000 to $50,000 by only 6 percent to 8 percent. It was sure to be attacked by Democrats as another giveaway by President Reagan and the Republicans to the wealthy. Nevertheless, the president liked his chief of staff's arguments and agreed to the lower gains rate.

The oil-and-gas provisions also were on the agenda. Chief of Staff Regan argued oil ought to take a bigger hit than Baker proposed. But the oil industry was defended by Baker's fellow Texan, Vice President George Bush, who attended the meeting. Bush argued that the plan ought to be *even more* generous to the oil and gas industry than Baker's proposal. In one of his rare involvements in the tax-reform debate, the vice president pointed to the president and said: "This man and I campaigned on a platform of keeping the energy industry strong. Mondale and Ferraro were the ones who wanted to go after the oil industry!" Bush argued that the oil and gas industry was essential to the nation's security. All oil-and-gas tax preferences must be preserved.

Troubled by the split among his advisers, the president muttered, "Oh, Lord," but in the end, he decided in Bush's favor. The oil industry, one of the largest beneficiaries of tax preferences in the existing code, was allowed to keep virtually all of its favorite tax breaks. Once again, the politics of oil had proven too powerful to be tangled with.

Right up to the last day, Darman was still trying to get the rate below 35 percent. Even 34 percent, he thought, would be worthwhile. It would enable the Treasury officials to claim they had gotten the rates lower than the president wanted. But Chief of Staff Regan defended the Treasury I rates. He repeated his earlier argument: other mixtures of rates sounded like "football calls" or the "combinations for a lock." The 15-, 25-, and 35-percent rates were best, he said, and the president agreed.

In the end, the new plan was much less pure reform than Treasury I had been. It retained many tax breaks, but it ended or reduced many others and brought down the top tax rate dramatically to 35 percent. Most important, the new plan had the full support and approval of the president of the United States. With Ronald Reagan solidly behind it, tax reform could no longer be ignored.

The President unveiled the new plan in a nationwide television speech delivered from the Oval Office on the evening of May 28, with the grand rhetoric that had become his hallmark:

My fellow citizens, I'd like to speak to you tonight about our future, about a great historic effort to give the words "freedom," "fairness," and "hope" new meaning and power for every man and woman in America. . . .

No other issue goes so directly to the heart of our economic life. No other issue will have more lasting impact on the well-being of your families and your future. . . .

Death and taxes may be inevitable, but unjust taxes are not. The first American Revolution was sparked by an unshakable conviction—taxation without representation is tyranny. Two centuries later, a second American revolution for hope and opportunity is gathering force again—a peaceful revolution, but born of popular resentment against a tax system that is unwise, unwanted and unfair. . . .

Let's not let this magnificent moment slip away. Tax relief is in sight. Let's make it a reality. Let's not let prisoners of mediocrity wear us down. Let's not let the special interest raids of the few rob us of all our dreams. . . . We can do it. And if you help we will do it this year.

Chapter 5

"Write Rosty"

A week before President Reagan's televised plea for tax reform, House Speaker Tip O'Neill called Ways and Means Chairman Dan Rostenkowski to ask if he would deliver the Democratic response to the president's address.

"Not really, necessarily," Rostenkowski grumbled in reply, and the answer was natural enough. The often scowling, gruff-voiced chairman of the Ways and Means Committee was not exactly telegenic. He was big, brash and bellowing—a door slammer and, at times, a bully. He was reared as the kind of beef-eating, ward-heeling machine politician who considered the blow-dried world of TV to be sissy stuff.

Okay, said O'Neill. The Democrats in the Senate were eager to put their own man up for the job. If Rostenkowski did not want it, a senator would be happy to make the televised response.

"Whaddya mean?" Rostenkowski shot back. The mere thought of some self-important senator stealing the limelight got his back up. He felt that *he* was the Democrats' number-one man on taxes. If anyone was going to talk about tax reform, it should not be a member of the Senate; it should be Dan Rostenkowski, chairman of Ways and Means.

"Goddamn right I want to do the response," he blustered. And so, in a fit of pique and pride, he consented to put the nation on notice that he and the Democratic party were reformers too.

In truth, Rostenkowski had decided some months earlier to join forces with President Reagan to fight for tax overhaul, but his agreement to, in effect, link arms with the president in consecutive appearances on national television raised the stakes of that commitment. The prime-time display of bipartisan cooperation on the issue symbolized a new political reality: With the support of the top House tax-writer, tax reform had a chance.

The speech was scheduled for May 28, and Rostenkowski and his staff took the task of preparation very seriously. They knew the risks were high, and the odds against them were great. Tax reform was still a tough issue, with little support yet among the public or members of Congress. On top of that, the history of Democratic responses to Reagan addresses was abysmal. Many of the previous replies failed to stir public sentiment, largely because they attacked the enormously popular president. Pitting mere politicians against the "Great Communicator" was inevitably a mismatch.

So Rostenkowski took a different tack. Instead of picking a fight, he decided to embrace both Reagan and tax reform. It would be a partisan speech, blaming the Republicans for making a mess out of the tax system, but it also would position the Democrats as allies of the president in the battle against the special interests. "All I wanted to say was, 'This is my president too,' " Rostenkowski recalls. "If he wants to pass this one, Democrats will support him. We *should* support him."

To ensure that the rough Rostenkowski made a smooth TV appearance, John Sherman, Rostenkowski's speech writer, hired Joseph Rothstein, a media consultant. Rostenkowski had not dealt with such people before, but he realized this time was different, and he was willing to endure the training. "John," the chairman told Sherman, "this son of a bitch down at the White House talks in simple language that people understand. He gets on the couch in the living room of every person that watches. I want to get on that couch with him. I want to say to the people, put my arm around 'em and say, 'Our president wants what's great and best for you—and so do I.' "

Joe Rothstein had never met Rostenkowski, but on the Sunday morning before the speech, he saw a television interview with the chairman that made him realize what a monumental task he faced. Here was a politician who clearly was not made for television. He had a tough-guy demeanor and the kind of gravelly voice that others can imitate only after shouting at the top of their lungs for two or three hours. He was prone to mumbling and stumbling and mashing clichés. Malapropisms were his trademark. When presented in a speech with the word *hyperbole,* he pronounced it hyper-bowl. He referred to the dapper lobbyists who populated the hallways outside his committee as "pencil-striped," and when explaining the delicate decisions necessary to steer a bill through Congress, he said he was "walking through an egg field." After watching Rostenkowski's performance, Rothstein's wife turned to her husband with a knowing glance and said, "Good luck."

The goal of Rothstein and the Rostenkowski advisers was to transform this big-city, arm-twisting pol into a man of the people. They decided to shun anything artificial. Rostenkowski, for all his hardball reputation and coarse manner, possessed a peculiar kind of vulnerability, a sort of charm. On the flip side of the scowl that could curdle milk, there was a beaconlike smile that made his round, expressive face boyish and oddly compelling. Sherman and Rothstein worked to tap this softer side, to make the tough-as-nails power broker appear on television as a cuddly teddy bear.

They also strove to highlight Rostenkowski's ethnic roots, to reach back to his northwest Chicago neighborhood. The strategists wanted to evoke the sense in the audience that Rostenkowski was one of them—just a guy— a Polish friend from the neighborhood who did well but never forgot where he came from; an emotional man, a family man, and a man who wore a medallion around his neck engraved with the birthdates of his four daughters. Sherman wrote the speech almost as if Rostenkowski were to deliver it to his chums at old St. Stan's Church, across the street from the big brick house in Chicago his grandfather built, in which he and his family still lived.

Rostenkowski and Rothstein were an odd couple. Rothstein was an elfish man with graying hair and a gentle smile that matched his manner. The blustery chairman, on the other hand, stood six-feet two-inches tall and weighed more than 225 pounds. Normally, if his aides could get Rostenkowski to read over a speech just once before he delivered it, they felt lucky, but this time, Rothstein and the chairman worked together for six hours, going over the text, and practicing the presentation. They worked in the Capitol building itself, using the two offices that the chairman kept on the first and second floors of the three-story structure. Sherman, who had toiled as Rostenkowski's press aide since 1981, penned the draft. The former newsmagazine correspondent had developed a knack for authentically impersonating his boss's speaking style. With a few alterations by Rothstein, every word slipped naturally off the chairman's tongue.

By the end of the day on that Tuesday, Rostenkowski was ready. He was calm, he knew what he had to do. At one point, when the final minutes were ticking away before his big face would be broadcast into millions of homes, he suddenly jumped to his feet. "Shit," he shouted, "I'm not gonna do it!" The camera crew gasped, but Rostenkowski broke into a smile. Just kidding, he said, and sat back in his seat. Ronald Reagan finished his own address, in which he had labeled tax reform "a second American revolution." Then, Rostenkowski was on the air.

Good evening, I'm Dan Rostenkowski from Chicago. Let me read you something that pretty well explains what tax reform is all about, and what Democrats are all about.

Rostenkowski coolly picked up a book and read from an open page. Rothstein was pleased; the chairman was doing better than in any of the rehearsals.

"The continued escape of privileged groups from taxation violates the fundamental democratic principle of fair treatment for all and undermines public confidence in the tax system." That was Harry Truman's message to Congress thirty-five years ago.

Trying to tax people fairly: That's been the historic Democratic commitment. Our roots lie with working families all over the country, like the Polish neighborhood I grew up in on the northwest side of Chicago. Most of the people in my neighborhood worked hard in breweries, steel mills, packing houses; proud families who lived on their salaries. My parents and grandparents didn't like to pay taxes. Who does? But like most Americans they were willing to pay their fair share as the price for a free country where everyone could make their own breaks.

Every year politicians promise to make the tax code fair and simple, but every year we seem to slip further behind. Now most of us pay taxes with bitterness and frustration. Working families file their tax forms with the nagging feeling that they're the biggest suckers and chumps in the world. Their taxes are withheld at work, while the elite have enormous freedom to move their income from one tax shelter to another. That bitterness is about to boil over. And it's time it did.

But this time there's a difference in the push for tax reform. This time, it's a Republican president who's bucking his party's tradition as protectors of big business and the wealthy. His words and feelings go back to Roosevelt and Truman and Kennedy. But the commitment comes from Ronald Reagan. And that's so important and so welcome.

He nestled into the last words as if reclining into a La-Z-Boy chair.

Because, if the president's plan is everything he says it is, he'll have a great deal of Democratic support. That's the real difference this time. A Republican president has joined the Democrats in Congress to try to redeem this long-standing commitment to a tax system that's simple and fair. If we work together with good faith and determination, this time the people may win. This time I really think we can get tax reform.

As he neared the end of the speech, Rostenkowski asked the audience to send letters of support, and he uttered the words that would become the symbol of his effort to overhaul the tax system. The lines were written by Sherman, but were withheld from the speech by other aides who thought they sounded too gimmicky for the powerful chairman of Ways and Means. At Rothstein's insistence, however, they were added back shortly before the performance.

"Even if you can't spell Rostenkowski, put down what they used to call my father and grandfather—Rosty." He pronounced it "rusty," the way his childhood friends used to. "Just address it to R-O-S-T-Y, Washington, D.C. The post office will get it to me. Better yet, write your representative and your senator. And stand up for fairness and lower taxes."

When the speech was over, and the microphones were turned off, the camera crew did something Rothstein had not seen before: They broke into applause. "That was my first clue we hit it over the fence," Rothstein says.

The second was a telephone call from the White House. It was Don Regan to congratulate Rostenkowski on his speech and to pass along a comment from the president. "Jesus," Regan quoted the president as saying, "he's got me with Truman and Kennedy. Does he know I'm in the Roosevelt room watching his response?" Said Rostenkowski sometime later: "The president, I think, was pleased. At least the chairman of the Ways and Means Committee was willing to take a shot to support him."

The ultimate measure of the speech's success was taken by the Postal Service. More than seventy-five thousand people responded to Rostenkowski's plea to write "Rosty, Washington, D.C." One person sent a wooden two-by-four beam to help the chairman beat back the special interests. Another envelope contained a yards-long, computer-generated banner that read MY PARENTS NEED TAX REFORM. "Write Rosty" buttons and bumper stickers were printed quickly, and everyone from Treasury Secretary Baker to Bill Bradley wore them proudly in public appearances. A photo in Sherman's office showed a WRITE ROSTY sign on the front of a parked limousine.

In a single eleven-minute four-second performance, Rostenkowski, the consummate inside player of the dark, back corridors of the U.S. Congress, transformed himself into a kind of folk hero of federal taxation. His speech stirred something deep inside a skeptical public, and put the Democrats— and Rostenkowski—back on the tax-reform map. "I really took over the party on that 'Write Rosty' speech," Rostenkowski says—with a touch of hyper-bowl. "I took over the direction of the Democratic party."

"I must admit," the chairman said the morning after the speech during a breakfast interview at *The Wall Street Journal*'s Washington office, "I am on a high."

Ever since Treasury I emerged from the inner sanctum of the Treasury Department in November 1984, the Ways and Means chieftain had been forced to define a position for his committee, and his party, on the tax-reform front. That position, at first, was ambivalence. Rostenkowski tentatively embraced reform but said that it should not divert Congress from its main priority: deficit reduction. "Tax reform is a noble cause," he said soon after Treasury I was unveiled. "Deficit reduction is a demand."

The House leadership was skeptical of reform, and Rostenkowski also had his doubts. But President Reagan had locked the Democrats into a wrenching dilemma. Reform had always been a Democratic battle cry— they were supposedly the party of the little guy, the working man, the middle and lower classes; the Republicans were the party of privilege, the country-club set, the fat-cat corporations. In an attempt to usurp the Democrats' party-of-the-people mantle, President Reagan and the GOP were now turning things upside down.

Many of Rostenkowski's friends urged caution, but Rostenkowski did not believe he had the luxury to say no. He thought he had to defend tax reform, which he regularly called "the biggest plank in the Democratic platform."

"I thought Ronald Reagan was trying to outpolitic us," Rostenkowski says. "I'm not a reformer. But I'm a Democrat. And if the Democrats are for reform, then I'm a reformer."

Staking out the territory of reform-mindedness was especially important given the Democrats' drubbing during the 1984 presidential election. Walter Mondale's promise to raise taxes had hurt the party and enabled President Reagan to seize the initiative on the tax issue. Many Republican strategists were arguing that tax reform could turn the tables and make their party the majority party for decades to come. They thought they could make the Democrats the party of special interests and the Republicans the party of the average American. It was a threat that serious-minded Democrats could not ignore.

Though Treasury I was widely regarded as politically inept, it was such pure reform that it was difficult for Democrats to debunk on political grounds. "How can you put a Democratic stamp on something that's so fucking Democratic with respect to reform that if you go further to the left, you're a Communist?" Rostenkowski asked. Indeed, one of the staunchest liberals on the Ways and Means panel, Representative Charles Rangel, Democrat of New York, introduced a slightly altered version of it under his own name as a bill in the House. "You could go to the bottom drawer of the most liberal reformers, you could take out all their lists, and few would eclipse Treasury I," said Sherman of Rostenkowski's staff. "Democrats were just stunned."

The chairman and his staff gradually realized that even though Treasury I stood little chance of enactment, it made tax reform into a major issue that was not likely to go away. As Ways and Means chief counsel Joseph Dowley put it, "The genie was out of the bottle, and there was no putting it back."

The backing of tax reform by the conservative Ronald Reagan gave Democratic reformers a shot at accomplishing what they had sought for decades. It was the sort of unexpected gesture, like President Nixon's 1972 trip to Communist China, that dramatically altered the politics of the issue.

After Treasury I was unveiled, Rostenkowski and his people flew to Chicago for a day. At a downtown hotel, Rostenkowski convened a round-table meeting of his businessmen buddies, people he had known and grown up with in Chicago politics. On that gray December day, he and his aides witnessed a near explosion of outrage. The real estate developers were particularly incensed, and their vehemence took the Rostenkowski crew by surprise. They knew that businessmen would not like the Treasury plan, but they had not imagined the depth of their feeling.

The experience showed Rostenkowski that tax reform would be a perilous undertaking, but he also believed the reaction presented a unique opportunity. "I started to realize that, brother, I've got a lot of friends in the business community. I realized at that point that I was their salvation, because I wasn't going to move as far as Treasury I." Like Baker and Darman, Rostenkowski saw that the original Treasury plan gave him a rare chance to be a reformer *and* a friend to business at the same time.

The chairman unsheathed his newfangled reformist streak gradually. He first put the business community on notice in a speech in late February to the Economic Club of New York. There at the New York Hilton, looking distinctly uncomfortable in black tie, the hulking Ways and Means chairman said: "To those who are preparing to stand against the change, I have a warning: Don't underestimate the public; demand for reform is growing." At that speech he also withdrew his earlier insistence that Congress focus on deficit-reduction before turning to reform. Instead, he said that all tax breaks, "even the most popular," must be on the table for possible elimination.

The tax-reform bill was the greatest challenge that the chairman had ever undertaken. The effort would entail cracking open the entire tax code and rearranging its delicately balanced choice of winners and losers. Every interest blessed with a benefit would be forced to defend it to the death. Every interest that wanted a break would have a chance to create it. Rostenkowski's decision to answer Ronald Reagan with a yes incited the income-tax equivalent of world war.

No one, not the president, not his aides, not Rostenkowski himself, fully appreciated the difficulty of this task. Ways and Means top tax lawyer Robert Leonard tried to give a hint. He approached his chairman several times in early 1985 bearing a copy of the Internal Revenue Code of 1954, the standard text at the time. It was hundreds of pages in small print. "Boss," Leonard told him, "that's what we're going to change." After he had done that a couple of times, Rostenkowski said, "It began to penetrate this thick skull. I said, 'Holy Jesus, this is a monstrous task.' But by then we were already in it; you get to the point of no return."

Notoriety had come late to Rostenkowski. He was fifty-seven years old when he delivered the "Write Rosty" speech and had already served in the House for twenty-seven years. His career to that point had been marred by setbacks and disappointments. He had been laboring under a particularly dark cloud ever since he assumed the chairmanship of Ways and Means in 1981.

That year, he planned a party to celebrate the passage of his first tax bill, but the bash turned out to be more of a wake. The usually ebullient chairman left the House floor grumbling bitterly after his committee's bill was clobbered by a different measure backed by President Reagan. In 1982, Rostenkowski was dealt an even larger blow. The Senate Finance Committee, led by Robert Dole, managed to approve a tax increase, while Rostenkowski was unable to get his own members to act. In 1983, yet another Rostenkowski tax bill went nowhere, killed on the floor of his own chamber, the victim of a procedural vote.

With tax reform in 1985, Rostenkowski saw his chance to shine, to avenge his earlier losses. In 1983 he helped pass a bipartisan overhaul of Social Security, and in 1984 he managed to get a big deficit-reduction package through Congress, but those were not imposing enough achievements. He needed a big win to reestablish himself and his committee as legitimate legislators. Tax reform was the Big One. It was Rostenkowski's opening.

In pushing reform, he was taking a huge gamble. If he lost, his already tarnished reputation, and that of his committee, probably would be sullied for good. If he allowed the bill to die in the House, President Reagan and the Republicans would never let the Democrats, who were in control there, live it down. What's more, the chance for Democratic-style tax reform probably would be gone for decades. So Rostenkowski decided to work with the president. "I laid my reputation on the line," he said later.

If Rostenkowski had not been a politician, he might have been an excellent ball player. At St. John's Military Academy in Delafield, Wisconsin, the young Dan Rosten, as he was known in high school, won fourteen letters in four sports. He liked baseball best, and in 1949 was invited by Connie Mack, owner and manager of the Philadelphia Athletics, to try out for the team. But that did not last long. Rostenkowski's father called him home to return to school and join the family business—politics. His grandfather was a Polish immigrant who ran once for local office. His father, Joseph, was an alderman and ward committeeman from the same "Polish corridor" region of Chicago that his son still represents. When Poles fresh in town from the old country were asked who was the president of the United States, they would sometimes say, "Joe Rostenkowski."

Rostenkowski's first post was virtually inherited from his father. He became the Thirty-second Ward committeeman, a post he still held during the tax-reform debate. At the age of twenty-four, he became the youngest member of the Illinois House. At twenty-six, he became the youngest member of the State Senate. He was elected to the U.S. House from the Eighth District in Illinois in 1958 at the age of thirty.

Rostenkowski's decision to leave the Windy City and go to Washington was unusual for a machine politician. He came from a tradition where politicians bided their time and worked their way up the local-party ladder until someday, perhaps, they could reach the pinnacle of public service— mayor of Chicago. Cook County Democratic dinners looked like wedding cakes, with the local dignitaries stacked up at the top in a strict hierarchy. Only aged and retired politicians ever left to do service in Washington.

Rostenkowski had to do some persuading to convince his mentor, Mayor Richard J. Daley, the virtual despot of the city, that he could use a young man in the nation's capital.

As Daley's "errand boy," Rostenkowski drove to Chicago every Thursday night to brief the mayor on political happenings and tell him what he was learning as an eager backbencher in the highly stratified world of Congress. Rostenkowski and an aide would manage the 11½-hour overnight trip by alternating naps on a mattress in the rear of their station wagon. Daley would tease Rostenkowski by referring to him as the "speaker of the House." But Rostenkowski's briefings did not take on great significance until 1964, when he was appointed to the influential Ways and Means Committee.

Then, as now, Ways and Means wrote tax law, but more important to Rostenkowski and his mayor, it also made committee assignments for members of the House. Rostenkowski's job was to help dispense committee seats, a potent form of patronage that he and Daley well understood—and utilized.

In that same year, 1964, Rostenkowski was chosen by Lyndon Johnson, a Rostenkowski hero, to second the televised nomination of Hubert Humphrey as Johnson's vice president at the Democratic National Convention in Atlantic City. Johnson called him over and said, "That nice, long Polish name on the screen, 'Dan Rostenkowski.' Smart move, wasn't it Dan?" It was Rostenkowski's first major television success, and it helped encourage him twenty years later when he was asked to answer the president's tax address.

The next nominating convention in 1968, however, would nearly be Rostenkowski's undoing. In his own hometown of Chicago, the Democratic party was torn apart by protest over the war in Vietnam. While police and students battled in the streets, the convention also was unruly. It was too much for the man in the chair, Representative Carl Albert of Oklahoma, to handle. So Lyndon Johnson telephoned Rostenkowski, who was sitting on stage, and told him to rein in the convention. In front of the television cameras that had been his friend four years before, Rostenkowski wrested the gavel from the diminutive Albert and hammered the throng to order.

Albert never forgot. When House Speaker John McCormack of Massachusetts retired in 1970, Albert succeeded him. Rostenkowski was the choice of Hale Boggs, the new majority leader, for the position of Democratic whip, the top vote-counter in the House. But Albert vetoed Rostenkowski, and instead, chose Tip O'Neill. Adding insult to injury, Rostenkowski was upset that same year in his fight to remain chairman of the Democratic Caucus in the House, a leadership position he had held since 1967.

Eventually, after Boggs died in a tragic plane crash and Albert retired, O'Neill moved into the job that Mayor Daley had teased his young disciple about one day holding—speaker of the House.

In 1976, Rostenkowski's world changed, and he emerged again as a force in the House. He was a key vote-getter for Representative Jim Wright, a moderate Democrat from Texas, who was elected majority leader after a fierce four-way fight. Rostenkowski was compensated for his role with the job of chief deputy whip. On Ways and Means that year, Rostenkowski, for one of the first times, concentrated on tax matters. The panel had lost its power to make committee assignments during a congressional reform movement in 1974. Rostenkowski was no tax technician, but during a crucial House-Senate conference, he stayed up late one night studying a portion of the tax code. He was finding arguments to defeat an amendment by Senator Abraham Ribicoff of Connecticut that benefited several insurance companies in the senator's state. To the surprise of almost everyone, Rostenkowski marshalled this newfound knowledge and managed to win enough votes to kill the provision.

Rostenkowski's excursion into tax policy, however, was not done for the good of the code. Rather, the Chicagoan was settling an old score. During the 1968 convention, Ribicoff had criticized the "gestapo tactics" of Mayor Daley and his riot-helmeted police, and Rostenkowski never forgot. "I went in the room and just kicked the brains out of them," a grinning Rostenkowski told *The Washington Post* some years later about the Ribicoff tax break. The incident contributed to Rostenkowski's image as a politician who plays hardball.

In later years, Rostenkowski became well-known for his long memory and his eagerness to wreak revenge. In 1981, Ways and Means Representative Kent Hance, Democrat of Texas, led a revolt that ultimately defeated Rostenkowski's own tax plan on the House floor. In the following weeks and months, Hance became a committee pariah. During a committee trip to Baltimore, he was assigned a seat in the back of the bus, behind the staff. The chairman also refused to allow him to travel with the rest of the committee to China. Even during committee meetings, Hance was humiliated. He was, quite literally, grounded; Rostenkowski made sure his chair, unlike the others', did not have wheels. "If you cross Danny Rostenkowski," Representative Trent Lott, a House Republican leader, warned a colleague, "he'll get your ass!"

The pivotal event of 1976 for Rostenkowski came at the tail end of the year, far away from the intramural intrigue of Capitol Hill. On December 20, Mayor Daley died. The man who had become synonymous with the city, who controlled it for more than two decades and molded it to his personal style, was gone. It was a particularly painful blow to Rostenkowski, who learned his craft at the feet of the master and served loyally as his eyes and hands in Washington for so many years. At the mayor's house after the funeral, Daley's widow pulled Rostenkowski aside and pressed her husband's money clip into his mitt-sized hand. "He wanted you to have this," she said. Rostenkowski still carries it with him.

The death, in a way, liberated Rostenkowski. Instead of stripping him of his power, it allowed him to become his own man, to come into his own as a leader in the House. It was the passing of an era and the start of a new one. Rostenkowski began to pay more attention to Ways and Means and to focus more on the lessons he had learned over the years from its influential chairman, Wilbur Mills of Arkansas. "I am at his knee," Rostenkowski would say years later of Mills. From Mills, Rostenkowski learned some basic legislative skills: the art of controlling a committee, of angling always to win. Indeed, one of Rostenkowski's most central goals was to get and maintain control. Some critics charged that Mills never took gambles, always played it safe. He worked under weak speakers, and had the luxury of "closed rules" on the House floor that prevented amendments on his bills. The chairmen who came after him did not have it so easy. Nevertheless, Mills became a model for Rostenkowski and taught him some important lessons that came in handy during the wrenching battles for tax overhaul.

In 1980, the Reagan landslide swept many senior Democrats out of office, and Rostenkowski was faced with a critical choice. He could move up from his position as deputy to become Democratic whip, using his well-honed skills of vote-counting, arm-twisting, and log-rolling; or he could take the chairmanship of Ways and Means, which was vacated by the defeat in Oregon of Al Ullman. Rostenkowski, it turned out, was not ready to settle down, was not willing to allow himself to be branded as a political hatchet man, a palooka from the Illinois Eighth. To the surprise of many, he chose the more cerebral, and challenging, job: He chose to enter the big-time world of Ways and Means, one of the nation's least known but most important centers of power and influence.

Ways and Means stands at the vortex of two worlds. One is the world of government and its awesome power of taxation; the second is the business world, in which the whims of Ways and Means can mean the saving—or losing—of millions, even billions, of dollars a year. This fact elevated Rostenkowski, as chairman, to the equivalent of American royalty. Everywhere he went, he was fawned over and fêted, hosted and pleaded to, sought after and feared by the best, the brightest, and the richest of the capitalist elite. Maître d's, lobbyists, and hangers-on of all sorts would clamor to assist "Mr. Chairman." He rarely had to pick up the check, and in fact, attracted hundreds of checks of a different sort. One of the ways Rostenkowski kept the loyalty of his Ways and Means members was simply to attend their fundraisers. Wherever he went, thousands of dollars of campaign contributions followed. For some people, merely being seen in his presence would count as money in the bank.

But there was one public office that the chairman held in esteem—indeed, he viewed it with near-reverence: the office of president. Rostenkowski's father traveled from Chicago to Washington to let his son witness Roosevelt's third inauguration, an experience that deeply moved the young man. In his own congressional office, Rostenkowski displayed several photographs of himself with more-recent presidents. Among them was one photograph of Mount Rushmore, with Rostenkowski's own face pasted next to the sculpted countenance of George Washington. Its handwritten inscription reads: "Dear Danny, It looks good to me. Say hello to George for me. [signed] Ronald Reagan."

The obstacles to reform began piling up in Rostenkowski's path the day that Baker and Darman delivered the details of the president's plan to Capitol Hill—Wednesday, May 29. Rob Leonard, Rostenkowski's tax aide, dropped his clipboard in disgust when he saw the complete plan. He immediately saw there was a problem with revenue. There was no binding-contract rule, a tradition in tax legislation. In addition, the Treasury's business-recapture provision was quickly recognized for what it was: a desperate grab for revenue that did not have a chance of winning approval in Congress. The committee would have to find some other way to raise the $64 billion in revenue over five years that would be lost by correcting those two problems. But even if one counted those sleight-of-hand revenue-raisers, the Treasury bill still wasn't revenue neutral. It was calculated to add $12 billion to the government's budget deficit over the next five years.

The bill "had elements of mirrors, and, if you want to be that hard about it, intellectual dishonesty," said Ways and Means chief counsel Dowley. Baker and Darman, he says, "weren't playing the game totally on the up and up."

In addition, Rostenkowski complained that the Treasury team had not gotten anything in return for what they gave away. Despite the billions of dollars' worth of concessions to interest groups made in turning Treasury I into the president's plan, Rostenkowski saw little increase in the number of groups supporting the plan. Moreover, Baker had defied Rostenkowski's most solemn warning: His plan retained virtually all the tax breaks for oil and gas drillers. It had another political shortcoming as well: It gave bigger cuts to upper-income taxpayers than to middle-income taxpayers, a fact that worried many politicians on the Hill.

Baker and Darman wanted Rostenkowski to finish drafting a tax bill by the August congressional recess. But the chairman knew that, with such big problems to overcome, the administration's schedule was a pipe dream. For one thing, the chairman insisted on holding hearings to allow groups a chance to air their complaints about the proposal. Baker and Darman thought such hearings were a waste of time. They thought the purpose was for show more than substance, but Rostenkowski insisted. "This is the people's house," he said.

The hearings droned on throughout the summer, as the committee heard from well over four hundred special pleaders, who once again demonstrated the intensity of opposition to tax reform. Committee members grew weary of the harangues and tried to avoid the meetings, but Rostenkowski ordered his staff to assign at least a few members the chore of sitting with him through every hearing. While the members paid half-attention to the numbing parade of witnesses, the Ways and Means staff listened intently for hints of where compromises might lie, where allies could be enlisted. They searched for what Rostenkowski described as the "middle," that place where deals could be cut and enough support garnered to squeeze the legislation through.

Meanwhile, a more serious struggle went on behind the scenes. In the chairman's hideaway office just off the House floor, Rostenkowski and Leonard carefully interviewed each member of Ways and Means to determine which tax preferences were most precious to them and which they would be willing to repeal. There also was a great deal of truth-telling in the back room between the Ways and Means staff and the framers of the president's plan. During one meeting, Dowley and Leonard grilled Pearlman and a few other Treasury officials about the bogus recapture tax. After several minutes of intense argument, Dowley recalls, "We started smiling, they started smiling." Then all of them broke into outright laughter. "Nobody could stop laughing," says Dowley. The recapture tax "just didn't make sense," and all of them knew it.

Outside of Washington, the great populist awakening that was supposed to sweep tax reform to victory remained only a yawn. Taxpayers disliked the existing system, to be sure, but they still weren't convinced Congress was going to make it any better. The only constituents that lawmakers heard from were those who complained about losing this or that tax break. Hardly anyone seemed to think that they might have something to gain by lowering rates. The average taxpayer was unmoved by the reform effort, and the warning of Ways and Means Republican Willis Gradison of Ohio was coming through in spades: "This inevitably will be an uphill fight. The potential winners are skeptical that Congress will ever enact reform and the potential losers are organizing."

This fact was evident everywhere, from the rural foothills of the Appalachian mountains to the middle-class neighborhoods of Islip, New York, and the corporate suites of suburban Minnesota.

In the Georgia mountains, Representative Edgar Jenkins, a respected Ways and Means Democrat and political pal of Rostenkowski, found little if any support for the effort. His sprawling district included Gainesville, Georgia, known as the "Broiler Capital of the World," a town that had a monument with a chicken on top and feathers strewn along the roadways. Questions to him from voters during a round of visits and speeches focused mostly on his personal crusade in the House to protect the struggling local textile industry from a flood of Asian imports. Some folks expressed more general worries that the budget deficit was running amok. But there was seldom a mention of tax reform. On the rare occasion that the tax bill itself was discussed, most everyone had a gripe. The possible repeal of the deduction for mortgage interest on second homes was seen as threat to the otherwise impoverished region's only growing business, vacation home sales. In addition, any trimming of tax benefits for small farmers was viewed with alarm.

"There is no enthusiasm down here for a tax bill," Jenkins concluded. "In a tax-reform bill, you step on everyone's toes to some extent, and everyone is looking for an excuse to oppose it."

Late in the summer, Representative Thomas Downey, also a Rostenkowski ally, convened a public meeting on the tax-overhaul bill in the sweltering auditorium of Islip High School on Long Island, New York. Big fans were whirring in every corner of the packed room, but the citizens' animosity toward the president's proposal could not be cooled. The Ways and Means Democrat asked how many people supported the president's plan, and only one hand was raised. The big problem: the proposed repeal of the deduction for state and local tax payments. New York Governor Mario Cuomo had raised that issue to the level of righteousness, and no politician in the Empire State could resist. In a rare show of comaraderie, Senator Alfonse D'Amato, the state's Republican senator, joined Downey on stage that night and together they whipped up the crowd about their fight to save the state and local deduction. "We're here tonight to underscore this is not a partisan issue," Downey implored the crowd. "It is a matter of survival."

The next day the young congressman told a long parade of local leaders and business owners who met with him in his office that he was sympathetic to each of their causes, which ranged from preserving the business-meal deduction to keeping the inside buildup on life insurance policies tax-free. But he said he had to focus all of his attention on the state and local issue and could not be counted on to champion any other cause. On the drive to La Guardia Airport later that day, Downey compared tax reform to an impressionist painting: "The further away from it you go, the clearer it gets. The closer you get, the more it looks flawed."

As Downey was encountering resistance from the man on the street, Representative Bill Frenzel, Republican of Minnesota, was hearing similar complaints from about eighty business executives during a dinner in the Minneapolis suburb of Bloomington. At the meeting of a group called Minnesota Business Partnerships, Frenzel heard a withering series of worries. They carped about the possible cutback in the amount that high-paid executives could contribute to their tax-free 401(k) pension plans. They were also concerned about such business breaks as the foreign tax credit, which was a candidate for reduction, and of course, about the state and local deduction. "It's obvious that every friend you make [with tax reform], you are going to make a few enemies," Frenzel concluded. "The chairman's enthusiasm here is a mile ahead of everyone else's."

Tip O'Neill, usually one of Rostenkowski's strongest backers, added his voice to those of the doubters. "I have found very little sentiment for the reform tax bill [sic], very little sentiment," the speaker told reporters after Congress's monthlong August recess. "The people in the street, they never even mention it." He predicted "great difficulty" moving a bill through the House unless President Reagan somehow managed to convert the nation's apathy to excitement.

Even some of the most ardent backers of the enterprise began to abandon ship during these summer doldrums. On a plane to Washington from Atlanta, a tax reporter ran into Missouri's Gephardt, who had just attended a fundraiser for ambitious Democrats. The cosponsor of the seminal Bradley-Gephardt bill inquired, almost incredulously, whether the reporter was still writing about taxes. When Gephardt got a yes in reply, he responded with blank surprise. "It's not that good a story," he said.

Despite his seminal role, Gephardt dropped the ball on tax reform while the legislation was experiencing some hard times. Gephardt had remained true to reform for at least two years after he signed onto the bill with Bradley in 1982. During this period, he talked up the proposal with fellow Democrats in the House, traveled to promote the idea, and worked closely with Bradley to revise parts of the second version of the bill introduced in 1983. But his dedication did not last.

In May 1985 Gephardt sided with several tax-reform opponents and supported a proposal that would have used the revenue raised by a stiffened minimum tax to reduce budget deficits rather than help tax reform's effort to lower tax rates. In the fall, when Congress, spurred by newsmagazines' cover stories, rushed to pass some sort of protectionist trade legislation, Gephardt helped to lead the charge. At the time, he confided privately that he thought tax reform was going nowhere and that trade was the issue of the hour. Later, when Congress moved away from trade to focus on the Gramm-Rudman-Hollings law as a way to appear to be doing something about reducing budget deficits, Gephardt was out front again. He spent a lot of his time on the budget problem while other members of Ways and Means were working on tax reform.

Gephardt's time for tax reform also was crowded out by his frequent trips across the nation. In 1985, the young lawmaker was spending spare moments advancing the cause of his own nascent presidential campaign. Gephardt contends that he never abandoned tax reform and that he played key roles in developing the Ways and Means proposals and in counting votes to help pass the finished product. But when it came to the day-in, day-out efforts to muster support among wavering members of the House, Rostenkowski didn't rely on Dick Gephardt, whom he sometimes disparaged as one of the "blow-dried guys."

While the average taxpayer seemed apathetic toward Rostenkowski's effort, the average interest group was intensely involved. Loud and persistent complaints came from groups that ranged from one-man lobbying crusades to multifaceted and expensive coalition efforts.

Thomas Franks, the thirty-one-year-old lobbyist for the American Land Development Association, spent his days in 1985 talking to members of Congress about a sore point: the importance of preserving the mortgage-interest deduction for second homes. The developers he represented with his $60,000-a-year job were worried that their high-toned tourist developments might be squeezed by plans to do away with the deduction, and Franks had a $250,000 budget to fight it.

Franks paid out thousands of dollars for public-relations campaigns and even some extra lobbying help. He also made campaign contributions to tax writers such as John Duncan of Tennessee. Franks explained that he had no choice but to attend a $500 a head fundraiser for Ways and Means's top Republican because, "I couldn't go to his office without having contributed." Making arguments to members was the heart of his one-man show.

Popping a Certs mint into his mouth, Franks said: "I can't have bad breath, can't smoke, can't perspire. In this line of work, I can't afford to offend anyone." He worried that his message was not getting through. "Getting congressmen to take a stand against a provision of this tax bill is more difficult than I've ever seen. They would rather talk about anything else right now. It's paranoia on the Hill. They're scared to appear to be caving to special interests."

To help make his argument, Franks called in Jesse Abraham, an economist with Data Resources Incorporated, a Massachusetts-based consulting firm, to conduct a study on the economic effects of the proposed second-home limitation. Such supposedly objective studies were a standard part of the Washington lobbyist's repertoire. "What do you think you'll find?" Franks asked. Abraham responded, "First of all, I don't have a contract with you or a check from you." After Franks ordered up a check and a contract, Abraham inquired, "What do you want us to find?" (Asked later what he meant, Abraham said: "Well, I was interested in seeing what he expected the market impact would be. As an industry person, he has a strong feeling on what will be the market reaction, which can be useful for my analysis.")

Data Resources was only one of a host of hired guns who made hay preparing studies on the supposedly disastrous effects of tax reform. When added together, they suggested the president's tax bill would create a cataclysm. According to various studies circulated on Capitol Hill, the bill would force "a dose of Jonestown-type cyanide" on the construction industry, raise apartment rents by 20 percent to 40 percent, destroy old urban neighborhoods, and jeopardize "the oral health of the American people." Horse breeding would fall 18 percent, American Samoa would be devastated, and canned tuna would become obsolete. The president's tax plan, according to these studies paid for by anti–tax-reform lobbyists, would precipitate all evils short of famine, pestilence, and plague—even plague wasn't entirely out of the question: The National Council of Community

Hospitals submitted a report claiming that taxing private-purpose revenue bonds would threaten health care for the poor.

Jobs would become scarcer than congressmen-in-August if these many authoritative-sounding reports proved true. "Millions" of workers in export industries would be out on the streets, along with 350,000 construction workers, 224,841 Puerto Ricans, 144,000 restaurant workers, 69,000 oil men, and 44,000 country club employees. In Beaufort County, South Carolina, alone, 28,000 workers would get the ax, according to one survey. To the congressmen and their aides deluged with such reports, it seemed that tax reform would devastate every American industry save one: the economic consulting and research business, which produced all these forecasts of disaster.

The consulting firms insisted their work was unbiased. "Nobody is ever going to buy us," said Norman Ture, former Treasury undersecretary who headed an organization called the Institute for Research on the Economics of Taxation, which raised money from corporations to fund anti–tax-reform studies. As James Wetzler, a congressional tax aide who left the Hill in 1984 to become an investment banker, put it: "Most people who get into this game are big boys and realize they're not being paid to do a study that goes against the guy who funded them. They know which side their bread is buttered on."

Consultants were available to study almost any potential problem the tax plan might create. Economics Research Associates, a Los Angeles–based consulting firm, earned $45,000 from the American Horse Council for a study showing the tax plan's effects on horse mating. The firm also got a contract from Thomas Franks's group to study the effects on vacation homes. The results of the studies, although frequently stated in very precise-sounding terms and numbers, were seldom rock-solid. The study concluding that horse breeding would drop 18 percent was done simply by surveying horse farmers, who opposed the tax plan because of its proposed changes in capital-gains taxation. Anxious to alter the tax bill, the breeders may have simply overstated the effects, or they may not have really known what the effects would be. "You can poke all kinds of holes in our survey research," conceded Steven Spickard of Economics Research. "This isn't the kind of ironclad econometric analysis with ten years of historical data we would like to be using."

Despite their shortcomings, such studies played an important role in the tax debate. "I know they're hired guns," said Connecticut Democrat Barbara Kennelly, a member of the Ways and Means Committee, "but I've got to tell you that I was just putting one of those studies in my stuff to read tonight. I feel nothing wrong with reading them. Are they slanted? Of course. But you know that, and at least they give you a glimpse of how the plan will affect an industry."

Tom Franks was, for the most part, a soft and solo salesman. But one of the biggest and best-financed lobbying efforts, staged by a high-powered group of New Yorkers, was not so gentle. In conjunction with a determined Governor Mario Cuomo, the coalition pulled all the stops out to save the deduction for state and local taxes.

The New Yorkers' lobbying drive began in the spring of 1985 with an urgent mailgram to several hundred of the richest and most important people in New York City. The mailgram was an invitation to a meeting on an issue that, it said, threatened nothing less than the future of the city and the state. The mailgram was signed by David Rockefeller, former chairman of Chase Manhattan Bank; James Robinson III, chairman of American Express; and Laurence Tisch, chairman of Loews Corporation.

The featured speaker at the meeting, held in the lavishly appointed Harley Hotel in Manhattan, was Senator D'Amato. The topic: tax reform. The Treasury's plan would repeal the deduction for state and local taxes, and its effect on New York, the state with the highest taxes in the nation, would be severe, D'Amato said. Each of the people attending the meeting had plenty of their own complaints about the controversial tax overhaul; most had business interests that would be hurt. But D'Amato's message was clear: The proposal to eliminate the state and local deduction needed their undivided attention. "You've got to focus on this and this only, because if you don't, we'll get killed," he said.

Thus began one of the most persistent and pervasive lobbying campaigns of the tax reform story. During the next year and a half, these wealthy New Yorkers doled out more than $1.5 million to protect their precious write-off.

Lewis Rudin, a New York real estate manager, was named to head the campaign. He enlisted Jay Kriegel to help run it. A fast-talking lawyer, Kriegel had served as chief of staff and special counsel to former mayor John Lindsay of New York. Kriegel later opened New York City's Washington office and lobbied Congress extensively in the early 1970s for revenue-sharing benefits. He knew the ways of Washington well.

From the start, Kriegel realized that saving the state and local deduction would be no small task. Eliminating the deduction raised $150 billion in revenue over five years and was a keystone of the Treasury plan. Baker and Darman repeatedly insisted there could be no bill without its repeal. Furthermore, the Reagan administration seemed to revel in the criticisms of New York's Democratic Governor Cuomo. If tax reform ended up as a fight between New York and the rest of the country, the administration strategists thought, New York would surely lose. To some GOP political analysts, a loss for Cuomo would be especially welcome, because he was a potential contender for the Democratic nomination for president in 1988.

"They wanted to isolate us, and there was a grave risk they would succeed," Kriegel said later. "Given the nature of the attack, from the president on down, it was clear that the usual response wouldn't be adequate. Unless we did something significantly bigger, we were going to lose."

The determined New Yorkers decided that they had to broaden their base of support and get other states involved. "The only way we could win was to prove this was not just a New York issue," said Kriegel. They opened an office near the Capitol and hired a young Democratic fundraiser, Bob Chlopak, to head it. They began to accumulate a national base of support. They ran eye-catching television commercials that pictured a large man in a wading pool trying to telephone his congressman to complain about the repeal of the deduction for property taxes. Other groups quickly joined the effort. Public-employee unions were the first to sign on, providing some of the money needed to fund the campaign. Organizations like the Conference of Mayors also soon joined. The group, started by a handful of rich New Yorkers, gradually became a national coalition, calling itself the "Coalition Against Double Taxation." A research director was hired to crank out studies showing how eliminating the deduction would affect every state. When representatives of the coalition met with a congressman from Georgia, they showed him detailed information on how it would affect Georgia services, Georgia taxes, and what it would do to everyone in Georgia. When they met with someone from Connecticut, they unveiled the same detailed figures about Connecticut.

Unlike the insurance industry, which conducted a scattershot lobbying campaign designed to hit every member of Congress, the cleverly run state-and-local group aimed carefully at important tax writers. They sent grassroots organizers into the California congressional district of Democratic Representative Robert Matsui, for example, and set up a committee of community leaders opposed to repeal to put pressure on the Ways and Means member. They ran advertisements in local newspapers saying the proposal to repeal the deduction of property taxes would hurt every homeowner. DO YOU WANT TO PAY MORE FOR YOUR OWN HOME? the ad asked. "If not, call Congressman Bob Matsui today." The hard-nosed tactics were repeated in the districts of key Ways and Means members across the country.

Early on, both Rostenkowski and the Treasury recognized the state-and-local issue was especially controversial and would probably require some sort of compromise. Baker and Darman continued to argue, however, that they could not afford to give up the entire provision. If the deduction were retained, tax writers would have to look elsewhere to find a large chunk of revenue. The alternatives were not happy ones for the Treasury officials: Either tax rates would have to rise above the level they recommended, or business tax breaks would have to be curtailed even more than the Treasury request.

With so much on the line, the appearance of Cuomo before the Ways and Means Committee in July was a particularly tense event. He was scheduled to testify about the president's proposal, and the day began with an informal breakfast gathering in the book-lined library in the rear of the Ways and Means hearing room. The library was dominated by a thirty-foot-long mahogany table, inlaid with black slate around its oval-shaped rim. Embedded in the slate were brass plates bearing the names of previous Ways and Means chairmen, starting with THOMAS FITZSIMMONS, PA., FEDERALIST, 1789–95 and sweeping around to the plate in front of Rostenkowski's own seat that read DAN ROSTENKOWSKI, IL., 1981—. Such private breakfast sessions were among the best attended and most informative of the Ways and Means Committee's events, much more so than the public hearings that followed them. Rostenkowski used these sessions to expose his members to corporate chief executives who backed tax reform and to let his tax writers know that at least some corporations were their friends. But this day, state-and-local day, the breakfast featured an unwavering opponent of the president's reform.

Cuomo's message was loud and emphatic, especially in the cramped quarters of the library. His arguments were marshalled with eloquence, but they were forceful—too forceful, some members thought, for the setting. They were the verbal equivalent of fist-pounding: a fiery sermon about the rectitude of the state and local deduction. Members of the committee felt they were being lectured to, and they did not like it.

The ill-feelings that began in the library spilled over into the public hearing later that day. It did not take long for Cuomo to get into a row. His victim was one of the most mild-mannered and courtly members of the committee, John Duncan. During the New York governor's testimony, members speculated about whether some high-tax-state taxpayers might move to low-tax states if the deduction were taken away. "I've never met anyone from Tennessee who retired to New York," Duncan said. Cuomo shot back, "Maybe after they retired they denied they were from Tennessee."

The arrogant quip angered committee members. "If we had a vote on it [the state and local deduction] at that point," speculates Joe Dowley, "it would have been a lot easier to dispose of the issue." No votes were taken, however, and the issue got even stickier as the weeks went by.

In August, the Coalition Against Double Taxation made a critical decision that threatened to foil the plans of Rostenkowski and the Treasury and scuttle tax reform. Acting against the advice of some of their most savvy political advisers, Kriegel and Chlopak convinced others in the coalition to adopt a "no-compromise" strategy: They decided to refuse to settle for half a loaf. Washington is a city that operates on deals, but the coalition was saying it would not deal. The group wanted to retain the *entire* state and local deduction and decided compromise would not do.

Cuomo echoed this sentiment to the New York members of Ways and Means during a special meeting in the state's offices in Manhattan's World Trade Center. There, with the help of other statewide politicians, he laid down the law: no compromise. Rangel, a senior member of Ways and Means and a close ally of Rostenkowski, was not eager to accept the stance, but the lawmakers left the meeting speaking with one voice on the pivotal issue.

The strategy risked incurring the wrath of Rostenkowski, but Kriegel felt by that point that the coalition would ultimately prevail. If he was right, the entire tax-reform effort faced a serious threat.

By September, after a summer's worth of rising complaints and little support for tax reform, Rostenkowski thought it was time to lay down some laws of his own. On Saturday, September 7, he packed up his thirty-six-member committee, a handful of economists, and some top Treasury officials, including Baker and Darman, and set off for a weekend of sublime seclusion in the Virginia hills. In the spacious, sunken living room of a house on the grounds of a convention center called Airlie House, away from the prying eyes of the press and the crush of lobbyists, the chairman tried to breathe new life into tax reform.

It was not easy. Harvard economist and former Reagan adviser Martin Feldstein argued strenuously at the retreat that the tax plan would harm heavy, rust-belt industries like steel. Members raised other thorny concerns: Does the proposal encourage adequate savings and investment? Will the package produce a short-term economic recession? Might it hamper America's already-lagging international competitiveness? New York Republican Raymond McGrath said that "two of the three people in America who favor tax reform are in this room, and only one of them has a vote"— a reference to Rostenkowski and Baker, who were present, and President Reagan, who was not. There also was mostly hushed talk about trying to kill the bill. In an aside, Bill Frenzel of Minnesota warned his colleagues that if they wanted tax reform dead, they had better give it "a good karate chop, or it will come back and beat the shit out of you."

Most ominous of all, one of Rostenkowski's earliest, and most private, fears was coming to pass. His members were beginning to form political marriages that, if successful, might block his bill. During some of the quieter moments at Airlie House, lawmakers from high-tax states like New York, who were worried about the state and local deduction, made preliminary overtures to those from oil-and-gas regions like Texas, who feared Rostenkowski would attack their favorite industry's tax breaks. Together, the disaffected lawmakers might form a coalition that could stop any bill.

Baker added his own impediment by outlining four issues on which, he said, the president would not compromise. He described them as "lines drawn in the sand"—a curious metaphor for unyielding demands, but it was clear he meant business. The four were: reducing the top individual tax rate to 35 percent from the existing 50 percent, removing low-income families from the income-tax rolls, retaining the mortgage-interest deduction, and keeping the entire proposal revenue neutral compared with existing law. The only guideline that was in dispute was the top tax rate; the committee was not as wedded to so low a top rate. Representative Frank Guarini, Democrat of New Jersey, asked his colleagues to vote that day to "lock in" 35 percent as their first decision on the bill, but no one responded to the suggestion.

Amid all this resistance, Rostenkowski's closing statement provided the retreat's one shining moment for tax reform. In the sunken living room that looked out through a picture window on the tartan hills, the chairman delivered an impassioned appeal. His words were borne out of his own conviction that the time was right for reform, but also out of the frustration he was feeling. His own members, he knew, were turning their backs on him.

He reminded them that they had been through a lot together, and that if they failed this time, it could well be the professional disappointment of their lives. It would cast a pall on the committee that might never be removed. He spoke about the need for reform, the chance to bring fairness into the code. Although not a reformer by nature, Rostenkowski did have a desire to pursue tax justice. When uncertain about how to go on a tax issue, he would frequently turn to his advisers and ask, "What's the right answer?" He told his committee members about his own daughters, who, he said, were working hard to make ends meet, but who paid more in taxes than some millionaires. Three of them were airline stewardesses, the fourth was an office assistant. Tears came to his eyes at the mention of them. "We have an opportunity to etch what little we can in the history books," he said. "It's not going to be easy, but it's doable."

At the end, under the blue-eyed gaze of their chairman, few of the members were willing to say no, either to Rostenkowski or to his drive for reform. The weekend's windup appeared to be the start of a new era of good feeling.

Any good feelings among the Ways and Means committee members were short-lived, however. Tax overhaul encountered new obstacles as soon as the members returned for work in the House. The first problem was the rush of interest in tackling another national problem that fell under the wide reach of the Ways and Means Committee—the trade deficit. Georgia's Ed Jenkins put his colleagues on notice that tax reform was not his top priority, that he would attempt to attach a textile-protectionist amendment to every bill the committee tried to pass. Faced with a similar wave of interest from a growing number of members not on the committee, Rostenkowski was forced to delay the start of work on the tax-reform bill until he pushed Jenkins's textile bill out of committee and onto the House floor.

When Rostenkowski announced his plans to move the trade bill first, he owned up to a "hesitancy" among his members to dive into reform. Jenkins was more direct: "The members of the committee simply don't feel the rising tide from the public or from other members of the House for a comprehensive tax-reform bill. They don't want to be leading the train with no boxcars back there."

Tax reform's troubles did not end after the trade issue had been dealt with. An influential group of liberal House Democrats called the Democratic Study Group came out strongly against the president's demand to lower the top tax rate to 35 percent. They feared such a steep decline from 50 percent would produce a windfall for the richest Americans. They also could not see the reason for turning the tax code inside out without raising some revenue to attack the nation's number-one problem: budget deficits.

In early September, President Reagan began to tour the nation in an attempt to rouse the public from its indifference over tax reform. It was his first speaking tour since his operation for intestinal cancer that summer, and it met with little success. Speaking in his shirt-sleeves outside the Jackson County Courthouse in Independence, Missouri, the president conjured up images of Harry Truman. "It's the working men and women of America who pay the taxes, foot the bills, and make the sacrifices that keep this country going," he told the crowd. "And I'm here to talk to you about a long-overdue change in our tax laws, a change that is aimed at benefiting you. . . . I think Harry would be very pleased."

The president traveled as well to Concord, New Hampshire; Raleigh, North Carolina; and Athens, Tennessee, to sell his reform package, but the takers were few. Reagan acknowledged that the battle to win public support for tax reform would be difficult. The American people, he said, have "heard too many promises by too many politicians about how their lives are going to be made better. They have been hurt too many times by elected officials who promised better and delivered worse." The president insisted that this time, "I promise you we are going to win." But skepticism continued, and polls showed that those who opposed the president's tax reform effort were as numerous as those who supported it.

Meanwhile, Rostenkowski hoped to create some new enthusiasm, at least among his own members, by presenting them with a new tax-reform plan drafted by his staff. The president's plan had been so thoroughly discredited in the minds of the committee members that some new starting point was needed if the process were to move ahead. Indeed, the many political problems with the president's plan might well have contributed to the continuing public disinterest.

When the Ways and Means plan was unveiled in late September, however, it was greeted not with praise, but with resentment. "Almost none of the members felt any allegiance to it," Dowley recalls. "Few of them felt it was a product of their making." Even the chairman was reluctant to put his name to it at first. It was called the "staff option."

The plan eliminated the president's controversial windfall recapture tax—to the relief of almost everyone. It also compromised on the state and local deduction, preserving a large share of the write-off, but the compromise was not enough. Members immediately rejected the proposal as inadequate.

To keep the president on board the plan, the top individual tax rate was set at 35 percent. The top corporate rate was placed at 35 percent, up from the president's 33 percent. In addition, the top capital-gains rate, which the president wanted to reduce, was increased to 21 percent from the existing 20 percent. The New Right's insistence on a $2,000 personal exemption was cut back. Only taxpayers who did not itemize their deductions would get the full $2,000 exemption; itemizers would get only $1,500.

Depreciation write-offs were made significantly less generous compared with the president's plan; and oil-and-gas tax breaks, along with other benefits for specific industries, were socked hard. Compared with the president's proposal, the Ways and Means plan gave a smaller tax cut to the very wealthy and a somewhat larger one to families earning between $30,000 and $100,000 a year. And, as with the Reagan plan, millions of working-poor families were removed from the income tax rolls.

Rostenkowski made clear that the document was only a starting point and that he expected it to be changed by the committee. In fact, many of the provisions were written with the understanding that they would eventually be watered-down. But the vehemence of the complaints provoked by the plan took the chairman and his staff by surprise. It was clear that a deeper resistance to tax reform lay at the root of the grousing.

Rostenkowski needed help. His efforts to appease his members had fallen flat, and members outside the committee were even less impressed. During lunches with lawmakers from various geographical regions, the chairman got almost no positive reactions. If constituents did not clamor for the bill, and many of the affected groups only complained, many members asked, "Why bother?" To help answer those questions, Rostenkowski turned to his friend in the Senate, Bill Bradley.

When he played basketball, Bradley was known as one of the best in the game at moving around the court without the ball. This was an attribute that proved helpful in Congress as well. As a junior member of the Senate and the Finance Committee, Bradley was seldom in command. As the result of the institution's seniority system, he had limited ability to advance legislation and was beholden to more-experienced lawmakers to achieve many of his goals. He was forced to believe in the adage that there's no end to what a person can accomplish if he lets others take credit. When it came to taxes, he well understood that Rostenkowski was, as he put it, "the king." Tax measures originate in the House, the Ways and Means Committee writes the laws, and Rostenkowski was its chairman.

Even before Treasury I was unveiled, Bradley tried assiduously to arrange a meeting with the chairman. While giving a speech at a hotel in New Jersey in November 1984, Bradley finally got word that Rostenkowski, who was in Chicago at the time, would see him. Standing at a bank of pay telephones in the hotel, he tried to make arrangements for the meeting on one phone while booking an airplane flight to Chicago on the other. Two hours later, he was on his way, and he met with Rostenkowski in downtown Chicago that very same day. Bradley told the chairman he was willing to help in any way he could. It was an important meeting that helped both men advance their thinking about how desirable and *doable* tax reform was.

Bradley also tried to keep in close contact with the Reagan administration. Shortly after Christmas in 1984, Bradley drove from Palm Beach, Florida, where he was vacationing with his parents, up the coast to John's Island, where Regan had a home. The two men talked for three hours, first at Regan's house, then over lunch at the nearby golf club. Bradley went away convinced that the Reagan administration was serious about reform; Regan left feeling certain that the New Jersey Democrat would help the president's effort. "We had an understanding there that we could and should push tax reform," Regan said later. "It was a very significant meeting."

Bradley lobbied for his brainchild in numerous meetings with senior members of the House. Picking his targets with the aid of Ari Weiss, a tax-reform advocate who was one of Speaker O'Neill's top aides and an expert in the workings of the House, Bradley met with the speaker, House Majority Leader Jim Wright of Texas, House Whip Thomas Foley of Washington State, and Representative Tony Coelho of California, who chaired the House Democrats' campaign fundraising organization. When deliberations at Ways and Means heated up later in 1985, Bradley placed himself at the disposal of Rostenkowski. The senator's top aide, Marcia Aronoff, was in constant contact with Charles Mellody, one of Rostenkowski's top men. Together they would decide where the senator could be best utilized. He met with almost every Democratic member of Ways and Means, and as well as many others not on the committee, including the liberal Democratic Study Group (DSG). He helped persuade DSG members to back the bill, despite their doubts about lowering tax rates at a time when budget deficits were pressing.

It is extraordinary for a senator to try to influence the members of the House in such an overt way. The Senate considers itself the upper chamber and its members, many of whom graduate from the House, often think of themselves as superior. Not so with Senator Bradley. At one point, in the House gym, Bradley played his first serious game of basketball since ending his professional career. Many of his opponents were Ways and Means Democrats. He took care not to humiliate his less-athletic rivals, but he still wound up popping a leg muscle. He did not much mind; at least he scored some points for tax overhaul.

On September 30, the eve of the first drafting session, Rostenkowski invited Bradley to deliver another pep talk to the Ways and Means Democrats. Such a visit from a senator was exceptional and his message was partisan. Tax overhaul, he argued, is a natural Democratic issue. If the Democratic-controlled House passed a bill, he asserted, tax reform would be labeled a Democratic initiative no matter what the Republican-controlled Senate did. And, he added pointedly, "Republicans in the Senate don't want to have to deal with the issue."

Bradley wanted tax reform to become law and hoped the Senate would somehow find a way to pass it. Rostenkowski, however, never believed the strongly pro-business Senate would swallow a tax-reform bill, and he used that belief to try to persuade his members to keep his own bill alive. Republicans would have egg on their faces when the Senate killed tax reform, he told his colleagues, and the Democrats would score a public relations victory. Bradley's comments provided a first-hand account of just how hostile the other chamber was to reform.

The Ways and Means Committee finally got down to serious work on the tax-reform plan on Tuesday, October 1. All of the chatter and complaining about the legislation began to come home to roost. This was the moment of truth. Members had to put their votes where their mouths were.

Drafting sessions, known on Capitol Hill as "markups," were held behind closed doors, and neither the press nor the armies of lobbyists were allowed in the ornate Ways and Means Committee room. The room, which was numbered 1100 and dominated the first floor of the Longworth House Office Building, looked more like a vast, gilded arena than a hearing room. Dangling from the center of the nearly forty-foot-high ceiling was a gigantic, triple-tiered chandelier, topped by an eagle. There were statues of eagles, too, atop twin pillars in each recessed corner of the room. Everywhere there was gold. The eagles in the corners were gilded, and a gold-colored velvet curtain concealed the wall behind the double-terraced dais where the thirty-six Ways and Means members sat.

For the tax-reform markup, the members' seats were arranged in a wide circle on the hearing-room floor so that they could face each other—a sign that Rostenkowski meant to get down to business. Despite the closed doors, the lobbyists and their assistants crowded the halls, waiting desperately for any brief opportunity to corner committee members or their aides. To get in and out of the closed meetings, members had to run the gauntlet of these highly paid loiterers. Lobbyists would try to hand the members position papers or urge on them a point or two.

Although they were closed out of the markup, these denizens of the hallway still made their presence felt. Many of the committee members worked hand-in-hand with certain favored lobbyists, presenting problems for the beleaguered chairman. Staff aides emerged periodically to brief the lobbyists on issues that were important to their clients, and the lobbyists passed instructions back into the room for members who were championing their causes. Sometimes, a representative would walk out of the hearing room, crook a finger in the direction of a lobbyist in the hallway, and then disappear for a few minutes into a back room for a strategy session.

Many of the committee members, in fact, eagerly became the standard-bearers for issues that lobbyists pushed. Often, the member's interest coincided with his or her constituency. Representative Barbara Kennelly, Democrat of Connecticut, who was otherwise a rigorous reformer, for example, defended the tax breaks that helped the insurance companies that resided in great numbers in her district. Representative James Jones, Democrat of Oklahoma, was one of several oil-state lawmakers who fronted oil-company causes. Other members backed issues that were broader than their own districts. Bob Matsui of California, for example, was the tax-exempt-bond man, and Ronnie Flippo of Alabama championed commercial banks.

These allegiances made many Ways and Means members reluctant reformers at best. Each of them had a few key interests that they felt bound to protect from the tax-overhaul knife. As a result, Duncan said at the beginning of the markup that there were not enough votes to pass a bill. Rostenkowski was quick to defend the effort, however. "Don't let yourself get misled by the negative rumors," he told a group of health-industry executives. "The tax-reform train is moving. It is picking up speed, and there's a real danger that doubters will be left behind at the station."

The train was painfully slow in leaving, however, and the panel's reluctance to move ahead sprang to the surface immediately in the form of "staff bashing," a term turned by David Brockway, the moon-faced staff director of the Joint Tax Committee and one of those who was most often bashed. Brockway served as Congress's chief tax expert and had an uncanny ability to formulate policy proposals that fit political needs. He played a critical role in fashioning the House bill, and later, the Senate bill. Members did not want to criticize Chairman Rostenkowski directly, and they were loathe to take on the smooth-talking Treasury secretary, who also attended the early meetings. Instead, Brockway and other staff aides became the natural focus for their generalized complaints about the proposal, about the process, and indeed about the entire tax-reform enterprise. The staff was accustomed to criticism from members, but this time the attacks were more severe than usual. "It was the worst I'd ever seen it, really, at Ways and Means," Brockway said.

The harshest words came from Representative Sam Gibbons of Florida, the panel's second-ranking Democrat and an unbridled opponent of reform. Gibbons got so upset at times that he threw temper tantrums. His face turned red and he pounded the table to complain about this or that point in the proposal, almost all of which he abhorred. Such outbursts from Gibbons became commonplace during tax-reform sessions. Other members also complained about the details of the plan as the staff read through the proposal.

As the time drew near for actual voting on the plan, members switched their complaints from substance to procedure. The enemies of reform attacked the manner in which the legislation was to be considered and won a major victory right off the bat.

Rostenkowski believed that the rules of procedure should require that any amendment be revenue neutral—any proposed change that would lose revenue had to be paired with another change that would raise the same amount of revenue. The chairman thought his members had agreed to that procedure at their Airlie House conference. The rule would place a difficult burden on any member who wanted to alter the package. If members wanted to help out one particular interest group, they would have to pare back the benefits of some other group.

The restriction proved too harsh for Ways and Means members. They wanted more freedom to fiddle with the proposal. They did not want so massive a measure to be simply dictated to them by the staffers who were its prime authors. They were members of Congress, with no lack of pride and self-esteem, and they wanted to place their imprint on the document. So, on October 2, the proposed rule was cast aside, making the chances of holding the plan together slim.

Members were clearly being dragged kicking and screaming into tax reform. Led by Gibbons, a group tried that same night to get Rostenkowski to accept a second, and even more menacing change in procedure. They argued that the committee should use existing law, rather than the staff option, as the starting point for its deliberations. That procedure meant the committee would have to vote to curtail or eliminate each and every tax preference in the code necessary for reform, and each vote would subject them to severe lobbying pressure. In contrast, if the staff option were used, members could simply accept it as a package and not be forced to go on record offending individual interest groups. Votes would be taken only if someone on the committee demanded that a particular tax break be restored. Furthermore, since amendments can be defeated by tie votes, if the committee started with existing law, tie votes would favor the status quo. If it started with the staff option, tie votes would be votes for reform. There was a world of difference between the two procedures. By taking the Gibbons approach, the tough task of writing a tax-reform bill would become even tougher.

In a lapse, Rostenkowski agreed to the damaging procedure. He was immediately rushed by his frantic staff into Dowley's office across from the hearing room. "Look, you can't do this, this is bullshit," Brockway said. "You're not going to be able to markup under this set of rules. It's going to be a goddamn disaster." The aides importuned the chairman to reverse himself and start with the staff option. Also, they said he should stop calling it the "staff" option; he should accept it as his own to give it the credibility it needed to move forward.

The next day the chairman worked to reverse the decision to accept the damaging procedure. Baker, sensing serious trouble for tax overhaul, even urged Republicans on the committee to support the chairman's package as the starting point. After a long day's effort, the procedure was changed, and the staff option—which from then on was called the "Rostenkowski plan"—became the basis for the committee's work.

The bill got off to an agonizing start. The committee made a few small gestures in the direction of reform: It voted one day to tax all unemployment compensation benefits, and on another day to repeal income averaging, which allowed people to offset taxes on high incomes in one year by averaging them with low incomes in other years. But for the most part, the committee seemed more eager to abandon the chairman's reform proposals than accept them. When the first vote to go against the chairman's package was taken—a vote to exclude from taxation workman's compensation and black-lung disability benefits—several members applauded. The panel then went on to expand a tax break for racing horses. Rostenkowski carefully skirted the big issues, fearing he would lose and thus endanger his entire effort. For two weeks, the committee nibbled about the edges of reform. Support for the chairman remained tentative, and the lack of action led to rumblings that the bill was dying a slow death.

The final straw for the dying plan fell on Tuesday, October 15, the day after Columbus Day, thanks to an amendment offered by Alabama Democrat Ronnie Flippo. The son of a working-class family, Flippo had been a construction worker, even though his father died doing the same job. He might have remained an ironworker all his life had he not, as a young man, plunged fifty-five feet onto a concrete floor and been confined to bed for eighteen months to heal his broken bones. Afterward, he was prevented from lifting and hauling, so he set out instead on a new life. He was elected to Congress in 1976 after proving himself the top man in a ten-person field.

A trained accountant, Flippo was sympathetic to the arguments of banks that they would be hurt by proposals to cut back on the bad-debt-reserve deduction, the biggest tax break enjoyed by financial institutions. He offered an amendment that went in the opposite direction, actually expanding the bad-debt-reserve tax break. The amendment was the antithesis of reform; it represented old-time tax legislation at its worst, giving out goodies to favored interests rather than taking them away. If the amendment succeeded, it would be clear to the world that this tax bill was no different than any other. It would be clear that the Ways and Means Committee had no desire to enact real reform.

On the Thursday before the vote, Frank Toohey, an aide to Flippo, met another tax aide and a curly-haired bank lobbyist named David Rosenauer in the hallway outside of room 1100. Rosenauer joked that the amendment

Toohey's boss was pushing to help commercial banks did not stand a chance, but Toohey disagreed. With tax reform adrift in the committee, he thought, even the generous new tax break for banks might succeed. "If you get off your ass and do something we can win this thing," Toohey told Rosenauer. Flippo himself conveyed the same sentiment to bank representatives during a meeting on the brown-leather chairs in the room behind the dais of room 1100.

Flippo's banking amendment was the first order of business on Tuesday. Over the long holiday weekend, home-state bankers had busily telephoned members of Ways and Means and their staffs to seek support for the proposal. Even Toohey got a call. The previous week, Toohey had counted only about a dozen votes for the proposal on the thirty-six-member committee. By Tuesday afternoon, he had a feeling it had a chance.

When the chairman called for a vote on Flippo's amendment, the ayes started coming from unexpected directions. First he tried a voice vote, then a show of hands, and finally a roll call. Each time the outcome was the same. Rostenkowski's aides, who usually stood over his shoulder like falcons ready to be dispatched by their falconer, went swooping down on members who had voted for the outrageous amendment. Even traditional Rostenkowski backers, like Matsui and Downey, were supporting the banks. Something was seriously awry.

The Flippo amendment was adopted 17–13. It ripped a gaping hole in the Rostenkowski tax plan, losing $7.6 billion in revenue over five years compared with the plan's targets. More important, it served as a measure of the discontent that had been festering in the committee from the very beginning. Eleven of the panel's twenty-three Democrats either didn't cast a vote or voted for the amendment. Downey voted aye because he wanted the chairman to know how strongly he felt about the deduction for state and local taxes. Matsui voted aye because he didn't know where the effort was going; he did not want to cast a hard vote for an effort that was bound to fail. All but one of the Republicans voted aye, because they felt left out of the process. Others had similar stories. The bank vote proved that the chairman needed to gain control of his committee if he was going to get a bill.

The chairman was livid and threw down his pencil in disgust. He told Deputy Treasury Secretary Darman to look at the vote count and see for himself that only one Republican, Gradison, had backed his position. "If the administration wants this tax bill, they had better get us Republican votes," Rostenkowski shouted. Flippo approached Rostenkowski and tried to assure him that he had not expected his amendment to win. Ways and Means aides scurried to try to change some votes around.

Word about the vote quickly reached a knot of bank lobbyists outside. "We won! We won!" David Rosenauer shouted, and the lobbyist's cry of victory echoed in the hallway. The bank's win was the biggest defeat yet for tax overhaul, leaving the bill teetering on the brink.

Chapter 6

The Phoenix Project

In the moments after the bank vote, an odd silence filled the committee room. Some members clustered around the chairman. Others sat without moving. Everyone was shaken, surprised. The dissatisfaction and uneasiness that had been building for weeks suddenly had reached a crescendo. Staffers wracked their brains to figure out where they could find the votes to defeat the bank amendment. They urged the chairman to move to reconsider it right away. But Rostenkowski told them to cool down.

"This one's gonna hang out there," the chairman said. "Just let them stew in it for a while."

The delay was a gamble. The bank vote marked a threshold on the rocky road to tax reform in the House. The committee would either have to step across it, or stop and allow the effort to die. Many members were clearly leaning toward the second option.

But Rostenkowski put his faith in an idea he had tossed around with John Sherman, his speech writer and press aide. Tax reform, for them, was the "phoenix project," named after the mythological creature that rose from the ashes of its own destruction. Like the phoenix, tax reform would rise to its most spectacular success only after it had first crashed in flames. Rostenkowski would ask jokingly, "Is it bad enough yet, John?" And Sherman would respond, "No, not yet, Boss, it's not bad enough."

The savvy chairman took the jest seriously. He sensed that tax reform was propelled largely on the strength of a negative motivation. The populace was too distrustful of government to believe that Congress would produce a bill that improved the tax system, and as a result, the polls showed only mild support for the committee's efforts. Tax reform was, as Rostenkowski put it, "the bill that nobody wanted." At the same time, however, the taxpayers' distaste for the system was so deep and so strong that no politician could afford to be perceived as working to make it worse. Anyone who stood in the way of reform would be tagged in the press as having sold out to special interests; that was a harsh label few were eager to accept.

The bank vote marked the burning of the phoenix. Rostenkowski now hoped to shame his members into making it rise again. In the weeks that followed the vote, Rostenkowski would have to use all his skills to turn a losing enterprise into a victory.

Newspaper and trade publications did their part to help. They humiliated the committee by reporting the gloating words of the bank lobbyist: "We won! We won!" The embarrassment was compounded by a scathing article by tax reporter Anne Swardson in *The Washington Post* headlined: TAX REFORMERS TURN RECIDIVIST; BANK LOBBYISTS WON ANOTHER BREAK FROM WAYS AND MEANS. The piece featured pictures of members who voted for the offending amendment with their lame explanations as to why. The story was exactly the kind of public pulverizing the chairman was counting on to help turn his members around. "The last thing that any of these guys want," explained one aide, "is for it to be written that tax reform dies in the Ways and Means Committee because sleaze-bag politicians want to take care of First National City Bank so the average public gets screwed."

In the wake of the bank vote, the conflicting pressures on committee members mounted. They were forced to choose between two distasteful alternatives: They could either turn their backs on the interest groups they had always supported and push for reform; or they could forget reform and risk being viewed by voters as panderers to the big-money interests. Unwilling to make the choice, members grew frustrated, and their tempers flared.

Deputy Treasury Secretary Darman was an early victim of the anger. In a meeting several hours after the bank vote, he began to lecture the committee on the nature of their enterprise. Tax reform meant siding with the general interest against the special interest, he scolded. Members simply could not continue to give away billions of dollars in new tax breaks to banks and other special pleaders and still get reform; they had to curtail those breaks to pay for lower rates.

The speech was more than Flippo could bear. Flippo sincerely believed that the write-off for bad-debt reserves helped preserve the financial integrity of banks. So when Darman, an outsider, a Republican, a nonelected administration official, tried to impose his thinking on the members of Congress, Flippo rebelled. He gave voice to the feelings that other members had bottled up for weeks. He accused Darman of being hypocritical. He reminded him that he and Baker had taken a "pure" tax-reform plan, Treasury I, and watered it down for six months with political deals and giveaways to their own constituencies. Were the groups favored by the Ways and Means Committee members any less worthy? For Baker and Darman even to suggest that the House of Representatives should blindly accept the Reagan version of tax reform, Flippo said, was ridiculous.

The testiness did not stop there. Two days later, the committee defied Rostenkowski again on a separate piece of legislation. The panel narrowly approved, over the chairman's objection, a small, broad-based excise tax on manufacturers to finance the Superfund toxic-waste-cleanup program. The levy was a form of value-added tax that Rostenkowski thought would spell political trouble for his Democrats in the long run, but his committee members disagreed. During that meeting, Representative Henson Moore, Republican of Louisiana, lashed out at the diminutive Pearlman of the Treasury, calling him a "son of a bitch," and Sam Gibbons unleashed yet another tirade against the staff and their proposals.

Those kinds of outbursts proved to Rostenkowski that the phoenix project needed help. Members were afraid of killing reform, but they still needed encouragement before they could bring themselves to support it; shame alone would not suffice. Committee members were overwhelmed by reform; it hit too many interests that were dear to them. Rostenkowski would have to use all of the tricks in his politician's repertoire to save the effort.

The biggest challenge to Rostenkowski and his bill clearly was the curtailment of the deduction for state and local taxes. Many members, particularly liberal Democrats, who might otherwise have been natural reformers, were so disturbed by the proposal that they could not bring themselves to support tax reform because of it. The fate of the bill and the treatment of the state and local deduction were closely intertwined. Joe Dowley expressed it this way:

The bank vote was merely symptomatic of the greater problem. Tax reform was dead unless we got some movement on the state-and-local issue. We advised him [Rostenkowski] after the bank vote that some arrangement had to be made on state and local. There weren't enough votes aligned to the core idea of tax reform at the time.

The advice was well informed. New Yorkers and oil-and-gas state lawmakers were firming the kill-the-bill alliance that they had begun to discuss at Airlie House. Rostenkowski's people knew there was trouble for sure when Democratic Representative James Jones of Oklahoma wrote an op-ed piece for *The Washington Post* that demanded the retention of the deduction for state and local taxes. State taxes in Oklahoma were so low that President Reagan had chosen Jones's home state to make his biggest pitch for repeal of that deduction. He argued that the write-off represented a subsidy by low-tax states like Oklahoma to high-tax states like New York, but Jones wasn't buying that line.

For political expediency, Jones and other "oilies" had joined forces with New York Jewish groups to protect each other's tax breaks. The strategem had roots in an organization developed by Representative Tony Coelho of California, the chairman of the Democratic Congressional Campaign Committee. The initial purpose of the group, called the Council for a Secure America, was to boost both Israel and the U.S. oil industry by discouraging U.S. imports of oil, especially from Arab states. But the contacts made through the organization proved to be useful in the fight against tax reform. It was an unholy alliance that paired Jewish political activists, many of whom lived in high-energy-consuming states in the Northeast and ran businesses dependent on tax breaks, with oil-and-gas drillers, who were eager to maintain or enact special breaks that helped keep energy profits high. Both sides of the group opposed the tax bill for their own reasons, and both saw the New Yorkers' struggle to keep the deduction for state and local taxes as the most effective way to reach their goal.

For many lawmakers, preserving the state and local deduction was a euphemism for killing the bill or making sure, at least, that it was all gift-wrapping with nothing inside the box. The deduction seemed to be the plan's Achilles' heel. Rostenkowski's proposed curtailment of the deduction raised nearly $65 billion over five years, and that revenue was thought to be essential to writing a bill that fit the parameters set by President Reagan. Baker and Darman insisted that the committee could not draft an acceptable bill without eliminating at least part of the popular deduction. As a result, many of the interest groups who joined the effort to save the deduction thought that by doing so they could help destroy the whole measure.

Jenkins of Georgia was one of the first to realize that the administration's strategy of pitting low-tax states against high-tax states was not working. Serving as a kind of Rostenkowski scout, he devoted hours during the fall to pulling colleagues aside along the back rail of the House floor to test their resistance to the proposal. To his own amazement, Jenkins discovered that members opposed fiddling with the deduction no matter how low their own state's taxes were. He sent that message to the chairman: Any bill that clipped the deduction, he warned, stood to be defeated on the House floor. To emphasize the point, Republican Representative Ray McGrath of New York presented Rostenkowski with a list of 208 names of House members, nearly half of the entire 435-member House, who would vote against any tax-reform bill that tampered with the deduction.

Still, the New York lobby was not convinced that its battle was won. They were determined to make Rostenkowski fold completely. After the bank vote, to ensure their success, they enlisted the aid of Representative Marty Russo, the chairman's own protégé from Illinois.

Russo was a surprise choice for the role of convincing Rostenkowski to preserve the state and local deduction. He was one of the chairman's closest allies. The two men were seen everywhere together in the House. They possessed one of the strongest and most visible mentor relationships in an institution that has many. Russo was almost a younger version of Rostenkowski. Both gestured broadly and spoke loudly. They were products of similar working-class, ethnic roots. They were both inside dealers, political animals. The tall Russo functioned as Rostenkowski's lieutenant and political progeny. They often confided in each other and, it was commonly believed, always worked on the same side. There was no one more loyal to Rostenkowski on the committee.

Russo lived in a group house with three other Democratic members of Congress who left their families at home: Representative Charles Schumer of Brooklyn and Representatives George Miller and Leon Panetta of California. Earlier in the century, that kind of living arrangement was the rule, rather than the exception, for federal lawmakers. In those days, new congressmen were given steamer trunks to symbolize their temporary stay in the nation's capital, and their workweek extended only from Tuesday to Thursday. The steamer trunks were a thing of the past, but the close friendships that developed among housemates persisted. When one asked another for a favor, the request was taken seriously; they were almost like fraternity brothers.

Schumer, like all the New York representatives, was committed to preserving the state and local deduction, and he became the New York lobby's link to Russo. Jay Kriegel, the kingpin of the New York group, telephoned Schumer to say that he was worried: As far as he could tell, there were only fourteen solid votes to retain the deduction on the thirty-six-member Ways and Means Committee. The determined Kriegel wanted a majority. What could he do? Schumer suggested that Russo might help and promised to try to enlist his support.

Russo had a reputation as one of the House's better vote-counters and deal-cutters. Having Russo as an ally would be a big plus for the lobby. But would he cross Rostenkowski? Schumer sat with Russo one night soon after the bank vote in the living room of their two-story, Capitol Hill townhouse, a short two blocks from the Longworth Building. On chairs and couches around the television set, they discussed the New Yorkers' woes. First they thrashed out the merits of the provision. Then they concentrated on the politics, on the pitfalls the issue presented to Rostenkowski, and on the committee. The talk began at 11:00 P.M. and drifted well past midnight. It was punctuated by frequent trips by Schumer, a big eater, to the refrigerator.

"The New York community is desperate," Schumer told Russo. The problems with the state and local deduction "were holding up reform." The New York representative tried to appeal to his housemate's sense of loyalty to Rostenkowski, arguing that a major defeat loomed on the House floor for the chairman if he didn't alter his course. Russo had already heard plenty of complaints about curtailing the deduction and was disturbed by the proposal himself, but he hesitated to go against Rostenkowski. He said he would think over the request.

Two days later, Russo decided to join the New Yorkers' cause. Upon reflection, he came to believe that Rostenkowski would indeed suffer an embarrassing loss if his bill came to the House floor with the deduction trimmed back. He wanted to spare his mentor that setback if he could. Paradoxically, working against the chairman seemed the only way to save him. At the same time, Russo also was anxious to broaden his own base of support in the House, to become known as something more than a Rostenkowski clone. A chance to help save the important deduction was another way to distinguish himself from his mentor.

The New Yorkers were happy to have Russo on board. Kriegel jetted to Washington to talk to him, and afterward, Russo began lobbying the committee, looking for new, solid votes. In a matter of days, he collected enough names to claim majority support on the committee for retaining the deduction. He took this intelligence to the chairman.

Rostenkowski was not pleased. He and Russo had a long, intense talk, fraught with the tension inherent any time a younger man questions the wisdom of his elder. Nevertheless, for Rostenkowski, the signs were hard to resist: The outcry to retain the deduction had come from almost everywhere, and now it was even coming from his most loyal members.

The repeal of the state and local deduction had become an easy reason for members to vote against reform. It served as legitimate cover for whatever other special interests the opponents of reform wanted to protect. Rostenkowski felt it was time to clear that cloud. He had resisted buckling sooner because he feared that the Reagan administration would walk away from the legislation if he did. The many billions of dollars lost by keeping the preference would have to be made up, in part, with a top individual tax rate higher than the president's demand of 35 percent. Dizzying questions swirled through the chairman's head. Could he retain the deduction and, somehow, also give the president what he wanted? By agreeing to keep the popular deduction, would he be ending any hope of support from the president and, therefore, any hope for bipartisan tax reform?

On the Sunday after the bank vote, October 20, Rostenkowski's staff got the first inkling from Darman that the president wouldn't jump ship if the 35 percent "line in the sand" shifted a bit. In the oval-shaped conference room of the Joint Tax Committee in the basement of the Longworth Building, Darman met with Joe Dowley, Rob Leonard, David Brockway, and other congressional staffers. The elegant room adjoined Brockway's own crowded office and was a frequent spot for weekend skull sessions on the tax bill. It had an elaborate terra-cotta and gold-leaf ceiling, with a ponderous, brass chandelier badly in need of polishing that looked as though its pointed base was about to fall into the red-felt top of the table below it. During that meeting, Darman hinted to Rostenkowski's aides that the top individual tax rate could go higher than 35 percent. Dowley recalls the conversation: "I don't remember Dick Darman ever actually conceding that, but he allowed as how maybe the rates could go up and it wouldn't be the end of the world. There was a constant concern about the president walking away from the bill. It was extremely helpful to know there was a crack in the armor there and that, being realistic, they wanted a bill."

That opening provided enough room for the staffers to try to put together a plan that saved the state and local deduction and had a chance of winning the committee's approval. It was the green light that Rostenkowski had been waiting for.

Brockway and Randy Weiss, the Joint Tax Committee's top economist, had already discovered a trick that allowed them to raise much of the revenue they needed to cover the huge gap created by preserving the state and local deduction. Tremendous amounts of revenue could be gained, they found, by lowering the income levels at which the new tax rates kicked in. Up until then, everyone had focused on the rates themselves. But lowering the rate "break points" had the same effect as raising the rates on many middle- and upper-middle-income taxpayers, and was not as noticeable. By starting the 35-percent bracket at about $45,000 in taxable income, instead of the $66,000 starting point suggested by the president, Brockway and Weiss discovered they could raise enough money to pay for retaining the state and local deduction. They might still need a fourth rate slightly above 35 percent to keep the plan from giving too large a tax reduction to the wealthy, but they would not have to go to rates of 40 percent or higher, as Baker and Darman privately feared.

Armed with assurances from the staff that the top rate could be kept below 40 percent, Rostenkowski made the watershed decision to give in and retain the entire state and local deduction. Unbeknownst to Baker and Darman, he began to tell members that he would work to save the deduction, and he asked for their loyalty in exchange.

The concession to the state-and-local lobby took a huge obstacle out of the path of tax reform, but it still wasn't enough to get it rolling. The effort needed a strong hand to guide it, and that was what Rostenkowski provided. At times, he bullied his members; at other times, he cajoled and begged them. When necessary, as with the state and local deduction, he simply bought their support. It was the kind of one-on-one wheeling and dealing that the Chicago pol knew best.

Rostenkowski's methods were rooted in something that transcended traditional explanations of legislative success, such as seniority or leadership position or political quid pro quos. The methods were wrapped up in the man himself. There were times when a Rostenkowski bear hug or a cold-edged glare was enough to change votes and move legislation. Congress is not a bureaucracy that moves by rote and form letter; it is a place where one person can make a difference and often does. When it came to tax reform, Rostenkowski was such a person. He was a force unto himself, a character to be dealt with.

The Congress is filled with ambitious and extroverted men and women who, most of the time, vote for legislation because they have to—their district needs a water project, their party's leadership demands their vote, or they fear a position won't sit well with their constituents. They vote for partisan reasons or take stands because they want to avoid blame for missing some new trend. But every once in a while, a legislator such as Rostenkowski wins votes by the force of his personality. In Congress, and in politics in general, charisma can be a palpable commodity, an energy that can be felt. When some lawmakers talk, listeners simply can't stand too close.

Such was the case with Lyndon Johnson when he was Senate majority leader. He intimidated his colleagues simply by bringing his big face with its huge ears down to their eye level. Legislation moved when he wanted it to. The white-maned Tip O'Neill, who wore 52-long suits, had the same kind of effect on his colleagues in the House. A speech by him in the well of the House chamber or a chat in the cloakroom off the House floor could turn a vote or change a mind and make a difference in the end. Dan Rostenkowski possessed elements of this kind of presence. Members outside the committee would sometimes prefer to deal with his staff rather than face the man himself. When he walked into a room, his own committee members grew silent. Once, he made clear that Representative Harold Ford of Tennessee was not enjoying his favor. Thereafter, the other members tried not to be caught near Ford in the chairman's presence. "You didn't want that odor on you," a Ways and Means member recalls.

By Monday, October 21, five days after the damaging bank vote, Rostenkowski was ready to launch his reconstructed phoenix. True to form, he did so in person. Early that morning, he marched into Flippo's office unannounced and demanded to see the congressman right away. Such a visit was highly unusual, but the request could hardly be denied. It was the kind of terrorizing tactic that would send shivers down the spines of any member involved. It was like the top executive in a corporation bursting into a subordinate's office to demand an instant accounting.

A meeting was hastily convened, and Rostenkowski got right to the point. "Your amendment set the wrong tone," the chairman charged and then asked, "What can we do to get you to back off?" It did not take much. The big man had come to ask a favor, and that could not be ignored. Flippo quickly consented to work with the chairman and agreed to make the motion himself to reconsider the bank vote. The proposal that would substitute for the original bank amendment, they concurred, would be one of Flippo's fallback proposals, which would take the special bad-debt deduction away, but only from the biggest banks.

Rostenkowski met that day with other members who had made the retention of the state and local deduction their top goal. He summoned Tom Downey of New York to his office in the Capitol building off the House floor and laid out the deal straightaway, demanding that Downey begin to support him in return. Downey agreed.

"I'm glad we're allies," Rostenkowski said with a toothy grin.

"I'm glad I'm an ally rather than a guerrilla warrior," Downey replied. "I don't find that comfortable."

Ray McGrath, the Republican from New York, was also given the word, and his reaction was all the chairman could have hoped for. From then on, he voted with Rostenkowski on almost every issue. "When I'm bought," he said privately, "I stay bought." His loyalty to the Democratic chairman became a bitter joke among his Republican colleagues. Once, when Rostenkowski called for a caucus of Democrats during a drafting session, a Republican sneered into a microphone: "Ray, you better go too."

The bank vote was overturned on Wednesday, October 23, eight days after the initial debacle. Flippo moved to reconsider his old vote, and Democratic Representative Pete Stark of California offered the new compromise amendment that already had been worked out by Flippo and Rostenkowski. The compromise passed 14–7, with the support of the state and local rebels. It was one of the most important votes in the entire tax-reform debate; for the first time, it looked like tax reform might start to move.

"That was it. That was the first indication that we were going to get a bill," Rostenkowski said. "The members started to realize that they were going to bite the bullet. The element of being cute evaporated." Rostenkowski now had a solid core of unwavering supporters, and he was ready to go forward.

At six o'clock that evening, Darman met with Brockway, Dowley, and Leonard. The Treasury official was happy that tax reform was being rejuvenated, but he wondered what had caused the change. Rostenkowski had not told the Treasury that he had given in on the state and local deduction, but Darman was suspicious. Halfway through the meeting, Rostenkowski stuck his head through the open door, and Dowley commented briefly to him that Ray McGrath had been won over "totally." Darman knew McGrath cared only about state and local taxes. If McGrath had been brought aboard "totally," then surely the state and local deduction must have been saved. "Uh oh, shit," Darman thought, "these guys have already struck the deal."

Darman was still convinced that retaining the state and local deduction would be the death of tax reform, or at least the death of a reform bill the president could support. If Rostenkowski failed to eliminate some of the deduction, Darman feared, the House plan would need a top rate as high as 40 percent in order to raise the same amount of money as the existing tax system. The president might be willing to support a bill that edged a point or two above the 35-percent top rate he demanded, but not a bill with a top rate of 40 percent or higher.

The next day, the rumors of Rostenkowski's concession were everywhere. Baker was furious, feeling the Democratic chairman had not leveled with him. He telephoned Rostenkowski, who was in North Carolina to attend a fundraiser for Democratic Representative Charlie Rose. Their exchange was heated. Rostenkowski refused to concede that he had made a deal to keep the deduction, but Baker and Darman knew he was lying. Newspaper stories the next day quoted lawmakers from New York boasting about their conversations with the chairman. On Friday, Baker and his entourage confronted Rostenkowski in person at the Ways and Means Committee office. There was shouting, but still no admission of a deal. Bad blood began to boil between the two men.

After the angry meeting, Baker and Darman went to Andrews Air Force Base outside Washington to brief Chief of Staff Regan and his legislative aides on the committee situation. The meeting was held at the out-of-the-way locale because other White House staffers, such as Communications Director Patrick Buchanan, opposed the Ways and Means effort, and Regan wanted to avoid unproductive sniping. For the Treasury officials, tax reform had become a two-front war. They had to try to keep the Ways and Means Committee moving in the right direction, but they also had to keep the White House on board. The White House staff was hearing endless complaints from House Republicans about the tax effort, and there were those on the president's staff who thought it was time to, as one put it, take the bill "to the swamp and drown it." In addition, there was the continuing tension between Regan's staff and Baker's staff; the new Treasury chief continued to get rave reviews while the new chief of staff was under heavy criticism.

Darman prepared a memo for the meeting. "There is no realistic chance of a fully satisfactory bill coming out of Ways and Means," it began. The top rate would probably be 37.5 percent, he concluded, and could go all the way to 40 percent if Rostenkowski insisted on giving up state and local entirely. (Baker and Darman still thought the chairman might relent on his deal.) The memo suggested two alternatives for the Reagan administration: It could keep working to improve the Ways and Means package and hope to fix it in the Senate, or it could "punt now"—blame the Democrats for going astray and promise to try tax reform again another year.

Regan agreed to the first approach, but he and his aides were worried. Tax reform wasn't going well in the House, they thought, and the president might eventually have to abandon ship.

Discouraged by the House actions, Darman had already begun plotting a contingency—a "minimal" tax-reform bill. In an elaborate drawing that looked like an electrical diagram, he linked together the few pieces of reform that might be pushed through the Ways and Means Committee to pay for a small lowering in the top rate—perhaps to just 45 percent, down from the existing 50 percent. He also schemed out what he called the "Dole-Packwood hero option." After fundamental tax reform failed in the House, Majority Leader Dole and Finance Committee Chairman Packwood might rescue the bill and turn it into a plan with a top rate of 30 percent, paid for by enacting some sort of a national sales tax or value-added tax, which many senators were known to favor and which Darman favored as well. The Treasury official even discussed the hero option with Packwood's trusted aide, Bill Diefenderfer, who said the plan might work, but only if the president first endorsed the value-added tax. Given the president's strong opposition to new taxes, however, the option was a long shot. Time was running out for tax reform, Darman feared, and faith in Chairman Rostenkowski's ability to achieve acceptable reform was on the wane.

Unaware of this planning in the highest reaches of the Reagan administration, Rostenkowski worked busily in his own element, making the backroom political concessions necessary to get the bill moving. In many ways, tax reform for him had become like any other tax bill. Deals had to be cut to keep the special interests from overwhelming the effort; votes had to be paid for with favors and special tax breaks. "I'm a negotiator," Rostenkowski said proudly. He built his bill by compromise, doing whatever was necessary to raise the revenue needed to pay for lower rates. He made no pretense of purity. "Tax reform," he said, "like all major changes in policy, is negotiated, not dictated. Like it or not, tax reform ends up a series of compromises. No compromise, no reform. . . . We may have to yield more to powerful interests."

A central element of Rostenkowski's strategy was to divide his committee into "working groups" to deal with the delicate issues. Each group was asked to trim enough tax breaks in its assigned area of the code to reach a revenue-raising target set by the chairman. In most of the working groups, the membership was stacked to give the chairman an easy majority, but the working-group members were given wide discretion to reach the chairman's revenue goal in whatever way they wished.

This arrangement immediately gave Rostenkowski some new headaches. His first major challenge arose in the working group assigned to deal with tax-exempt bonds. There, the carefully planned balance of power was disturbed when Representative Wyche Fowler, Democrat of Georgia, joined the panel even though he had not been assigned to it by the chairman and his aides. Fowler was one of the members who made it clear that his support for reform would have to be bought with concessions. He put the congressional tax staff on notice that he planned to fight for a long list of special tax breaks, one of the longest compiled by any Ways and Means member.

The reason, he told tax staffers, was his impending race for the Senate; carrying water for special interests would undoubtedly help raise money for the expensive effort. His fundraising strategy apparently worked: During 1985, Fowler received $539,575 in campaign contributions from a host of special-interest groups and wealthy donors with keen interest in the tax bill, including tax-shelter promoters in New York and oil drillers and real estate developers in Texas. Hamilton Jordan, Fowler's chief rival for the Democratic Senate nomination in Georgia, once was asked what would most help his campaign. "A few days on the Ways and Means Committee," he instantly replied.

The cool half-million that Fowler raised was only the third-highest total among Ways and Means Committee members. He was eclipsed by the two other senatorial aspirants on the committee: Henson Moore of Louisiana, who raised $1.4 million in 1985, and Democratic Representative James Jones of Oklahoma, who raised $616,624. Indeed, as they considered every nook and cranny of the tax code, members of Ways and Means became quick favorites of lobbyists and campaign contributors of all sorts. Some members even raised their per-person rates for fundraisers to as much as $1,000 from the more usual $250 or $500 rates. All told, the thirty-six Ways and Means Committee members raised approximately $7 million in 1985 and did so without apology. "That's just the way the world works in terms of politics," said Representative Moore.

The taxation of municipal bonds was one of the most intensely lobbied parts of the tax bill. Bond lawyers huddled in a great mass late into the night outside of room 1129 in the Longworth Building, where the working group met. The room was down the hall from the ornate Ways and Means hearing room and stood in sharp contrast to it. It was a small, simple conference room furnished sparingly with a schoolmarmish desk, a plain oval conference table, and about thirty chairs that would fit the décor of a Howard Johnson's restaurant.

The focus of the working group was bonds issued by state and local governments to fund private development. Municipal bonds issued for use by the governments were not taxable at the federal level, and Rostenkowski was not proposing to change that. But in recent years, state and local governments had begun to issue tax-exempt bonds for use by private industry. Rostenkowski tried to pare those bonds back in 1983, but opposition was so strong that he failed to win a majority on the floor to agree to bring his measure up for debate. Some curbs were enacted in 1984, but tax-exempt financing continued to expand at a rapid pace. The total amount of tax-exempt bonds soared to $71.7 billion from $8.9 billion a decade earlier; fully two thirds of the tax-exempt bond market consisted of bonds used for private purposes. While state and local officials defended the break vigorously (and enjoyed the political rewards of passing out what amounted to low-interest loans to their friends in the business community), reformers saw this proliferation as a rip-off of the taxpayer under the guise of civic do-goodism. "It's pretty straightforward," said Bob McIntyre, of Citizens for Tax Justice. "The federal government puts up the money in the form of interest subsidies, and corporate executives spend the cash."

Private-purpose tax-exempt bonds were especially important to Wyche Fowler, whose home area in Atlanta used them to construct airport facilities. They were important to other members as well, who were under pressure to avoid new bond curbs from the governors and mayors who dispensed them, the securities firms that sold them, and the bond lawyers who did the legal work. Bob Matsui of California was the champion of a coalition of bond groups and managed during the hours-long meeting of the working group to win many of the coalition's demands. Each victory for the bond people marked a defeat for Chairman Rostenkowski.

Tempers in the bond group frayed almost to the breaking point. Flippo, who was supposed to be one of the chairman's allies in trying to limit tax-exempt bonds, voted instead to retain the use of the bonds to finance ports, which were important to his state of Alabama. Henson Moore felt betrayed by the move, and complained that he had been taking some tough votes that helped the chairman, but now members of Rostenkowski's own party were going against reform. Moore used the occasion to propose removing all limitations on tax-exempt bonds issued by universities and hospitals, which was his own pet cause. The move prompted an explosion. Moore made a remark to Flippo that questioned his intentions. In reply, Flippo suggested that they "step outside to finish the conversation." Others intervened before the lawmakers came to blows.

Word about the blowup in room 1129 reached Joe Dowley, who was monitoring three separate working groups from his Ways and Means office at the other end of the hall. At about 10:00 P.M., he hustled over to the bond group to try to regain control. His target was Representative William Coyne, Democrat of Pennsylvania, a quiet bachelor from Pittsburgh. He asked Coyne, on behalf of the chairman, to vote for the chairman's position. But on the very next vote, Coyne defied the chairman's emissary and voted the other way.

Dowley immediately put a call into Rostenkowski, who was traveling out of town. Rostenkowski, in turn, telephoned the working group and demanded to speak to Coyne. The Pennsylvanian was beholden to the chairman for his seat on the working group and for his recent assignment to the full committee as well. After a thorough talking to, Coyne agreed to change his allegiance. The group disbanded for the evening, while the staff worked to put together a new package.

In order to ensure support for the package, Rostenkowski's staff included numerous special breaks to appease the members. Fowler won an exemption for airport facilities, McGrath was able to keep a break for bonds used to build solid-waste disposal facilities, and Flippo and Coyne were allowed to revive some so-called small-issue industrial development bonds, the type of bonds used most often to benefit companies directly. Port bonds also got easy treatment. The chairman's badgering and the carefully constructed new package softened the opposition, and the working group was finally able to reach agreement.

The chairman used a more direct approach to win the support of Matsui, leader of the bond rebellion. One morning, after the full committee approved the bond changes, the chairman telephoned Matsui to say he wanted to talk. "I want to see you right away," Rostenkowski said. "I'll be right over."

The chairman stormed into Matsui's small office, sat down on a chair, and said, "I'm going to have to rely on you." He went on to pitch tax reform as "one chance in a lifetime" and, as at the Airlie House retreat, expressed his outrage at the idea that his daughters paid more in taxes than their bosses or large and profitable corporations.

"I'm going to need your help," he said with feeling. "I'm asking for your help."

Rostenkowski did not need to push too hard, especially since he already had defeated Matsui's effort to preserve markets for certain tax-exempt bonds. "Mr. Chairman, I'm going to help you," a flustered Matsui replied. "I sure appreciate your asking me." In return for Matsui's loyalty, Rostenkowski aides offered to preserve a break for a type of bond used frequently in California to finance urban redevelopment. Matsui told them he didn't need the quid pro quo, but the bond change was made anyway.

As Rostenkowski slowly gathered his reluctant members into the tax-reform corral, a bill began to take shape. The chairman kept the tax writers in town during the weekend of October 26 and 27—a beautiful fall weekend—and made substantial progress. The full committee not only voted to approve the bond provisions, but also agreed to clamp down somewhat on the use of the tax laws to subsidize low-income housing and to make it more difficult for wealthy families to avoid taxes by shifting income to their children. The decisions were made by members wearing casual attire, amid the pervasive odor of aging empty pizza boxes.

After that weekend, the process continued to be one of careful compromise, with favors being granted to those who played along with the chairman. The corporate advocates of "reform" found that they were granted special tax breaks that weren't reform at all, in return for their support. To cement the support of small-businessmen, for instance, the committee voted for special low rates and a new, generous accounting system for smaller companies. To reward big corporations that supported the reform effort, like Procter & Gamble and IBM, the committee agreed to accept a scaled-back version of the president's proposal to allow corporations to write-off a portion of the dividends they pay.

Even when it agreed to cut back breaks, the committee still inserted provisions carefully targeted to benefit certain favored constituents. A compromise that chopped timber-industry tax breaks didn't harm a sliver of businesses owned by relatives of Representative Beryl Anthony of Arkansas, who proposed the compromise. Cutbacks in estate taxation included a "Gallo amendment"—an exception sought by the famous owners of the Ernest and Julio Gallo Winery in California that would allow their grandchildren to inherit more than $80 million without paying a proposed generation-skipping tax. The progress of that amendment was closely monitored by Representative Tony Coelho, who was the Gallo's local congressman and the chief fundraiser for the House Democrats. (The Gallo clan had contributed more than $130,000 to the Democrats during the previous four elections.) The amendment was offered by the wily Ed Jenkins of Georgia, who claimed at the time: "I don't know Mr. Gallo [which he mispronounced gay-low], never met him. Are there more than one of them? Are they brothers?"

At times, the committee moved faster than members imagined possible for such a weighty piece of legislation, and in the process, some reform proposals were shunted aside, particularly if they didn't lose much revenue. Representative Anthony expended many words defending an amendment to restore a tax break for employee stock-ownership plans, only to have his amendment accepted by a perfunctory voice vote. He turned to a colleague after the vote and said in astonishment, "Did you see that?"

Rostenkowski pulled his committee forward, taking big swipes at some interest groups while steering clear of others. The committee voted to repeal outright the investment tax credit, as well as the completed-contract method of accounting used by military contractors to postpone taxes. It put new restrictions on another accounting practice that enabled many businesses to defer taxes, but excepted doctors, lawyers, and accountants from the tough new restrictions. It also extended the credit for research-and-development expenditures and preserved the write-off for mortgage interest paid on second homes. Some real estate tax breaks were cut back, but not as much as the chairman had proposed. Said Representative Stark, who chaired the real estate working group, "I was just outgunned by a real estate lobby that knows no limits to its greed."

Tax reform was moving ahead, though in the rough fashion demanded by the nature of Congress. "We're doing some good," concluded Democratic Representative Byron Dorgan, a former tax commissioner from North Dakota, "but we're not doing as much reform as I had hoped. It's a little disappointing."

Still, a new mood had taken hold. Members no longer questioned the seriousness of the effort; they were finally convinced that Rostenkowski could not be stopped. The chairman publicly predicted a conclusion to the markup by Thanksgiving. Those on the committee who had battled against the chairman tooth and nail, like Sam Gibbons, had reason to fear they might be the subject of the chairman's revenge in the final bill. Representative Harold Ford of Tennessee, who had frequently opposed the chairman, commented to other members during a weekend session, "Boy, am

I in a lot of shit with the chairman right now." Representative Charlie Rangel, who overheard the comment, shot back, "If you're in shit, you're standing on Sam Gibbons's shoulders."

The Republicans on the Ways and Means Committee watched the bill progress with a feeling of helplessness. They were a powerless minority, outvoted nearly two to one by the Democrats on the committee. Few of them had any real interest in reform. They were, for the most part, conventional Republicans, not members of the new supply-side breed, and they believed in retaining many of the business tax breaks that Rostenkowski was paring down. They had not sought seats on Ways and Means to take away tax benefits; they were there to promote breaks that helped their business constituents.

The alienation of Ways and Means Republicans was especially intense because Treasury officials were working more closely with the Democratic chairman than with the members of their own party. Adding insult to injury, the Republican National Committee sent letters into the home districts of a number of Ways and Means Republicans urging voters to complain to them for failing to support tax reform. McGrath's mother was one of those who received a letter. "Pretty shabby work," groused Bill Frenzel of Minnesota.

Baker and Darman tried to assuage the group's hurt feelings, but their efforts were viewed, in the words of one member, as "a little too little too late." The GOP members did not trust the Treasury officials and expressed anger at being left out of the process. During the course of the markup, Republicans endured the defeat of amendment after amendment as the committee worked long hours late into the night. "You could hear taps being played whenever they offered an amendment," Representative Tom Downey said. Frenzel became physically ill from the frustration. "The Republicans are spectators mostly," he lamented. "There is a feeling that whatever comes out of committee, the Treasury will support. The Treasury seems willing to support almost anything just to keep a bill alive. They're more interested in working with the chairman than with us."

Most of the Ways and Means Republicans simply did not want reform, and Rostenkowski was getting predictably little support from them. On a good day, only four of the thirteen Republicans would vote with him on any given issue; on most days there were only two, Gradison and McGrath. The chairman worried that Baker and Darman couldn't deliver any more Republicans for the final vote. What was worse, he realized it would be difficult, if not impossible, to get the bill through the House without the support of the president and some members of the GOP. So in early November he decided he needed to speak to the president directly to test his sentiment and to warn him about his own Republicans' resistance to the reform cause.

Rostenkowski and the president earlier had made an agreement of silence about the drafting sessions; the White House would refrain from criticizing the committee until its work was through. But with the Republicans so distressed, Rostenkowski wanted to make sure that the president would not pull the rug out from under his bill.

Rostenkowski called Don Regan. As he recalls it, the conversation went as follows:

"Don, I have to see the president."

"Well Danny, what is it you want to see him on?" Regan asked, obviously hesitant to grant the request.

"Do I have to tell you?" Rostenkowski responded.

"Well no, but the president's preparing for the summit," Regan said referring to the president's upcoming meeting with new Soviet leader Gorbachev, which was less than two weeks away. Rostenkowski was fully aware of this, since he had just returned from a visit to the Soviet Union himself.

"Well Don, I'm not getting any support from the Republicans, and I think I ought to share that with him. It's his bill," Rostenkowski insisted.

"Well Dan, Jesus, I don't think we can squeeze it in."

"Don, I can do the *Today* show and *Good Morning America*, get on and say I've spent four and a half hours with Gorbachev, and he's only been the general secretary of the Soviet Union for about three weeks. I can say that I'm the chairman of the Ways and Means Committee, and I can't even get in to see the president of the United States, and I haven't even been in his company for more than two hours in the five or six years that he's been president. I could say that."

"Can I get back to you?" Regan asked.

"Don, listen to me, nothing technical," Rostenkowski assured the chief of staff. "I just want him to know who it is that he's screwing with, I want him to know who I am and what I am. I want to talk to him about the lack of Republican support, but I promise you there'll be nothing technical."

"Call you back," Regan said and hung up.

The next afternoon at about three o'clock Rostenkowski went to the White House. He hoped he could wrest some secret assurance from the president that it was okay to allow the full deduction of state and local taxes or that the top rate could rise above 35 percent. He first went to Regan's office, to be briefed in preparation for his visit with the president. Then he rode up the small elevator to the president's private residence.

President Reagan was waiting at the doors of the elevator, and he warmly greeted the Ways and Means chairman. The two men went into a living room, and Rostenkowski sat on a flower-print sofa while the president sat in a chair to his left. The president served Rostenkowski a cup of coffee, and then they began to talk. Although originally scheduled for only fifteen minutes, the meeting went on for nearly three quarters of an hour. A presidential aide opened the door occasionally to remind the president of the time, but Reagan waved him away.

Rostenkowski recalls the conversation. "Mr. President," he said, "you know you're talking about state and local taxes—I can't go with it. I can't get any place. You told me that I couldn't get down on the rates and not have state and local taxes, and I've done it. But I've got other complications, and I'm not really getting a lot of help from your people. And I can't do it without going to thirty-seven percent."

"Oh, no, thirty-five percent," the president said and recounted again the stories about his days in Hollywood, when he and other actors were faced with marginal tax rates exceeding 90 percent.

"Well, I can't do it," Rostenkowski said. "But you know, Mr. President, you and I have come to power at the same time. We're really defining the economic destiny of this country. Are you suggesting that two percentage points are going to deny you and me a place in history? I can't believe that—two percentage points?"

Rostenkowski remembers that the president just sat there, somewhat uncomfortable. "Mr. President, two points—thirty-five percent to thirty-seven percent—history—two Illinois members of government. Mr. President, just don't say no."

"This is presumptuous of me," Rostenkowski recalled later, "but I think he enjoyed my company, because I sure enjoyed his—even though I didn't get a goddamn thing from him."

In fact, Rostenkowski got less than nothing. Despite the plea for help, Reagan broke radio silence and criticized Rostenkowski and his committee a few days after the White House meeting. "We need the kind of tax reform we originally proposed, and not some of the waterings-down that are taking place as they discuss it up there," the president said. The comment was only a glancing blow and didn't hinder progress, but soon thereafter Treasury officials indicated Baker was "boycotting" the Ways and Means drafting sessions because he was angered over the retention of the state and local deduction. Ways and Means aides tried to make light of the situation by saying they did not know about any such boycott and had not much missed the secretary anyway, but a rift with the Reagan administration was a serious problem.

Relations between Rostenkowski and Baker grew even more strained on Monday evening, November 18, when the Treasury secretary weighed in against the chairman on one of the most contentious issues of the entire tax debate: oil and gas. While still boycotting the committee meetings, Baker was invited by oil-state lawmakers to meet with them and a group of oil-and-gas lobbyists on Capitol Hill to discuss their negotiations with Rostenkowski. Baker did not hesitate to attend, and when he got there he was not the least bit shy about saying where he stood. He was so much a booster of oil drillers' views that members would often remark sarcastically that he must harbor ambitions of running for governor of Texas. Baker had already defied Rostenkowski once by largely preserving the industry's tax breaks in the president's proposal. Now he was fighting to keep them during the Ways and Means markup too. On that Monday night, before this group of oil-industry lobbyists and their partisans on the Hill, Baker pledged his help and said flatly that he would not ask the president to sign any bill that contained the harsh cutbacks in oil tax preferences that the chairman sought.

Fights over oil and gas are always among the liveliest in Congress. On few other issues is the nation so clearly divided along geographical lines: the Northeast and Midwest against the South and Southwest. Word of the oil meeting enraged Rostenkowski. Baker had been avoiding the Ways and Means Committee for more than three weeks, and the first time he came back to the Hill was to try to undercut the chairman on this bellwether issue. "It stinks," fumed one of the chairman's top staffers.

Baker returned to his office after the meeting and telephoned Rostenkowski. "I'm going to have a very difficult time delivering votes," Baker warned the chairman. "You and I are going to have to sit down and talk energy." Rostenkowski launched into extended shouting, and Baker removed the phone from his ear to wait for the barrage to stop. Rostenkowski demanded that the energy industry pay its fair share of the cost of reform, and Baker shot back, "Why don't we have energy pay as much as state and local." The chairman complained that GOP members weren't supporting the reform effort, and the secretary groused, "I can't deliver Republican votes when you won't give on Republican issues."

Baker and Rostenkowski spoke by telephone several times the next day, and negotiations continued between the oilies and Rostenkowski's staff. The meetings were turbulent. In the middle of one, Rostenkowski stormed out of his Capitol Hill hideaway, leaving behind a flabbergasted phalanx of congressmen. As the chairman strode down the hallway toward the House chamber, he shouted back: "This is the last time I'm speaking to them. If they want to beat me, they can beat me. The bottom line is right there."

The bottom line was a compromise, agreed to the next day, that trimmed oil-and-gas tax incentives by $4 billion over five years, which was less than half of the $9 billion cut originally backed by the chairman and a fraction of the $40 billion cut proposed in Treasury I. It was approved with bipartisan support, 29–4. With so large a vote, Rostenkowski and his aides believed—incorrectly—that their oil problems were behind them.

The toughest issues were saved until the last few days of the markup, and the period could not have been a harder one, personally, for Chairman Rostenkowski. His youngest daughter, Stacy, had long suffered from kidney problems and earlier in the year had rejected a transplant. During the last week of the markup, Rostenkowski and his family were shaken by the news that none of them could serve as a suitable donor for her.

The chairman wanted to give her his kidney, but was told he could not. At the time of the markup, the family was caught between doctors and conflicting advice about how to improve Stacy's faltering health.

During the same period, Rostenkowski faced other troubles as well. He and his committee were under heavy pressure to produce budget savings to help reduce the deficit and also to help draft the controversial deficit-reduction law called Gramm-Rudman-Hollings. "I'll be surprised if I don't have a nervous breakdown," he confided to his colleagues.

The most severe tests of the drafting session began on Thursday, November 21—just one day before Rostenkowski hoped to finish the bill. That evening, the committee took up the chairman's proposal to allow deductions for only 75 percent of the cost of business meals, and for only 50 percent of entertainment expenses, such as theater or sports tickets. The proposal was opposed by an extremely powerful coalition, which included big companies like American Express, as well as unions, hotels, professional sports teams, and the tourism bureaus of some of the nation's largest cities. So heated was the lobbying that the issue was taken up in full committee without the recommendation of a working group. The coalition's members worked hard. One New York representative was told by an executive in the Mets baseball organization that the team might have to sell Dwight Gooden, its star pitcher, if the deduction were cut back too far. Opponents of the Rostenkowski plan argued that thousands of jobs and billions of dollars of business would be lost from their arenas and restaurants.

An amendment to undermine the chairman's position was offered by Wyche Fowler of Georgia. It would keep the deduction at 100 percent, but would add a new set of compliance measures to assure that deductions were taken for legitimate business expenses only. The Fowler plan was welcomed by the lobbying coalition, but it raised far less revenue than the $13 billion Rostenkowski wanted.

As debate on the issue began, the chairman was informed by his staff that he would probably lose to the Fowler amendment by two votes. The loss would be a severe blow, dashing the chairman's hopes for keeping the top individual tax rate in a range acceptable to the president and possibly inspiring other dissidents to bring forth their own, expensive amendments to further undercut the enterprise.

Before he asked for a show of hands, Rostenkowski made an extraordinary plea for support. This was a difficult issue for him. His Illinois protégé, Marty Russo, sided with his opponents. Bob Juliano, a longtime friend from Chicago, was a head lobbyist for the coalition. But Rostenkowski had said time and again that everyone's tax breaks had to be placed on the table for reform to succeed; it was important that this one not be taken off.

Everyone knew that another watershed vote was at hand. The chairman spoke in a low, measured voice. The entire hearing room was rapt. He reminded his members that they were engaged in tax reform. The purpose was to rid the system of "unfairness." The tax code had become a monster, he said, and the average American didn't trust it any longer. Few things contributed as much to their disgust with the system, he said, as expense-account living. While the average guy took his lunch to work in a pail, and the secretary took hers in a brown bag, some big shot down the street could go to a fancy restaurant and deduct his lavish meal. That was unfair, Rostenkowski said, and could not be left untouched in any reform worthy of the name. He warned that three-inch-high newspaper headlines would scream out criticism of the committee if the members failed this test.

Amid the high rhetoric, Rostenkowski also inserted a short but pointed warning: There was going to be a bill, he said, and as chairman, he would decide who got—and who didn't get—transition rules. Transition rules sound like something minor, but in fact, they are one of the most important and least understood elements of tax writing. Ostensibly, they ease the transition between existing tax law and the new law, but in fact, they serve as legislative favors that the chairman can dole out to help win over enough votes for his legislation. They provide billions of dollars' worth of special, targeted tax benefits for members' home-district companies and localities and are always highly valued. Rostenkowski's threat to deny transition rules to any member who crossed him could not be ignored.

Whether it was Rostenkowski's plea for reform or his threat to withhold transition rules that caused the change, the committee majority shifted after the speech. Representative Hal Daub, Republican of Nebraska, and an apparently chastened Harold Ford of Tennessee, changed their votes. Rostenkowski won the issue, and after a series of votes, accepted a compromise that would allow a deduction for 80 percent of business meals and entertainment expenses—the formula that eventually became law.

The next day, Friday, November 22, was to be the last, and it began with preparations designed to ensure a happy ending. Starting at 7:00 A.M., Rostenkowski and Rob Leonard sat with a stack of papers and a telephone in the library in the back of the hearing room, dispensing more than $5 billion in special transition-rule favors. "What do you need?" the chairman asked each member. In general, friends of the effort were rewarded with lots of transition-rule relief. Others, who the chairman hoped could be encouraged to support the effort, also got special treatment.

A key target of the chairman's transition-rule largesse was Representative Claude Pepper, the aged chairman of the House Rules Committee. Pepper, a Democrat from Florida, would have influence in dictating how the Ways and Means bill would be debated and voted upon on the House floor. Rostenkowski, like Wilbur Mills before him, wanted a "closed rule" for the debate, which would permit few if any amendments to the vast piece of legislation. Too many amendments, he knew, could unravel his tightly wrapped package. He hoped that his many favors to Pepper would make him more compliant with the request. These breaks included exceptions to tax-exempt-bond limits for a new stadium for the Miami Dolphins football team, a convention center in Miami Beach, a midtown Miami redevelopment project, and two new heating and cooling systems for the Florida region.

Other transition breaks were given to Rangel, for New York's Metropolitan Transit Authority; to McGrath, for a new headquarters for Merrill Lynch; and to Guarini, for a sports facility in the Meadowlands of New Jersey. The chairman reserved some of the benefits for himself, including one of the largest—a $200 million break for Commonwealth Edison, an Illinois utility.

As was common practice, the benefits were concealed in language designed to prevent the public from figuring out the beneficiary. For example, the Miami convention center transition rule for Pepper read as follows:

An exception from the repeal of authority to issue I.D.B.'s for convention centers would be provided for a specified amount of bonds issued for expansion of a convention center with respect to which a convention tax was upheld by a state supreme court on February 8, 1985.

Only one convention center in the country met the description: Miami's.

The list of transition rules was completed and distributed by evening. For a time, it looked like the tax-reform act might be put to bed early.

Tax bills, however, almost never finish during decent hours. There is something mystical about the hours of three o'clock or four o'clock in the morning for tax-writing lawmakers. Perhaps it is the thrill of seeing the sun rise over the Capitol dome—or, more probably, the natural inclination of humans to procrastinate until a deadline is reached and passed—but tax bills don't ever seem to come to an end without at least one sleepless night.

Rostenkowski warned his members that he wasn't going to allow them to leave until the deal was done. In response, Representative Andy Jacobs, a zany and unpredictable Democrat from Indiana, passed out disposable urinals—white plastic bags designed "for men and boys." They were meant, he explained, to make it easier for the members to remain in the hearing room for long hours without being followed into the lavatory by anxious lobbyists.

The panel had a lot to do: There was a major package of provisions that the chairman would present at the very end with the rates, the personal exemption, and other major features of the individual tax system. Before dinner, the package was ready, and the Democrats retired to the library to review it. They wanted to be sure the distribution of tax cuts among income groups was "right"—giving a bigger percentage reduction to the middle- and low-income categories than to the upper classes. They saw, for the first time, that the state and local deduction was preserved in full, that the chairman made good on his assurances. The plan included a fourth tax bracket for individuals of 38 percent, a top capital-gains rate of 20 percent and a top corporate rate of 35 percent—a number that was worked out in advance with Rostenkowski's tax-reform supporters in the corporate world. The package also taxed employer-provided group-term life insurance benefits, a slap at labor and at fringe benefits' chief congressional supporter, Senate Finance Chairman Packwood.

Debate on the document didn't get far. David Brockway, the director of the Joint Tax Committee, approached Rostenkowski with a dour expression on his face. "Sorry, Mr. Chairman," he said, "I'm afraid I fucked up here. We're short $17 billion."

Instead of being revenue neutral, as expected, the plan added an estimated $17 billion to the government's budget deficits over the next five years. Like the Treasury before him, Rostenkowski was hit with a last-minute revenue shortage.

Brockway was told about the bad news by his revenue estimators, who had found the glitch just moments before. Rostenkowski took it calmly. He directed the staff to fix it and they quickly vanished into the sixth floor of a cramped office building across the street, which was actually a converted hotel. They worked there feverishly with the estimators' computers trying to find a new combination of proposals that would bring the plan back into balance.

A second serious problem arose over the plan to tax employer-provided life insurance. Democrats were hearing strong complaints in the hallway from their allies in organized labor, who were staunchly opposed to any taxation of fringe benefits. Democratic members did not like the thought of going against their friends in the labor movement, and some of the chairman's allies also feared that the provision would cost the bill Democratic support on the House floor. At the time, hopes of winning GOP support for the bill were fading by the moment, as the Ways and Means Republicans, meeting down the hall from the Democrats in room 1129, grew increasingly enraged about how they had been ignored throughout the process. They convinced themselves that whatever the chairman was about to present to them would be unsatisfactory. That meant Rostenkowski could scarcely afford to lose any of his Democratic allies.

Worried about the prospects, Rostenkowski's protégé, Russo, asked Secretary Baker how many Republicans could be expected to vote for the bill.

"About the same percentage of Republican votes on the floor as it will receive in the committee," Baker answered.

"What does that translate to, eighty or a hundred?" Russo estimated.

"No," Baker replied, "more like forty or fifty."

"That's all?" Russo asked, disbelieving. There were 182 Republicans in the House.

"Well, maybe closer to thirty-five," Baker said upon reflection.

With so little Republican backing, Russo knew the bill had to keep Democrats on board. By irritating labor, the fringe-benefit proposal might spell real trouble. During a meeting of the Democrats in the library, Russo sat in the back and encouraged other members to walk up to Rostenkowski and tell him that the loss of labor could be a problem for the bill. He wanted to send the message that there was going to be trouble on the House floor if the chairman persisted in trying to tax fringes.

At that point, someone asked how much revenue a one-percentage-point increase in the corporate rate would raise. Rob Leonard answered about $10 billion over five years—approximately the same amount as the fringe-benefit proposal.

"Well, that's it. That solves it," said Byron Dorgan of North Dakota. Russo bolstered the idea of the trade-off by revealing what Baker told him. By taxing fringes, Russo asserted, the bill probably would lose far more Democratic votes than it would gain in Republican support. The wiser course, he argued, would be to raise the corporate rate. Other Democrats, especially Rangel of New York, chimed in with their support for the switch.

By this time, Brockway and the other tax aides had found ways to fix the $17 billion problem. They pushed down some of the rate "break points" a bit further, and they increased the top capital-gains rate to 22 percent. But now the problem was the life insurance proposal, and Rostenkowski was at his wit's end. The hours had flown by; it was after midnight, and his day had begun at the crack of dawn. The trade-off his members were seeking flew in the face of his strategy. He had promised his corporate backers that the top rate for businesses would be 35 percent and no higher. He had, in fact, planned an elaborate show of corporate support for the tax-reform bill based on that figure.

Without the knowledge of reporters and most lobbyists in the hallway, Finn Caspersen, the chairman of Beneficial Corporation, was waiting in Joe Dowley's office across from the hearing room. When the package was completed, he was to emerge triumphantly and declare that, despite the huge increase in business taxes, the bill did have business support. IBM had a public affairs officer on hand, who was carrying a sheath of press releases lauding the bill. The lobbyist from Procter & Gamble even distributed a few of his company's releases extolling the bill before the bill was done. But all of this orchestrated elation was contingent on the 35-percent corporate rate.

Back in the library, Rostenkowski, who was sitting on a couch in an alcove of the room, made a plea to keep the corporate rate where it was. He was so wracked with fatigue that some members remember seeing tears come to his eyes during the speech. When he asked for a show of hands on the fringe-benefit issue from the members who were huddled around him, however, the vote went against him: thirteen or fourteen hands, an easy majority of his twenty-three Democrats, were raised to keep all fringe benefits tax-free. Most of the Democrats wanted to back labor and raise the corporate rate. "There goes the bill," Rostenkowski said and stood up and started to leave.

But during the long, hard trek toward reform, Rostenkowski had engendered loyalty among his committee members and won the control he cherished. So when they saw his despair, they began to relent. As if in one voice, they called him back and asked him what he wanted them to do. He was the chairman. It was his bill. He had won their respect and deserved their support.

One of the first to speak was Charlie Rangel, the chief backer of tax-free fringes. "Mr. Chairman," he said, calling to Rostenkowski from off to his right, "we've got the votes but you're our leader—what do you want us to do?" Representative Cecil Heftel of Hawaii, who had not been much of a reformer up to that point, chimed in from the left: "Look, Mr. Chairman, we're all on the same team. We're all pulling together here. I think we ought to be with you. You've carried the load for us, you put us back in the ballgame on this issue." Others followed suit, including Russo, who was standing not far from Heftel. At that moment, some time after 1:00 A.M. on Saturday, the Democrats, who had for so long fought Rostenkowski and his bill, rose up to back him, even though many of them feared he was wrong.

By now, the chairman's voice was choked with emotion, and his eyes were red and teary. He made a deal with his members: They would allow him to pass his package intact—with the 35-percent corporate rate and the taxation of life insurance fringes—but only if the Republicans permitted a voice vote, so the Democrats would not have to go on record by name opposing labor. If the Republicans insisted on a roll-call vote, Rostenkowski said, the Democrats could feel free to vote to retain tax-free life insurance benefits. "If there are recorded votes," the chairman repeated, "all bets are off." The Democrats left the library like a football team charging onto the field from the locker room, ready for the second half.

Rostenkowski entered the hearing room expecting to put the final touches on the historic legislation. Aides had told the chairman that the Republicans were willing to approve the package on a voice vote and keep the corporate rate from being pushed up. Rostenkowski was triumphant. Henson Moore compared the chairman's efforts to those of a master violinist: "He's played the committee like Yehudi Menuhin plays the Stradivarius. It was a virtuoso performance."

It was not a flawless bill. Indeed, the tinkering that was done to pay for retaining the state and local deduction and to make up for the $17 billion shortfall had narrowed the tax rate cuts for many middle-income Americans so sharply that some taxpayers would actually have *higher* marginal tax rates than under existing law. But overall, the Ways and Means bill ended more tax preferences than any legislation had in decades and made a substantial cut in the top rate. It was still more reform than anyone had thought possible. If approved, it would mean that Rostenkowski's reputation, long under a cloud, would be rejuvenated. Against the odds, the chairman had taken on Ronald Reagan and saved the issue for the Democrats.

Rostenkowski was more than ready for an end. He had stretched his endurance to the limit. He and his aides were almost staggering with fatigue. His daughter was seriously ill. He had finally reached the end of a very long journey. During the course of the markup, Rostenkowski had sat in his tiny, Spartan apartment not far from the Capitol and written a long letter to himself detailing the hard lessons he had learned along the way. It began, "If at any time in the future you want to go through this process again, you're committed to read the following. . . ."

Rostenkowski took his seat to bring the gavel down on the final session of the tax-reform bill. Then came the bad news. Ken Kies, the Republicans' top tax aide, informed Joe Dowley that the Republicans would demand recorded votes on pieces of the package. The Republicans were tired of being pushed around by the chairman. The decision would destroy his elaborately laid strategy.

No one remembers for sure what Dowley's words were in response, but his intention was clear. The usually calm, cerebral aide threatened to smash Kies in the face. Kies shouted back. The scene was ugly.

Rostenkowski called another caucus of the Democrats and assured them that he would make good on his promise. Back in the hearing room a few minutes later, he offered the amendment to raise the corporate rate one percentage point to 36 percent from 35 percent. Rangel moved to keep life insurance fringes tax-free and even to extend the exemption for some benefits that had expired. Only Republicans voted nay.

After the vote, the Procter & Gamble press release was solemnly retrieved from reporters. The IBM spokesman was sent home. Finn Caspersen had already boarded his corporate jet and winged away. Nick Calio, a lobbyist for the Tax Reform Action Coalition, a large collection of pro–tax-reform companies eager for the 35-percent rate, kicked the wall and took a long walk around the corridors.

At 3:30 A.M., a weary Rostenkowski emerged into the teeming hallway to declare that the tax reform act had been completed. "The fat lady sang," he said to the cameras, putting forward a brave face. "We have not written a perfect law. Perhaps a faculty of scholars could do a better job. A group of ideologues could have provided greater consistency. But politics is an imperfect process."

He and his members disappeared into the front office of Ways and Means and quietly shared some champagne. It tasted bittersweet. "It was the most emotional night in my life, divorced from my family," Rostenkowski remembers. "I was boiling inside."

And the battle had hardly begun.

Chapter 7

---◆---

The Bear Takes One

in the Back

As the Ways and Means Committee neared completion of its monumental tax-overhaul bill, President Reagan and his chief of staff were meeting in Geneva with Soviet leader Mikhail Gorbachev. It was the first summit conference in six years between leaders of the world's two most powerful nations, and it was an exhausting event. The return trip was especially grueling; the president had a twenty-hour day on Thursday, flying to Brussels to brief allied leaders on the meeting, then flying home for a late-night address to Congress. Both President Reagan and Chief of Staff Regan were tired; their minds were on questions of war and peace. Neither had thought about taxes for days.

The next day, still suffering from jet lag, the president and Regan met with Baker and Darman. It was Friday, November 22, and Chairman Rostenkowski was just twelve hours away from completing his massive rewrite of the nation's tax laws. The meeting was held in the White House Oval Office, and the four men gathered around the president's desk along with White House legislative strategist Dennis Thomas and chief congressional lobbyist M. B. Oglesby. It was an important meeting. The fate of tax reform once again rested in the hands of the president; his handling of the explosive issue would determine the bill's prospects on the House floor. During the next four weeks, the president and his men would first bungle the delicate effort, driving tax reform to the edge of extinction, and then launch a desperate, eleventh-hour effort to rescue it.

Dennis Thomas played a crucial role. As one of Regan's most trusted aides, he acted as the chief of staff's eyes and ears on Capitol Hill. The forty-one-year-old former congressional aide was a mild-mannered man with wire-rimmed glasses, a rapidly receding hairline, and a low-key attitude that was often a welcome antidote to Regan's impulsive nature. He had worked for Secretary Regan at the Treasury Department and returned to Regan's White House staff in mid-1985, after doing a brief stint as a lobbyist with the accounting firm of Touche Ross & Company. His cautious manner sometimes served as an even keel that helped keep the stormy White House crew afloat. But on other occasions, Thomas was far too cautious and prevented decisive action. This Friday would be one of those occasions. The yellow lights were flashing in his head. He had been listening to House Republicans complain vehemently about the Rostenkowski plan, and he was worried. Nevertheless, he sat through the meeting with the president without expressing those fears.

Baker and Darman gave the president a brief overview of the bill that was about to be approved by the Ways and Means Committee. To be sure, they said, the measure fell short of the president's goals. The top tax rate for individuals was not 35 percent, but 38 percent, and the bill offered very little in rate cuts for many middle-income taxpayers. The $2,000 personal exemption, which had been a battle cry of pro-family conservatives, was limited to taxpayers who did not itemize deductions—those who itemized would get only $1,500. There was little reform on the personal side of the tax code: Most of the deductions, exclusions, and credits enjoyed by individual taxpayers were left untouched. On the business side, the plan was far tougher than the president wanted, raising corporate taxes by about $140 billion over five years, rather than the $120 billion hike in his own plan.

Nevertheless, Baker and Darman argued, the fact that the House panel was approving a bill at all was a tremendous accomplishment. Only a few weeks earlier, around the time of the bank vote, the common wisdom in Washington was that tax reform was dead. Now, Rostenkowski was completing a measure that included many of the same reforms that the administration had sought, particularly on the corporate side of the ledger. More important, the bill brought down tax rates considerably, which was what the president wanted most.

The choices for the president were clear: He could either withdraw his support for the bill and blame the Democrats for ruining tax reform, or he could back the bill despite its flaws and hope to do better in the Senate.

Without the president's support, tax reform would die. Rostenkowski would have a tough—perhaps impossible—time getting the measure approved by the full House if members thought the president had abandoned him. Even if the House passed the bill, it would be ignored by the Republican Senate, whose leaders were not about to invade the hornet's nest of tax reform unless the president was with them.

On the other hand, a nudge from the president would probably entice some House Republicans to support the bill and provide enough votes to send it to the Senate. The administration could then work with senators to fashion a measure more to its liking. House approval was only the first step in the process, the Treasury officials argued, and it was important to keep the bill moving. "This had been our strategy from day one," Baker said. "Get the best bill we could in the House, keep the process alive, and improve on it in the Senate."

For the president, still eager to be history's premier tax-rate cutter, the choice was easy. He decided not to embrace the bill itself, but to urge his party to support it and send it to the Senate to keep it from dying. The president had a "decision memo" on the table before him, and he wrote his initials—*RR*—in the box next to the first option. He was still firm in his quest for tax reform.

The group then agreed upon a plan of action. They decided that the president would personally call the ranking Republican on the Ways and Means Committee, John Duncan, at six o'clock that evening to convey his intentions. In addition, a letter from the president would be delivered to all the committee members. These two gestures, Baker and Darman knew, were extremely important. The president's efforts might secure as many as eight of the thirteen GOP votes on the committee for Rostenkowski's bill, and that in turn would encourage a good many Republicans to support the measure on the House floor. Without the president's backing, however, there would probably be only two or three Republican votes in Ways and Means and equally sparse support from Republicans on the floor.

After the meeting, Darman sat down outside the Oval Office and began drafting the president's letter. The president, weary from his travels, left the office early to retire to his residence. Darman finished the letter, checked it with Baker, and then handed it over to the White House staff. Everything seemed set for that Friday evening, November 22, the final night of the Ways and Means markup. As he returned to the Treasury Department, Darman felt satisfied with the administration's plan of action. He would never have guessed that the carefully laid strategy was about to be undercut by the White House staff.

Following the script, Bruce Thompson, the Treasury's top lobbyist, called Duncan aside at 5:45 P.M. and asked him to come into a back room where he was to receive the president's phone call. Thompson and Duncan waited for thirty minutes, but the call never came. Thompson was confused, wondering what had gone wrong. For the taciturn Duncan, it was just another insult in a long day filled with insults. He and his fellow Republicans already believed they were being steamrolled by Rostenkowski, who was working out the final details of the tax plan in private caucus with his Democratic colleagues. And Duncan was getting no help from Baker and Darman either, who seemed to him to be too eager to assure Rostenkowski's success.

Finally, at 6:15 P.M., Oglesby, the White House lobbyist, walked into the room where Thompson and Duncan were waiting. "It ain't coming," he said. The White House had changed its plan.

It was an astonishing reversal. When Darman heard about the foul-up at his Treasury office, he was furious. He knew the president had approved the call; he had even written *Call Duncan* in the margin of his decision memo. Still, Darman thought, all was not lost. The letter to the committee members was more important than the call to Duncan. It would be a strong and clear statement of the administration's position; after all, he had written it.

An hour and a half later, word filtered to the Treasury that there would be no letter either. Dennis Thomas, the cautious legislative strategist, had convinced Regan to withhold any sign of support.

Thomas had shown no visible signs of dissent during the meeting with the president earlier that day, but after the meeting, he had gone to talk to Regan. He pointed out that all of the top House GOP leaders were complaining about Rostenkowski's bill, including Minority Leader Robert Michel of Illinois, GOP Whip Trent Lott of Mississippi, and Republican Policy Committee Chairman Dick Cheney of Wyoming. The grousing was coming as well from tax-reform proponent Kemp, who felt the Ways and Means bill fell far short of his own reform goals. On top of that, bitter Ways and Means Republicans thought that Baker and Darman had been co-opted by Rostenkowski. Thomas asserted that it was dangerous to ignore all of these people. The Treasury had only to worry about the tax bill, he reasoned, but the White House had a much bigger array of issues on its plate. It could scarcely afford, in one blow, to knock for a loop every influential Republican in the House of Representatives.

"The question wasn't one of whether to withdraw support or hold it back; it was a question of timing," Thomas said later. "We wanted to get a better idea of what the bill was going to look like through that night and then make a final determination in a way that involved the House Republicans. The Republicans felt terribly alienated by Rostenkowski—and, I think unfairly so, by the Treasury Department." By withholding any immediate sign of support for Rostenkowski, Thomas hoped to mollify the House GOP.

Regan was willing to go along with the delay, in part because he resented Baker and Darman trying, as he saw it, to force a plan down his throat. His resentment for the Treasury team had continued to fester during the tax debate, and he welcomed the opportunity to exert his power. "I hadn't had time to study the plan," he said later. "I had been back less than twenty-four hours. And the fact that the Republicans were growing more and more intolerant and were hitting the flash point seemed to have escaped the notice of some people"—meaning, of course, Baker and Darman.

The two Treasury officials were incensed. In private, they had often questioned the wisdom and judgment of the new White House team. Baker, always the diplomat, had been very careful to keep his feelings out of public view; Darman had been somewhat less discreet. But this time, the actions of Regan and Thomas were too much. The president needed to send a strong signal to keep the bill on track. After all, if the chief executive was not sure he could support the bill, why should GOP members of Congress support it? It was sheer stupidity not to make a statement, Baker and Darman thought.

A series of heated telephone conversations ensued. Darman spoke to Thomas; then Baker spoke to Thomas. Baker asked to speak with Regan, but Thomas said the chief of staff had gone home exhausted from his postsummit travels and should not be disturbed. By 10:00 P.M., there was still no word from the White House, and Baker was growing impatient. The Treasury officials did not want to return to Capitol Hill until they knew what to tell Rostenkowski about the president's stance. In a conversation with Thomas, Baker exploded: "I'm not going forward on the strength of your say-so to announce an administration position. I want at a minimum to talk with Regan, and if I'm not satisfied, I'll talk with the president."

A few minutes later, Regan called Baker at the Treasury. The conversation was tense, but civil. An agreement was finally reached between the two men, but it was far less than Baker thought was adequate. There would be no letter or phone call from the president that night; he had already gone to bed. Baker would be allowed to inform committee members of the administration's support for the process, though not for every specific provision of the bill itself—*provided* there were no major changes in the legislation before it was approved. The president would then make a strong statement either in his regular Saturday morning radio address or in a press release on Monday morning.

It was not a good compromise, Baker thought, and would probably weaken support for the bill in the House, but it would have to do. The only alternative was to wake the president and get him to reverse the chief of staff's decision. "I started to call the president, and then I thought, no, life is too short to call him and wake him up. We'll clean it up ourselves," Baker recalls.

At about 10:15 P.M., Baker and Darman returned to Capitol Hill. The Ways and Means Democrats were still meeting in a private caucus, and the Republicans, feeling totally cut out of the tax-writing process, were steaming. It looked as though even the one or two GOP members who backed Rostenkowski's efforts might vote against the chairman out of anger. The Treasury officials hoped that word of the president's conditional endorsement would calm them down.

When Rostenkowski finally emerged triumphantly from the Democratic caucus, having temporarily quelled the revolt over his proposal to tax life insurance fringe benefits, Baker was waiting to see him in Joe Dowley's office across the hall from the hearing room. The president had his problems with the measure, Baker said, and wanted a chance to rework it in the Senate, but he planned to call the bill a "good start," and urge its approval. Provided there were no major changes, he said, Darman would make a statement to that effect when the committee completed its work.

For Rostenkowski, that was good news. He needed to have the president's support; without it, he knew, his bill might be viewed as a charade and go down in defeat on the floor of the House. Baker left the Ways and Means deliberations shortly after that conversation. He planned to go goose-hunting early in the morning on Maryland's Eastern Shore, and he wanted to get a couple of hours' sleep. Darman remained to see the bill through, and to read the administration's statement at the end of the markup.

Not long after Baker left, Rostenkowski's fringe-benefit deal exploded. The proposal to tax life insurance fringes was dropped, and the corporate rate was boosted one percentage point. It was not a huge change, but it was enough to convince Darman that he could not speak for the administration. It was too late to call Regan or the president, so Darman said nothing. He urged Rostenkowski to put off the final, recorded vote on the package until after the Thanksgiving break. By then, Darman assured him, the president would have made his statement, and the Republicans would have cooled off. The chairman agreed; his plan was approved in a preliminary way by voice vote, and a final, recorded vote was delayed.

Relations between Regan's White House and Baker's Treasury were stretched to the breaking point. On Saturday morning, after a few hours of sleep, Darman called Oglesby to ask if the president needed some information for his radio address encouraging support for the Ways and Means bill. Oglesby said no, the president was not going to make any kind of statement about the tax bill that morning. Darman then talked to Thomas. Did he need help putting together a statement for release Monday morning? Thomas replied that it might be better to wait until Tuesday, because the House Republican leaders would be meeting that morning and would have an opportunity to express their views before the president spoke out. On Tuesday, the delays continued. Treasury officials asked, "When will a statement be coming out?" White House officials replied, "Maybe tomorrow or the next day or the next." For ten long days, there was no word from the president. No statement was made, and newspapers were filled with speculation that the White House was going to let the measure die. Rostenkowski put in a call to President Reagan, demanding to know where he stood, but for several days the president did not even return the call.

The press, lobbyists, and legislators were stunned by the White House silence. The president had launched the tax-reform effort. He had carried it this far. And now it seemed he was ready to drop it. Darman recalls it this way:

The president at this point should have been advised to lead, not follow. His failure to be out-front was interpreted by everybody as a signal that he was about to pull the rug on tax reform. It emboldened the Republicans to organize against him—and reform. Politicians are extremely sensitive; their antennae are attuned to political signals. The last time they'd seen the president and Rosty talking about tax reform, they'd seen them both on TV, going forward together to the nation. Afterward, the president even advertised "Write Rosty." This time, though, Rosty comes forward, announces a tremendous victory, and there's dead silence from the president. No comment. As it continues for several days, the political world interprets this as a big, big, big signal. If anybody's thinking of running away from reform, then they'd better run because the president's about to saw the limb off.

Run they did. The vast majority of House Republicans wanted nothing to do with the bill. They certainly were not going to take on the army of special-interest lobbyists opposing the measure if they did not at least have the president backing them up.

The revolt was officially launched on the Tuesday after the Ways and Means Committee bill was completed, when the House Republican Conference voted overwhelmingly to oppose the measure. The conference includes all the Republican members of the House and is the forum they use to select their leadership and to consider party positions on major pieces of legislation. It was chaired by Kemp, and its vote to oppose the tax bill was a powerful statement.

When Rostenkowski finally held a roll-call vote on the bill in his committee on December 3, he got the support of only five of the panel's thirteen Republicans. Outside the committee, GOP support was even weaker. Every member of the House GOP leadership had vowed to work against the bill. Bruce Thompson, the Treasury lobbyist, tallied votes that same week and came up with an incredible result—only six Republicans in the entire House were definitely planning to vote for the tax bill, and only eight more were leaning toward supporting it. The remainder of the 182 GOP members were either undecided or opposed; and those opposed were not the least bit reserved in their opposition.

It was an extraordinary situation: Tax reform was the top domestic priority of a president who had been reelected a year earlier in a forty-nine-state landslide; yet his own troops in the House were now going all out to bury it.

The year had been a particularly trying one for the underdog House Republicans. A minority for three decades, they had long felt stifled, and 1985 brought those feelings to a peak. The year opened with a knockdown battle over whom to seat in a disputed Indiana congressional election. Republican candidate Richard D. McIntyre was certified by the Indiana secretary of state as the winner with a razor-thin thirty-four-vote margin. Citing election irregularities, a House task force recounted the votes and named Frank McCloskey, a Democrat, as the winner. Exercising their power to settle election disputes, the House Democrats voted to seat McCloskey rather than McIntyre, and the angry GOP members, in a rare and dramatic demonstration, walked out of the House chamber as the vote was taken. "Mr. Speaker, you know how to win votes the old-fashioned way," complained embittered Republican Representative Bob McEwen. "You steal them."

The House GOP also felt ignored throughout the year by their own Reagan administration. The Republicans had worked closely with the White House in 1981 to push through the president's economic program, forming alliances with conservative Southern Democrats. But in the 1982 elections, Republicans lost twenty-six House seats, and they regained only fourteen in the 1984 Reagan landslide. The ability of the minority Republicans to form a voting majority coalition with Democrats was weakened, and their power in the House had dwindled accordingly. The White House increasingly cut its deals with Republicans in the Senate, who, by contrast, were in the majority; the House Republicans seemed irrelevant. The *National Journal* magazine called them the "Rodney Dangerfields of American politics"—they got no respect.

The more moderate leaders of the House GOP, like Minority Leader Robert Michel, were still inclined to work with the administration and, when possible, with the House Democrats. But Michel's leadership was under challenge by a cell of younger, feistier Republicans—called by some the "bomb-throwers"—who thought confrontation was the only way to get noticed. Rifts within the party ran deep and added to the problems.

Tax reform stoked this fire of frustration. As the Republicans saw it, Baker and Darman had cut a devil's deal with Rostenkowski. The Treasury officials allowed the Democratic chairman to plow ahead with a bill that rolled right over the Republicans and their constituencies. It was the ultimate insult. The tax-reform bill struck at too many of the groups that they felt bound to protect. Despite the president's stumping around the country in favor of reform, the public seemed uninterested. The administration had put the Republicans in an untenable position by championing this awkward issue, and now they wanted to fight back.

The White House could have softened this rebellion if it had made its strong desire for tax reform known as soon as Ways and Means completed its work; the president's influence over his party was still enormous. But Regan and Thomas made a critical error in judgment: The ten days of foot-dragging clearly fed the rebellion. Even Baker and Darman began to fear that Regan and his staff had decided to let the bill die and just were not telling them. "After a while, we came close to concluding that they couldn't be that dumb, that they must be planning to dump the thing," Darman said.

Earlier that year, Darman had given a speech in which he compared the perilous course of tax reform to a target bear in a popgun shooting gallery. "It gets hit," he said. "It rises, pauses, turns a bit—and then keeps on going"—nothing was able to stop it.

This time, however, the tax-reform effort was under attack from the White House itself. The bear had taken one in the back, and the injury looked like it could be fatal.

Tuesday, December 3, ten days after Rostenkowski's committee finished its work, the White House finally began to put out the word that it was still interested in reform. President Reagan met privately with GOP congressional leaders and told them he was "committed to keeping tax revision alive in Congress." The next day, the White House released a tepid statement saying the president believed that "the legislative process must be allowed to go forward."

The president's weak statement was rendered even weaker by his refusal to choose between Rostenkowski's bill and the House Republicans' own alternative. The Republican plan was thrown together by Ways and Means Republicans who by and large opposed reform, and it was not considered a serious document. It appeased an array of Republican interest groups by retaining major deductions and credits, including the investment tax credit, but it trimmed the value of all those breaks to pay for a reduction in the top tax rate to 37 percent—a transparent attempt to do the Ways and Means bill's 38-percent top rate one better. The plan had no chance of passage; by suggesting he might favor it over the Rostenkowski bill in the December 4 statement, the president only contributed to the impression that he did not care much about reform.

Republican opposition to the Rostenkowski bill solidified. "House Republicans believe that the promise of tax reform has been betrayed," Kemp said. "The hard truth is that the Democratic bill is anti-family, anti-growth, and anti-investment." Kemp had staked out tax reform as a key issue in his efforts to win the 1988 GOP nomination for president, but after the Rostenkowski bill came out, he quickly changed course. That was in part because of serious problems he had with the Rostenkowski bill, but also because, as chairman of the Republican Conference, he could not easily defy that group's wishes.

The president kept promising to improve the bill in the Senate, but the promise had a hollow ring. Senate Republicans were even less interested in reform than House Republicans. "The phrase the 'Senate will fix it up' is the moral equivalent of 'I'll respect you in the morning,' " said Ways and Means Republican Bill Frenzel.

Rostenkowski was having trouble keeping the Democrats in line, as well. Tax reform, like so many previous tax bills, was splitting the House not just along party lines, but also along regional lines. Democrats from oil states opposed the measure, arguing the committee's concessions to the oil and gas industry were insufficient. Many Democrats from timber-producing and heavy-industry states also thought that Rostenkowski's bill was too tough on them. Most Democrats still supported the measure, but it was unlikely that Rostenkowski could carry the full House without at least some Republican help. Speaker O'Neill warned that the president had better start lobbying intensely "if we are to accomplish the historic, bipartisan overhaul in the tax system that he has promised."

Business lobbyists worked busily behind the scenes to defeat the measure. The legislation was opposed by the Chamber of Commerce of the U.S.A., the National Association of Manufacturers, the Business Roundtable, the National Association of Home Builders, the American Bankers Association, and a long roster of representatives of corporate America. They believed that the bill would harm the economy—and not coincidentally do damage to their own members' profit-and-loss statements.

But a small group of businesses endorsed Rostenkowski's plan and diluted the influence of the naysayers. Two groups—the Tax Reform Action Coalition and the CEO Tax Group—decided to lobby strongly for the measure, after a momentary hesitation when the corporate rate rose to 36 percent from 35 percent on the last night of the markup. Their members included such powerhouse companies as General Motors, IBM, and Procter & Gamble—as well as such organizations as the American Electronics Association and the National Association of Wholesaler-Distributors. Still, in the scheme of things, the corporate opposition to Rostenkowski's bill was immense.

Worried that the president's chief domestic initiative might falter, White House officials belatedly tried to step up their campaign. On Friday, December 6, Reagan's aides telephoned Rostenkowski to tell him they would turn up the heat on House Republicans the following week. On Saturday, the president used his weekly radio address to push for reform: "I hope the House will vote yes next week and allow the Senate to consider, debate, and to improve this important measure." On Monday, he sent a letter conveying the same message to each member of the House. Though support among Republicans still lagged, most Washington observers thought the popular president would be able to rally the necessary support. Noting the president's increased activity, O'Neill told reporters on Monday, "I would think we will pass it."

A vote was scheduled for Wednesday, December 11, on the "rule," which needed to be adopted before debate on the bill could begin. Rules are a crucial part of the legislative process in the House, and they are particularly important for tax bills. In the Senate, debate on a bill is virtually unlimited and amendments are offered without restriction. But in the much larger House, most bills cannot be considered without a rule, which sets the length of the debate and often restricts the amendments that can be offered. Tax bills generally are considered under "modified closed" or "closed" rules, which allow few or no amendments on the floor. These rules provide an important discipline to the tax-writing process. The alternative would be chaos. Without such a rule, each of the House's 435 members might be tempted to try and dip into the tax cookie jar to get favors for constituents.

Rules are written by a small panel known as the Rules Committee, which, because of its unique function in the House, exercises significant power. The Rules Committee is, in a sense, the gatekeeper for the House floor, deciding which bills will or will not be voted on and how they can be altered. In the late 1950s and the 1960s, the panel became a cemetery for civil rights legislation and other liberal initiatives, when Rules Chairman Howard W. Smith, a conservative Virginia Democrat, refused to act on measures drawn up by his Democratic colleagues. More recently, the committee has become an instrument of the House speaker, peopled largely by party loyalists, but its power remains substantial. Powerful chairmen of other committees are often reduced to beggars before the panel as they seek a favorable rule to guide debate on their bills. "You have a lot of leverage with the committee chairmen," says Democrat David Bonior of Michigan, a member of the panel. "Those guys are always looking to please us."

The rule approved by the committee for tax reform allowed only five hours of debate, an exceptionally brief period for a bill that promised to be the most far-reaching measure considered by the House in years. That was because the legislative session was nearly over, and members were anxious to leave for the holidays. Moreover, the rule allowed only three amendments to be offered on the floor. One was the Republican alternative, a salve to the disaffected Ways and Means Republicans. Another created a generous, expanded tax credit for campaign contributions to candidates for the House or Senate. The third amendment was a minor measure affecting the tax codes of U.S. island possessions—a proposal that was added to assuage some jurisdictional squabbles between Rostenkowski and other committee chairmen.

The rule also made one important change to Rostenkowski's bill in an attempt to douse a simmering controversy. The Ways and Means bill repealed a provision in existing tax law that allowed all federal retirees to get tax-free payments from their pension plans in the first three years after retiring. Rostenkowski had quietly slipped in a line exempting members of Congress and their staffs from that change—a relief to Speaker O'Neill, who was planning to retire at the end of 1986, and to many others as well. Rostenkowski hoped no one would notice the self-serving provision, and his staff had drafted it in such a way that it was very difficult to find in the tax document. But on December 7, *The Washington Post* ran a story pointing it out. Anxious to avoid further public embarrassment, the Rules Committee wrote the rule so that when members voted for it, they would also be voting to strike the exception.

Because the rule was largely a procedural vote, it was expected to create little controversy; such measures usually win enough Democratic support to guarantee a majority. Treasury officials thought this rule in particular would be easy to pass, because members who voted against it would, in effect, be voting *for* the provision that exempted them from the pension change—a self-serving vote which could easily be flaunted by election opponents.

But on the morning of the vote, several Democratic lawmakers began attacking the rule. They charged that the change in the treatment of federal pensions ought to be dropped from the tax bill entirely. For the most part, these complaints came from members whose districts had large populations of federal workers, but their position was winning sympathy from other members who knew that their *own* retirement benefits would be hit as well. What's more, some Democrats saw the pensioners' issue as a good excuse to vote against the bill.

Huddled in a tiny room off the House floor, a group of Republican leaders—including Robert Michel, Trent Lott, Dick Cheney, and Jack Kemp—listened intently as one Democrat after another rose to criticize the rule. They recognized in the budding Democratic dissent their own opportunity to attack the bill. Lott remembered that in 1983, the Republicans had defeated a Rostenkowski tax bill by going after the rule; perhaps this time, they had an opportunity to do it again. Representative Newt Gingrich, a Georgia Republican who joined in the discussions, recalls, "It suddenly hit us at 10:30 A.M., if we pushed hard enough, we could defeat tax-overhaul."

Thanks to Bob Packwood, the House Republicans were more eager than ever to scuttle the tax measure. The Senate Finance Committee chairman had appeared on television that morning and shattered the administration's promise to "fix the bill in the Senate." He told a television interviewer that he doubted his committee would make many changes in the bill if it passed the House—a comment that reinforced the worst fears of the Republicans. It was a blatant and disingenuous attempt to kill the bill. Packwood knew his committee would substantially alter the measure if it ever reached the Senate, but he apparently hoped to contribute to its problems in the House so he wouldn't have to deal with it.

The rule was a tempting target for the Republicans. Members were hesitant to vote against the bill itself, fearing they might be saddled with the blame for killing reform, but the rule offered a chance, as Lott put it, for members "to get rid of the bill without putting their fingerprints on the trigger."

For the next hour and a half, the GOP leaders worked feverishly to get out the message: "Defeat the rule." Republican Whip Lott was responsible for rounding up votes for the GOP leadership. Usually, his fine-tuned whip organization promoted the president's initiatives; this time it was launching a guerrilla attack against the White House and against Rostenkowski. "It was one of those occasional cavalry charges that the House Republicans make to let everyone know they still exist," Lott says.

Working out of his chandeliered Capitol office (located down the hall from Rostenkowski's), Lott sent out a flurry of messages to the GOP members through a "rotary" phone system, similar to the kind used by volunteer fire departments to call firefighters during an emergency. An electronic beeper-system used by many members also conveyed the message. A meeting was hastily convened of the twenty-one members who served as part of the whip organization. "We have an opportunity to kill this snake before it gets out of the hole," Lott said and began to array his troops.

When the vote was called for shortly before noon, Lott's whip team was ready. The fifteen minutes allowed for the vote were a critical time, and Lott's fine-tuned machine took full advantage of it. He stationed members at each door of the House chamber to collar their colleagues as they entered and urge them to oppose the rule. Lott coordinated the effort from the "well" of the House, standing in front of the Speaker's podium and dispatching his two lieutenants, who stood at either shoulder. He had to keep as many of his Republicans from supporting the rule as possible, and he assigned members of his team to put pressure on anyone who wavered.

From his position near the center of the semicircular House chamber, Lott knew where almost all of the 435 House members could be found. To his right, at about the three-o'clock position, was the so-called Pennsylvania corner, where rust-belt Democrats tended to congregate. To his left, at the nine-o'clock position, were the Northeastern Republicans, who tended to be the moderates in the wide spectrum of the House GOP. In the back of the chamber, to the right of the high-noon position, just next to the narrow aisle that separated the two parties, were the "boll-weevil" Democrats, the conservative Southerners. This group was critical to Lott's effort; they were less tied to the Democratic leaders of the House than were many of their colleagues and more prone to support the GOP in a party-line procedural vote. Lott dispatched his skilled deputy, Republican Representative Tom Loeffler of Texas, to work this group of renegade Democrats and to help win over their support.

As members voted on the House's electronic system by inserting credit-card-like devices into designated slots along the aisles, Lott's lieutenants brought him reports from a vote-counting computer located in the center of the Republican side of the chamber. They carried up-to-the-minute tallies that told him precisely how every member was voting. The count looked good. The GOP was holding firm; only a handful of Republicans were supporting the rule. Oil-state and boll-weevil Democrats were also opposing the rule, as was the entire Maryland Democratic delegation, whose members were concerned about the federal-employee pension change. Seeing the frantic activity in the well, Rostenkowski walked up and asked, "Lott, you rascal, what are you doing to me?"

But it was too late. The surprise attack had been a success. Lott and his lieutenants had defeated not only their Democratic rivals, but also their own president. The rule went down by a vote of 223–202. All but fourteen of the Republicans voted with Lott against the rule, and against Reagan.

As he was leaving the podium after the vote, O'Neill turned to his trusted aide and strategist, Kirk O'Donnell, and said, "Today Ronald Reagan became a lame duck on the floor of the House."

As the vote was being tallied, Rostenkowski put in an urgent phone call to Secretary Baker, who was attending a lunch at the State Department. The Ways and Means chairman had frequently complained that Baker participated only in the big battles and was never around for the many smaller ones. "He doesn't watch the guys fight to get the pennant," Rostenkowski said, "he just goes to the World Series games." When the secretary picked up the phone, Rostenkowski spared no words. "Goddammit," he shouted, "the rule is going down."

At about the same moment, Senator Bradley, who had been urging House Democrats to vote for reform, put through an exasperated call to fellow-reformer Kemp to find out why in the hell he had opposed the rule. Kemp tried to assure Bradley that his goal was not to defeat the bill, only to get the president's attention. But the senator was dumbfounded. The guerrilla attack threatened to do considerably more than get the president's attention. It could spell the death of tax reform, and Kemp, the Republican's leading reformer, was helping to wield the murder weapon!

The defeat of the rule was a major loss for the president. His top domestic initiative had been beaten by a near-unanimous vote of his own party. It also was a blow to Baker; the administration's legislative wizard had failed to foresee the House revolt. White House spokesman Larry Speakes tried to brush off the blame, "It is the members of the House that will have to answer to the American people, not the president." But O'Neill's remarks were more to the point: "Today, with glee in their faces, Republican congressmen voted to humiliate the man who led them to victory. They showed their contempt for the White House by voting overwhelmingly against the tax-reform process."

Some House Republicans crowed about their victory, wearing buttons that read: RON AND DAN, TRY AGAIN. Others were more contrite. Even the GOP leaders who had led the attack had not expected to be quite so successful. "We did better this morning than we thought," Dick Cheney said.

In the wake of the debacle, White House aides quickly forgot any reservations they had about the tax-reform effort. There was some finger-pointing between the White House and the Treasury, but that quickly disappeared in the face of the greater threat that they both now faced. The rule vote was a challenge to the president's power and influence in his second term. The administration had to reverse it, as a matter of presidential pride and prestige. President Reagan was said to be angry and perplexed. An extraordinarily partisan politician, he did not understand how so many members of his own party could desert him.

The Treasury and the White House immediately launched a joint rescue effort. Baker got on the telephone and began to call House Republicans. Some were summoned to meet with the president. A few of them caved under the pressure, some claiming they "wouldn't have voted against the rule" if they had known the president was going to lose. Others vowed to continue their battle and urged the president not to fight back.

It had been a close vote. Only eleven members needed to switch their positions to reverse the outcome. But there was also a new problem to cope with—a very serious one. The defeat of the rule had put the fate of tax reform in the hands of one man: Speaker O'Neill. He was the only person with the power to bring up the rule for a second vote, and it was not at all clear he wanted to do that. The Democrats, after all, had the political advantage. They had accepted the president's challenge to draft a tax-reform bill that ended tax breaks and lowered tax rates. They had pushed it through the committee, over the objections of members of the president's own party. A large majority of Democrats had supported the rule on the House floor—188 of the House's 253 Democrats voted aye. They had, indeed, done everything necessary to assure that their reputations as reformers went untarnished. If the bill failed now, there would be no one to blame but the Republicans.

To help keep the speaker on board tax reform during the floor fight, Rostenkowski asked former O'Neill aide Ari Weiss to come back to Washington. An Orthodox Jew, Weiss had left O'Neill's staff in November to live and work in Israel. Although only thirty-two years old, he had been with the speaker since he was twenty and was a skilled operator in the politics of the House and also a brilliant analyst of the substance of legislation. Weiss believed deeply in reform, and the speaker had great respect and affection for the young aide. He treated him like a son, calling him unabashedly "the most brilliant kid I've ever known." Rostenkowski had hoped that with Weiss around, the speaker's support for tax reform would not wane. Rostenkowski also did not hesitate to use his own close personal friendship with the speaker, a golfing chum, to assure his loyalty to the cause.

Rostenkowski still wanted his bill to pass the House. If it were going to be killed, he preferred that the Republican Senate be left holding the knife. Shortly after the failure of the rule vote, Rostenkowski declared that the president would have to find thirty Republican supporters before the bill could be brought up again. Later that afternoon, however, O'Neill upped the stakes: "As soon as the president informs me personally that he has a list of fifty to seventy-five Republican votes for passage of the bill, we will begin moving ahead with the bipartisan reform process." It was a big demand—thirty votes was a struggle; fifty votes was a mammoth task. By setting a goal for votes, O'Neill signaled that he had been persuaded by Weiss and Rostenkowski to give tax reform another try. But he was not about to let the president off without extracting his pound of flesh. "The speaker thought we could jump six feet," Dennis Thomas said later, "so he put up a nine-foot hurdle."

O'Neill had mixed feelings about the tax-overhaul effort from the start. A big, hulking man with a bulbous nose and a thick thatch of white hair, the seventy-three-year-old speaker was an old-time pol who preferred politics to policy. He spent much of his time talking strategy with his friends over poker or golf. For Republican partisans, he had come to symbolize the worst of the Democratic party: the living embodiment of government run amok. But for those who knew him better, and for much of the public at large, the speaker also represented the best in the Democratic party. His understanding of complex policy issues was limited, but he believed deeply and sincerely in the need for a government that was compassionate and fair. He also was supportive of the younger Democrats who were searching for "new ideas" for the party, and he had been a booster of the seminal Bradley-Gephardt plan. Thanks to prodding by Weiss, he came to realize that the existing tax code was a travesty and he recognized the need for reform. But as a politician who had spent a quarter-century in the House and nearly a decade in the speaker's chair watching numerous attempts to reform the tax system collapse in early defeat, he had little faith in its legislative prospects.

"Tip O'Neill didn't want the fight, the aggravation," Rostenkowski says. "He was jelly in some respects."

O'Neill thought tax reform was just too radical. "I always thought that the bill was a good idea," he said, "that it had some merits and some dismerits, but I thought it was eight years ahead of itself. You just don't come up with a revolutionary idea and make it fly in its first [session of] Congress. I just thought it would be six or eight years before it would actually come."

The speaker was also under pressure from Democrats who were anxious to scuttle the whole effort. House Majority Leader Jim Wright, a Texan who worried about the bill's effects on the oil industry among other concerns, wanted to see it defeated. Other Texas members fanned out on the House floor after the rule was voted down to urge their colleagues to leave the bill where it lay. Some members worried about the effect that a reform bill would have on the money-starved Democrats' ability to raise much-needed campaign funds from special interests. The Republican revolt had removed the Democrats from the difficult box that the president's call for tax reform had put them in, these members argued, so the party no longer needed to worry about being blamed for selling out to the special interests. Why put themselves back in that box?

On Thursday, December 12, the day after the rule went down, Baker, Darman, and Chief of Staff Regan had a tense two-hour meeting on the Hill with House Republican leaders. The Republicans used the opportunity to express their frustrations and to give the administration team a thorough dressing-down. At the meeting's conclusion, Kemp and Michel asked if the president would consider sending them a letter in which he would agree to veto any bill that did not meet certain specifications.

Kemp and Michel had little in common; indeed, there was considerable resentment between the two men and their staffs. Kemp was a member of the upstart breed of supply-side Republicans; Michel represented the more traditional Republican views that Kemp was trying to supplant. Nevertheless, both men were eager to find an excuse for reversing their votes against the rule. Kemp, by this time, realized that the rule vote might tarnish his reputation as a tax reformer and possibly hurt his chances for the 1988 presidential nomination. He wanted to be able to say that he saved reform, not that he killed it. Michel wanted an excuse to switch votes because he was a loyal party man and did not like opposing the president's chief domestic initiative. The institutional pressure on the minority leader to back his president was intense.

In the meantime, Rostenkowski and the speaker waited for word that the president had rounded up fifty votes. It did not come that day. GOP support still fell far short of the mark. Late Thursday afternoon, the speaker recessed the House until the following Monday. It was clear there would be no answer from the White House before then.

On Friday, Baker and Rostenkowski met with O'Neill in the Capitol. The meeting took place in the speaker's private office, his "inner sanctum," filled with mementos of his life, his family, and his party. On the walls there was a drawing of his wife, Millie, and a photograph of a Thanksgiving dinner in Ireland with the O'Neills' extended family. There was a case full of autographed baseballs. And everywhere, there were various-sized replicas of donkeys, the symbol of the Democratic party. Sitting across the desk from the speaker, the Treasury secretary was like a mouse in a den of cats. The Democrats had him over a barrel; they knew it and he knew it. He was there to ask for a favor, and he had no choice but to beg. He tried to steer the discussion away from partisan banter and to appeal instead to O'Neill's liberal instincts. "Mr. Speaker," he asked, "when in your lifetime will you have the chance again to take six million poor Americans off the tax rolls?"

The Democratic leader was unmoved. Baker explained that the Republicans needed an excuse to switch their votes, and he asked if the speaker would agree to change the rule in order to allow a vote on a Republican amendment increasing the personal exemption to $2,000 for all taxpayers. O'Neill said no. Baker asked if the speaker would allow some smaller change in the rule. It did not have to be big, he said; the Republicans who voted against the rule simply needed a "face-saving" change that would

give them an ostensible reason for reversing their votes. O'Neill still refused. "You know this is your bill, this was your idea," the speaker said.
"Now you've got to produce the votes for it."

It was a long meeting, and for Baker, a frustrating one. The only change
the speaker would agree to was to allow a vote on a largely meaningless,
nonbinding resolution sought by Michel that urged Congress to change the
bill's general effective date from January 1, 1986, to January 1, 1987. It
was clear by now that Congress would not complete a tax-overhaul bill
until well into 1986, and Michel was afraid the prospect of a retroactive
effective date would create uncertainty and turmoil in the business community.

The Michel resolution was a thin reed for Republicans; it could hardly
justify a vote reversal. Nevertheless, it was all the speaker was willing to
give. Baker walked out of the meeting unsure of O'Neill's intentions. Ari
Weiss had returned to Israel shortly after the failure of the rule vote and
was no longer around to remind the speaker of the importance of the
effort. To be sure, O'Neill was not usually an obstructionist, but this time,
Baker thought, the Democratic leader was teetering, and the fate of tax
reform was teetering with him. It was one of the bleakest moments in the
two-year struggle for tax reform. Baker was really worried. "That's where
tax reform had the best chance of going down the tubes," he recalled later.

Meanwhile, Lott continued to prime his whip group on ways to fight the
bill. The president's strong appeal was weakening the resolve of some
Republican members, and they needed to know how to answer the tough
queries they were getting from the administration and from their constituents. Seminars were convened to coach reluctant members.

QUESTION: How could a good Republican oppose the administration's top domestic priority?
ANSWER: Since my president said he'd veto this bill if it came to his desk, I voted
against it.
QUESTION: How could anyone oppose a bill that takes six million poor people
off the tax rolls?
ANSWER: It may take six million off the tax rolls, but 1.5 million of them will
be unemployed.

Desperate for support, the White House decided to take the rare and
risky step of sending President Reagan into the lion's den. The president
agreed to go to the Hill to meet with the House Republican Conference,
the group that had helped start the revolt in the first place. It was a big
gamble: By going to the Capitol, the president was putting his reputation
on the line. Nevertheless, Darman and Thomas both argued strongly that
the move was necessary; there was no other hope of getting the fifty votes
the speaker demanded.

The president met with the GOP conference at 2:15 P.M. on Monday,

December 16, in a private session, sealed away from the public and the press. Going into the meeting, the administration had rounded up only about thirty-eight votes for the bill, and many of those were uncertain. The speaker had given the president until 8:00 that evening—less than six hours away—and time was rapidly running out.

In introducing the president, Kemp was unrestrained in his criticism of the Ways and Means bill:

Mr. President, we all appreciate your gesture in coming here, and we would like to respond by being equally gracious and candid. As you know, all of us revere your leadership. The vote on the rule last week, in the view of some of us, prevented a choice presented by the House Democrats—between a bad tax bill or no tax bill. In its current form, the Rostenkowski bill fails to fulfill the pro-growth, pro-family promise of your original proposal. And Bob Packwood was quoted the morning of the vote as saying he did not believe the Rostenkowski bill would be substantially changed in the Senate. I would like to emphasize that it is the substance of the bill, on items like the $2,000 personal exemption and incentives for investment, which is at the root of concern about the bill.

The crowd was ready to take on the president, but in classic Reagan style, he disarmed them. He had just returned from Fort Campbell, Kentucky, where he had attended a memorial service for 248 Army soldiers who had died when their transport plane crashed into the woods of Newfoundland. Before even mentioning the tax bill, the president, visibly moved by the emotional experience of that morning, called for a moment of silent prayer. "That took the sting out of our bite," Lott recalls. "That changed the whole mood in the conference."

After the prayer, the president made a few brief remarks, urging the group to support the tax-reform process. As soon as he was finished, he was assaulted by questions from members who were clearly hostile to the bill. The first speaker criticized the 38-percent top rate; the second complained about the personal exemption; the third hit the oil-and-gas provisions, and the fourth complained about the effect on heavy industry. It seemed as though everyone in the cavernous room was lined up against the president and reform.

The president was sympathetic. He too wanted a $2,000 personal exemption, he said; he too wanted better investment incentives; but tax reform was important to him and important to the Republican party. If the House let it die now, there might never be a chance to resurrect it. If the House passed the bill, on the other hand, the president himself would make certain that it was changed before he signed it into law. If it did not meet his concerns about investment incentives, about the personal exemption, about the top rate, he would veto it, he said.

The first break in the barrage of criticism came from Illinois Representative Henry Hyde. A large man and an impressive debater, Hyde had been a member of the House for more than a decade and had impeccable conservative credentials. He had been an outspoken opponent of the tax bill and the rule, but after listening to the president for a while, he rose to speak: "Mr. President, if you say you'll fight for the $2,000 exemption, the rate reduction, effective dates, and a lower capital-gains rate, I don't need a letter. I'll vote for it."

Hyde's comments were just what Reagan needed. The meeting changed from a debate over the tax bill to a show of loyalty for the popular president. A few other members followed Hyde's example, speaking in favor of the president and pledging their support. Reagan's presence made an impact. The Republican rebels had been willing to complain mightily about the White House, about Regan, about Baker, and especially about Darman, but when it came to the president, their defiance seemed to melt. As Thompson and Oglesby watched the crowd, they could see some of the members warming to the president's request, clapping loudly at each pause in his answers. They jotted down the names of those who clapped most vigorously and made notes to telephone them right after the meeting to ask for pledges of support.

At the end of the meeting, a secret ballot was taken. Forty-eight members indicated they would support the bill. It looked as though there might be enough votes to satisfy the speaker's demand. Still, the blind ballot was only a rough count. Members were under the spell of the president at the time; their positions could easily change in a few hours or even a few minutes. Moreover, the administration head-counters had to have the names of those who were willing to support them and most of those who had been swayed by the president's speech were not talking. "If he changed minds," Representative Gradison said after the meeting, "the changed minds were attached to quiet bodies."

The White House still needed to nail down fifty firm ayes, and it had little time left. Many GOP leaders who normally corralled votes for the administration were unwilling to help this time; indeed, most of them were still rounding up opponents to the bill. That meant the Treasury and the White House had to hunt for votes themselves.

Baker, Darman, Thompson, and Oglesby set up shop in an office in the corner of the Capitol, off the rotunda, that housed the staff of Minority Leader Michel. They worked the phones, calling those members they thought might be willing to support the president. "Anyone who didn't tell us to go to hell, question our ancestry, and throw us out of the door, we put down as undecided," Dennis Thomas recalls. Even with such a broad definition of undecided, the undecideds and supporters together totaled only sixty-five names. The administration had to win over fifty of those into the solid supporters' column.

The Treasury and White House officials called every lawmaker on their list. When members said they were still undecided, they would get another call in thirty minutes to see if they had decided yet. If members could not be reached by telephone, White House lobbyists would wander the hallways and catch them as they went to vote, or as they left the House floor to go to the rest room. Baker did much of the calling himself, contacting more than twenty members in the few hours before the deadline. In his calm Texas style, he let the Republican members know the consequences of defeating the president's top priority. He was not harsh or demanding, but he was persistent. "The president really needs you," he would say. "We can't be the ones to kill the bill. We'll fix it up in the Senate. And if we don't fix it up, let me tell you right here, I'll recommend a veto."

Members who were still sitting on the fence saw this as an opportunity to swap their votes for favors from the White House, and they began horse trading. Eager to get fifty supporters, the administration team was more than willing to deal. Representative Steven Gunderson of Wisconsin said he would support the tax bill if President Reagan would promise to sign the farm legislation his rural district needed; the White House agreed. Representative George Gekas of Pennsylvania said he would change his vote if the administration would take a look at his proposal to have staggered filing dates for tax returns; Baker agreed. Representative Nancy Johnson of Connecticut promised to switch if the cabinet would consider placing import quotas on machine tools; Baker promised to look into that as well. California Representative Al McCandless asked for Treasury figures showing how typical taxpayers in his state would fare; Thompson had those quickly prepared. One congressman asked Baker to come to his state and help in his reelection campaign; Baker said he would. "Boy, they weren't bashful," Baker recalls.

The count fluctuated from moment to moment. Sometimes, a member would agree to vote for the bill, but then word would leak back down to the administration head-counters that he had changed his mind. Names came on the list, then went off again. Getting a firm count proved exceedingly difficult. Representative Marjorie Holt told the White House she would vote for the rule, but only if her vote was absolutely necessary to make the goal of fifty. "It was an excruciating process," recalls Oglesby. "We didn't have many happy voters."

By 6:00 P.M., the administration team had rounded up forty-eight votes. They were still two votes down, and they were running out of possibilities. Despite the shortfall, Baker called Regan to tell him they had the votes and to have the president call O'Neill. Baker pushed for the call because time was running out and he was reasonably confident that he could make the promise of fifty votes come true, but, as Lott would say later, tax reform at that point was within two votes and two hours of death.

Shortly after six o'clock, the White House operator made a call to O'Neill's office, saying the president wished to speak with him right away. Aides promised to get the message to the speaker, and finally got through to the telephone in his car, but O'Neill did not call back. The eight-o'clock deadline passed, and no return phone call came from O'Neill. Another hour went by; still there was no call. For nearly four hours, the president and his aides waited, not knowing where the Speaker was or why he was refusing to return the call. Baker was nervous; he felt certain the speaker had decided to let the bill die. Why else would he ignore a call from the president of the United States? The strenuous effort of the last week seemed ready to go up in smoke.

Finally, at 10:00 P.M., the Speaker returned the president's call. He had been dining at the University Club with a friend, his aides said later, and had taken his time in calling back. Said O'Neill, "I didn't call back because I had other things to do at that particular time." The two aging symbols of their respective parties spoke only briefly. President Reagan said he had the fifty votes; O'Neill said, "Okay, Mr. President, we'll bring her up tomorrow."

A meeting of the Rules Committee was hastily convened for that night, and at 11:45 P.M. a new rule—virtually identical to the first one except that it allowed a vote on the nonbinding Michel resolution—was approved by the committee and sent to the House floor for action the next day.

Earlier that same evening, the White House sent a letter to Kemp and Michel, promising not to sign any bill that failed to meet certain minimum requirements. The letter had been worked out over several days between Darman and the two House members. Treasury was particularly anxious to have the support of both men—Michel, because he was minority leader; Kemp, because he was, in Darman's words, "the Republican definition of tax reform." In the letter, the president promised not to sign any bill that did not establish a $2,000 exemption "at least for those individuals in the lower and middle income tax brackets." He also said he would not accept a bill that did not include basic tax incentives for American industry or that had a top individual rate higher than 35 percent. Baker and Darman later boasted privately that the letter committed them to nothing new: The president was already adamant about the 35-percent top rate, the "lower and middle income" language gave them plenty of room to compromise on the personal exemption, and "basic tax incentives for American industry" was vague enough to allow almost anything. Nevertheless, the letter provided important cover for Kemp, whose Republican conference was still insistent upon opposing the bill and who still needed a reason to reverse his prior position. With the president's letter in hand, Kemp decided to change course and support the measure.

Still, the game was not over. There would be three votes the next day: one on the rule, one on a motion to recommit the bill to the committee for further work, and one on final passage. The administration had to keep its fifty reluctant Republican supporters in line throughout all three votes. That was not going to be easy, especially with Lott's efficient whip group doing all it could to win the fifty back.

To police the floor the next day, Baker decided to put together his own ad hoc whip organization. He chose the members for the group carefully. There were three pro-reform members of the Ways and Means Committee who knew the substance of the bill: Guy Vander Jagt of Michigan, Hal Daub of Nebraska, and Bill Gradison of Ohio; moderate Republican Claudine Schneider of Rhode Island, who would help bring in other Northeasterners; and a few older, well-respected members of the party like Henry Hyde of Illinois and William S. Broomfield of Michigan.

Before the voting began, O'Neill came down from his podium, stepped into the well, and gave a moving speech. The chamber was filled; they all knew that a historic vote was about to happen. When the speaker began to talk, the large room fell silent.

Before I came to Congress, when I was actively interested in politics, I remember the Tax Department during the war coming up with a comprehensive tax-reform bill. It was during the war, so it never saw the light of day.

People clamored for it, and people said we needed it. Wilbur Mills, during the 1950s, held hearings. The hearings got nowhere. My own beloved Jack Kennedy came forward with a tax bill—tax reform and a tax cut at the same time. In order to stimulate the economy at that time, Congress approved the tax cut but forgot about tax reform. Jimmy Carter, his heart and mind set on tax reform, did not get it. We came out with a tax cut. That has been the history of tax reform for the last forty years. We are closer to it now than we have ever been before.

The result of forty years of only talking about reform is that the American people have lost confidence in the fairness and the integrity of our tax laws. Our country used to have the greatest voluntary tax system in the world. Americans paid their taxes with pride. But along the line, this voluntary tax system of ours has been threatened, threatened by a widespread perception that some segments of our society are not paying their fair share of the costs of this Democracy.

Let me say this to you, Republicans on that side and Democrats on this side: All of us Americans, America, the people are crying for fairness in our tax code. . . . I ask you to vote for the rule. I ask you to vote for the bill. I ask you to send it to the other body so that ultimately both parties can work out the final passage.

Any misgivings the speaker had about the tax-reform effort had by that time disappeared. The rule passed 258–168, with the help of seventy Republicans—including Michel and Kemp. A solid majority of Democrats backed the rule, though fewer than half of the Republicans did the same. A few hours later, the Republican effort to "recommit" the bill, or send it back to the Ways and Means Committee, was defeated 256–171, with only forty-nine GOP members voting against it.

Then came the day's unexpected climax. At 10:55 P.M., the speaker, now in his chair looking over the House floor, called for a vote on the bill.

As is customary, he called first for a voice vote, expecting the Republicans would then demand a recorded vote. "The question is on the bill," he said in a perfunctory manner. "All those in favor say aye, opposed no, the bill is passed." He then looked to the Republican side of the chamber, expecting to see a Republican member rise and call for a roll call, but no one moved. The speaker banged his gavel, and it was done.

The Republicans, in a moment of confusion, had missed their only opportunity. A few Republicans made a show of complaining that the speaker had gaveled too quickly, but any fair witness could see that the Republicans had simply made a mistake. Six days after the president had suffered an ignominious defeat, the overhaul of the nation's tax system—numbered H.R. 3838—was approved by the House of Representatives without even a recorded vote.

The House action defied the predictions of countless pundits. The bill was less than most reformers had hoped for, to be sure. It left many tax breaks untouched, and many others were only slightly trimmed. It was, in many ways, a massive halfway measure. But the House bill had shown that under the right conditions, members of Congress would cast a vote for a tax bill that was in the general interest, even though it went against the wishes of legions of powerful lobbyists. It showed that, under the right circumstances, the special interests could be defeated.

After the vote, Rostenkowski held a press conference and a celebration. Secretary Baker, who stood near the chairman, was asked if he wanted to join the festivities. "No," he replied, "this is Rosty's night."

At the press conference, Rostenkowski raised a glass of champagne, poured for him by a lobbyist from his pro-reform coalition, and gave the following toast: "To an accomplishment of the House of Representatives and to a bumpy ride in the Senate."

He, like many other students of Congress, thought the Senate would be the graveyard for tax reform.

Chapter 8

The Gucci Boys' Revenge

As the House thrashed over tax reform on the night of December 17, Senator Packwood hosted his office Christmas party. It was a festive event, held in the Commerce Committee hearing room, just a few steps down the hall from Senator's personal offices in the Russell Building. The congressional session had lasted far longer than anyone expected that year, and the last few weeks had been hectic. The year-end recess was finally about to begin, and Packwood's staff was ready for a celebration. The beer and wine flowed freely, and staffers gathered around a piano, filling the room with slightly off-key renditions of popular Christmas carols.

But the senator, who usually had a hearty appetite for such parties, was out of sorts. He joined the caroling only in spurts. Every few minutes, he drifted away from the lighthearted crowd and walked down the hall to his office, where a television set was tuned to the raging debate on the House floor. For a long time, Packwood had tried to ignore the tax bill, judging that its chances for survival in the House were slim. Now the House was about to finish its work, and the political hot potato was going to be tossed into his hands. Neither he nor most of his Finance Committee members wanted anything to do with the controversial legislation, but once the House passed the bill, they would be under pressure to act. "We held our breath to the last minute," an aide recalls, "hoping something would go wrong."

The House passed the sweeping measure that evening, denying Packwood's Christmas wish and putting him on the spot. He and his committee had to fashion a tax-reform bill of their own now, or they would be accused by the president and the press of scuttling reform. Few people in the Senate seemed to have any interest in tax reform, but institutional politics dictated that the Senate, and Packwood in particular, somehow produce a bill. The Finance Committee chairman had been backed into a corner, and for the next six months, he would be consumed with the effort to extricate himself from that uncomfortable position. The odds were against him, and it would be only with great difficulty, after coming perilously close to failure, that he would succeed at the task.

The smart money in the Washington establishment was betting against Packwood. His Finance panel was a bastion of pro-business sentiment, heavily favored with the attentions and cash of the nation's wealthiest business executives and special-interest groups. There was no place in Congress where tax breaks were more treasured or where a corporate tax hike of the magnitude proposed in the House bill—$140 billion over five years—was less welcome. The committee had traditionally been a lobbyists' haven, and the opponents of reform knew it was their last and best chance to stop the bill. They had never expected tax reform to pass the House, but they felt certain that an all-out lobbying effort could halt it in the Senate.

The amount of time, money, and effort expended on tax lobbying throughout 1985 and 1986 was enough to overwhelm even the most cynical congressional observer. With billions of dollars of tax breaks on the line, major corporations, trade associations, and pressure groups hired the biggest names in Washington to protect themselves. The result was perverse: The populist tax bill, an all-out attack on the special interests that swarmed over the nation's capital, was producing a huge windfall for the lobbyists who represented those interests. Some wags began to refer to the bill as the "Lobbyists' Relief Act of 1986." Fred Wertheimer, president of the citizens' lobby Common Cause, quipped, "It's not clear yet what the tax-reform fight is going to mean for the average taxpayer, but Washington special-interest lobbyists have just landed in hog heaven."

Many of the lobbyists were former members of Congress and former aides, whose stock-in-trade was their expertise in the system and their access to old colleagues and bosses. The lucrative allure of tax reform caused ever more of these people to join the lobbyists' ranks. Congressional and administration officials were transformed, almost overnight, from being the people sought out for tax favors to the people who were doing the seeking. They traded power for money. Two of Rostenkowski's former top aides—John Salmon and James Healey—were included among their ranks; both had left the Hill after many years to earn the big bucks of lobbying. Salmon represented a liquor company and one of the nation's largest tax-shelter syndicators; Healey worked for Allied Signal, Exxon, Johnson & Johnson, Chrysler-Mitsubishi, Union Pacific, Bethlehem Steel, and the investment banking house Salomon Brothers. Buck Chapoton, the former Treasury tax official, also used his expertise to secure a highly paid lobbying position for commercial banks. Roderick DeArment, formerly Dole's staff director on the Finance Committee, lobbied for a group of chief executive officers who favored reductions in corporate tax rates, as well as for the Solar Energy Industries Association and for a trade association of cellular-telephone companies.

Tax lobbyists were a virtual who's who of the once-powerful in Washington. There were mini–alumni associations that comprised lobbyists who had once worked in the Senate for Russell Long, Bob Dole, or Lloyd Bentsen of Texas. Their world was a kind of inbred village, in which everybody knew everybody else, and in which information swirled like gossip. It was a tightly knit network of tax insiders and former insiders. Everyone talked the same language and sought the same facts. "All of us have just come off the Hill. We worked with the people we lobby. They're our friends," explained lobbyist Denise Bode, a former aide to Senator David Boren, Democrat of Oklahoma.

There was plenty of work for everyone: U.S. Steel hired Kip O'Neill, the son of House Speaker Tip O'Neill; Senator Dole's daughter worked as a lobbyist for the real estate sales firm Century 21. Companies were tripping over each other to get their points across. The law firm of Patton Boggs & Blow, which was run by Tommy Boggs, the son of late House Majority Leader Hale Boggs, housed two hostile, corporate coalitions: the Coalition to Reduce High Effective Tax Rates, which favored reform's goal of abolishing tax breaks to pay for lower rates, and the Basic Industries Coalition, which favored retaining corporate tax breaks, even if it meant higher rates.

There was so much business that the best-known lobbyists in town complained about a flood of new competition. J. D. Williams, a former aide to the late Senator Robert Kerr of Oklahoma, groused that he was losing business to upstart "boutique" lobbying firms. "They are doing well because the established firms are getting more business than they can possibly handle," he said.

Lobbyists—or often their young, lower-paid legal assistants—lined up early each morning to get seats at the tax-writing markups. At Ways and Means, before the sessions were closed to the public, some eager committee-watchers would arrive as early as 5:30 A.M. to get at the head of the queue and have a chance for a front-row seat. The line sometimes stretched the entire length of the hallway, a city block long, and then wrapped around the corner. There were so many people that it looked like the committee was giving something away—which, at times, it was.

The lines were immense each day, no matter what subject the committee was discussing. Representative Pete Stark, Democrat of California, devised a formula to explain the phenomenon, which was equally pronounced in both the Senate and the House: "The fewer the number of taxpayers affected, and the more dull and arcane the subject, the longer the line of lobbyists." Some of those standing in the hall or sitting in the Senate's wired-for-sound auditorium two floors below billed their clients upward of $400 an hour for their loitering. Others charged as much as $10,000 a month per client.

The involvement of lobbyists extended beyond the sterile halls of congressional office buildings. Washington was a virtual money machine, and lobbyists provided much of the fuel. Fundraisers of one kind or another were held almost every night of the week, and lobbyists would stuff checks in their pockets and jump from one to another. It was as if there were a nightly sale, and the members of Congress were the merchandise. Evenings were filled with so much drinking and eating at fundraiser cocktail parties that several of the biggest lobbyists in town had to put themselves on "controlled fasts" under the care of a diet doctor during the tax-reform effort. J. D. Williams, Tommy Boggs, James Free of Charls E. Walker Associates, Robert Barrie of General Electric, and Geoffrey Peterson of the Distilled Spirits Council all decided that they did not have to be the fattest corporate lobbyists in town to be the most successful.

Staying slim was not an easy discipline to maintain. On one night alone in 1985, whole troupes of lobbyists sped the half-mile from a $500-a-head fundraiser for John Duncan of Ways and Means to another $500-a-head event for Chairman Rostenkowski's PAC. In addition to shrimp, ice cream, and beer, those who attended the Rostenkowski fundraiser received buttons that read: I DID BETTER THAN WRITE ROSTY.

The results of this spree were obvious to anyone who paid a visit to the public-disclosure room of the Federal Election Commission in downtown Washington. The crowded, bustling office was located at the far end of the K Street corridor where many of the capital city's twenty thousand or so lobbyists kept their posh offices. There, in row upon row of photostats and microfilm, were the detailed records for the millions of campaign dollars that each year flowed from special-interest PACs into the campaign chests of the nation's elected representatives.

The largesse was gruesome in its volume. Lawmakers from an earlier era would probably have been ashamed to collect so much money from so many special pleaders or, at least, to allow the public to know that they did. But times had changed; expectations were different in 1985 and 1986. Politics and money were as inseparable as salt and pepper.

During the eighteen months that ended June 30, 1986—the period that encompassed most of the congressional tax-reform debate—PACs contributed the staggering sum of $66.8 million to House and Senate candidates, according to a *Wall Street Journal* tabulation. That was a 32-percent increase from the record $50.7 million they had given to congressional candidates during the comparable period in the previous election cycle. That, in turn, was more than double the amount that was given two years earlier.

As the favored targets of money-laden PACs, members of the congressional tax-writing committees found it particularly easy to fill their campaign coffers. In 1985, congressional tax writers received $19.8 million in campaign contributions, a remarkably large sum considering there was not even an election that year. What's more, that was double the amount they raised in 1983, according to Common Cause. Of this total, $6.7 million came from special-interest PACs, which was two and a half times their 1983 giving. The twenty members of the Senate Finance Committee banked a total of $11.8 million in 1985, up from $6.4 million in 1983. The thirty-six members of the Ways and Means Committee received nearly $8 million in 1985, up from $3.5 million two years earlier.

Tax bills brought out the greed in everybody involved, and tax reform was the ultimate tax bill. Iowa Republican Charles Grassley explained the surge in giving that occurred between 1983 and 1985 this way: "We didn't have a tax bill in 1983," the senator told the *Los Angeles Times*. "Now people are anticipating a major tax bill." The effort promised to leave no corner of the nation's massive tax code untouched, and that meant billions of dollars of special breaks were on the chopping block.

Members were eager to cash in. In normal times, a ticket to a congressional fundraiser would cost $250. But with tax reform, the admission price doubled and sometimes quadrupled for Ways and Means and Finance Committee members. Representative Frank Guarini, Democrat of New Jersey and a junior member of Ways and Means, hosted breakfasts that commanded $1,000 per person. Representative Ronnie Flippo, Democrat of Alabama and a relative newcomer to Ways and Means, threw large cocktail parties and dinners that cost $500 and $1,000 a shot. Guarini explained the premium pricing to *The Washington Post:*

So many different industries and groups stand to be affected by this, and there's a lot of anxiety. When there's that much concern, the opportunities for fundraising increase. People want to have access. They want to put their two cents in. Or their thousand dollars.

The hunger for money was insatiable. The ascendance of expensive television advertising made the cost of getting elected astronomical, even for candidates from the most rural states and far-flung districts. Expenditures of hundreds of thousands of dollars were routine in House elections; many millions of dollars were spent on Senate races. Even politicians with secure seats sought contributions. The more money they had, the more they could contribute to their colleagues. The more they gave away, the more powerful they could become in Congress. Members like Representative Jim Wright of Texas did not have any worries about their own reelections, but they hoarded hundreds of thousands of dollars as "leadership funds," which they distributed to fellow House members to help secure votes for their own moves up the leadership ladder. This generosity helped to elevate Wright from majority leader to speaker at the end of 1986.

From January 1, 1985, to June 30, 1986, the top recipients of PAC contributions in the Senate included Finance Committee members Bob Dole ($839,319), Steve Symms of Idaho ($870,560), and Charles Grassley of Iowa ($668,526). During 1985, while Ways and Means was considering tax reform, the top PAC recipients in the House included Ways and Means members Sam Gibbons of Florida ($317,096), Henson Moore of Louisiana ($333,620), James Jones of Oklahoma ($343,592), and Wyche Fowler of Georgia ($223,060).

So much money was floating around Washington that even lawmakers themselves began to look askance. Rostenkowski, whose own panhandling missions to Los Angeles, New York, and St. Louis brought him more than $500,000 during the tax-reform years, told *The Wall Street Journal* that he was "nauseated" at the influence that campaign money seemed to have on some of his own Ways and Means members. GOP Senator Barry Goldwater of Arizona, who was always one to speak his mind, agreed: "It is not 'We, the people,' but political action committees and moneyed interests who are setting the nation's political agenda and are influencing the position of candidates on the important issues of the day."

When normal channels for this lucre were tapped out, members and contributors resorted to more creative—and more questionable—routes. Federal election laws that limited contributions were routinely circumvented to channel even more money into the coffers of politicians. New terms were invented to describe the different routes. There was *hard money:* straight contributions subject to federal limitation; and *soft money:* indirect gifts of services, such as telephone banks and studio time, which were not subject to any legal restraint and which aided candidates without going directly into their treasuries. In addition to campaign funds, members also received "honoraria" for giving speeches, or in some cases, just for showing up at meetings with well-heeled pleaders—that money went directly into the lawmakers' pockets. Tax writers regularly jetted all over the nation to address groups that wanted favors done in the tax-reform bill, charging two thousand dollars a pop.

Occasionally, even top aides to tax-writing members dipped into this brimming money pot. Bill Diefenderfer, Packwood's big-bellied top man at the Finance Committee, moaned about his loss of income when he left a job as a lobbyist to return to Packwood's service during tax overhaul. But he managed to supplement his lower salary ($72,000 a year) by accepting honoraria for giving speeches in such places as New York, Chicago, and Boca Raton, to groups with an interest in tax overhaul. In 1985, he gave fifteen speeches and pocketed $14,250. He spoke to Northwestern Mutual Life, the Real Estate Tax Institute, the American Trucking Association, and the Grocery Manufacturers of America, among others.

In 1985, the top honoraria recipients in the Senate, according to Common

Cause, included tax writers Bob Dole ($127,993), John Chafee of Rhode Island ($57,606), Charles Grassley of Iowa ($55,460), and Bill Bradley ($46,800). In the House, big honoraria recipients included Ways and Means members Bill Frenzel ($48,500), Pete Stark ($47,800), Bob Matsui ($38,250), and James Jones ($35,834). Some of this money was given away by the members to charity, but not all of it.

The benefits from the lobbyists went beyond honoraria. An investigation by Common Cause found that, in addition to the typical $1,000 or $2,000 speaking fee, some groups also picked up the tab for members and their families during extended stays at the posh resorts where speeches were delivered. Senator David Durenberger, Republican of Minnesota, and his two sons got the equivalent of more than $5,000 in travel costs for a six-day trip to Puerto Rico from groups seeking to keep the island's tax credit. Senator Max Baucus, Democrat of Montana, and Representative Phil Crane, Republican of Illinois, and their wives received separate week-long Caribbean cruises from cruise-line companies. Representative Barbara Kennelly, Democrat of Connecticut, and her husband received a six-day stay in Pebble Beach, near Carmel, California, at the expense of the Connecticut Business and Industry Association, according to Common Cause.

The top honoraria recipient in the House in 1985 was Rostenkowski. He took thirty-six trips and had earnings of $137,500, most of which went to charity. He did not disclose the destinations of his trips, having been burned in the past by revelations of his excursions at special-interest expense. Instead, he listed "travel" or "travel and lodging with spouse" beside the name of each trade association or business group that picked up his tab.

When it came to raising money from special interests, Senator Packwood was the champ. As Finance Committee chairman, he possessed enormous power, and as a result, he became a magnet for campaign contributions from almost every monied interest and political action committee in the nation. He was Congress's top PAC-man. During the eighteen months of the tax-reform effort, Packwood outpaced any other member of Congress in special-interest PAC receipts with $992,017.

Contributions came from almost everywhere; he received the maximum $5,000 contribution allowed by law for his primary campaign from ninety-six different interest groups, according to one calculation. Between 1981 and the time of his general election in 1986, he had collected from all sources well over $6 million, which was nearly nine dollars for every person who eventually voted for him in the general election.

Packwood put together a sophisticated system to haul in this loot. He hosted exclusive breakfast meetings of insurance executives, union leaders, and anyone else who would contribute $5,000 to his campaign. The contributors got the benefit of Packwood's opinions during the monthly meetings in his office, and Packwood, in turn, got the benefit of using the groups as a base for further fundraising. Packwood also had an aggressive direct-mail drive that targeted groups that supported his pro-Israel, pro–women's rights, and pro-abortion stands. That effort raised more than $3 million.

In addition, Packwood was the beneficiary of a gaping loophole in the campaign-contribution laws. In 1985, a committee of successful insurance salesmen funneled more than $168,000 into Packwood's reelection fund. The group, called Alignpac, was formed to beat back reform proposals to tax inside buildup on insurance policies and deny deductions for interest paid on money borrowed against policies. Alignpac managed to circumvent the federally imposed $5,000-per-election limit on PAC-giving by urging its members to make checks out directly to Packwood rather than to the PAC. The committee then bundled the checks together and sent them out to the lawmaker's campaign headquarters.

In 1985, Packwood hit the road and held a series of ten $1,000-a-plate fundraisers at the nation's big-money centers. The stops included the Helmsley Palace in New York City, the Loews Anatole Hotel in Dallas, the Mayflower Hotel in Washington, and the Ritz Carlton Hotel in Chicago. The spree netted $2.4 million, and during one night at the Century Plaza Hotel in Los Angeles, Packwood raised half a million dollars, which was more than he spent in his entire first campaign for the Senate in 1968.

"Raising money for Bob Packwood is like making love to a seven-hundred-pound gorilla," Lester Pollack, a longtime Packwood friend, told *The Washington Post*. "It doesn't make a difference when you get tired."

Over the years, Packwood's contributors were amply rewarded for their check-writing stamina. Like most of his colleagues on the Finance Committee, Packwood was no champion of tax reform. Reform meant cleansing the code of credits, deductions, and exclusions. Packwood saw his job as doing the exact opposite. An unabashed advocate of using the income tax to give incentives to private industry and to promote social action, he managed to enact so many tax preferences that his staff thought of the long list as a kind of "Packwood plan."

Though Packwood claimed to be as "predictable as the sun rising" when it came to taxes, there was little else predictable about the aggressive chairman. He was a man with a long history of doing the opposite of what people expected him to do. Indeed, few members of Congress were harder to understand or to categorize than Robert William Packwood. He had a bright, if sometimes undisciplined, mind; a bulldog nature that refused to accept defeat; and an openness, some say a naïveté, that permitted him to take huge risks.

Packwood's family history possessed more than a hint of this volatile nature. His great-grandfather was an adventurer and a con man, an opportunist and a legislator. Bob Packwood loved to tell his story. It goes like this:

William Henderson Packwood, a native of Illinois, joined the army and served in California at the time of the great gold rush. The temptation of riches was too much to pass up, and he promptly deserted to seek his fortune. But he did not find gold. He was captured and sentenced to serve a term as a prison laborer in the godforsaken wilderness north of California known as the Oregon Territory. As luck would have it, he was shipwrecked en route off the coast of what is now Curry County in southernmost Oregon. He put down roots there long enough to prosper and get elected to the fledgling state's constitutional convention in 1857. He traveled to Salem to attend the conclave and liked the city so much that he never returned to the remote outback he came from. He did travel, however, to eastern Oregon, where he allegedly bilked gold miners in a scam that involved a waterway that he promised, but never built. Despite these undertakings, he managed to remain prominent in state politics.

Bob Packwood's father—William Packwood's grandson—was not a criminal, but he was a lobbyist and was closely involved in the political life of Oregon all his life. Frederick William Packwood worked for thirty years representing the interests of the Associated Oregon Industries, a business group, before the state legislature. A bitter dispute over the organization's stand against workmen's compensation caused the elder Packwood to leave the organization and to make a startling change in his allegiance. Frederick Packwood was fired from the business association and promptly went to work for the nation's largest labor group, the AFL-CIO. Years later, his son would become one of the few politicians who backed the causes of both organized labor and business.

Following in his father's footsteps, Bob Packwood showed an early interest in politics. He studied political science at Willamette University, where one of the teachers was Mark Hatfield, later Packwood's senior colleague from Oregon in the Senate. He attended faraway New York University Law School on scholarship, did a brief stint as an Oregon Supreme Court law clerk, and then went to work as a labor lawyer, representing management. At age twenty-seven, he became the Republican county chairman in heavily Democratic Portland. Three years later, in 1962, he was elected to the Oregon State House by dint of his political savvy and a studious avoidance of issues. His sparsely worded campaign brochures featured an oversized photograph of Packwood with his golden hair coiffed like the youthful Jack Kennedy. He served in the legislature for three two-year terms before attempting a dark-horse candidacy against Senator Wayne Morse, an Oregon institution in the U.S. Senate since 1944.

When Packwood started his drive for the Senate, only 10 percent of the electorate had any notion who he was, but that did not stop the ambitious young legislator. He positioned himself to the right of Morse, especially on the issue of the U.S. involvement in Vietnam. He criticized the senator for voting to cut off funding for the war, and he made an issue out of Morse himself. Packwood successfully painted the senator as an outcast in his own party, unable to win federal money for the state. He also played up the advantages of his own youth against Morse's sixty-eight years. It was a finely tuned political campaign effort, which included an army of young volunteers and plenty of lawn signs and bumper stickers. Packwood won by the narrow margin of 3,293 votes out of the 814,000 cast. He was sent to the Senate as its youngest member, at the age of thirty-six.

Most freshman senators try to start slowly, and to concentrate on things close to home. Bill Bradley's first bill, for example, was a plan for a new waterworks in Paterson, New Jersey. Brash Bob Packwood was different— his initial piece of legislation was a proposal to abolish the seniority system for committee chairmanships. It was an act of rebellion for a junior member of the collegial Senate, and it angered his senior colleagues. The proposal went nowhere.

Packwood always took pride in his outspokenness, reasoning that Oregon voters tolerated—indeed, appreciated—an iconoclast. During a White House meeting at the height of the Watergate scandal, Packwood looked President Nixon straight in the eye and said, "Your weakness is credibility. This has always been your short suit with the news media and the general public."

The young senator went on to strike the first of many liberal poses that quickly branded him as a maverick in the Republican ranks. He played a key role in helping the Democrats kill President Nixon's nominations of Clement Haynesworth and G. Harrold Carswell to the Supreme Court. Next, he turned his attention to the powder-keg issue of abortion and sided with those who wanted abortions legalized. In 1970, three years before the landmark Supreme Court decision that gave women the legal right to have an abortion, he introduced a model law that would have both sanctioned and regulated abortions in the District of Columbia. He also introduced a bill that would have legalized abortions nationwide. Neither bill attracted a single cosponsor.

The measures earned him the everlasting enmity of anti-abortion groups across the country, which labeled him "Senator Death." (When he became Finance Committee chairman, a political opponent expanded that to "Senator Death-and-Taxes.") After his first decade in the Senate, he had gained a reputation as a gadfly, and he seemed forever afflicted with high staff turnover. He fancied that his views might have a rejuvenating effect on the GOP, but he seemed to be one of the few Republicans who thought so.

In 1978, Packwood began to play a more mainstream role as a member of the Commerce Committee. He wrestled with the difficulties of deregulation—in trucking, broadcasting, and passenger airlines—and found a platform to espouse his developing economic vision. "There's no reason why we should be controlling capitalistic acts by consenting adults," he said. In 1981, Packwood was elevated to the chairmanship of the committee when the Republicans took control of the Senate in the wake of the Reagan landslide. He also became more adept at manipulating the Senate rules to win favors for his home state. Budget Committee staffers coined a verb to describe his skill at inserting pork-barrel amendments into spending bills: *Packwooding.*

Even as he climbed the ladder of Senate leadership, gaining more seniority and responsibility, Packwood maintained his penchant for candor and independence. He became one of President Reagan's most visible antagonists.

In 1981, Packwood, a longtime supporter of Israel, led the fight in the Senate against the Reagan-approved sale of advanced radar planes, or AWACs, to Saudi Arabia. It was a long, fierce, and dirty battle. After a meeting between Packwood and the president in the Oval Office, White House aides put out the word that Packwood had been rude and had bluntly warned that backing the sale would lose Jewish contributions and votes for the GOP. In the end, Packwood was defeated and the sale went through.

His problems with President Reagan worsened considerably in 1982. That year, Packwood did more than oppose the president's legislation; he viciously attacked Reagan's intelligence and judgment. Serving at the time as chairman of the Senate Republican Campaign Committee, the rebellious senator publicly accused President Reagan of chasing away blacks, Jews, women, and blue-collar workers from the Republican party with what he derided as Reagan's "idealized concept of America." He portrayed Reagan as a buffoon who told mindless anecdotes in answer to serious questions. After listening to Reagan stories, such as one about poor people buying vodka with food stamps, Packwood said he and his colleagues would "just shake our heads."

"The Republican party has just about written off those women who work for wages in the marketplace. We are losing them in droves. You cannot write them off and the blacks off and the Hispanics off and the Jews off and assume you're going to build a party on white Anglo-Saxon males over forty," Packwood said. "There aren't enough of us."

Packwood's tirade was too much for the president's backers. The Oregon Republican had been remarkably successful as head of the party's Senatorial Campaign Committee, raising money through direct mail to expand the committee's take to $40 million in 1981–82, from a mere $2 million in 1975–76. But that success was not enough to save his job. The day after he made his comments, Packwood was forced to apologize to the president. Joseph Coors, the arch-conservative brewer, started to organize a boycott of the campaign committee.

After the 1982 elections, Packwood was voted out of the campaign committee job, at the behest of the White House, and was replaced by the more compliant Senator Richard Lugar of Indiana. "Being a maverick is great," said Senator Paul Laxalt of Nevada, the president's best friend in Congress and the agent of Packwood's undoing that year, "but it's a luxury you can't afford in leadership."

Packwood was an obsessively organized man who demanded that things be done his way. He sometimes arrived in his office at six in the morning to study the loose-leaf briefing books that his staff painstakingly compiled for him each day. Each page in the briefing books was triple-punched and double-spaced as he instructed. The books themselves had to have metal hinges because, Packwood explained, they made the binders easier to handle, especially for the volume of material he had to digest as chairman.

The willful Oregonian never did anything halfway. Years before tax overhaul, when he was afflicted with cataracts and unable to read, he had tax law read to him each morning. Even after surgery improved his vision, his eyesight remained less than optimal. He had to ask the television networks to use filtered lights during Finance Committee markups, because the glare hurt his eyes. In normal office light, Packwood sometimes had trouble recognizing people who were standing across a room.

Details were important to him, and time was never wasted. When he campaigned at home, Packwood took a secretary with him in his big white van, dubbed the "White Whale," so that thank-you notes to the previous host could be written before he reached the next stop. His driver recorded almost every campaign stop with a video camera. At the end of the day, Packwood recorded his thoughts on a tape recorder for a diary that was transcribed by a friend.

Details were also preserved in meticulous briefing books that covered each of Oregon's thirty-six counties. Each book contained the county's history, its federally funded projects with dollar amounts, and a record of Packwood's own past appearances there. The county books also had long lists of names, with red dots next to business leaders whose correspondence needed to be answered quickly.

Packwood was a man of intensity and flawless precision in everything he did. At home, his music cassettes were always in alphabetical order. He kept a stopwatch on his steering wheel to time his trips. Even games for him were more than just fun. He had been known to play squash with bloodied knees. Once, his friends set him up for a practical joke by giving him the phrase *motherfucker* to act out in a game of charades. Packwood went at the task with vigor: He easily got the players to guess the first word by making a rocking-cradle motion with his arms. For the second word, he got right down on his stomach and made rapid, up and down motions. After a long while, Packwood's wife, Georgie, who was not in on the joke, shouted, "Mother push-ups!"

Packwood's favorite movie was *Lawrence of Arabia,* and he idolized the eccentric lead character in that film as "a man with a zealous discipline intent upon pursuing a goal that he's already decided on." Like anyone whose life was so orderly and rigid, Packwood sometimes acted impetuously when crossed. He berated aides mercilessly when they disagreed with him, or even when he thought they did. He did not suffer fools gladly. Even small infractions would chafe him: Driving in heavy traffic through downtown Portland in 1985, he repeatedly barked orders about alternative routes he insisted would speed the journey. He suspected his friends of working against him. During the tax debate, Packwood once said of his allies in the Reagan administration, "They'll sell me out in a minute." These tendencies inspired some congressional staffers to give him the name "Cap'n Bob," after the paranoid Captain Queeg in *The Caine Mutiny*.

For all this harshness, Packwood had a soft side. Staffers he once chewed out would later become his friends; all would be forgotten. To his own staffers, he was incredibly loyal. He helped them get jobs elsewhere in the Republican administration, and when they went to work as lobbyists, he did not hesitate to tell their clients what a fine choice they had made in representation. "He wanted to be thought of as a work-oriented genius," Diefenderfer said, but added that in many ways, Packwood was really "a Jekyll and Hyde."

In his off-hours, Packwood was a beer-drinker and a belly-laugher. He listed his favorite food as pork chops, and he was once asked to leave a pizza parlor for laughing too loudly. In Portland, one of his favorite restaurants was a college hangout called The Cheerful Tortoise, where he knew he could get a pile of nachos and a pitcher of beer and enjoy himself without being bothered by anyone. On weekends, he drove a battered old car and walked around in tattered clothes. In preparation for his high-profile fling with tax overhaul, his wife and staff forced him to endure an overhaul of his personal appearance. The treatment included a new wardrobe—new suits, new stiffly starched shirts, and power-suspenders.

Packwood was also a very private man. He liked to sail, but alone, in one-person boats. He also liked to conceal his ambition to become president of the United States with stories—true ones—about how much he valued his privacy. "I'm not prepared to give up the last shred of privacy I have," he told *People* magazine. "I want to [be able to] go to Shakey's Pizza with my family without being recognized."

Packwood became chairman of the Finance Committee when Bob Dole, his predecessor, was elected majority leader of the Senate in late 1984. Dole had run the committee in a strongly partisan manner, cutting the Democrats out of important tax-writing decisions. Packwood had a very different vision of how to run a committee, which was colored by his admiration for Russell Long, the panel's top Democrat, who had chaired the committee for fifteen years in a bipartisan fashion, and who, during that time, was one of Washington's most powerful people.

Packwood was a student of Long, and at critical junctures throughout the tax-reform debate, he relied on Long's advice and counsel. Long had once told Packwood this basic rule: "When the Congress organizes in January, you want to know where you want to be a year from September. If you know that, you know what you want to achieve, then you can structure all your thinking and organization, planning and everything toward that end."

On the list of things that Packwood initially hoped to achieve as Finance Committee chairman, tax reform did not rank very high. At a breakfast with President Reagan shortly after the release of Treasury I, Packwood said: "I hope you're not going to push simplification for simplification's sake. Simplification for the sake of simplification is to beat your brains out. To go through the whole process and wind up without a dime's dent in the deficit just doesn't make sense."

When Secretary Baker was revising the Treasury plan in the spring of 1985, Packwood threatened to kill the proposal not once, but twice. The first was over the issue of health-insurance fringes. On tax day—April 15—Packwood vowed to a meeting of building trade unions that if the final Reagan plan taxed employer-provided fringes, "I will do everything I can to defeat the bill, no matter what else is in it."

The second threat was over the potential loss of some timber tax breaks. A few days after a potential rival for his Senate seat, Democratic Representative Ron Wyden, held hearings on the president's proposal, Packwood declared: "This isn't tax reform. It's the deliberate act of sabotaging an entire industry and thereby the state of Oregon." "If the breaks were not retained," he said, "I will do everything possible to kill the entire bill." The next day, Packwood retracted the death threat after Secretary Baker made an appeal for moderation. The senator's aides tried to take blame for the belligerent tone of the timber remark, but Packwood later confessed, "I wrote it myself."

If Packwood was not a tax reformer before the House passed its tax-reform bill, his views began to change immediately afterward. First of all, he was chairman of the Finance Committee, and taxes were his arena. He had an institutional responsibility to approve a tax-reform bill, despite any personal inclinations to oppose it. Second, he was up for reelection, and he had to be extra careful to avoid doing anything that would jeopardize his chances. "It's like the gallows focusing the mind," said Deputy Treasury Secretary Darman, describing Packwood's change in attitude after the House sent its bill to the Senate. "There's a different view of capital punishment when the noose is around the neck."

President Reagan had made tax reform his chief domestic initiative for his second term, and as the Republicans' top tax writer in the Republican-controlled Senate, Packwood could not let him down without suffering the consequences. Like Rostenkowski, Packwood had an obligation to his party not to drop the tax-reform ball. To be sure, Packwood had defied the president in the past, but he had suffered for his rebelliousness and had no interest in repeating the mistake. After the 1984 election, he had given

Jim Baker a handwritten note to deliver to the president, which stated that he wanted to be a team player in Reagan's second term, and that he was willing to help the administration in any way he could. Later, at a meeting of senators who were up for reelection, the president called Packwood aside and thanked him for the good wishes. In politics, Packwood says, "you learn there are no permanent enemies or friends, just temporary alliances. You don't bear grudges."

Packwood had ample reason to make amends with the president. He faced a tough primary election challenge in the spring of 1986 from Joe Lutz, a smooth-talking Baptist minister. The common wisdom in Oregon was that the primary was the best opportunity to knock off Packwood, because his support among hard-core Republicans was thin. His pro-choice position on abortion left him open to an attack from the political right wing, and Lutz was going to be a serious rival from that faction of the party.

The chairman's strategy to beat Lutz was to avoid, at all costs, crossing the popular President Reagan, and instead, to hide behind his coattails. "Every year there is one candidate that the press says can't be beat that's beaten," Packwood said, explaining his cautiousness. "I'm trying to make sure that isn't me." If the president wanted to push for tax reform, then Packwood, in 1986 at least, would be a reformer. He pledged his support to the president's effort, and in return, the president praised Packwood in a television commercial made for use during the primary campaign.

In preparation for his new role as reformer, Packwood sat down and thought hard about which of the multitude of tax breaks in the existing tax system he really cared about. He tried to decide which he felt he could not vote to eliminate, even in the name of reform. He came up with only two. They were (1) protecting the tax-free status of fringe benefits and (2) saving tax breaks for the timber industry, which was a staple of the Oregon economy. If a tax-reform bill could be drafted that preserved both of those, he thought, then he could be for tax reform. Packwood, as chairman, wielded enormous authority over the fate of the tax system; yet his tax philosophy boiled down to just these two items: fringe benefits and timber.

Packwood was a zealot for the tax breaks to encourage employee fringe benefits, largely because he hated the idea of national health insurance—an opinion that endeared him to the political action committees of the insurance industry. He feared that unless private employers were given incentive through the tax code to provide health insurance for their workers, the federal government would have to step in to provide it. As a result, he used his monthly breakfast meetings with insurance and labor lobbyists to help coordinate efforts even in the House to fight taxing fringes. On behalf of the insurance industry, he also participated in trade-show films and put his name to newspaper advertisements that promoted the preservation of tax-free fringes.

The timber issue was a matter of political survival. A lawmaker from

Oregon had to support timber the way that a lawmaker from Texas had to support oil. And Packwood was never bashful about stumping for timber. In preparation for a meeting with timber representatives on tax reform in 1985, Packwood's staff prepared a memo that suggested he emphasize four points: "(1) your continuing and unwavering support for their cause; (2) the need for unity among timber concerns; (3) the strong support among various Finance Committee members; and (4) the need to avoid overconfidence merely because they have you on their side. They need to keep up the fight in order to insure that the proposals [that hurt the timber industry] are defeated."

Surely, Packwood thought, it would be possible to draft a reform bill that preserved fringe benefits and timber tax breaks. If he could do that, he could support the president and push hard for reform. Although once the darling of special-interest lobbyists, Bob Packwood decided he must transform himself into a proponent of the most radical overhaul of the tax code in history. It was a remarkable and unexpected reincarnation, but the circumstances that were sucking him into the anomalous role of a leader of tax reform were just too strong to resist. Packwood tried to explain his way out of the situation this way: "The only constant in history is change. I don't write off the possibility that anything can happen. I've been in this business long enough that nothing surprises me."

On the snowy Friday and Saturday of January 24 and 25, 1986, Packwood took a page from the Rostenkowski tax-reform textbook, and packed his committee into a bus for a private retreat in the woods. The Finance Committee retreat was held at a quiet inn in Berkeley Springs, West Virginia. There, Packwood and his members spent twenty-four hours airing the many reasons they did not like the House bill. The crisp mountain air was filled with rhetoric about "international competitiveness" and "savings, investment, and capital formation"—all buzzwords for keeping rather than trimming back corporate tax preferences.

During this formative stage, most of the discussion amounted to posturing, but the group did make one important decision—where to begin. Only one member, Senator John Chafee, Republican of Rhode Island, wanted to use President Reagan's plan as the starting point for the panel's work, and only three Democrats, including Senator Bradley, favored beginning with the House-passed plan. Arch–tax-reform foe David Boren of Oklahoma suggested that the committee direct Packwood to devise a new document that they would use as the basis for the markup.

Boren was betting that a satisfactory document could never be written, that the president's parameters were just too tight. How could anyone devise a plan that would meet all the druthers of the parochial-minded senators, get the top individual rate down to 35 percent from 50 percent, and still manage to raise as much revenue as the existing law? Packwood, Treasury Secretary Baker, and several committee members told reporters after the gathering that they believed it could be done. But hard work lay ahead.

At first, Packwood tried to convince Russell Long to join him in designing the sensitive starting-point document, but the Democrat avoided that trap. The responsibility rested with the chairman, he told his colleagues at Berkeley Springs, "I'm not trying to be co-chairman of this committee."

With the burden on his shoulders alone, Packwood returned to Washington to continue a process that his staff had begun late in the previous year. He interviewed each of his members to find out what they needed in the way of tax breaks to win their support for a bill. In front of the crackling fireplace in his book-lined Senate office, Packwood spent a total of seventy hours meeting with each of his nineteen members. Tax reform was the taking away of breaks to pay for lower rates, but Packwood's theory of building a majority tried to avoid the painful part of the exercise: He wanted to buy tax reform by pleasing his members with giveaways.

Packwood and his staff made long wish lists to use as a guide in this endeavor. One list stated that George Mitchell, Democrat of Maine, wanted to protect tax breaks for three solid-waste disposal facilities back home; that John Danforth, Republican of Missouri, cared about tax-free financing for a St. Louis Cardinals' sports stadium; and that Charles Grassley, Republican of Iowa, hoped to preserve "a growing Christmas tree industry in Iowa." The first three items on the list of Steve Symms of Idaho consisted of one word each: *mining, agriculture,* and *timber.*

The few broader-minded comments contained in the lists were, for the most part, critical of the entire venture. Boren, the Oklahoma Democrat, "opposes tax reform"; David Pryor, Democrat of Arkansas, "found no support for it" at home; and David Durenberger, Republican of Minnesota, believed "the deficit is the top concern."

Still, Packwood plunged ahead. In checking his lists, one fact became clear: He needed a new source of revenue, such as a new sales tax or an oil-import fee, if his plan was going to add to zero. He and his members demanded the retention of too many expensive breaks for the rates to be reduced far enough to satisfy the president. His wish lists were far longer than his hit lists. "No matter how you jimmy it and pry it, you just can't get there by moving the shells around," Packwood said. So the hunt for a new source of revenue began, and tax reform's troubles quickly multiplied.

While Packwood saw no alternative, Bradley thought that the search for a new source of revenue was sending tax reform down the wrong path. The key to success was to focus on the attractiveness of low rates, he thought, not on the pain of eliminating deductions. But he was in a distinct minority. From experience he knew there were a lot of excuses for avoiding tax reform and every one of them could be traced to the kind of dilemma

Packwood was trying to overcome. Bradley placed tax-reform opponents in three categories: those who like the tax code the way it is, those who try to make tax overhaul part of a tax-increase effort, and those who advocate a new form of tax. Over the next several weeks, the tax bill ran into each form of opposition.

The first objection came from a number of senators, mostly Republicans, who argued that reducing the burgeoning budget deficit was far more important than tinkering with the tax code. They saw the massive reorganization of the tax system as a luxury the country could scarcely afford, given the fact that the nation's most crying need was to stanch the flow of red ink that topped the staggering sum of $200 billion a year. Not coincidentally, these senators also were bothered by the massive tax increase that the bill would level on their traditional business constituencies, such as real estate and mining. Senator Rudy Boschwitz, Republican of Minnesota and an expert in campaign fundraising, argued that the budget deficit should be addressed first and that tax reform should be delayed until later. In fact, his proposal was a thinly veiled effort to kill tax reform outright. His allies included Senate Budget Chairman Pete Domenici, Republican of New Mexico; Senator Slade Gorton, Republican of Washington State; and later on, Majority Leader Dole.

A letter drafted by Boschwitz attracted the signatures of fifty senators—half of the Senate—including seven Finance Committee members. It read in part: "Until a firm, definite budget agreement has been reached between Congress and the White House, we do not believe that tax reform should be considered or debated by the United States Senate." White House Chief of Staff Regan was so worried about the letter that he paid a personal visit to Dole's hideaway near the Capitol rotunda to complain about the anti–tax-reform effort, but the sentiment was too strong to stop. Even as the Finance Committee began to draft the bill, the Senate overwhelmingly passed a resolution saying that tax reform should be kept off the Senate floor until the senators first took some action to reduce the deficit. Bradley derided the nonbinding measure as a "delaying tactic by opponents of tax reform," but thirteen of the twenty members of the Finance Committee voted for the resolution, including Dole. Dole took this complaint a step further and demanded that any new tax devised by Packwood be used to reduce deficits—not to lower tax rates as part of reform.

Dole had his doubts about the reform effort from the start. He had worked to plug loopholes in 1982 and 1984, when he was Finance Committee chairman, but he thought that a comprehensive reform bill was too ambitious. Congress had passed a tax bill almost every year since President Reagan took office, he thought, and maybe it was time to slow down. Besides, as Rostenkowski had predicted, other Senate Republicans were not buying the idea. "It seems to me we don't move too quickly around this place and that was a pretty big undertaking," Dole recalls. "He [Packwood] didn't have a majority of the Republicans on the floor for the concept. It was going nowhere. I think a majority of members would say it was a real turkey for a while."

Senator John Heinz of Pennsylvania, a Finance Committee member and the chairman of the Senate Republican's fundraising committee, did not hesitate to criticize reform. Heinz was worried about the effect a tax bill would have on the declining rust-belt industries in his home state, and he was an early partisan against taking away heavy industry's tax favors.

Even when he met early in the year with a group of corporate chief executives who supported the bill—the CEO Tax Group—Heinz did not attempt to hide his opposition to reform. The executives included some heavy-weights, such as John Akers of IBM, John Richman of Dart & Kraft, Finn Caspersen of Beneficial Corporation, Howard Goldfeder of Federated Department Stores, John Smale of Procter & Gamble, and Allen Jacobson of 3M. The meeting occurred in a small conference room in the Dirksen Office Building—so small in fact that the door could hardly open when everyone crammed inside. Heinz did most of the talking. He lectured the CEOs about the importance of the tax breaks that they wanted to get rid of in order to pay for lower rates. He accused them of taking their position for purely selfish reasons. The executives tried to argue their point of view, but Heinz would not let up. An exasperated Caspersen finally interjected, "Senator, you're not talking to a bunch of high school students." The meeting dissolved with the red-faced executives stomping out into the hallway. Later, Caspersen told lobbyists that the Heinz performance was "a sophomoric display." Akers of IBM was even less forgiving: "If that guy worked for me," said the man who oversaw a company with 369,545 employees, "I'd fire him."

Despite the opposition, Packwood was unrelenting. He was being inexorably drawn further and further into the enterprise. He deflected demands to enact deficit reduction prior to tax reform by saying he would be willing to turn his tax bill into a tax increase, if that were the will of the Senate, but he continued to scramble to put his plan together throughout February. He was on a desperate search for revenue of his own; he needed to find enough loopholes that the senators on his committee would allow him to close in order to pay for the sharply lower tax rates that the president demanded.

The process was fraught with flirtations and disappointments. Ideas would rise and fall, float and sink, lasting only a few days or sometimes a few hours. Some proposals were more serious than others; tax amnesty, which would have given tax cheaters immunity from prosecution if they paid their back taxes, was a serious contender until the revenue estimators said the idea would raise almost no money. Oil-state senators who wanted an oil-import fee went so far as to get a green light from the White House staff to try to round up enough votes for their idea, but when the count of supporters fell short of a majority on the Finance Committee, that proposal also disappeared.

Improbable ideas came to the surface, sending shock waves through the business community. Everyone knew Packwood was in desperate straits, and no one was discounting any possible revenue-raisers. A number of proposals surfaced that serious tax reformers did not consider reform at all; they would simply have denied businesses the ability to deduct legitimate business expenses. Diefenderfer tested out the idea of preventing corporations from deducting all of their interest expenses. That one drew an almost-audible gasp from K Street. In fact, Diefenderfer now says the idea was broached mostly to lure the approval of the supply-side Republicans who were pushing the radical notion, and whose support Packwood hoped to co-opt. A proposal to disallow the deduction for some advertising expenses also found its way onto a Packwood-plan summary, but the suggestion was soon dropped as well.

The ultimate solution to the revenue dilemma was designed by Packwood's top tax aide, John Colvin. It was one of the most cynical and misleading proposals in the entire tax-reform debate. Colvin, a staunch staff man completely loyal to Packwood, was lying on his living-room floor one evening, combing through lists of tax breaks, when he noticed that corporations could deduct from their income taxes the excise tax and tariff payments they make to the federal government. Those payments were generally considered by tax experts to be a cost of doing business; they had to be deducted from a firm's "gross" income, like any other expense, before getting taxable net income. Something clicked in Colvin's mind: Disallowing that deduction could solve a lot of problems all at once, he reasoned. For one, it would raise an enormous amount of revenue: $62 billion over five years. For another, it would be counted as a corporate tax increase, even though it was really nothing more than a backdoor increase in the excise taxes and tariffs themselves. What's more, almost all of that increase would probably be passed through directly to the consumer, without burdening the corporations themselves—a goal of the pro-business members of the Finance Committee. That meant that Packwood could argue that he was increasing corporate taxes, while, in fact, sparing corporations much of the extra burden.

On the surface, the hokey idea seemed an ideal solution. It was a sort of consumption tax, which would appeal to many Republican members of the committee. Senator Roth, and some others on the panel, had been arguing for years that consumption, rather than income, should be the basis of taxation. Roth favored a value-added tax, a kind of consumption tax, as the proper route to take.

Packwood, as well, was attracted by a broad-based consumption tax, but he was wary of the political risks. Oregon voters had turned down by a decisive margin a proposal to establish a sales tax for their state. In addition, Representative Al Ullman, an Oregon Democrat and former chairman of the House Ways and Means Committee, had been defeated for reelection in 1980 after he advocated imposing a value-added tax nationwide. Denying the deduction for excise taxes offered the possibility of achieving the same goal without the political risk. It was a clever, if poorly disguised, trick.

When Colvin broached the idea with his boss, Packwood said, "Gee, John that's not going to fly." On second thought, he decided it might. It had a "patina of plausibility," he said, that served his purpose.

When Packwood briefed Baker and Darman on the excise-tax proposal in his Senate office in early March, the two Treasury officials immediately liked the idea. Darman favored consumption taxes and thought a value-added tax would ultimately be needed to close the budget deficit. Colvin's backdoor excise-tax increase also appealed to Darman's Machiavellian instincts. It was a Darmanesque idea; indeed, after the plan was released, the Deputy Treasury Secretary was frequently accused of authoring it.

More important, Baker and Darman liked the idea because it meant Packwood could at least get a plan down on paper. Their objective, as always, was to keep the process moving. They were supremely confident that somehow, in the end, they would be able to save the bill and produce the victory they craved.

On March 11, Packwood took his plan to the president. The meeting went smoothly, and the president, unperturbed by the strange excise-tax proposal, expressed his own enthusiasm. That view was not shared by all of the president's top advisers, who wanted to study the proposal more carefully. But Packwood was not taking any chances. As soon as the meeting was over, he dashed over to the White House press corps to announce the president's support. He proclaimed, "By and large he likes the bill and will support it." It took the White House itself somewhat longer to come to generally the same, though less exuberant, conclusion.

Packwood let out the details of the plan sparingly. Over a few days, he met with his members one-by-one to tell them its contents, but he did not let them take copies away from the briefings. Bradley got half of his twenty-minute glimpse at the package while walking alongside Packwood on the way to the Senate chamber for a vote. Despite the inconvenience, however, the pertinent parts did not remain secret long. The excise tax proposal, in particular, created such a ruckus that a whole new army of lobbyists lined up against it, even before the plan was officially unveiled.

The massive lobbying effort against the excise-tax proposal included, ironically, some of the House tax plan's strongest advocates. The companies hardest hit by the excise-tax proposal included many of the same companies that suffered from high effective tax rates under existing law. These were the firms that were more than willing to trade tax breaks for low rates and were thus the segment of the business community Rosten-kowski held up as exemplary tax-reform advocates—tobacco companies, for instance, and trucking firms.

The biggest excise taxes were levied on cigarettes, gasoline, and alcohol, but, in fact, the excise-tax proposal seemed to anger almost everyone.

Former top tax aides to Dole and Rostenkowski, who were then lobbyists, were enlisted to put together coalitions to fight the proposal, and Washington was quickly awash in corporate executives seeking relief from the proposal. They included Ernest Gallo of the California wine-producing family, David Roderick, chairman of U.S. Steel, which owned Marathon Oil, and August Busch III of Anheuser-Busch, the big brewer. They argued that the elimination of the deduction would mean a big increase in their companies' tax bills and would probably lead to higher prices for their customers.

That argument forged an odd alliance. The corporate chieftains were joined in the fight by their usual nemeses, consumer advocates. Groups such as Citizens for Tax Justice, the Consumer Federation of America, Ralph Nader's Public Citizen, and the American Association of Retired Persons agreed that the Packwood proposal would increase prices, and they worried that the burden of the price hikes would fall disproportionately on poor people.

The uproar over the provision was an example of the potency of the chairmanship. When a tax-writing-committee chairman makes even the most modest reference to a possible change in the law, an upheaval can result. "You meet the power people of America if you just sit there as chairman," Dole once said. "If you want to meet someone bad enough, just indicate you're going to look into a part of the tax bill that affects them. You don't even have to leave home, they'll be right in to see you."

Russell Long knew the power of the chair well. "The chairman should, and usually does, have far more power than anybody on the committee," he said.

My guess is he has more power than any two or three people on the committee. To get something done, I need to have the cooperation of the chairman. He can make things move or slow them down or not move at all. If he runs his committee in a democratic way, then every senator will get the opportunity to add his suggestions. But there are all sorts of ways available to him that are not available to the average person to see that something either doesn't move or moves very slowly, if he doesn't want it to happen.

When asked once if he liked being chairman, Packwood broke into one of his deep, whooping belly laughs. "I love being chairman," he said. "It's a privilege."

But the chairman is not omnipotent. If he champions a lame proposal, he too can lose. Packwood tried valiantly to defend the excise-tax proposal, but after a while, his heart was not in it. He clearly did not have the votes. At the first markup session, on March 19, Packwood called the plan "the engine that makes the rest of the bill possible," but eleven of the twenty members of the committee expressed serious misgivings. "That's not going to happen," predicted Senator Daniel Patrick Moynihan, Democrat of New York, during the session. "I can feel it around this room."

The Packwood plan was not viewed as real reform. The trick of tax overhaul was to pay for lower rates by eliminating loopholes. Packwood had used the excise-tax proposal as a crutch: It enabled him to retain many of the egregious tax preferences that any tax-reform bill would surely curtail. These included existing tax breaks for the oil, timber, and mining industries, and for steel, shipping, and other heavy industries. Even officials in the Republican administration who had been involved in the early for-mulation of reform attacked the product. "It's hard to call it tax reform if you have to go to a new source of revenue to pay for lower rates," said Buck Chapoton. Ron Pearlman, who had left the Treasury at the end of 1985, agreed, "It has become a political document."

Once again, the tax-reform effort seemed to have stalled. Back in their home states, the senators were hearing little but complaints. George Mitch-ell of Maine, for example, pushed his policy of meeting any constituent with a gripe to the absolute limit during tax reform. He was forced to schedule appointments every fifteen minutes for entire afternoons and sometimes had to extend his office hours late into the night to accommodate the overflow. "If I can keep this policy going through this year," he said, "I'll be able to keep it forever."

During a visit home to Portland, Maine, in still-chilly April, Mitchell was besieged with pleas for help. At a breakfast meeting in a roadside motel sponsored by the Maine Chamber of Commerce, he was urged to save tax breaks for the timber industry, which comprised nearly one third of Maine's economy. "To look at timber as a special interest isn't accurate," said Edward Johnston of the Maine Forest Products Council. The politician could not help but agree. "I strongly support current law," he said. That afternoon, at his dreary government office, Mitchell heard similar carping from local realtors, corporate-pension managers, a utility-company exec-utive and even a former mayor of Portland. A hulking Maine trucker, wearing a loudly checkered sports coat, came to the senator's office, along with a lobbyist all the way from Washington, who was resplendent in a navy-blue suit with a white hankerchief in the pocket. At the end of the long day, Mitchell concluded: "It follows a predictable pattern. They all want 100 percent" of their existing tax breaks.

Under similar pressure from their constituents, most members of the Finance Committee decided that was what they wanted too: 100 percent. Even though Packwood had taken pains to include in his starting-point plan the most cherished items on each of his members' wish lists—including his own—none of the members were satisfied. The bill was not taking much away from anyone; that being the case, the members thought to themselves, why should they give up anything at all? Packwood quickly grew frustrated. "I discovered that if they have priorities one, two, and three, and you give them one, two, and three, then four, five, and six become their most important priorities," he said.

The panel began drafting the tax bill on March 24, in its hearing room in the Dirksen Building. While not as big as the giant chamber used by the House Ways and Means Committee, the Finance Committee room was more old-worldly than its House counterpart, with stern, classical proportions, tall windows, and stately wood paneling. It was in this setting that the committee reluctantly set to work on the tax plan.

The panel's very first action attacked a central tenet of the tax reform effort: The committee voted unanimously to remove from the Packwood plan the requirement that income from municipal bonds be taxable under the minimum tax. The tax-free treatment of municipal bonds had enabled many wealthy people to escape taxes altogether; if a minimum tax was to work properly, it had to curtail that tax-exempt income. But the revelation a week earlier that Packwood's plan contained such a provision had sent Wall Street bond dealers into a panic, and had caused the tax-exempt bond market to all but collapse. Gun-shy Finance Committee members immediately began scurrying to remove the offending proposal from the plan. Packwood at first defended the proposal, then tried to blame the Treasury for devising it. The Treasury, in turn, blamed Packwood. In the end, the beleagured chairman joined with his colleagues to kill the offending proposal. It was only the first of a long series of retreats.

The part of the Packwood plan that was the most chock-full of parochial interests was the natural resources section, and that was the committee's second order of business. The Packwood package retained existing law for almost every tax break associated with the timber, mining, agriculture, and oil and gas industries. Those preferences were usually considered prime targets for any reform effort, but Packwood had secretly formed a conspiracy among a majority of his committee members to keep the preferences intact. One of his chief confederates was Lloyd Bentsen of Texas, with whom he had earlier held a colloquy during a hearing in which they congratulated each other for believing so firmly in the use of the tax code for incentives. "I don't think parochial interests are a bad thing at all," Packwood said, and Bentsen nodded his assent.

Some of the reform-minded panel members tried to object to keeping all of these industry-specific breaks. John Chafee of Rhode Island complained that the oil and timber industries were not contributing to the cause of lowering rates. Bradley made a similar charge; but Packwood was quick to retaliate. He reminded Chafee that he was one of the committee's champions for tax credits used to rehabilitate historic and old structures, and to Bradley he threw back his advocacy of tax-free bonds to finance solid-waste disposal facilities. Packwood seemed to be warning, "Don't throw stones." He brought down the gavel, and without a vote, retained existing law for natural resources industries.

"It keeps getting lonelier and lonelier," Bradley said a few days later, as he tried without success—and almost without any support—to trim at least some of the natural-resources provisions. "None of us is committed to tax reform," said Senator Malcolm Wallop, Republican of Wyoming, at the same markup session. "We've abandoned it a long time ago. We're not going to retrieve it."

One outrage followed another. On April 10, the committee adopted a crazy-quilt depreciation system that ostensibly gave more generous write-offs for machinery and equipment that were used in "productive" purposes than for those that were not. This dubious distinction was the invention of lobbyists Charls Walker and Ernest Christian and their heavy-industry allies in the Carlton group that represented major rubber, steel, aluminum, and petroleum producers. The system, in fact, was largely a ruse to mask the committee members' frenzy to aid the industries they were beholden to. The special "productivity property" class included airplanes, many of which were built in Dole's home state of Kansas, and mining, paper manufacturing, farming, and oil-and-gas equipment, which were important to the same block of members who pushed through the retention of existing law for natural resources.

The depreciation scheme lost buckets of revenue—at least $11 billion more over five years than the already generous write-off system that was included in the Packwood plan. It also created bizarre effects. Trucks that carried "nonproductive" assets, such as hamburger buns or baseball gloves, would not get the richer write-offs, but if the very same trucks carried "productive" assets, such as knitting machines and printing presses, they would. "It's nuts for us to sit down and decide which are productive assets and which are not," Senator William Armstrong, Republican of Colorado, confessed to *The Washington Post*.

The trend of giveaways, once begun, could not be slowed. Each day, the committee not only failed to eliminate or curtail tax breaks, but they approved new breaks that were more generous than existing law. It was the kind of special-interest spectacle for which the Finance Committee was well known. The bill was supposed to be the most ambitious piece of tax-reform legislation since the inception of the modern income tax, but instead of taking away tax benefits, the committee spent two straight weeks adding them back at a terrifying pace. When Bentsen's tax aide, Jim Gould, visited a friend at a downtown lobbying firm, he was jokingly greeted as "Santa's helper."

The committee played Santa Claus for almost everyone who asked. Bradley looked on, wide-eyed with horror, as both senators from Nebraska pleaded before the committee to give a single, Omaha-based company, Enron Corporation, a $100 million tax subsidy. The committee postponed taking the action, thanks in part to Bradley's vehement protests, but they did not demur on most other giveaways. At a cost of $4.5 billion over the five-year period, they expanded the types and volume of tax-exempt bonds that could be issued. They raised Packwood's limits on the amount of tax-free contributions to 401(k) pension plans, increasing the benefits for highly paid executives. And, at the urging of Packwood himself, the committee retained a tax shelter for homebuilders called "builder bonds" that one of the biggest developers in the nation, Trammell Crow of Dallas, described as a "scam."

"We're sliding deeper and deeper into the abyss," warned Chafee, after the committee agreed that the proper longevity of an oil refinery for tax purposes was five years. It was a ridiculously short depreciation period for such a long-term asset, but it meant big write-offs for refineries and lower taxes as a result. (Steel mills also got the preposterous five-year write-off.)

Sick and tired of the giveaways, the usually reform-minded Chafee decided that the exercise was a failure and that the least he could do was protect the groups he thought deserved a break. As a former governor of Rhode Island, the senator chose government workers. The Packwood proposal included the government pension provision that had caused a fight on the House floor, but on Wednesday, April 16, the day after tax day, the committee decided by voice vote to accept a Chafee amendment that eliminated the tax increase for pensioners that the House bill mandated. The action, which helped 17 million federal and state workers, punched a $7.4 billion hole in the Packwood proposal and ended any chance that there might have been for salvaging the tax-reform bill. It was a watershed day: One of the few tax reformers on the committee had inflicted one of the deepest wounds that the legislation had suffered to that point. Thereafter, there was clearly no way to stop the attack. "With friends like that," Diefenderfer remarked to Packwood after the Chafee vote, "who needs enemies?"

The panel's goal was to close enough loopholes to bring the top tax rate down to 35 percent, but it was already $29 billion short of the revenue needed to meet that goal, and even bigger shortfalls lay ahead. The bill was hemorrhaging revenue with every decision, and no end was in sight. Newspaper reports brutalized the panel for its giveaways, for its pandering to special interests. *The New Republic* magazine took aim directly at Packwood; it headlined a highly critical piece about the markup, SENATOR HACKWOOD.

As bad as events had been, Friday, April 18, promised to be far worse. The markup schedule dictated that the most costly individual tax items were to be voted on that day. With the downhill slide of the markup thus far, Packwood's chances of winning those votes were shaky at best. Friday was shaping up as the day of reckoning. Huge sums were on the line, and the fate of the entire enterprise hung in the balance. Some $70 billion worth of tax breaks that Packwood wanted to pare were scheduled for a vote in the morning, and it was clear to Diefenderfer that the chairman was likely to lose.

Armstrong had collected enough votes to keep the current deduction for business meals. In addition, Moynihan had teamed with tax-reform opponents to gather enough votes to save the deduction for sales taxes, a big-money item that was vital to preserving revenue neutrality. Dole was on Moynihan's side, and even Bradley was so discouraged that he decided to vote with Moynihan.

Diefenderfer stayed late that Thursday, trying to figure a way out. He frantically contacted senators' offices, trying to find some support, but there was none. It was well past dinner when he called his boss. "It doesn't look good," he told Packwood. "We have problems."

Early the next morning Diefenderfer and his assistants made their way to Packwood's office in the Russell Office Building. Starting at about seven-thirty, they manned the telephones, trying to scare up a vote or two, trying to save the floundering effort, but it was to no avail. The calls only confirmed the fears of the night before. Discipline had broken down. The bill was a goner.

"We'll pull it down," Packwood concluded in his matter-of-fact, businesslike style.

By that time, reporters and staff aides had already gathered in the committee's hearing room and were awaiting Packwood's arrival. They gossiped about the tax-reform carnage the day might produce. Surely there would be plenty. Armstrong's people were crowing about their boss's imminent victory; he had even canceled a trip to see his amendment through. There were whispers as well about Moynihan's potential coup. Two floors below, dozens of lobbyists settled into their seats in the auditorium. Packwood, who was usually punctual, had not arrived and the lobbyists wondered what was delaying him. No one was prepared when he finally entered, took his chair in the center of the horseshoe-shaped hearing table in the front of the room, and delivered his message in rapid-fire fashion.

"I don't want to give any impression that we have any idea of quitting," Packwood said, "but I did not want to run the risk of killing this bill. What I was afraid of today is that if we held votes, it would be the end of the bill." There would be no votes today, he said. There would be no votes for some time to come.

Some lobbyists listening downstairs started to cheer.

To many, Packwood's action signaled the end of reform. The Finance Committee was clearly too wedded to its many tax breaks to accomplish such a massive rewrite of the code. A pessimistic Moynihan declared the effort "in ruins," and said, "it has clearly failed in the Senate." Secretary Baker, the administration's top gun for tax reform, was equally distressed: "We're in the soup."

David Pryor, the folksy Arkansan who was the most junior member of the committee, summed it up best: "We're all riding a lame horse right now. We have to decide whether we want to keep riding it or trade it in. I frankly think this is a horse that's so lame we can't continue to ride it."

The tax bill had reached its lowest ebb.

Chapter 9

The Two-Pitcher Lunch

About fifteen minutes after the markup disbanded, Packwood telephoned Diefenderfer from his office. "Lunch?" Packwood asked. "Sure," the aide replied.

Diefenderfer enjoyed his occasional long lunches with the boss, but on this day he knew the conversation would be as gloomy as the overcast skies. They were facing the greatest setback of their many years together on Capitol Hill. Diefenderfer had been Packwood's top aide at the Commerce Committee before moving to the Finance Committee, and the two men had been through many tough battles, but this was the biggest and the hardest to solve. They left the Capitol grounds together, making small talk, trying not to dwell on their failure. They walked the few blocks to their favorite saloon, The Irish Times.

The Irish Times is the kind of place that people go to get drunk. Neon signs on the window flash BUDWEISER and STROH'S, and above the door, a painted sign advertises: GIVE ME YOUR THIRSTY, YOUR FAMISHED, YOUR BEFUDDLED MASSES. Inside, a visitor's first impression is the odor of spilled beer; the second is the lighting—or lack of it. It is not the kind of place that engenders optimism. Even on the sunniest days, its checkerboard tablecloths are shrouded in darkness.

Packwood and Diefenderfer ordered two cheeseburgers, rare, and a pitcher of draft beer. "We're not going any place the way we're going," the senator said. "The bill is getting worse rather than better." Both men knew what vast understatement those words conveyed and solemnly began to review the bidding. It was their task, starting at that moment, to turn around what appeared to be an impossible situation. Tax reform—and Packwood's reputation—hung in the balance.

As they took their first sips of beer, Packwood suggested a new approach. Instead of writing a bill that reached into every corner and crevice of the massive tax code, he asked, why not select just a few, small pieces of the mammoth design and patch together a less far-reaching measure? Maybe it could consist of just a minimum tax and a few repealed deductions. At least it could be called reform.

Diefenderfer disliked that option. The stripped-down approach, he thought, would be considered a humiliating defeat among Washington scorekeepers. If Packwood was unable to persuade his panel to draft a sweeping bill along the lines the president was demanding—and the House already had passed—the press would label the committee a sellout and its fledgling chairman an impotent leader. Packwood would be relegated to the status of legislative loser, one of the worst fates to befall a big-time politician.

Diefenderfer was no tax expert, but he was extremely close to Packwood. His opinions carried tremendous weight. He was more than staff director at the Finance Committee; he was an all-purpose political adviser. It was his job to keep his boss out of trouble, and he usually succeeded. "Diefenderfer is in a category by himself with Packwood," Darman observed several months later. "When Diefenderfer tells Packwood what's on his mind, Packwood listens."

Packwood and Diefenderfer were almost inseparable, and they were a distinctive pair as they walked through the halls of Congress. Diefenderfer was a big, bearded, lumbering man of forty-one years, who was proud of his aggressiveness (he held a brown belt in judo) and his steel-country roots in western Pennsylvania. The shorter Packwood would often walk slightly ahead of Diefenderfer, striding with his high forehead jutting forward, looking oddly like the movie character E.T.

Diefenderfer's analysis of the problems of the stripped-down approach hit home with the ambitious chairman. The two men had often discussed how important it was for Packwood to prove himself a success. The senator's extensive library was stocked with books about great men in history, such as Disraeli and Jefferson, and his office was decorated with biscuit tins bearing likenesses of Winston Churchill. Packwood took the examples of these men seriously. If the Finance Committee failed to approve more than a pale imitation of reform, Diefenderfer argued, it would be three or four years before Packwood could regain his reputation as a leader, before he could recoup his power. This was a possibility that Packwood was loathe to ignore.

There was also Packwood's reelection to consider. On that day, April 18, 1986, Packwood was a month away from what he feared would be a close primary back home in Oregon, and his political opponents were beginning to make hay out of his committee's many giveaways. Representative James Weaver, the Democratic aspirant, gave a major address that asserted Packwood was "floundering" in his first major test as chairman, and that he was sucking up to "special interests." Oregon newspapers were also chiding him for taking huge campaign contributions from almost every interest group imaginable. He was quickly growing infamous as "Mr. Special Interest."

Another solution was vaguely in the minds of both men. They had discussed the possibility for months and had even done some preliminary research on it, but the notion was so drastic, and its likelihood of success so remote, that almost no one thought it anything but foolhardy.

Packwood and Diefenderfer called it the "radical approach": the paring away of enough deductions, exclusions, and credits in the code to halve the top individual tax rate to 25 percent from 50 percent. With a rate so low, Packwood reasoned, "people would cease to worry about whether or not the particular deduction or exemption they were concerned with stayed or disappeared."

The idea was an extraordinary but simple one. Although many Americans fell into tax brackets as high as 50 percent, few Americans paid more than 25 percent of their income in taxes; there was no reason for the top rate to be any higher than that. The proposal Packwood and Diefenderfer were plotting would be even more audacious than Bill Bradley's landmark proposal in 1982, and in some ways, even more far-reaching than the quickly dismissed Treasury I plan in 1984.

Packwood had dropped hints about his interest in the 25-percent solution before. During Finance Committee hearings, he had asked witnesses: "At what tax rate won't deductions matter anymore?" He had even mentioned a 25-percent plan to the president at a White House meeting with congressional leaders in the summer of 1985, but almost no one took him seriously. Eliminating enough tax breaks to get the rate down to 25 percent was, most everyone in Washington agreed, politically impossible. Packwood himself had originally thought a 25-percent plan would have to be accompanied by a consumption tax to raise additional revenue. Now, however, he was considering something more sweeping. The president had ruled out any new taxes as part of reform; that meant the low rate would have to be paid for by eliminating tax breaks.

During the first pitcher of beer, the two men hashed over the options. They were well into their second pitcher when it became clear there was only one course to take: the radical approach.

These two men—one who had never faced public election, the other who represented a state that had little more than 1 percent of the nation's population—were toying with the most massive redistribution of the tax burden in the nation's history. Hunched over their sandwiches, they were plotting to take hundreds of billions of dollars out of the pockets of those who had made heavy use of tax loopholes and bestow those billions on everyone who had not. It was a plan that would cause fundamental changes in the very structure of American society. It would subtly and deeply affect the lives of every American household and every American business. Packwood, who had spent much of his Senate career poking loopholes in the tax system, was now suggesting the biggest loophole-closing package in history.

To a large extent, the idea that crystallized over beer at The Irish Times was a political ploy. The two men thought it might help quiet the criticism of Packwood at home, and that certainly could not hurt his reelection chances. His political opponents could hardly criticize him for doing what they were demanding.

The plan also had its appeal in Washington. During his seventy hours of meetings with the senators on his panel, Packwood noted that almost every one of them said that they supported "reform—real reform," but of course, they always added, "real" reform was not politically possible. During the two-week deterioration of the markup, the members sometimes justified their piggish votes by claiming the initial Packwood proposal was not real reform anyway, so why should they hold back?

Well, Packwood now thought, if they say they want reform, I'll give them reform. A radical, off-with-their-heads tax-reform plan with a rate as low as 25 percent surely would call the bluff of anyone who was trying to conceal distaste for reform behind a reformer's rhetoric. It would be difficult for the self-righteous members of the Finance Committee to reject out of hand.

In addition, the radical approach had a substantive appeal for Packwood. By this time, he was convinced that 25 percent or thereabouts was a "magic" number for the top individual rate. If rates were that low, he believed, people would stop caring so passionately about their deductions and credits. He had come to believe that Bradley and Kemp were right: the lower the rate, the less political pressure for tax breaks and the more efficient the economy.

Packwood also liked the idea because it was bold, and the combative chairman enjoyed taking bold stands. Like his great-grandfather and father before him, he had a volatile nature. He cherished being unpredictable and independent-minded. If nothing else, the proposal would contribute to that image.

A more prudent lawmaker, steeped in the traditions and policy of tax law, would have concluded that the 25-percent idea would never work, that it probably was suicidal to even attempt it, but Packwood was in a desperate spot, and he chose a desperate strategy. Taking a half-inch-thick slice of onion from Diefenderfer's cheeseburger and placing it atop his own, Packwood looked at Diefenderfer and said, "Why not?" They finished their burgers and a second pitcher of beer and walked back to the Capitol rejuvenated. They had made their decision.

Neither of them knew where their half-crazed plan would lead them.

Later, in private, Packwood told several associates that he did not expect the 25-percent plan to succeed and that he was putting it forward mostly for tactical reasons. He and Diefenderfer both doubted the committee would go for it, but at least Packwood would have staked out the high ground on tax reform. Packwood conceded, "It was a long shot."

"I've often described it as sort of like the end of that movie *The Wild Bunch*," Packwood says. In the film, a gang of bandits sells out a young member of their crew to the other side, but later decides to undo the deed. "The next morning they get up and look at each other and strap on their guns and go to get the kid. They know they're going to be killed, but they've got to do this, they've got to try it. Bill and I just felt, OK, this is something we've got to try. If we fail, we fail at a great enterprise. No guts, no glory."

When Diefenderfer reached his office, he placed a call to David Brockway at the Joint Committee on Taxation. "David, we're talking about this radical structure," Diefenderfer said. "Give me a plan with tax rates of 15 percent and 25 percent, a 33-percent top corporate rate and make it revenue neutral. I don't have time to give you the outline; you know roughly where we want to go. I just want a plan to show them that this is possible."

Brockway was pleased—and shocked—to hear from Diefenderfer. Their relations had been strained. Brockway had been close to Rostenkowski in his struggle to get reform in the House, functioning as a de facto member of the chairman's senior staff. But he and Packwood had never gotten along. The Finance Committee chairman suspected that Brockway and his Joint Committee staff secretly wanted to tax his precious fringe benefits, and that alone was enough to make him distrustful. Indeed, at one of his first breakfast meetings with lobbyists after assuming the chairmanship, Packwood announced that he wanted to remove Brockway from his job, though he never acted on the intention.

Brockway was excited that Packwood might actually be interested in trying real reform. That was the kind of bill he and his staff had dreamed about for many years. But Brockway knew that his job did not rest on dreams. His honest, practical reaction to the radical idea, hewn from years of experience watching the tax scene in Congress, was pessimistic. Brockway knew that some of the most cherished deductions in the code, including those for mortgage interest and charitable contributions, might have to be on the chopping block to get the rate that low. "You realize," he told Diefenderfer, "that no way this flies."

At 2:15 P.M., Packwood and Diefenderfer met with Baker and Darman. The Treasury officials expected to find the senator and his aide in a downbeat mood. Darman had prepared an agenda for the meeting, as was his custom. The first item was designed to boost morale; it had new Treasury estimates showing the committee had not lost as much revenue as thought. The next few items were suggestions about how to build a new proposal with the help of a small group of senators, who might form a "core group." The last item, titled "shots across the bow," was the kicker. With the prospects for reform looking dim, Darman thought it might be time to use what he called "the big gun in the closet." It might be time for the administration to begin placing blame on some troublesome senators for trying to kill tax reform, for selling out to the special interests.

To their surprise, Baker and Darman found that Packwood had made up his mind to take a dramatic new direction: the 25-percent solution.

The Treasury chiefs cautioned the senator that his plan could never become law. To get the top rate down to 25 percent would require slaughtering too many political sacred cows. Nevertheless, they said, they were willing to back the idea; at least it was a new starting point. Like Packwood, they thought the plan would at least serve to "call the bluff" of those on the Finance Committee who claimed they would only support real reform and not a watered-down version. As usual, they were willing to go along just to keep the process alive, confident that, somehow, they could shape the bill to their liking in the end. "We weren't at all sure that it could be done," Baker said later, "but we were certainly willing to give it a try . . . Anything would be better than the course he was following."

Six days later, on Thursday, April 24, Packwood summoned his members to a meeting in the so-called exec room, behind the Finance Committee hearing room, where the committee held its private talks. Along the walls of the small, wood-paneled room stood several glass-doored cabinets that contained Senator Long's tax library. Otherwise, the only diversions for the members in the room were several telephones, a picture window looking out at the Russell Office Building, and a large photograph of the Teton mountains.

Lobbyists and reporters were massed outside the room, restlessly pacing the corridor's gray marble floors. All they knew was what Packwood had said publicly: that the committee was going to "start from square one" and that "nothing is sacred." The lobbyists were worried, and anxious to find out what was happening inside.

The members took their places around the fifteen-foot conference table. They were as much in the dark about Packwood's plan as those in the hallway were. They were handed two sets of papers. To the surprise of many, the first was a brief description of the original Bradley-Gephardt bill—the seminal document that launched the tax-reform movement four years earlier and that the Finance Committee had spent the past month repudiating. "This is the way Bill did it," Packwood explained. The paper listed the tax breaks that Bradley had eliminated or curtailed in order to get the top individual tax rate to 30 percent. The senators were surprised to see the Republican chairman pushing this Democratic plan, and there was muttering around the table.

Then Packwood passed out the real surprise: the 25-percent plan Brockway and his staff had drafted in secret. It was greeted with stunned silence. Since the day of the two-pitcher lunch, Brockway and his deputy, Randy Weiss, had worked with revenue estimator Steve Lerch to come up with the plan. It was bare bones and to the point. It eliminated every single deduction for individuals, including the most popular, such as those for mortgage interest, charitable contributions, and state and local taxes. It had only two rates: 15 percent and 25 percent. The corporate rate was slashed to 33 percent. The preferential treatment of capital-gains income was completely eliminated. To avoid reopening the battles of two weeks earlier, the new plan completely skirted the corporate side of the tax code. It simply assumed that about $75 billion in new revenue would be raised from unnamed changes in corporate taxes—far less than the $120 billion in the president's plan or the $140 billion in the House plan, but still a sizable amount. The plan also included a $25 billion increase in excise taxes to help pay for the drastic individual-rate cuts.

Even though it sidestepped difficult corporate tax reform issues, the 25-percent plan was still awesome in its scope. It was a collection of the toughest tax-reform provisions—at least for individual taxpayers—that had ever been seriously considered by any congressional body. Packwood's plan did more than call the bluff of his members; it blew them away.

"Any interest?" Packwood asked. Remarkably, there was.

Voices of support popped up from all corners of the table. It quickly became evident that Packwood was not the only Finance Committee member who was shamed and embarrassed by the panel's special-interest feeding frenzy of the previous few weeks. Many of the politicians had felt the sting of critical press reports; many realized they might suffer if their committee failed to act on the president's call for reform. As a result, the impossible was starting to happen: The phoenix of tax reform was beginning to rise again from the dead. Compared to the unpleasant alternative of killing reform, approving some sort of radical reform legislation looked like a good idea, even to the unlikely reformers of the Finance Committee.

As Moynihan put it later, "You shouldn't underestimate the ability for moral indignation, even among politicians." Packwood gave this explanation: "It was a cathartic process. Maybe we had to go through what we went through or we would not have gotten to where we are."

The 25-percent plan's central attraction was the low top rate. It was so low that the members began to focus on its attractiveness rather than on the pain that their constituencies would feel from the elimination of tax preferences. John Chafee of Rhode Island called the deep cut in the top rate "the siren's song" that lured support for the plan.

All of this was no revelation to Bill Bradley, who had pioneered the concept, so when Packwood associated his own plan with Bradley's, the New Jersey lawmaker was quick to join the chorus of praise. He also began to play an unaccustomed role for such a young senator: the elder statesman. He had been making the case for his own plan for four long years. He knew all the arguments for it and against it. In an instant, he was transformed from being a junior member of the committee's minority party—and, indeed, one of the few in that minority who favored reform—to a respected adviser on the most sweeping piece of tax law in over forty years. He began to help Packwood, his former nemesis, defend the radical approach. "Bradley was right," Packwood would say later, in simple explanation of the startling reversal.

The first newfound reformer to speak up at the meeting was, in many ways, the least likely. Malcolm Wallop of Wyoming, one of the most conservative Republicans on the committee, said he could be interested. He had fought the reform effort fiercely, but the simplicity and the low top rate of Packwood's plan attracted him. In public, Wallop had said repeatedly that he liked low rates and hated complexity. "Complexity," he said, "favors the most powerful among us." On that day in the exec room, Wallop made clear that he had not been joking.

John Danforth of Missouri was the next to praise the package. A tall, slow-talking preacher and scion of the Ralston Purina dog-chow fortune, he had a tuft of white in his brown hair that prompted his staff, secretly, to call him Spot. Danforth congratulated the chairman and told the group about a top New York executive who had approached him at a party recently and said, "I pay taxes, but nobody I know pays them." That was wrong, Danforth said, and something should be done about it. The 25-percent solution moved in the right direction, he said. Referring first to the old plan and then to the new one, Danforth concluded, "That was a bazaar; this is reform."

Moynihan, a former Harvard professor, ambassador, and White House adviser, also had some good things to say. He told the story that would become known on the committee as the "Grace Report." According to the 1985 annual report of W. R. Grace & Company, he said, the Manhattan-based conglomerate paid taxes to Muammar Qaddafi's outlaw nation, Libya, but got a half-million-dollar refund from the United States. That was an outrage, he believed, that had to be stopped. Nevertheless, the New York Democrat was pessimistic about the political prospects for so large a change as was envisioned by the Packwood plan. Legislatures were incrementalist by nature, he argued; perhaps the minimum-tax route would be a more realistic, if less attractive, alternative.

Even Lloyd Bentsen of Texas, one of the most respected conservatives on the committee and a friend to countless special interests, said he was intrigued by the plan. Some of the other senators quietly gasped when he declared that so low a tax rate could even compel him to agree to the elimination of the special low rate for capital gains—a truly stunning concession from the man who had helped popularize the term "capital formation."

But Bentsen reserved his support; the panel had to make a choice between two options, he said, and he personally was ambivalent about which option to take. The panel could either write a radical, low-rate plan, as Packwood was proposing, or it could write a stripped-down plan with a rate in the range of 40 percent, which did little more than impose a stiffened minimum tax and take families below poverty level off of the income tax rolls. Any middle-ground plan, he said, such as the one they had been suffering through, would be "the worst of both worlds."

Like Bentsen, most other members also were cautious. Chafee, a reformer by inclination, worried aloud that the 25-percent plan took away the most precious deductions enjoyed by the middle class. George Mitchell of Maine, also a reform-minded member, made perhaps the most telling point: The 25-percent rate was too low, he said; rich people should continue to pay a proportionately larger amount of their income to Uncle Sam than the less-well-off paid, and the progressive rate structure should be maintained. The income-distribution tables that accompanied the 25-percent plan proved Mitchell's point with a vengeance; the benefits fell heavily upon the highest-income Americans.

Bradley took the lead in saying that Mitchell's problem could be fixed. He had faced the same problem in fashioning his own plan, and he had solved it. Bradley-Gephardt kept an even distribution of the tax burden among income groups and still had a very low top rate. What's more, Bradley argued, the Packwood proposal, like his own, had the advantage of placing 80 percent of all taxpayers at the lower of the two tax rates.

Russell Long was far less enthusiastic. During his fifteen years as Finance Committee chairman, Long was considered one of the most wily manipulators of the legislative process in Washington. He was the master of compromise and political deal-making, and he had little inherent interest in reform schemes that would do away with the tools of his trade: deductions, exclusions, and credits. When the respected Long spoke, his colleagues listened.

Long argued that a Bradley-Gephardt–like plan would unravel if even a single preference were preserved. He compared it to a suit of clothes with a single, loose thread: one tug and the whole garment could come apart. So spare a system, he maintained, was not politically possible. The senator also began pulling on one of the plan's central threads. The deduction for state and local taxes, he argued, should not be eliminated as the 25-percent plan recommended. It was the taxpayers' constitutional right, he said.

Packwood disagreed with Long. The committee needed a new approach, he said. The old one, which involved giving away tax breaks to buy reform, had simply failed. "We tried that and it didn't work," he said. "We tried to take care of everyone's interest in the plan, and once that was done, everyone's interest became more generic and nonregional. Now I would like to try something revolutionary and see what happens." Bradley also rebutted Long. The panel, he said, should set some goals and do its best to move toward those goals. The result would be tax reform.

Packwood ended the meeting by asking for permission to take another crack at the radical plan, to solve some of the most serious problems voiced by the committee that morning. They would meet five days later, the following Tuesday, he said, to look at a revised proposal. "If the committee says no, we'll try again with a stripped-down bill," he said. "We can't sell anything on the Senate floor without Finance Committee support."

Packwood and Diefenderfer were encouraged. The comments at the meeting, as well as some whispered conversations afterward, indicated, to their surprise, that the radical approach had considerable support among the members. Diefenderfer called Darman to report the good news. He and Packwood were beginning to see the outlines of a "core group" they could count on to help them write a tax-overhaul bill. Their initial list of potential core group members included Packwood, Danforth, Chafee, Wallop, Bradley, Mitchell, and Moynihan. These four Republicans and three Democrats would form the nucleus for fashioning a plan that Packwood hoped could win a majority on the twenty-member panel.

At the conclusion of the Thursday meeting, Packwood asked his members to return the sheets of paper he had handed out. They were highly sensitive working documents and might cause a stir if disclosed to the lobbyists and reporters outside the exec room. The plan's distribution of tax cuts, which was skewed to favor the wealthiest people, was a particularly sensitive point. Indeed, during the meeting, David Pryor of Arkansas called the 25-percent plan "creative," but suggested that it "shouldn't go public now."

Secrets are seldom safe in Washington, however, especially in the inbred tax village. Newspapers carried details of the 25-percent plan the next day, including the damning income-distribution figures. Packwood was deluged with questions and complaints. He knew he would have to say something to answer to the outcry.

On Friday morning, Diefenderfer called Brockway to say there was going to be a press conference that afternoon. "You're going to have to go up there and present this," Diefenderfer warned him, and Brockway knew immediately what that meant. More staff-bashing was on the way. Packwood needed a fall guy, and Brockway had been selected.

Packwood and Brockway faced the overflow press conference together. At first, Packwood tried to defuse the tension of the event with some levity. A summary of the 25-percent plan that his staff had handed to reporters contained a mistake. The listings for "joint filer" and "head of household" were confused, so that one of the headings read instead, "joint head." Packwood quipped, "Joint head is not a bisexual toilet."

The joke flopped. Reporters began to shout questions to Packwood, who looked extremely uncomfortable under the hot camera lights. Was he abandoning his first tax plan? Did he really want to get rid of all those deductions? Why did he want to give rich people such a big break?

Packwood ducked all of those questions. The plan, he said, was not his own. It was Brockway's. It would be "easier to ask Dave to come up here and answer those questions," he said. Time and again, he stepped away from the bank of microphones, trying to shift attention to the slightly dazed director of the Joint Taxation Committee.

The chairman's evasiveness did not work. Each time Packwood tried to walk away from the microphones, reporters called him back. Packwood was forced to make other, even more lame, excuses. The plan, he said, was not a "specific proposal," but merely part of an "educational process" for his members. In sum, he did everything he could to distance himself from the plan. It was not a courageous display; he was disowning his own creation.

Just a week earlier, he and Diefenderfer, over two pitchers of beer, had decided to be bold and try the 25-percent solution. Now, faced with the task of defending that decision, Packwood flinched. Instead of taking responsibility for his scheme, he did the political thing—he tried to blame someone else.

Brockway was accustomed to rough treatment from lawmakers. They were his bosses, and he had come to understand that he made a better—and far easier—target for them than their colleagues made. "When all else fails, blame the staff" seemed to be the motto of many members of Congress. During the Ways and Means markup, so much abuse was heaped on Brockway's head that a fellow staffer gave him a crash helmet.

The forty-two-year-old Brockway was Congress's top tax brain. As director of the Joint Committee on Taxation, he headed a staff of forty nonpartisan economists, attorneys, and accountants whose offices were scattered on both sides of the Capitol. It was a joint committee because its staff was overseen by members of both the House and the Senate. It served as a reservoir of in-house tax expertise for the entire Congress, especially the two tax-writing committees. Joint Tax aides shaped and analyzed every change in tax law proposed by their bosses and often came up with suggestions themselves. Their revenue estimates on the changes were gospel. In tax reform, an exercise driven by revenue estimates and income-distribution charts, Joint Tax pronouncements were crucial.

Brockway was an unlikely leader for such a serious organization. His father was the chairman of W. W. Norton & Company, the publishing house, and he grew up in the affluent suburbs outside of New York City. He had a lust for life that did not extend into the classroom; he was the kind of kid who found learning easy, but playing around more fun. He was a self-described "wise ass." Despite frighteningly high standardized-test scores, especially in math, his high school recommended that colleges reject him because of his chronic discipline problems.

Cornell University ignored the advice and soon regretted it. At the end of his sophomore year, Brockway was academically ranked 848 out of a class of 849 students. He was asked to leave. "Up until I was nineteen, I was the happiest human in the history of the universe. Life was a gas. Everything was just great," Brockway says. "I just didn't have any self-discipline. I didn't study. I didn't show up for classes. I was goofing off and having a good time."

He was told that he had only a touch-and-go chance of ever being allowed to return, but the dean of students was sympathetic. He saw in Brockway that special intensity that was evident to anyone who had contact with him. He also saw in Brockway a bit of himself: The dean, too, had been thrown out of school once. He told the young man that what he needed to get himself square was a stint in the army. Perhaps for the first time in his life, Brockway did what he was told and joined up—along with his roommate, Gene DuBose, who had also been tossed out.

Brockway spent three long years, 1963 to 1966, "keeping the Russians away," as he put it, working as a radio-teletype operator in Germany. "I was at war with the army the whole time I was in there," Brockway recalls, "but by the time it was over, I could actually do sufficient work to get by and had a certain sense of responsibility. It took the piss and vinegar out of me. You never knew when somebody would send you to jail for failing to blouse your pants over your own boots."

He returned to Cornell a reformed character. In two years, he completed two and a half years' worth of credits and was accepted into Cornell's well-regarded graduate program in history, where he envisioned himself studying to become a professor of European history, but his old buddy DuBose changed all that. During the summer, he saw his former roommate at a party in Manhattan. DuBose had finished his first year at Harvard Law School and was accepted on the law review. He told Brockway that he was crazy to study for his doctorate in history. He, too, should go to Harvard Law.

Brockway thought the idea was absurd. It was already the middle of the summer, too late to apply for law school, but DuBose told him he would handle everything with the admissions office. This came at an opportune time for young Brockway; he was having second thoughts about whether history was his calling. He paid a visit to his history professor at Cornell, and found him in his office in the library stacks. That was where the man spent his life, Brockway realized, but that was not where the spirited Brockway wanted to spend his. "History I love," he thought, "but a life sitting in a library is not my personality. I want action."

So Brockway applied to Harvard Law School. Because his application was made so late, and the chances for its acceptance were so small, the school waived the usual application fee.

Fortunately for Brockway, Harvard gave special weight to scores on the standardized tests at which Brockway excelled. In August, they sent him a telegram of acceptance. "The fates were dictating that I ought to do that," he concluded. Besides, he thought, going to law school would put off growing up for another three years.

After graduation, Brockway joined a law firm in New York, but once again his restlessness prevailed. "Going to be a lawyer was an accident, not an objective," he told himself. "I want to spend a little time doing something of greater significance."

On February 1, 1976, he joined the Joint Committee on Taxation. He had long had an interest in broad policy issues, and he knew the reputation of the Joint Committee. He applied for a job and was hired. He spent five years as its expert in international taxation—one of the driest and most arcane topics in the dry and arcane tax repertoire, but also one of the most hotly lobbied. Brockway came to love the excitement of the tax-writing world. "It was the greatest thing that ever happened. Ideal. I couldn't have asked for anything more," he says.

In 1981, when Bernard "Bob" Shapiro left as staff director to join the accounting firm of Price Waterhouse, Brockway was made deputy director. And when Mark McConaghy, Shapiro's successor, also joined Price Waterhouse in 1983, to establish a kind of shadow Joint Tax Committee there, Brockway took over the real one on Capitol Hill. The position had a great tradition. For many years it was held by Larry Woodworth, a brilliant tax expert and patient teacher to any interested party. For more than a decade, Woodworth was considered the most influential staffer in Congress.

Brockway came into this position in the midst of a tumultuous period. At one time, the Joint Tax Committee was the preeminent voice on taxes in Congress. The tax-writing staffs of the Ways and Means and Finance committees were small and relatively unimportant. But during the 1970s, congressional committee staffs and personal staffs grew like Topsy, largely in reaction to the Nixon administration's cavalier treatment of Congress. When Dole took over as chairman of the Finance Committee in 1981, he beefed up its staff even more. In response, Ways and Means bulked up as well. The Joint Committee, which grew little during this period, saw its influence diminish.

In Congress, staff size is often a measure of clout. A member with a large staff is a member with large influence. By this gauge, the importance of almost everyone had grown dramatically. From 1947 to 1985, the number of staff members of standing congressional committees rose to 3,045 from 399, a 763-percent increase. During the same period, the number of staffers on Ways and Means rose to ninety-four from twelve, and staffers on the Finance Committee increased to fifty-three from six. The number of aides on members' personal staffs also increased gigantically. In 1947, there were 2,030 personal aides in Congress; in 1985, there were 11,665.

The raw numbers alone do not fully express the growing power of staffers. Indeed, elected members routinely groused that the staff possessed the real power in Congress. In a world growing increasingly complex, members were rarely experts on any single topic, and their talents were usually spread very thin. The only experts were the staffers. They briefed their bosses on the substance of any given initiative and often recommended what course of action to take. Particularly in the blindingly complicated subject of taxation, staff aides, called legislative assistants, functioned almost as personal priests to their bosses. Their advice carried tremendous weight, particularly in a town filled with so many contrary views and lobbyists who were willing to market them.

Aggressive staffers dominated much of the legislative process. They controlled the information, and that was what drove events. "Senators, I fear, are becoming annoying constitutional impediments to the staff," Senator Patrick Leahy, Democrat of Vermont, once complained. "Someday we may just allow the staff to vote and skip the middle man." Political scientist Michael Malbin even concocted a phrase to express this phenomenon: *staff entrepreneurialism*.

During tax reform, Darman was among the critics of staff participation. He contended that the lawmakers, left to their own devices, were far more willing to compromise and accommodate than were their aides. When aides were allowed into private drafting sessions, he contended, positions solidified and progress slowed. He derided this interference by legislative aides as "L.A. democracy."

Whatever their drawbacks, congressional staffers contributed greatly to the legislative process. The hardworking tax staffs, both on the tax committees and in the personal offices of the tax writers themselves, were among the Swiss guard of aides on the Hill. Rob Leonard on Ways and Means and William Wilkins on the Finance Committee's minority staff were as savvy tax attorneys and legislative operators as could be found anywhere. The Ways and Means tax staff included some able veterans who outshined the relatively green staffers brought in by Packwood on the majority staff of the Finance Committee. Nearly everyone worked seven days a week at all hours for interminably long stretches of time in order to make tax reform possible.

Brockway and his staff were not beholden to any single member. Their job was not political, and their bosses were many. They were sometimes suspected of having their own agenda, and that agenda did not always seem to jibe with those of the lawmakers they worked with. Packwood, in particular, distrusted the Joint Committee because of the staff's preference for tax reform. Indeed, one of Packwood's most famous shouting matches with staffers was a public dressing down of Randy Weiss, Brockway's deputy. During an open Finance Committee hearing in 1984, Packwood accused Weiss, one of the most sincere and best-liked aides on the Joint

Committee, of lying about the position of a fringe-benefit lobbying group. It was a cruel and embarrassing scene that soured many aides on the blustery lawmaker.

So when Packwood hung Brockway out to dry at the press conference on the 25-percent plan, no one who knew the temperamental chairman was too surprised. Many of Brockway's friends took great delight in addressing him afterward by a new name: "Senator Brockway."

Despite his shoddy treatment, Brockway knew that he had a job to do. The chairman's attempt to distance himself publicly from the 25-percent plan, Brockway believed, masked an interest in making it work. Brockway also knew that he and his people were the only ones in Congress with the expertise to do that. Diefenderfer could not do it, and John Colvin, Packwood's top tax aide, having been blamed for the failure of the first plan, was now largely being cut out of the picture. Packwood's pinning responsibility for the plan on Brockway, therefore, was true in one respect: All that stood between Packwood and failure was Dave Brockway and the Joint Committee staff.

Brockway's task was to turn the 25-percent solution, which still had elements that were politically unacceptable, into a tax plan that could pass muster in the committee and in the Senate. The top rate had to remain close to 25 percent, in order to retain the interest of conservatives like Wallop; in addition, at least some of the most popular middle-class deductions, such as those for mortgage interest and charitable contributions, had to be retained. That left Brockway with a double challenge: He had to find a way to raise the revenue to pay for the lower rates and retained deductions, and just as important, he had to make sure the sharp rate reduction did not cause the plan to unduly favor the wealthy. Ultimately, he struck on two obscure, but vital, twists of tax policy that solved his problems.

The solutions were worked out during the weekend of April 26 and 27. Brockway and his colleagues retreated into the cramped revenue estimators' office on the House side of the Capitol and started trying to fit the pieces together. The tax plan was like a huge jigsaw puzzle, and Brockway worked with Randy Weiss and revenue estimators Eric Cook, Steve Lerch, and Bernie Schmitt in an effort to find the missing pieces. Cook was the staff expert on a notion that Brockway himself found extremely attractive. It was a complicated and controversial concept, but Brockway knew that the idea could be the linchpin of the entire enterprise and the keystone of a new Packwood plan.

The idea was to launch a frontal assault on tax shelters by prohibiting the use of "passive" losses to offset other types of taxable income. Passive losses were losses on paper that went to investors who did not actively participate in a business. Such losses often resulted from limited-partnership arrangements, and provided investors in high tax brackets with large write-offs that reduced their taxes. Some of the most popular tax-shelter investments, such as real estate, cattle-feeding, and equipment leasing, produced paper losses two or three times the size of the initial investments.

The proposal would prohibit investors from reducing their taxable income with losses from passive investments. Earned income would then be subject to tax regardless of the extent of such paper losses. The screams from real estate interests to a similar proposal in the House had been so loud that the Ways and Means Committee had for the most part steered clear of it, choosing only to incorporate it in its minimum tax. Earlier attempts by Moynihan and Chafee to enact the idea in the Senate had also failed. But this time, Brockway's scheme had a chance. It neatly addressed the problem of the moment. Indeed, it seemed the perfect political solution to the puzzle that the 25-percent plan created.

The passive-loss provision accomplished several objectives at once. First, it raised a significant amount of revenue—in combination with a proposal to limit interest deductions, it was worth about $50 billion over five years. That helped solve one of the Finance Committee's most pressing problems: finding enough revenue to save the industry-specific tax breaks that its members cherished. Second, and more important, the disallowance of passive losses hurt wealthy people almost exclusively. That meant the provision would reduce the amount of tax cut that upper-income people received, despite the drastic reduction in the top tax rate. Keeping down the size of that tax cut for the rich was key to the political success of the tax-reform plan.

Brockway thought he could make everyone happy with his passive-loss proposal. The senators would not have to turn to some highly unpopular revenue source, such as excise-tax increases or complete repeal of the state and local tax deduction, to fund their tax-rate cuts. Instead, they could say—truthfully—that they were getting the money from rich people by killing "unfair" tax shelters. They also would be able to say—truthfully—that thanks to the provision they could chop the top individual tax rate nearly in half without giving a windfall to the wealthy.

When Brockway broached the subject with Packwood, he was careful to warn the chairman of the political risks. "Look," Brockway said, "you can do this, but I can tell you it's going to be controversial. A lot of people are going to scream." Packwood was willing to take the chance. "If you give me rates in the twenties," he replied, "no problem."

To help further reduce the benefit to the wealthy, Packwood urged Brockway to adopt another proposal, which was more along the lines of a tax-writing trick. First used in the Kemp plan, the provision made the top individual tax rate seem lower than it really was by "phasing out" tax benefits for high-income individuals. Under existing law, all taxpayers, no matter how much money they made, enjoyed the benefits of the lower tax rates on the first income they earned. In addition, all taxpayers got the benefit of the personal exemption. The Packwood proposal was to gradually eliminate those benefits for people whose incomes exceeded a certain amount. This would be accomplished by imposing a surtax of about 5 percent on incomes within a certain range, probably extending from about $75,000 to $200,000 a year. For taxpayers in that income range, there would be a "phantom" top marginal tax rate—the rate on each additional dollar a taxpayer earned—which would be considerably higher than the stated top rate. The scheme produced a perverse result: Families with moderately high incomes would have to pay higher marginal tax rates than would those with very high incomes. The device was a Darmanesque sleight of hand; in fact, it was similar to gimmicks advocated by Darman in his efforts to get a 30-percent top rate during the development of the president's plan.

Brockway and Weiss thought the idea was wacky, but they were under orders, and they complied. The main attraction of tax reform to the Senate was its low top rate, and the lower that rate was in appearance—if not in fact—the better chance the entire package had of winning approval.

Slowly, Brockway put together a plan that fit Packwood's demands. It was an intricate proposal, and in many ways, a house of cards. If the senators insisted on changing any major part of it, the whole thing might collapse. In order to drive the top rate into the twenties, as a clear majority of the committee preferred, the package had to contain a strong passive-loss rule, the tricky "phase-out" provisions, and also the repeal of the preferential treatment of capital gains, which was the favorite tax break of a broad coalition of businesses and investors. If any of those three tax benefits proved too resilient and was retained, the distribution of tax cuts would tip toward the wealthy and the plan would become politically unpalatable. Conversely, if the top rate was nudged up higher to increase the bite on the wealthy, many members would balk at taking such controversial steps as repealing the capital-gains benefit, which under existing law taxed long-term gains at 20 percent. It was an extremely fragile plan.

On Monday, April 28, Senator Dole, unaware of any of the plotting at the Joint Tax Committee, spoke the words that were on the minds of anyone who had watched the fiasco at the Finance Committee. Tax overhaul, he said, "is hanging by a thread." He added, "If we can't get a good bill, I would suggest we wait until next year."

But Packwood, secure in the belief that he had an emerging core group and a plan they might accept, refused to concede defeat. "All I can do here is plug away day by day," he said, and he continued to prepare behind the scenes for what he knew was a critical meeting the next day.

On Tuesday, April 29, the members marched into the exec room expecting the worst. What they found, instead, was a complete, and for some, pleasant surprise. "We came over to hear the eulogy on tax reform," said Senator David Pryor, "and we found some life in the old corpse."

Packwood handed out two more plans, one with a 26-percent and another with a 27-percent top rate, the variations Brockway and his staff had devised over the weekend. This time, Packwood did not shrink from taking a healthy chunk of the credit for Brockway's work. The plans went a long way toward meeting the objections of the members, and they did so without raising corporate taxes too high. The distribution of tax cuts was also politically acceptable: The middle-income categories did far better than the high-income groups did.

Both plans also retained some of the most cherished middle-class tax breaks that the 25-percent plan had eliminated, including write-offs for mortgage-interest payments, charitable contributions, and state and local income and property taxes. The 27-percent plan also kept deductions for state and local sales taxes. However, both plans repealed the extremely popular deduction for contributions to individual retirement accounts, which the tax-writing committees had expanded significantly five years earlier.

Inside the exec room, Bradley took the lead in explaining the delicate interrelationships that held the plans together. He pointed out how important it was to get the rate low and get rid of both the capital-gains and passive-loss benefits. He explained how much of a tax cut each income group would get and why. He concluded that the new plans were superior to the first one, and also better than existing law.

Bentsen, the most experienced businessman of the group, immediately caught the far-reaching import of the passive-loss provision. It was an extremely crude and blunt instrument of reform, and it would be painful to many investors and businessmen. Bentsen was filled with questions and concerns: Which losses would be disallowed, he wondered. Were any real, economic losses on the chopping block? How could eliminating the write-off for those be justified? What about a more gradual phase-in to prevent the severe dislocations that such a monumental change would cause? Despite his many concerns, Bentsen indicated he would probably be willing to go along, particularly if the top rate were no higher than 26 percent. He knew that an all-out attack on tax shelters would be a politically popular component of reform.

Other members were not as quick to decipher the impact of the new plans. The meeting was spent by most members simply trying to understand what was in the plans and what was not. Chafee inquired about the status of the mortgage-interest deduction: It was retained. Moynihan wanted to know about the minimum tax: A tough one was still included. Danforth wanted to know the status of pension-law changes: The committee's earlier decisions made in open session still held.

Nevertheless, the senators were clearly intrigued by the proposal. "How do we now proceed?" Danforth inquired.

Packwood noted that corporate taxes would still have to be raised by a substantial amount, although not as much as in the president's bill or the House bill. He brought out the first of many lists of revenue-raisers that, he said, could easily do the job. If the committee would agree to the changes on the individual tax items, Packwood said, he would start work on the corporate side. Although it would not be easy, he thought he could fashion a plan that would please a majority of the panel.

The attitude of the members was markedly changed by the meeting. Thanks to Brockway, Packwood had in his hands a workable alternative to his failed first attempt. His members considered the new plan "reform," and they knew they could sell it to their constituents that way. They began to believe for the first time that there would be a bill. The mood had shifted, and a momentum, similar to that Rostenkowski had created in the Ways and Means Committee when he turned around the bank vote, was taking hold.

Signs of this new awakening were immediately apparent. Dole emerged from the exec room to amend his earlier assessment that the bill was "hanging by a thread." This time, he concluded, it was "hanging by a rope." Bentsen also was more upbeat: "It is back on track." David Boren of Oklahoma, the tax-reform opponent, lamented: "Just when I thought I got this bill in bad trouble, he pulls something out of his hat."

Packwood was effervescent with optimism and said he planned to work through the weekend. "If it looks like we're this hot, let's keep going," he said. "You seize the moment when it's there."

The next morning, Wednesday, April 30, Packwood began a ritual that he repeated each weekday until the bill was completed. He met at 7:30 A.M. with his own staff and Brockway and Weiss. Then, at eight-thirty, he met with his core group of senators. At about ten o'clock, the rest of the committee convened in the exec room for private consultations that mostly involved slogging through lists of provisions that would raise enough revenue to pay for the dramatically lower rates.

The most important meeting that Wednesday, however, was an afternoon gathering in the Capitol offices of Majority Leader Dole.

The majority leader's offices are in the oldest part of the Capitol, midway between the Senate chamber and the Rotunda, and they are steeped in the history of the Republic. When the Capitol was still under construction, the rooms served as the meeting place of the House of Representatives. Later they were the robing chambers for the Supreme Court. The ceiling of Dole's own office contains one of the first fresco works in America, a miniature of Michelangelo's "Creation of Adam" done by the man who touched up the Sistine Chapel for the pope. During the War of 1812, the Senate stored books from the Library of Congress in this room, and when British soldiers stormed the Capitol in 1814, they used the books to start a blaze that eventually burned down most of the city. On a little table in Dole's office is an engraving depicting British soldiers gleefully tossing books into the marble fireplace that still stands nearby.

For the most part, Dole had been cool to the whole idea of tax reform.

He had even suggested to White House officials that they drop the initiative, and instead claim victory due to the rate cuts in the 1981 bill and the "reforms" contained in the tax bills he helped shepherd through Congress in 1982 and 1984. He was frequently absent from the Finance Committee meetings because of his own hectic schedule, but when he did arrive during the earlier markup process, his vote was frequently cast in opposition to reform.

After seeing the 26- and 27-percent plans, however, Dole began to change his tune. He was intrigued and impressed. During a private briefing on the intricacies of the proposals, he repeatedly brushed aside reservations expressed by his aide. "This thing," he said, "is going to pass." He told Packwood the same thing during a meeting on the balcony outside his office, which commanded a breathtaking view down the Mall to the Washington Monument and the Lincoln Memorial. Dole's opinion carried a lot of weight. His support for the tax-reform effort would be crucial not only for its success in the Finance Committee, but also for its reception on the Senate floor.

When Dole convened the meeting of the Republican members of the Finance Committee that Wednesday afternoon, his views of the radical new plan were not widely known. Baker and Darman, who were also invited to the meeting, came with a feeling of trepidation. They feared that Dole had called the meeting to bury tax reform, not to praise it.

That worry was soon dispelled. The participants sat in a conference room around an inlaid table. Baker and other supporters of the radical plan gave pep talks. "We talked a lot about lower rates and how this could be something that people could get excited about," Baker recalls. The Treasury secretary also used the same distinctly negative motivation that had propelled tax reform all along: He reminded the Republican senators that it was particularly important that they not be seen as killing tax reform.

Dole sat at the head of the table and for the first time began to send out clear signs of support for the bill. The majority leader usually talked in brief quips, and it was sometimes difficult to tell exactly where he stood on any issue, but this time his witticisms suggested he would support the effort. "Well, there are eleven of us," he noted at one point. "We can just vote it out."

The senators still voiced concerns. They were particularly troubled by two components of the Packwood plan: repeal of the capital-gains preference and the elimination of the IRA deduction. Those were two tax breaks that the president himself had expanded in his own version of tax reform; the Republican senators asked Baker if the White House was now willing to see both eliminated. They did not want to cross the popular president. In 1985 the president had abruptly backed out of a deal with the Senate Budget Committee to support a tax on Social Security benefits as a way to reduce deficits. The members did not want to have the rug yanked out from under them on tax reform in the same way.

In response, Baker gave a glowing dissertation on the concept of reform and on the attractiveness of low rates, but he could not answer the question. It was clear once again that the Treasury secretary was walking a narrow line. He wanted to encourage the senators, but could not speak for the president. He knew that the new White House team was unpredictable and could well decide to withhold the president's support, as they had in the House. The best Baker could do was to assure the Senators he would urge Reagan to support their bill.

The meeting helped convince the Republicans that it was time to support tax reform. With Dole on board, Packwood felt confident he could complete his bill. Two days later, he announced that he was "reasonably certain" that he had enough votes to pass it in committee.

Baker and Darman were scheduled to leave on Thursday, May 1, for an economic summit in Tokyo. After the Dole meeting, however, Baker saw that a critical point was at hand. "Should I delay until Friday? Should I delay until Saturday?" Baker kept asking Packwood. No, Packwood finally concluded, go to Tokyo, but leave Darman behind. Although a controversial figure during the Ways and Means markup the year before, Darman had become a valued adviser to Packwood and the Finance Committee's "core group." The clever Treasury official was skilled in picking his way through the tax minefield, and Packwood publicly referred to him as a "gem." Starting on Thursday morning, Darman began to attend both the seven-thirty and the eight-thirty private meetings, and he became an integral part of every large and small meeting that Packwood conducted in the interest of tax reform.

At about this time, Kemp attended a Packwood fundraiser and showered praise on the Finance Committee chairman. He compared Packwood's gutsy effort to cut tax rates to General MacArthur's Inchon landing in Korea. Soon thereafter, syndicated columnists Evans and Novak, whose column was a font of supply-side propaganda, used the Inchon-landing analogy to bolster the tax-reform effort. The new plaudits from supply-siders indicated that the two warring factions of the Republican party were converging in their opinion of Packwood's bill. Dole praised it from the traditional moderate point of view, and Kemp from the supply-side right. To any Republican, the signal was clear: This was legislation that deserved support.

On Friday, May 2, a lengthy explanation of the passive-loss provision appeared in *The Wall Street Journal*. The 980-word story was so long that it was continued deep inside the paper. The article concluded:

The effect [of the passive-loss rule] would be to nearly wipe out tax shelters that are a major force in financing commercial real estate construction, oil and gas drilling and certain agricultural activities, such as cattle feeding.

By coincidence, the story ended just above an advertisement that caught the attention of the Finance Committee. It read:

FEEDING CATTLE COULD REDUCE YOUR TAX BITE

Alta Verde Industries, a longtime South Texas custom feed lot is now placing cattle on feed for sale in early 1987. The ratio of 1986 expense to equity required is approximately three to one. If this interests you as an individual or closely-held corporation, check with your accountant, tax attorney or professional financial advisor and write or call for more information with no obligations.

The juxtaposition of the article and the advertisement so tickled the committee members that photocopies of the two were passed out during their exec-room session that day. The joking reflected a new esprit de corps that was developing among the members as the legislation began to pick up steam. Cloistered in the exec room, isolated from the hordes of lobbyists in the hallway, members of Packwood's core group began to develop a real interest in reform. Out in the hallway, many lobbyists were still betting the effort was dead, but inside, it was alive and well and gathering strength by the hour.

In a ploy to keep the effort from stalling, Packwood announced to the hallway loiterers—reporters as well as lobbyists—that there would be no sessions over the weekend. The hallway erupted with applause and cheers. In fact, first thing Saturday morning, the Finance Committee chairman secretly convened his core group for the most serious bargaining session of the entire process. It was a beautiful morning—the kind, Packwood would say later, that members would rather have spent pruning rose bushes or playing golf. Instead, Packwood, Brockway, Darman, Diefenderfer and the core group sat down in the Dirksen Senate Office Building, its hallways now deserted, and began to fill in the details of the most sweeping tax-reform bill in American history.

Danforth, Chafee, Mitchell, and Moynihan all arrived before 10:00 A.M.; Bradley came later in the day. The New Jersey Democrat was giving a speech in Kentucky that morning and turned down an invitation to the Kentucky Derby in order to return to the tax-writing session. Dole and Wallop did not attend, but were represented by staff.

Packwood began the day by proclaiming that the group had to find $35 billion worth of revenue-raisers over five years. That would be no easy task. Treasury officials offered up a "hit list," but nearly every item on the list struck interests dear to at least one member of the Finance Committee. Reform was not going to be painless, but the eight senators represented there were increasingly determined to produce a bill.

The first tax breaks to go were those favored only by committee members *not* in the core group. Those who had not embraced Packwood's plans were made to suffer for their reluctance. A provision providing special treatment for inventories was eliminated by the core group, despite its support by Charles Grassley of Iowa. A scheme providing tax-free bonds to finance municipal bus service, favored by John Heinz of Pennsylvania, was also excised. Oil refineries were taken out of the lucrative five-year depreciation category—a blow to David Boren of Oklahoma.

Even senators in the core group gave up some cherished tax breaks to make the plan work. Packwood himself sacrificed the preferential treatment of individual capital gains, an important break for the timber industry. Moynihan acquiesced to the repeal of the sales-tax deduction. Each of the core-group members anted up something to the cause of lower rates. As they made these tough decisions, they also developed an inside joke that helped justify their positions: When they chose to remove a tax break dear to any specific industry, the senator who should have been fighting tooth and nail to prevent the change would ask for "a note from the chairman." That meant that the lawmaker could tell the lobbyists in the hall that he had put up a valiant fight for the break, but that the chairman had taken it away anyway. The lobbyists could then blame the chairman.

Although they had to give up some of their favorite tax preferences, core-group members suffered far less than others. They were rewarded for their loyalty to the chairman. They each got to keep a few items that were dear to them. "If we were going to be the people supporting this bill, we were going to look after our particular interests," Moynihan said at the time.

Packwood agreed to repeal a withholding tax on foreign investors to please Wallop. (The Wyoming senator thought the tax depressed land values by discouraging foreign buyers.) "I gave it to him because he was a good soldier," Packwood explained. Danforth was allowed to keep the completed-contract method of accounting that was a fiscal boon to the military contractors who were big employers in his home state of Missouri. Even Bradley got a special deal: Limits were removed from the amount of tax-free bonds that could be used to finance the construction of government-owned solid-waste disposal facilities. As in the Ways and Means Committee, support for tax reform in the Finance Committee was, in part, bought with concessions.

Danforth was one of the wealthiest men in the Senate, and he opposed a new proposal that would increase taxes on income earned on money that grandparents gave to their grandchildren. He was supported in this position by Treasury, particularly by Baker. The Treasury secretary was himself a multimillionaire and did not like the idea of the government taxing away gifts to grandchildren. During meetings at the Treasury, he would erupt in displeasure whenever the "kiddie tax" topic arose. He even called from Tokyo to check on the status of the provision. A Treasury official was once asked why Baker was so adamant on that issue; he responded, "Because he's rich." In any case, Danforth and Baker prevailed, and the change was not adopted.

The group also spent considerable time debating possible ways to soften the controversial passive-loss rule. Rich Belas, Dole's aide, who had sacrificed a trip to Bermuda to attend the extraordinary weekend session, voiced Dole's preference for a long phase-in of the tax-shelter-killing provision. He floated the idea of imposing a new surtax on high-income individuals to pay for the more gradual passive-loss disallowance. Mitchell, who as chairman of the Democratic Senatorial Campaign Committee was the chief fundraiser for Democrats in the Senate, knew the passive-loss provision would anger big-money Democratic contributors in the real estate business; he also backed a slow phase-in. In the end, the senators agreed to ease the pain of the passive-loss rule somewhat by phasing it in over four years.

By the end of the day, the plan was taking shape: The top rate for individuals would be lowered to 27 percent. The special tax break for capital gains would be eliminated, there would be no excise-tax increases, and taxes on corporations would be increased by $100 billion over five years, with the top corporate rate set at 33 percent.

Before the meeting ended, the members of the group made a pact: They would keep each other informed about their intentions about the bill, and they would work together whenever possible to keep it intact. Moynihan announced that he would offer an amendment to save the sales-tax deduction. Mitchell said he would try to impose a third top rate for wealthy individuals, but would wait to offer the amendment on the Senate floor rather than foul up the committee's deliberations.

When the meeting ended late that afternoon, Packwood, Diefenderfer, and Darman retreated into Diefenderfer's office to watch the running of the Kentucky Derby. Bill Shoemaker won a 17–1 long shot astride a horse named Ferdinand. Darman made a note to himself that the victory was a good omen for the long-shot tax-reform plan.

The next afternoon, William Wilkins, the Democratic staff director of the Finance Committee, and Karen Stall, Senator Long's tax aide, went to visit Long at his apartment in the Watergate building. The apartment had once been owned by John Mitchell, the attorney general during the Nixon years, and was the place where Mitchell's wife, Martha, claimed she was held captive during the Watergate scandal. Its living room had a magnificent view of the Potomac River. The two aides sat down with Long in the living room to review the core group's decisions of a day earlier.

Hunched over the coffee table, Wilkins and Stall told Long that they felt it would be politically difficult for him to oppose the bill fashioned by the core group. As a primary architect of the tax code that would be replaced by the radical plan, Long had to be especially careful of being perceived as an opponent. If he fought the plan and won, or worse, if he fought it and lost, he might be cast as the villain, a sellout to special interests.

Sitting in his cream-colored lounge chair, Long made it clear he did not need a lecture about politics. He understood that a "pure" Bradley-Gephardt–like bill might be the only way out of the corner into which the committee had painted itself. He saw that the politics had shifted in favor of reform. Early in the Senate tax debate, he had begun to prepare for this moment by headlining a newsletter for constituents: LONG SUPPORTS REFORM. He was also a faithful friend and backer of Bob Packwood, the young man he helped train in the ways of tax legislation, and who, in turn, was always careful to keep Long and his interests in mind.

During the one-and-a-half-hour briefing, Long was most interested in hearing the major details of the plan. He liked the low rates. He liked removing poor people from the tax rolls, for he was always a sort of populist, a lasting legacy from his father. In general, he liked much of what he heard, and more important, he knew it would sell.

As Wilkins and Stall were leaving, Long asked, "Do you know Lloyd Bentsen's number at the farm?" He wanted to spread the news.

At five-fifteen, Monday morning, Senator Pryor, the Finance Committee's junior Democrat, was awakened by the insistent ringing of a telephone. "Evidently, someone has the wrong number," he thought, still misty with slumber. "I'm not going to answer that phone."

After what seemed like the fortieth ring, Pryor stumbled downstairs to his den and picked it up. "Hello," he said.

"Hey man, you weren't asleep were you?" said the rapid-fire voice on the other end that was immediately recognizable as Russell Long's.

"No," Pryor said, recovering quickly, "I was standing here waiting for you to call."

"Well," Long continued at a breakneck pace, "I wanted to tell you, David, Senator Packwood has a bill that is a good bill, it is a fair bill, and we ought to work with him to get it passed."

Other Democrats also got early-morning phone calls. The message for all of them was the same, and the import was clear: Packwood was going to get a bill. The tax-reform train was starting to move, and it was time to jump on board.

Later that day, the Finance Committee returned to public session on tax reform for the first time in two weeks. It was a brief meeting, but the rhetoric reflected the sea change in outlook. "We have an opportunity that is given to few," Packwood began. "If we march up that hill and fail, it will not pass our way again for another decade." His words were echoed by some of the same members who voted against him in the first phase of the markup. Danforth said that allowing rich people to pay no taxes was "just plain wrong." Chafee added that "it's insanity the way the current system is working out." Even the balky Heinz gritted his teeth and said, "I am very close to supporting this legislation."

Tuesday, May 6, was to be the final day of the public markup, but a tax bill would not be a tax bill without a last-minute crisis. In this case, the crisis was created by some of the most senior and powerful members of the tax-writing panel. Early that morning, the troublesome politics of oil began, once again, to rear its ugly head.

A secret meeting was called in the spacious Capitol hideaway of Senator Long, not far from the offices of Majority Leader Dole. The walls of the private hideaway were decorated with Audubon prints, and an imposing armoire made of Honduran mahogany stood to the right of the door. Long sat on a beige daybed in the corner, next to the telephone. Over the years, he had spent so many hours in that spot that the fabric on the sofa arm was worn from chafing. Surrounding Long, in horseshoe fashion, were most of the Finance Committee members who had a stake in the nation's oil patch, including Senators Dole, Bentsen, Boren, and Pryor.

In quiet tones, the group discussed their strategy. They were worried that independent oil and gas drillers might be put out of business by the stringent passive-loss provisions. Much of the money raised by independent oil drillers to finance their operations came from "passive" investors. The oilies wanted an exception for these investors, who invested in drilling by acquiring a so-called working interest in a well.

The meeting was not flashy. There were no rhetorical flourishes. The lawmakers simply had to decide what exception to seek for oil producers and how best to win an eleven-vote majority. The old pros—Long, Dole, and Bentsen—dominated the meeting. They decided to go for a broadly defined provision that would exclude all working-interest investments from the passive-loss rule and would cost the Treasury $1.4 billion over five years. They knew that tampering with passive losses, the linchpin of the package, was risky, but they also understood how important the exception was to the people they represented. Oil politics went beyond the numbers; to these legislators from oil-producing states, it was almost a religious matter. Passions ran high when oil was discussed, and reason was cast to the wind. The assembled senators were ready to fight to kill the bill if they did not get their way.

Meanwhile, Packwood was on the phone trying to round up support for a rule he hoped would impose discipline during the final hours of the committee's proceedings. The rule, which neither he nor Rostenkowski had been able to enforce previously, would require that each amendment offered would have to pay for itself. If a senator wanted to restore a certain tax break, he would have to take away another break to pay for it. Packwood believed that he could hold eleven votes, a majority of the panel, if he could enforce that amendment-by-amendment revenue-neutrality rule. "That's what I really worked on," he says. "We had almost generic agreement among the core group on almost everything, but it could come undone if we didn't require revenue neutrality."

To entice support for his effort, Packwood even made a few more concessions. To Roth, for instance, he promised to allow generous write-offs for chicken coops, which exist in abundance in Roth's home state of Delaware. The spadework paid off. When the committee finally convened Tuesday morning, Packwood called for a vote on his proposal to require revenue neutrality for the remainder of the markup. It passed without a single objection. A smile swept across Packwood's lips.

The fight was not over, however. In quick succession, Packwood had to beat back two efforts to retain the sales-tax deduction. Two weeks earlier, such amendments would have won easily, but now, the momentum of tax reform had begun to take hold. Both amendments lost by votes of 13–7. Packwood also defeated efforts by Heinz to weaken the corporate minimum tax.

The toughest vote came on an amendment to eliminate restrictions on deducting business-meal and entertainment expenses. It was the same issue that had come close to sinking Rostenkowski's plan in the Ways and Means Committee. Only two weeks earlier, William Armstrong of Colorado had been secure in the knowledge that he had the votes to pass his amendment. Whether he still had those votes was unclear. Packwood was not sure he could defeat Armstrong: if he did not, his bill could be in trouble.

Initially, there were ominous signs. Long supported the amendment, which was paid for by an increase in the corporate rate to 34 percent. He did so in his inimitable, homespun style. "Entertainment," he said, "is to the selling business as fertilizer is to the farming business." The stately Bentsen also was a backer. He justified his vote by saying, "I rarely pick up the check, [so] I can be totally objective." Packwood began to rest easier, however, when Dole spoke up. The majority leader said he believed in the entire package, thought it should be kept intact and would vote with the chairman against the Armstrong amendment. When the roll was called, the Armstrong amendment lost on a tie vote, 9–9. Dole was the deciding vote.

The members retired into the exec room, out of public view, where they still had a good bit of last-minute tinkering to do. They needed to find some more revenue, and there was still the slippery oil problem to solve. The revenue was found through some painful last-minute changes—they decided, for instance, to repeal the investment tax credit retroactive to the first of the year. They also engaged in some more sleight of hand—somehow the estimators found about $5 billion extra in the passive-loss rule. They found another $1 billion in a provision that no one on the panel had ever heard of. Roger Mentz, the assistant Treasury secretary, suggested extending the application of section 338—a section of the code dealing with premium prices paid for business assets—to raise the money. The senators, having no idea what section 338 was, agreed with a shrug.

The hassle over working interest was not so sedate. Bradley, Mitchell, and Chafee were violently opposed to the special carve-out for oil companies. They asserted that the hole in the passive-loss rule would serve as a magnet for tax-sheltered investments in the oil and gas industry and would provide an unfair benefit to the oil states. Oil-state senators protested that a working interest was very different than the usual limited-partnership tax shelter. Under a working-interest plan, they argued, investors carried full liability for the project and had to ante up more money if the drilling called for it. The investment was not "passive," they said.

Packwood took a risk on the issue. He knew the dispute was a major challenge to the success of his venture, yet he firmly opposed making any exceptions to the tax-shelter-killing provision. To make his point, he stood at the head of the exec-room table throughout the long debate. Darman sided with the oil-state senators, reflecting the preference of Secretary Baker, who was still thousands of miles away in Tokyo. Gradually, it became clear that the oilies had forged some important alliances. The oil interests beat back efforts to compromise their exception in the private meeting. So inflamed were the passions over the issue that Bradley insisted the committee vote again when the senators went back into public session at nearly eleven o'clock that evening.

Looking exhausted from the long day, members repeated their oil arguments when the public session convened. Bradley was particularly vociferous during the debate. It was as if the provision were a personal insult to him, a matter of pride. Dark circles made the bags under his eyes seem even heavier than usual; he was badly in need of a shave. He refused to let up on the issue, demanding that votes be taken even though the decision clearly had already been made and he had lost.

While other members looked as tired as Bradley, Long was still animated. He had spent most of the evening in New York City making a speech to businessmen and had flown back by helicopter. Keying off a charge by George Mitchell that the exception was unjustified, Long launched into the broad-gauged oratory that he learned from his legendary father:

Mr. Mitchell is a great lawyer and a great judge. He had a lifetime job as a federal judge, and he sacrificed that to serve in the Senate. Why a man would do that, I don't know.

There was laughter in the crowd and a growing excitement as the audience realized that Long was about to roll.

From a legal background, a life in the judiciary, he tends to look upon this tax law as that statue over there in front of the Supreme Court.

He pointed vigorously, as if out the window, his arms pulling out of his shirtsleeves.

They have a lady holding a scale. She's blindfolded. She doesn't know whose weight is on the left-hand side and whose is on the right-hand side. And that's how they're supposed to decide cases over there: not knowin' who they're helpin' and who they're hurtin'. Whoever puts the most weight on his side, wins. To say that we ought to pass laws the way they decide cases over there is as wrong as anything can be.

He pounded the table and waved his hands.

We fellas are lawmakers. We're supposed to know who we're helpin' and do it deliberately, and know who we're hurtin', and do that deliberately. Now the people in the oil and gas b'ness are the most depressed industry in the United States.

As he talked about the industry, he pounded his chest with both fists, speaking with such force as his tirade reached its climax that his voice started to squeak.

If you're sittin' over there in that court, I can understand your sayin', "I'm blind-folded. I'm gonna treat them all the same. This fella is broke, down and out. God knows he needs help. But the hell with him. I can't do anything about it." If you're a judge, that's how you'd do it. If you're a lawmaker, you'd say, "That poor fella needs help, let's help him."

With that, the vigor left the drive to kill the working-interest exception. Bradley looked angry, but defeated. There was no use in rebutting Senator Long—his rhetoric couldn't be matched. More important, he had the votes.

It was the last major hurdle of the evening. A few minor amendments were offered at the end, and in the rush to finish, Packwood accepted one by Senator Steve Symms, Republican of Idaho, even though it was not revenue neutral and lost $50 million. With his tie askew, Packwood began to stammer when he realized his mistake. "We're making unwise decisions when we start down this path," he said. Wallop, seeing Packwood's distress, made an almost unprecedented offer: He said he would agree to alter the repeal of the withholding tax on foreigners that Packwood had given him for being "a good soldier." The change would net $400 million, and more than pay for Packwood's oversight. Packwood accepted the generous offer with great fanfare. The audience murmured in disbelief.

Packwood then asked Darman, who was sitting at the table in front of the senators, if the administration had anything to say before the vote. The deputy Treasury secretary had spent much of the day on the phone, trying to hammer out a statement acceptable to the White House staff. Once again, the White House aides were dragging their feet. They were worried about the plan's repeal of the capital-gains tax break and its cutback in IRA deductions. Rather than endorse the bill, they wanted a cautious statement that called the committee proposal "a major step toward mean-ingful tax reform." Darman grew angry at their stubborn intransigence and said it would be better to say nothing at all than to make that kind of mealy-mouthed statement. This is a great and historic moment, he argued, and the president should take his share of the credit. Darman called Baker in Tokyo to complain, and Baker took up the matter with Chief of Staff Regan, who was also at the Tokyo summit. Finally, after much long-distance fighting and gnashing of teeth, a statement of support was agreed to. When Packwood gave the cue, Darman said the president had decided the Senate Finance plan generally fit his requirements for meaningful tax reform. "We congratulate you," he concluded, "and the distinguished members of the Senate Finance Committee, for your bold tax-reform proposal."

When Darman finished, Bradley quipped: "The president knows how to steal a headline ten thousand miles away."

Then Packwood called for the historic vote. He expected at most 16 ayes, but the night had gone remarkably well. Although he had lost the working-interest battle, Packwood had won the votes of all the oil-state senators as a result. Everyone voted aye. Pryor had told his staff earlier that he was going to vote nay, but his was the last name called, and faced with near-unanimity, he meekly pronounced aye along with the others. No one was willing to be hung out alone to be ridiculed for pandering to special interests.

Packwood called the unanimous, 20–0 vote, a miracle, and in a way it was. Two and a half weeks before, Packwood pulled off the table a plan so badly battered by special-interest amendments that it was about to collapse of its own weight. Six days later, he unveiled a new proposal so radical that he was forced to disown it. Buried in that radical plan had been the rudiments of success—a rate structure so low that even the Finance Committee could buy it.

The unanimous vote made it clear that a tax-reform bill was going to become law. Dole later characterized the event perfectly. In just a few days' time, he said, "the bill went from immovable to unstoppable."

Chapter 10

Politics Is Local

The night after his unanimous victory, Packwood was on a plane headed home. The senator's Republican primary was less than two weeks away, but he rested comfortably during the six-hour journey, secure in the knowledge that he had left his biggest reelection problem behind him. After weeks of dawn-to-midnight days, he had turned a huge potential liability into an important political asset. Prior to that flight, the Oregon senator had heard only complaints about tax reform in general and about his earlier bill in particular. But now that was all changed. Passenger after passenger walked up the narrow airplane aisle to congratulate him for his good work. "Thank God somebody's done it," one traveler said as he shook Packwood's outstretched hand.

On the ground, Packwood got the same reaction. The criticism that had been poured on his head for his failed effort the previous month was gone. Instead of peppering Packwood with complaints about his huge campaign hoard and his giveaways to special interests, the local news media began to praise him. Prior to the triumphant final vote, a cartoon in the *Oregonian,* the state's major newspaper, had ridiculed a devilish-looking Packwood for having "seventeen versions of tax reform." Afterward, a follow-up cartoon pictured a more benign-appearing Packwood on Bill Bradley's shoulders throwing a tax-bill basketball through a hoop as the press exclaimed, "Incredible shot!" *Oregonian* editorials went so far as to concede that Packwood had "confounded the skeptics, including us" by producing a bill that would mean "real reform."

"There is special interest after special interest that is hit in this bill," Packwood gloated, pointing out that many of the injured groups "contributed to my campaign." It was a true boast. Packwood's victory was encouraging proof that moneyed interests could not always buy their way to success in Congress.

For the first time, polls unearthed a budding interest in tax reform among the populace. A *Wall Street Journal*–NBC poll showed a significant rise in public optimism about the effects of reform. Although the public still worried about losing favorite deductions, 47 percent of those asked in June 1986—after the Finance Committee had finished its work—said they thought the legislation would help them personally, up from 39 percent in November 1985, during the Ways and Means markup. The House bill actually provided the average taxpayer with a bigger tax cut than the Finance Committee package, but it was the strong allure of lower rates that apparently won over public sentiment.

Despite the swelling support, however, the battle for tax reform was far from over. The bill's next hurdle, the Senate floor, had always promised to be one of its toughest challenges. Although the Senate operates with a veneer of gentlemanly decorum, it is often an unruly place. Its members were privately referred to as the "animals" by Majority Leader Dole, whose tough task it was to keep them under control. Tax bills, in particular, had traditionally caused near-chaos in the Senate, as the senators struggled to win special favors for their constituents. The whole idea of tax reform was an affront to their way of operating; it threatened to take away many of the goodies that they had tucked away in the income-tax code for the benefit of the folks back home. Holding together the fragile tax-reform package on the floor would not be easy. As Bradley put it: "Sometimes the Senate's a little like jazz. You can't predict what's going to happen."

The founding fathers intended the Senate to be the great deliberative body of the legislature. Statesmen like Daniel Webster, John Calhoun, and Stephen Douglas made their mark there. The grand oratory of those nineteenth-century senators had become rare by the time of the tax debate in 1986, but long-winded rhetoric had not. Modern-day senators were the sort of people, one Senate aide observed, who could give a speech in the shower. Unlike House members, who had to walk to a microphone before speaking, each senator had a microphone at his or her own desk and could rise at any moment to join in the debate. For anyone who watched the Senate, the sight was a familiar one: A senator would rise, button his jacket as if by reflex, raise his chin, and then begin. The speeches could go on for hours. The light at the top of the Capitol dome would often be seen shining late into the night, signifying that the Senate was still in session.

Unlike the House, the Senate has few rules to limit debate, or to restrict amendments. Senators may filibuster a bill—talk endlessly to prevent a vote from happening. They may delay a bill by offering amendment after amendment. Former Majority Leader Mike Mansfield once observed that a single obstinate senator "can tie up the Senate for days, and if he allies himself with a few other senators, he can tie up the Senate for weeks."

In such an unrestricted environment, tax bills were open season. During the 1981 tax bill, the senators debated for 102 hours and adopted eighty-one amendments. During the 1982 tax bill they debated for thirty-four hours and adopted forty-nine amendments. And they debated the 1984 tax bill for 111 hours, adopting eighty-six amendments. Offering a big tax-overhaul bill on the Senate floor was like tossing a piece of bread to a flock of seagulls: Everyone wanted a bite.

Although the course through the Senate would be perilous, the tax-reform bill had several important forces working in its favor.

First of all, the 20–0 Finance Committee vote had convinced highly paid business lobbyists that the tax bill now had unstoppable momentum. Their first response to the vote was shellshock. "Terror and disbelief is the reaction," said Wayne Thevenot, president of the National Realty Committee, an association of big real estate developers. "At least our people have nice, big buildings of their own to jump from." But most business lobbyists quickly concluded that it was pointless to keep fighting the bill. The Senate Finance Committee had been their last chance, and they had lost. As DuPont Chairman Richard Heckert put it: "At some point, you stop lying in the street and kicking and screaming, because nobody gives a damn anyway."

With tax reform clearly on its way to passage, the most savvy lobbyists decided it was time to jump on board. Packwood's bill, for most of them, was the lesser of two evils. It raised corporate taxes by $100 billion, while the House bill raised corporate taxes by $140 billion. That gave corporate lobbyists $40 billion worth of reasons to support Packwood's plan. Overnight, almost every business group in town became ardent supporters of the Finance Committee proposal. Even Charls Walker, who had fought tax reform at every turn, now saw the futility of opposing the entire effort, and voiced support. "The Packwood tax plan deserves early passage," he said.

The most virulent opponents of the effort became born-again reformers. During the Ways and Means debate in November 1985, the Chamber of Commerce of the U.S.A. said the House tax bill "would be disastrous for the American economy, American business, and the American worker." But the Finance Committee bill, it said a half-year later, would "on balance have a positive effect on long-term economic growth and job creation." Likewise, the National Association of Manufacturers, which thought the House bill would "pose extremely high risks for the economy," urged the Senate to pass the Finance Committee bill—without alteration.

The high-sounding rhetoric masked the real reason for supporting the bill—it was the lobbyists' last chance to save themselves and at least some of their favorite tax breaks. Every interest group in Washington wanted to show support for the measure in hopes of currying favor with Packwood and his committee. The Senate bill, they knew, would not be the final bill. The ultimate fight would come later, after Senate passage, when representatives of the Ways and Means Committee and the Finance Committee sat down together to reconcile the two bills in a House-Senate conference. Many corporate interest groups already had made an enemy of Rosten-kowski by fighting his bill in the House. They still had a chance, they thought, to make amends with Packwood and win some concessions in the final negotiating.

Another factor that helped the cause of reform was that fact that the bill would be one of the first major Senate debates broadcast on television. The House had been on the air for years, but the stodgy Senate had resisted until the summer of 1986. The Senate was an exclusive club, with customs and practices that senators feared might seem odd to the outside world. Television was viewed as an undignified intrusion, especially by old-timers like Senator Long. But even the U.S. Senate could not block progress forever, and it finally agreed to a trial run. As the debate on tax reform approached, senators hired media consultants to spruce up their wardrobes (red ties and blue shirts were preferred) and to coif and dye their hair. Packwood even checked the camera locations to see what spot on the semicircular floor would afford him the most flattering angle. (As it turned out, the place he chose was the wrong one. It was too close to the brown leather couches in the rear of the chamber where staffers always sat; as Packwood spoke, a constant stream of scurrying aides could be seen over his shoulder.) Thanks in part to the prying eye of television, members were leery of appearing to obstruct reform. They feared that their usual long harangues might look unseemly to the public. Few wanted to risk appearing in full color on the evening news as a defender of "special interests."

The prospects for reform also got a boost from the new Gramm-Rudman budget law that had been enacted a year earlier. Under the law, amendments that increased the budget deficit could be blocked by an objection from any member of the Senate. For technical reasons, that portion of the budget law was not in place in the early summer of 1986 when the tax debate began, but the spirit of Gramm-Rudman prevailed, and the senators were under pressure to keep all amendments revenue neutral. That meant senators wishing to restore a tax break would also have to propose a way to pay for that break. It was a new discipline for the senators. A similar rule had helped the bill win approval during the final day's proceedings in the Finance Committee, and it was sure to help the measure on the Senate floor as well. Often, the Senate could tie itself in knots over the most minor tax legislation, but with this new requirement of revenue neutrality, the chances of approving major amendments diminished significantly.

To help propel the bill through the Senate, Packwood began organizing his rapidly growing band of supporters. Once again, he turned to Bill Bradley for help. Thus far in the tax-reform debate, Bradley had nudged his brainchild along mostly by giving credit to others: first to the president, then to Rostenkowski, and then to Packwood during the second and ultimately successful phase of the Finance Committee markup. "There's plenty of credit to go around," he was fond of saying. As a basketball player, Bradley said, "I always got as big a kick out of giving an assist as making a basket." Now it was time for Bradley to go to the hoop himself. He became a key coalition builder among Democrats on the Senate floor. With typical energy, Bradley reached out—one at a time—to his fellow Democrats to recruit them to join a bloc of tax-reform backers.

Bradley also worked to convince Packwood to adopt an important strategy: to build a coalition to oppose *all* amendments. Packwood had initially thought his bloc of supporters should be sworn only to oppose amendments that were paid for by raising rates, but Bradley urged a tougher stand. He reasoned that any exception to a solid front against all changes to the bill would lead to the disintegration of the entire pro-reform coalition. An amendment that saved one tax break, he argued, might be paid for by eliminating a break that was important to other members of the group, causing dangerous schisms. The bill was fragile, and keeping it from falling apart was going to be a delicate task. As a show of good faith, Bradley even abandoned his own plans for an amendment to kill the oil drillers' tax-shelter loophole.

Packwood believed amendments would probably be inevitable on such a major bill; nevertheless, he bought Bradley's recommendation. The two men began rounding up other senators who were willing to pledge to fight every amendment. Baker and Darman also persuaded the president to back the no-amendment strategy. By the end of May, just three weeks after the Finance Committee reported its bill to the Senate floor, Packwood and Bradley had convinced thirty-two of the Senate's one hundred members to stand with them.

To help keep that bloc of senators together, and to gather even more votes, Packwood and Bradley sought to tap the growing support among lobbyists. Bradley had begun this process in early 1986, working closely with many of the same groups that had supported the Rostenkowski bill. He kept in contact with the CEO Tax Group and the Tax Reform Action Coalition—business groups that wanted a lower corporate rate—as well as "good government" groups, such as Common Cause and Citizens for Tax Justice, and also various anti-poverty groups.These groups became the nucleus for a far larger coalition patched together by Packwood and one of his top Finance Committees aides, Mary McAuliffe. The 15-27-33 coalition—which took its forgettable name from the all-important individual and corporate rates in the plan—grew rapidly. By the end of May, less than a month after the committee had approved its bill, the 15-27-33 coalition had expanded to well over six hundred companies and organizations, including some of the most vocal opponents of the House bill. For example, the Independent Petroleum Association of America and the General Contractors of America were members in good standing, and for good reason: Tax breaks precious to both groups were retained in the Finance Committee bill, but were curtailed by the House.

The pro-reform coalition was extremely diverse. It ranged from Amway Corporation to the Children's Defense Fund, from Church Women United to the Irish Distillers Group, from Philip Morris to the Consumer Federation of America. There were eleven groups whose name began with the word *national,* including the National Council of LaRaza, the National Puerto Rican Coalition, the National Black Child Development Institute and the National Coalition of American Nuns. Another five began with the word *American,* including the American Association of University Women and the American Frozen Food Institute. The coalition even included the Sisters of the Humility of Mary. Only a few months earlier, Senator Armstrong of Colorado had said of tax reform, "Nobody wants it." Now, the list of members of the 15-27-33 coalition made it look like everyone wanted it.

In late May, a week before the start of the Senate floor debate, Dole announced that senators who sought to make major changes in the bill would simply be "out of luck." Tax reform had a good head of steam, and looked like it could chug right through the Senate. "In all the years I've been here," said Senator Paul Laxalt, Republican of Nevada, "I've never seen such unanimity on a piece of legislation. Most senators sense this is almost historic."

Still, tax overhaul had been burdened with problems and setbacks all along its way, and Bradley, for one, was taking nothing for granted. "You don't start worrying about the next season if you are heading to Boston to play the Celtics in the Eastern Final," the former New York Knick said. "You've got to get through the [Senate] floor. . . . Frankly, I'm very pleased that the bill is where it is, but it's still got a long way to go. And it's not over 'til it's over. Until the bill is finished, entrenched opposition always has a counteroffensive."

Faced with such strong support for the broad outlines of the Senate bill, many senators began shifting their attention to the smaller issues. The Finance Committee bill was a massive document with hundreds of provisions. The amounts of money involved were so immense that provisions costing less than $100 million were referred to derisively by tax writers as "zero point one." Those costing less than $5 million were denoted simply by an asterisk. But the spare change of tax writers was a holy fortune to anyone else, and as the Senate floor debate approached, the scramble among senators and lobbyists to get some of that change became intense.

Speaker O'Neill was fond of reminding his colleagues that "all politics is local." The grab for tax-bill favors was proof of that adage. Forgetting about the overarching significance of the tax-reform bill, senators worked hard to win special tax relief for certain friends back home.

The common practice for a Finance Committee chairman is to come to the floor with a kind of slush fund under his control for the purpose of dispensing transition rules. In past years, transition rules were included in the bill for the benefit of specific constituents, but were drafted in ways that would also aid others who were similarly situated. The tax-reform rules, however, were frequently written like rifle shots to benefit only the constituent companies or individuals—and no one else. That meant that two companies or people with exactly the same tax situation could well be treated very differently under the bill. The mere volume of these special handouts in the Senate alone also was unique at a staggering total of $5.5 billion. Still it was not enough. Every time Packwood ventured onto the Senate floor, his colleagues stuffed pieces of paper into his jacket pocket, with additional requests for transition rules.

All told, the Finance Committee bill granted generous transition rules to 174 beneficiaries. Many of them were corporations, such as Avon Products, General Motors, RCA, Pan American World Airways, MCI Communications, General Mills, and Control Data. Others were cities and municipal facilities such as the New Orleans Superdome and the University of Delaware. There also were some oddball winners, such as five biomedical researchers in Rochester, New York, and the estate of James H. W. Thompson, a wealthy silk merchant who mysteriously disappeared in Malaysia in 1967.

In addition to the transition rules, there were other narrow tax-law changes designed to benefit a few lucky taxpayers. Page Wodell was one of the biggest winners. A provision buried in the Finance Committee bill would save Wodell about $5 million. He had lost a bid in tax court to escape that much in tax on his grandmother's estate. Unwilling to call it quits, Wodell turned to his Yale University classmate, Senator Chafee, who added the amendment to the Finance Committee bill. "It was just plain unfair," the Republican tax writer said of his schoolmate's problems.

The *Houston Chronicle* was also a winner. The Texas newspaper was owned by a tax-free foundation and was threatened by the 1969 law that prohibited such foundations from running large businesses. For seventeen years, the newspaper had been trying to get around the law. Texas Senator Bentsen, a man who well understood the value of good relations with the press, was always happy to help. He had tried repeatedly to sponsor amendments exempting the *Chronicle* from the 1969 law, but his amendments had always been dropped. When the tax-reform bill came along in 1986, he decided to try his old chestnut again. "What would a tax bill be without the *Houston Chronicle* amendment?" joked John Salmon, the Ways and Means Committee's former chief counsel.

Then there was the "Marriott amendment," a name designed to convey the provision's importance to the hotel industry. Sponsored by Dole, who was a popular and well-compensated speaker at convention banquets, the amendment stated that "business meals provided as an integral part of certain convention programs would be fully deductible in 1987 and 1988." That meant that extravagant dinners at meetings in Las Vegas and Hawaii would be fully subsidized by taxpayers, while a salesman's working lunch would be limited to 80 percent.

Dole also secured an exception to protect the tax benefits for a giant renovation project in a blighted area in downtown Manhattan on behalf of the junior senator from New York, Alfonse D'Amato. On his own behalf, Dole won a special rule for the redevelopment of another downtown Manhattan—in his home state of Kansas.

Not all special-interest breaks were as easy to decipher as these. A time-worn tradition of transition rules was to camouflage their beneficiaries in indirect language. For example, General Motors was not named directly in the transition-rules sections of the bill. It was described as "an automobile manufacturer that was incorporated in Delaware on October 13, 1916." A rapid-transit line to Dulles International Airport was called "a mass-commuting facility that provides access to an international airport." A drilling project by an Alabama firm called Sonat was listed as "a binding contract entered into on October 20, 1984, for the purchase of six semi-submersible drilling units." And a tax break designed to attract outside investors to finance citrus farmers who suffered freeze damage was described this way:

The rules governing expensing of costs of replanting groves, orchards or vineyards destroyed by freezing or other natural disasters would be extended to replanting on land other than the land on which the plants were destroyed and to businesses having new owners who materially participate in the business so long as the new owners hold less than 50 percent interest.

Transition rules and other specialized relief were an inescapable part of every congressional tax bill; most senators dipped into this pork barrel without hesitation. One senator, however—Democrat Howard Metzenbaum of Ohio—took it upon himself to crusade against the most unsavory of these favors. A self-made millionaire who earned his fortune in the parking-lot business, Metzenbaum had developed a reputation during a decade in the Senate as the liberal master of obstruction. He was the self-appointed guardian of the "general interest," and tax-bill provisions that benefited narrow business interests were among his favorite targets. He regularly fought the ones that he and his able aide, David Starr, deemed the most egregious. Dole liked to refer to the gadfly senator as the "Commissioner." On more than one occasion, Dole, when he was Finance Committee chairman, used the obstreperous Metzenbaum to winnow away tax subsidies that he had granted in his committee or on the floor, but he secretly wished to discard. "When you prepare an amendment or a bill, subconsciously you're thinking about Howard Metzenbaum," Senator Pryor said. "Will it pass the Metzenbaum test?"

On the floor, the white-haired Ohioan unveiled a long list of what he considered the most disgraceful transition rules. For a bill that carried the title "reform," the list was startling. Senators had slipped in one provision after another benefiting small constituent groups and home-state employers. Senator Boren had included an exemption from a multimillion-dollar pension-fund withdrawal penalty for Phillips Petroleum, which was a major employer in his home state of Oklahoma. Senator Long had sponsored an exemption from tax for a fund set up by Manville Corporation for victims of poisoning from one of its main products, asbestos. Senator Armstrong had championed a rule that allowed a small group of investors to save an estimated $1 million each by retaining special capital-gains treatment for their stake in a Colorado coal company.

Metzenbaum even took aim at a tax break for Bermuda that was traced to Packwood himself. Under existing law, convention trips to certain countries were deductible, but only if those countries gave the United States their banks' records for use in tax audits of American citizens. Bermuda had consistently refused to hand over such information. Nevertheless, the Finance Committee tax bill extended to Bermuda the special convention benefit. The Finance Committee staff claimed that the provision was inserted in the bill at the request of the White House because of "foreign-policy considerations." No doubt Packwood and his wife were fully briefed on the situation in July 1985, when they were flown to Bermuda in a government plane for a weekend of what a White House spokesman called "sensitive and important discussions."

Despite his crusading rhetoric, even the Commissioner did not walk away from the fray with unsoiled hands. Metzenbaum personally advocated transition rules for North Star Steel of Youngstown, the Cleveland Dome stadium, and convention centers in Columbus and Akron. In addition, he excluded from his published list of heinous transition rules the largest transition rule of the bunch, and surely the most controversial—the steel rule.

The steel provision was championed by Senator Heinz at the urging of Packwood's aide, Diefenderfer, a native Pennsylvanian. It provided to steel companies a $500 million refund of their unused investment tax credits. Steel companies at the time were suffering losses and therefore paid no tax, so their credits were worthless. The refund provision promised them ready cash in exchange for the extra tax breaks. Metzenbaum's home state of Ohio was filled with troubled steel mills; he steered clear of attacking that one.

The insertion of such a large transition rule raised the ire of several senators from states that were not big steel producers. Pryor was so angry that he wrote a letter of protest to Packwood. The steel break "looks bad, smells bad, and is bad," he said. Chafee called it "a major change in tax law that went beyond what I'd call a transition rule." Still, Packwood defended it and beat back what amounted to a halfhearted effort by Pryor to take it out. By holding tight to the provision, Packwood made some steel-state and steel-company friends for tax overhaul.

The Finance Committee was far from alone in hiding special giveaways in its tax bill. The Ways and Means reform bill, as well, was chock full of transition rules. Its most colorful example was sponsored by Representative J. J. Pickle, Democrat of Texas, and was dubbed the "turkey-buzzard amendment." Tucked away in the voluminous Ways and Means measure, the provision was worth $800,000 to Hill Country Life of Texas, an insurance company in Pickle's Austin district. The firm's emblem was a turkey buzzard and its motto seemed to fit transition-rule politics: "Keep turning over rocks and you'll eventually find some grubs."

"Grubs" such as the turkey-buzzard amendment sullied the noble intentions of tax reform, but these little tax favors kept the tax bill moving through Congress. The Treasury Department wisely turned its head when it came to the dirty business of negotiating transition rules. Even the most committed congressional reformers realized that these relatively small provisions were a necessary price to pay. If ten or fifteen billion dollars in temporary transition rules would enable Congress to close several hundred billions of dollars' worth of permanent tax loopholes, then they were willing to go along. Metzenbaum would continue his crusade, but with little success. The transition rules were a necessary evil; they would help assure passage of the bill.

The Senate debate began on June 4. It was a beautiful early summer day, before the stifling humidity of midsummer had set in. The first senators to speak made largely laudatory comments about the bill and its chances for rapid approval. Packwood called it "an opportunity that will not come this way again in a generation. It's not often this brass ring will swing by." But the rhetoric masked the serious challenges to the bill that lay ahead.

The most pressing problem involved IRAs. Under existing law, workers could salt away as much as $2,000 in these retirement accounts each year and deduct the amount of the contribution. The Finance Committee bill proposed wiping out that deduction for people who were covered by employer-provided pension plans. IRAs were used by more than twenty-five million Americans to set aside money for retirement, and the Finance Committee's proposal would affect almost three quarters of them.

William Roth of Delaware was the IRA's most vocal supporter. A cosponsor of the Kemp-Roth tax cuts of 1981, Roth believed that the government needed to encourage savings as a way to increase the pool of capital necessary to spur investment. He contended that IRAs, which were expanded in his 1981 bill, were one of the most important savings incentives in the federal tax code.

Economists as eminent as Federal Reserve Chairman Paul Volcker disputed the contention that IRAs instigated more savings. He and others speculated that IRAs, for the most part, only caused savings to be shifted from other accounts into IRAs. "It is hard to see an impact on the overall savings rate" from IRAs, Volcker once told a congressional hearing. "In fact, the personal savings rate has gone down" during the period since 1981.

The real importance of IRAs was political. Lawmakers judged them to be the one tax shelter in reach of the middle class. In fact, more than 45 percent of all IRA deductions were taken by taxpayers with adjusted gross incomes exceeding $40,000 a year, a group which accounted for less than 11 percent of the taxpaying public. But the "middle class" in political terms was far different from the middle class in purely economic terms. While the median income of a family of four in the United States hovered around $33,000 a year, members of Congress frequently defined the "middle" to include people whose incomes were considerably higher than that—$50,000, $60,000, even $100,000 a year. It was this group, lawmakers knew, who were politically active back home and who were most likely to make campaign contributions.

So, it was with good reason that Roth and others began to preach about the need to restore the IRA deduction, even on the first day of the tax-reform debate in the Senate. "A lot of solid, middle-class people—not rich people—use IRAs as a way of providing for their retirement," Roth asserted. Senator D'Amato of New York, led a separate group that also pushed to save the IRA. The determined D'Amato called the no-amendment effort "absolutely ludicrous. . . . I didn't get elected and I don't think senators are elected to be rubber stamps." He and Senator Christopher Dodd, Democrat of Connecticut, both of whom were standing for reelection that year, made clear they would be angling soon to shoot down Packwood's IRA provision and help out the vast "middle class" back home. Of the more than thirty amendments that senators threatened to unleash, the IRA amendments stood the best chance of success and were the greatest challenge to the no-amendment strategy.

Roth, however, poorly understood the new political dynamic of tax overhaul. He chose to pay for partial retention of the IRA deduction by curtailing tax breaks that were dear to many of his colleagues. For example, his proposal trimmed the completed-contract method of accounting, which was important to military contractors, who were big employers in several states, including Missouri, Kansas, Connecticut, and Washington. To the chagrin of rust-belt senators, Roth's proposal also eliminated the $500 million transition rule for steel companies. On Tuesday, June 10, Dole prevailed on Roth not to offer his amendment. Roth, knowing he did not have the votes, agreed and promised instead to offer a nonbinding resolution that asserted the need to retain the existing IRA deduction.

Other pro-IRA senators refused to admit defeat, however. On Wednesday, June 11, D'Amato and Dodd took the floor to promote their own IRA amendment. They were much smarter about paying for their proposal than was Roth. Instead of going after other interest groups, they chose to slightly raise the rates in the corporate and individual minimum taxes. The provision left intact the top 27-percent rate for individuals and the top 33-percent rate for corporations. While the increased minimum tax would hit some capital-intensive industries such as steel and mining, the D'Amato-Dodd tack was much easier to explain to constituents: It simply raised taxes on those who were not paying their "fair share" to Uncle Sam.

Packwood was prepared. His block of thirty-two senators opposed to all amendments was solid. He needed to convince only nineteen other senators to vote against the IRA amendment in order to defeat it. President Reagan had also been pitching the no-amendment strategy every chance he got. With all that in his favor, Packwood cavalierly predicted that the D'Amato-Dodd amendment would be defeated.

The risk of failure was high. Packwood staked the success of his bill on his ability to beat back major amendments, and this was the most dangerous amendment he had to face. If it passed, the no-amendment strategy could backfire, and senators with gripes about the bill would be emboldened to propose other big changes. "We need to defeat this amendment so we don't start an unraveling of the bill," Dole concluded.

When the clerk of the Senate started to call the roll on a motion to "table," or kill, the IRA amendment, Packwood's boast about easy victory began to look premature. For every aye from Packwood's coalition, there was a nay from the IRA advocates. The well of the Senate, which was in front of the presiding officer's chair, was quickly filled with anxious senators curious about the outcome. Packwood was more than curious. He became extremely anxious.

In desperation, Packwood sought out a trio of Republican senators with whom he knew he could work in a pinch. Senators Slade Gorton and Daniel Evans of Washington State and Phil Gramm of Texas were ripping mad over the Finance Committee's repeal of the sales-tax deduction; their states had sales taxes and no income tax at all and stood to suffer immensely from the change. The hair-thin vote on the IRA amendment, however, gave them new and unexpected clout.

As Packwood sought their support, the sales-tax senators issued him a challenge. They said they would vote to kill the IRA amendment if he guaranteed them his support for their amendment to partially reinstate the sales-tax deduction. With the credibility of his no-amendment strategy on the line, and the votes mounting rapidly, Packwood made an instant decision. "OK," he said. "I'll buy it."

The three senators walked to the well, got the attention of the clerk who was recording the votes, and lent their names to the list of those who wanted to table the IRA amendment. A few minutes later, the importance of those three votes became evident. The D'Amato-Dodd proposal was tabled by a vote of 51–48. Had Gorton, Evans, and Gramm not struck a deal, Packwood would have been dealt a major defeat, and other senators would have been encouraged to take a run at changing the bill. Packwood managed to avert that disaster only by secretly selling out his own coalition.

The Senate then went on to approve Roth's IRA resolution. Dodd called the nonbinding resolution a "charade" and a "ploy" that meant "absolutely nothing." Senate Minority Leader Robert Byrd, Democrat of West Virginia, asserted that the resolution was designed to "make people believe that something indeed is being done," while, in fact, "the sense of the Senate resolution doesn't accomplish anything." Dole himself had previously referred to such nonbinding resolutions as "get-well cards"—a nice thought with no practical effect.

The next day, June 12, the sales-tax-state senators tried to collect on Packwood's promise of support, but Packwood had double-crossed them. Packwood had not called off his no-amendment coalition and they ran into a buzz saw of opposition. The senators' plan would have allowed taxpayers the choice of deducting either their state and local sales taxes or their income taxes, and paid for that change by closing a loophole in the bill that permitted the taking of second mortgages to finance consumer purchases.

The method of payment was, again, the amendment's Achilles' heel, and the coalition members attacked it brutally. Senators ranging from Democrat Wendell Ford of the high-sales-tax state of Kentucky to Bradley of New Jersey asserted that the proposal damaged the most sacred tax break in the code—the deduction for mortgage-interest payments. That preference, as they painted it, was almost an American birthright. The mere thought of tampering with it was unpatriotic.

During this barrage, Packwood was nowhere to be found, and the trio of senators was left without any recourse. At the urging of Dole, they withdrew the amendment to avoid certain defeat. Instead, they backed yet another meaningless resolution. "To put it mildly," Gorton said, "we were not happy with Packwood."

The defeat of the sales-tax proposal added steam to the drive of the no-amendment coalition. The operation was working like a clock. Packwood appeared able to defeat any amendment at will, and his resources seemed vast. He stationed his own personal army of lobbyists, the 15-27-33 members, in the Finance Committee hearing room. They were provided with telephones, television sets tuned to the Senate floor, and coffee. Whenever Packwood or his minions detected a wavering senator, they dispatched a pack of 15-27-33 lobbyists to plead for support.

On Friday the thirteenth, Packwood unloaded these big guns in an unusual effort to *approve* an amendment. While it appeared to run counter to the no-amendment strategy, the move actually proved to be a fierce display of force to show the consequences of not adhering to the Packwood line.

The Finance Committee chairman had placed into his committee's bill a transition rule for Union Oil Company of California (Unocal) worth about $50 million. The Unocal provision was sought by Senator Pete Wilson, Republican of California, but on the Senate floor, Wilson proved to be no friend of the Packwood bill. Despite the special favor, the California lawmaker voted against Packwood on several big issues, including IRAs and sales taxes.

With the help of the Commissioner, Packwood got his revenge. Metzenbaum argued that the Unocal rule had nothing to do with "transition" at all, but was a "fresh-off-the-shelf loophole" and an example of "simple greed." Many members of the no-amendment coalition could not help but agree. The provision was a tax break designed to help offset the extra debt Unocal amassed in the previous year to fight off a takeover attempt by corporate raider T. Boone Pickens. The rule was not only an exception to the committee bill, it also was an exception to existing law. Packwood, sensing the agitation of his no-amendment allies with some of the committee's special-interest transition rules, and angered by Wilson's votes on the floor, urged coalition members to support Metzenbaum's Unocal amendment. "When we asked Packwood how we should vote" on the Unocal matter, a coalition member told *The New York Times,* "he said, 'Sock him.'" The result was a rout. Wilson's Unocal rule was dropped from the bill by a vote of 60–33. It served as a warning to other senators not to defy Chairman Packwood.

In succession, Packwood disposed of every other major issue. He defeated an effort by Republican Senator Paul Trible of Virginia, a state heavy with federal workers, to ease the Finance Committee's tax increase on federal pensions. Packwood and his coalition also slaughtered the effort by George Mitchell of Maine to cut back benefits to wealthy individuals by imposing a 35-percent top rate. So daunting was the no-amendment bloc that advocates of the preferential treatment of capital gains chose not to even offer their nonbinding resolution. They feared that the margin of their victory, if they could even manage one, would be so paltry that it would kill any chance for better capital-gains treatment in the all-important House-Senate conference.

The fight dragged on for more than two weeks, with the sessions at times lasting until midnight. More than one hundred hours were devoted to the debate. When there were no amendments being contested, or when Packwood and Dole were trying to resolve problems off the Senate floor, a "quorum call" would be requested to kill time. The clerk would slowly and monotonously read through the names of the one hundred senators until someone asked that the quorum call be dispensed with so that debate could resume. At other times, Packwood would recite his version of the history of the tax code and tell why tax reform was so important. During this period, Packwood constantly paced around the chamber. He did this in part to stretch his legs, which were always tight from his almost daily games of squash, but he also walked so that members would be less inclined to stop him and ask questions.

Gradually Packwood's no-amendment strategy began to show some cracks. He was making enemies of those who resented his heavy-handedness. His manner chafed some members, but Packwood's actions were even more grating on matters of substance.

On Tuesday, June 17, the day he beat the Trible amendment, Packwood caved to pressure from his coalition to *accept* an amendment that stung two of his own committee members, Wallop and Bentsen. The amendment, cleverly crafted by Metzenbaum, restored the withholding tax on foreigners that the committee bill had repealed and used the $1.2 billion raised by the tax to pay for a special tax break for hard-pressed farmers and a medical-cost deduction for the elderly. The combination of taxing foreigners and helping farmers and senior citizens was irresistible to most senators. Wallop had been a loyal supporter of the tax package, and on the last night of markup he had even helped Packwood out of a jam by offering to amend the repeal provision so it would cost less revenue. But under pressure, the chairman turned his back on the steadfast Wyoming senator. He made his second exception to the no-amendment strategy and released the coalition members to pass the Metzenbaum proposal. A visibly wounded Wallop protested at length from his seat in the rear of the chamber. The more reserved Bentsen simply left the floor.

The sales-tax senators were also still fuming about Packwood's double-cross. Packwood defended himself by telling them that he had pledged only *his* vote for their amendment, not the votes of his coalition—a story that was hard to swallow. Contrite nonetheless, Packwood began to meet Gorton, Evans, and Gramm privately, often in Dole's office, to work out some sort of face-saving compromise.

At about the same time, D'Amato, the leader of the save-the-IRA drive, was beating the bushes to find support for another major amendment. He wanted to tie together several big issues that had been defeated by the coalition. He thought that lumping the most popular issues into one package would be so attractive that senators would be loathe to vote no. "I was working on an amendment that would have taken care of the IRAs and the pension problem," he said later. "There was some consideration, too, of the sales-tax problem." D'Amato and Trible were holding serious talks about how best to combine forces.

Word about D'Amato's triple-play "killer amendment" worried the members of the coalition. They feared he might well win. Frustration with the no-amendment strategy was beginning to bubble, and could come to the surface as support for the D'Amato-Trible package.

Senators were becoming increasingly resentful of Packwood and his Finance Committee for preventing them from altering this very important bill. Many members did not believe Packwood's claims that the package was so fragile that it would disintegrate if amendments were adopted. They were itching to assert their role as lawmakers, to take care of the interests of their own folks at home, and they disliked the sometimes sanctimonious way that members of the coalition advocated their no-amendment strategy.

These feelings erupted on the night of Wednesday, June 18. Senator Paul Sarbanes, Democrat of Maryland, derided Senator Danforth for giving a virtual "sermon" to his colleagues on the no-amendment strategy the night before. Sarbanes even read back into the Congressional Record Danforth's offending speech:

If you believe that the point of taxation is to take care of every group, and I am not putting down those interest groups, but if you believe that the point is to take care of them one after another as they come through the door, vote for this amendment and then the next amendment and then the next amendment and then the next amendment and then the next amendment, because there is no end of it. Once you say yes to one group you can never say no again.

Danforth had gone on to praise the 15-27-33 lobbyists and described their commitment in ringing terms:

We do not agree with every detail in this bill. We do not agree with some of the things you have done. We do not agree with what you have done with real estate or what you have done to the state sales taxes. We do not agree with this, that, or the other things in the bill, but the bill is right, the bill is right. For once you are doing the right thing in the Congress of the United States. This bill is right and we will stick with you.

Sarbanes was visibly disturbed by the sappy self-righteousness of this language. After all, he noted, Danforth's own special interest—Missouri-based military contractors—had been fully protected in the Finance Committee bill. Sarbanes, like Trible, represented a large number of retired federal workers, and was frustrated by the Trible amendment's failure the night before. He did not want to leave the debate with his protest unstated. "We were being put down last night because we were offering what I thought was a perfectly reasonable amendment with respect to twenty million Americans, who are going to, in effect, be subject to double taxation," he said. "Their concerns about the impact of this legislation were perfectly reasonable concerns and ought not to be dismissed as special interests."

Sarbanes was far from alone in his disaffection. As a sign of the growing protest, other senators began proposing more and more amendments in defiance of the no-amendment stance. Shortly after eleven on that same evening, Dole appeared on the floor to announce that "the number of amendments seems to grow rapidly. At eight o'clock there were twenty-some. Now we are up to fifty-some."

Tension mounted. Shortly before midnight, one of the Senate's crustiest members, Ted Stevens, Republican of Alaska, took the floor and embarked on a lengthy speech about the way the rest of the Senate was being treated by the elite Finance Committee and its chairman. Stevens attacked the surreptitiously composed transition rules. His complaints were similar to those of Metzenbaum, but his point was the complete opposite. He wanted some Alaskan transition rules in the bill. If constituents of so many other states were to be so blessed with favors, he argued, why not give more special breaks to the good people of Alaska too? In a tone that amounted to a growl, Stevens began to address himself directly to Packwood:

I would like to have my friend tell me who they are. Who are these people that have these projects that we do not name in the bill? . . . When we appropriate money for a project in Louisiana, we say where it is, who owns it, and if there is going to be a contract let for it, we say who the contractee is. We are not saying this is a project that is described in this paragraph that could fit almost anything. But you all know who they are. I do not know who they are. I do not know why I cannot try to fit some of my own projects into these exemptions already in this bill. If I can, I am going to try, okay?

In Packwood's defense, Senator Alan Simpson, Republican of Wyoming and the assistant majority leader, rose to take on the cantankerous Stevens. Simpson, a tall, balding man with intelligent eyes and a ready smile, was sometimes referred to as a modern-day Abraham Lincoln: His wit was quick and dry. He had a talent for indirection and exaggeration to make a point. He had tangled before with Stevens; the two lawmakers were not friends. Stevens's complaints about the way giveaways were handled in the tax bill were simply too much for Simpson to take without reply.

"Mr. President, I am very interested in this debate, and it is very fascinating—and a little heavy," Simpson began.

I have been here seven and a half years. I have watched with total admiration as the senator from Alaska does his work in the U.S. Senate. It should leave us all absolutely envious. Because I have seen him with his extraordinary skills insert more pieces of legislation into various bills for his state than any person that I have ever met in this place. I think the people of Alaska should be proud of that; that is why they return him here, only one of the reasons.

I have seen him work hard on the Appropriations Committee. I am not on the Appropriations Committee, but I have seen pieces of legislation come from that committee which were literally larded with material that had to do with the state of Alaska.

I am not going to get into one with the senator from Alaska because he is a pretty feisty cookie; but I can tell you if they wanted a bear to represent them in Alaska, they hired a grizzly. That is Ted Stevens.

I think that is great, but I do not think you can come in here and have a debate that has to do with talking about things and costs and so on, when I have seen things come here under the direction of the senator from Alaska which were of tremendous cost—railroads, unified commands. There is no limit to the extraordinary ways—he is the envy of us all.

I have seen him produce the most novel legislation. I have seen condition upon condition come from wherever this remarkable gentleman plies his trade, project after project, waiver after waiver.

The Simpson speech was a stunning put-down, but it was not enough to stop the growing dissent against Packwood and his no-amendment strategy. The snarling and sniping continued, and as the session came to an end in the early-morning hours, the floor leaders knew they needed to act quickly to quash the rebellion. They decided, in the words of Bradley, "to cut the core out of any growing interest in a bigger amendment."

On Thursday, June 19, Packwood took the floor to say that he had worked out an amendment with the three senators from Washington and Texas to ease the effect of eliminating the sales-tax deduction. Evans and the others introduced it, and it was adopted without objection. The provision allowed taxpayers to deduct 60 percent of their sales-tax payments, but only to the extent that the payments exceeded the amount of their state-and-local income tax liability.

The convoluted provision was drafted to help only states that had raised most of their revenue from sales taxes and to cost no more than the $1.6 billion that Packwood had found to finance it, but it served its purpose. It quieted the complaints of the sales-tax senators and cut the legs out from under the D'Amato-Trible triple-threat amendment. Dole and Packwood met with D'Amato and Trible outside the chamber in front of the large wooden timepiece known as the Ohio Clock. "Packwood made it clear that he would view our amendment as a hostile act," Trible recalls. The two dissident lawmakers already knew they did not have enough votes to beat the no-amendment coalition. They also concluded that pressing the point and then losing would so anger Packwood that they would have no leverage at all in the conference. "I realized if we tried and failed," Trible said, "our chance of gaining any relief would be lost forever. The chemistry of the situation had changed. . . . Events had passed us by."

It was the final challenge for the Senate tax-reform bill; from then on, the debate was mostly a mop-up operation. The Senate faced dozens of minor amendments, most of which were accepted as "conference bait"— provisions that would be adopted on the Senate floor, only to be dropped in the later House-Senate conference. Many of these were extremely local in focus, including provisions to benefit a truck-leasing company in Des Moines, a housing project in Massachusetts, and flood victims in West Virginia. Senator Stevens persisted in plying his "extraordinary ways"; he won a special tax treatment for Alaskan Indian tribe corporations and another for the income from reindeer, which Bradley said would better have been granted at Christmastime.

In the end, on Tuesday, June 24, only rhetoric remained. Dole attempted to trace the origins of the tax overhaul to his own tax bills since 1982. Bradley said the idea went back to the origins of the U.S. Constitution. Senator Joseph Biden, Democrat of Delaware, gave much of the credit to Bradley. Packwood gave credit to almost everyone: Rostenkowski, Reagan, Long, Bradley, Dole, Metzenbaum, the entire core group, and himself. He harkened back to the two-pitcher lunch and recalled saying to Diefenderfer, "Let's give real reform a try."

For the benefit of the cameras, Dole requested that the senators vote from their own seats rather than follow their usual practice of bunching up in the well. The final vote on the 1,489-page bill was 97–3, with three Democrats dissenting—Carl Levin of Michigan, John Melcher of Montana, and Paul Simon of Illinois.

"Nothing is certain in this life; the good Lord might call us home tomorrow," Russell Long said after the vote, "but if we're here on Labor Day, there'll be a bill on the president's desk."

Chapter 11

The Running Shoes
and the Sledgehammer

Just two hundred and fifty paces separate the Senate chamber from the House chamber. The short walk across the second floor of the Capitol building is like a quick passage through history. From the Senate, the route leads down an ornate hallway past the Old Senate Chamber, with its sixty-four desks, quill pens, and brass spittoons, where Preston Brooks of South Carolina brutally caned Charles Sumner of Massachusetts on the eve of the Civil War; through the great Rotunda, the nine-million-pound cast-iron dome that symbolizes the very heart of the nation's government, under which the bodies of Abraham Lincoln and John F. Kennedy lay in state; through a semicircular room lined with statues of sixty-six great Americans, including Frances Elizabeth Caroline Willard, one of the founders of the Women's Christian Temperance Union, who stares sternly across at Huey Long, a man not known for moderate habits; and finally down a quiet corridor to the House chamber.

Despite the proximity, the path is seldom trod by members of the House or the Senate. The two bodies are distinct institutions, and their members prefer to keep it that way. The one hundred Senators, who each represent an entire state and who serve relatively luxurious six-year terms, tend to feel superior to their 435 House colleagues; they maintain far-ranging interests and committee assignments. Members of the House, on the other hand, usually represent fewer constituents, run for reelection every two years, and tend to specialize in narrower areas of policy. Snobbery and resentment inflame the relationship between the two bodies, each taking pride in its own customs, its own rules, its own history, and its own ideas about how the nation should be governed. Disagreements between the two are common. It is because of those disagreements that many of the nation's laws are ultimately written in one of the most unusual, most difficult, and least understood institutions of American government: the conference committee.

For the tax bill, the conference would be crucial. The tax-reform debate had raged for four long years, and both the Senate and the House had struggled mightily to produce their own versions of the legislation. Now, virtually everything that had been done would be put on the conference table for a small group of senators and representatives to dispose of as they pleased. The two tax bills were in many ways mirror images: The House bill closed many corporate tax loopholes, but left the tax preferences used by individuals largely untouched, while the Senate bill made sweeping reforms on the individual side of the tax code, but left many of the biggest corporate tax breaks unchanged. That meant the twenty-two conferees had wide leeway to determine the final shape of the most comprehensive tax-overhaul bill in the nation's history.

Legislative conferences have their origins in fourteenth-century England and were also used by some of the colonial legislatures before Congress was created. They came of age in the United States in the mid-1800s, when the Senate and House grew increasingly antagonistic. By the turn of the century, conferences had become so critical that Senator George Norris of Nebraska, one of the legislative giants of the time, called the conference committee a "third house" of Congress and "often the most important branch of our legislature." Today, says Senator Mark Hatfield, the senior senator from Oregon who as chairman of the Senate Appropriations Committee attended dozens of these testy negotiating sessions, "more legislation is written in conference than in committees. It may be the most significant institution in the whole Congress."

Simple or otherwise noncontroversial bills can clear Congress without going to conference. If the differences between the House and Senate versions of a measure are small, they can be worked out by sending the bill back and forth between the two bodies until both find it acceptable. On major tax bills, however, conferences are inevitable. Taxes are not small matters. They alter the finances of countless individuals and corporations, and the conference is the last chance for those interests to soften the blow or boost the benefits. A conference committee is not provided for by the Constitution and is little understood by the public, but it is there that final decisions are made about who bears the tax burden. In often cramped and stuffy rooms, away from the gaze of the public, unpredictable events occur and tax laws are written.

The interplay of personality—always an important element in the workings on Capitol Hill—takes on magnified significance in conference. Conference meetings are like labor-management bargaining sessions, and the skill and stamina of the lead negotiators can be critical. A clever conference operator, like former Finance Committee Chairman Long, can make the most of these high-pressure dealings. Long once kept secret the fast-approaching date of his own marriage so that he would not lose leverage in a conference. If his House counterparts had known that Long had a deadline, they could have waited him out and forced concessions. They never found out—until Long already had won most of his issues.

For tax reform, the final decisions would rest largely in the hands of just two men: Bob Packwood and Dan Rostenkowski. The two had little in common: Packwood was a maverick legislator from a largely rural state; Rostenkowski was a machine politician from a big city. Packwood was cerebral, analytical, a collector of rare books and special editions; Rostenkowski was physical, a man of gut instinct, a devotee of red meat and golf. Packwood was new to his chairmanship and still uncertain of how to wield the power that accompanied it; Rostenkowski was accustomed to his high-ranking post and well-trained in the mechanisms of power. The differences in style between the two chairmen were symbolized by the gifts they received from the pro-reform lobby, the Tax Reform Action Coalition: Packwood was given a pair of running shoes; Rostenkowski, a sledgehammer.

These two, very different men, working mostly by themselves behind closed doors, would serve as the last arbiters for billions and billions of dollars' worth of tax breaks. Their decisions during a few, short weeks in the summer of 1986 would deeply affect every person and every corporation in America. The clash of their contrasting personalities would shape the tax code for years to come.

Packwood and Rostenkowski had met in conference before, and the results had been explosive. During a House-Senate conference over the 1984 tax bill, Rostenkowski criticized a fringe-benefit provision favored by Packwood. The red-faced senator—who was not yet chairman—responded by saying in open session that Rostenkowski "doesn't know what he's talking about." The observation might have been true: Rostenkowski was not always quick to grasp complicated tax matters. But it was an unwise comment for the Oregon lawmaker to make to the powerful House chairman. Rostenkowski said nothing, but with his head half-buried in his hand, his pinky ring exposed beneath his big chin, he slowly shifted his eyes to where Packwood was seated. The public insult had been registered, and the retribution was swift. Packwood lost the fringe-benefit issue.

The two clashed again in late 1985, when they both served on a major conference panel chaired by Rostenkowski. The bill was a budget measure that included a provision to finance a Superfund for cleaning up toxic waste. Packwood's Finance Committee wanted to pay for the Superfund by imposing a broad-based excise tax on manufacturers. Rostenkowski opposed such a broad tax, but many of his own House conferees sided with the senators. Eager to resolve the issue, Packwood called for a meeting of the conferees without asking Rostenkowski's approval. An angry telephone call from the House chairman quickly followed.

"You shouldn't have called the conference meeting without my permission," Rostenkowski growled into the phone.

"You can't control your conferees on Superfund," Packwood shot back. "They've got the votes to override you."

"You may be right, but you still shouldn't call the meeting without my permission."

"Well, I have called the meeting, I am calling the meeting, and we are going to put it [the broad-based tax] in the Superfund title over your objection—because we can."

The conversation came to an abrupt end when Rostenkowski slammed down the receiver.

The tax conference of 1986 seemed destined to continue this rocky relationship. Even before it got underway, a controversy erupted over who would chair the House-Senate committee. By tradition, the chairmanship of tax conferences alternates between the chairman of the Ways and Means Committee and the chairman of the Finance Committee. In early June, when it was Packwood's turn to chair a conference on a bill involving water projects, the senator tried to decline the post, hoping to leave himself poised to become chairman of the upcoming tax-reform conference. The ploy failed, and Rostenkowski became chairman of the all-important conclave instead, but the incident, at least for a while, deepened the gulf that already separated the two men.

Soon after the Senate passed its tax-reform bill, Packwood again snubbed his House counterpart. At a joint appearance before a group of women lobbyists and tax aides, each of the chairmen was asked to speak for a few minutes about tax reform. Packwood went first, talking for twenty-five minutes while Rostenkowski waited and listened. Then as Rostenkowski began his three-minute remarks, Packwood slipped out, unwilling to stay and hear his House colleague. Recognizing that trenchlike warfare lay ahead, the group presented each chairman with a World War I combat helmet. With these two in charge, the monumental task of melding two versions of tax overhaul was not going to be easy.

The first step for both chairmen was to choose their fellow conferees. It was an important decision; the final tax bill would reflect the preferences of this select group. Rostenkowski's conferees had undercut his position on the excise tax in the Superfund conference in 1985; neither he nor Packwood wanted a similar situation to arise during the upcoming tax conference. To succeed at their delicate task, both men needed to have fellow negotiators who would support them and give them room to make necessary deals. Rostenkowski wanted a majority of his conferees to be unswervingly loyal to him; Packwood knew he could not count on that kind of unquestioning support from the senators on his panel, but he wanted at least to be certain that his conferees supported reform.

By tradition, the chairman and the ranking minority member of the committees chose the conferees, and the speaker of the House and presiding officer of the Senate supported those selections in their respective chambers. Conferees were usually chosen according to their seniority on the committee, but when Rostenkowski came to see Speaker O'Neill in July 1986 to discuss the tax conference, the white-haired speaker asserted his authority.

"I want Gephardt on there," O'Neill said. Representative Gephardt had little seniority on the Ways and Means panel and had not been a major player in drafting the tax bill. But O'Neill knew that having Gephardt on the panel would highlight the Bradley-Gephardt bill and help focus attention on the Democrats' role in reform.

"I can't put him on there," Rostenkowski said. "I've gone on seniority."

The speaker's voice grew firm. "Dan, let me tell you something. Wilbur Mills never said that to Sam Rayburn when Sam Rayburn was speaker of the House. The rules say that the speaker shall name the conferees. I am the one that has the right and I want Gephardt on there."

"If you feel that way about it," replied Rostenkowski, "then you can name the whole committee."

"Look," said O'Neill, "this is a Democratic bill; we can't afford to have it defeated. I want you to put on members of the committee that you think will support it."

Rostenkowski then combed the committee list, choosing those most likely to support reform, tossing out those most likely to oppose it, regardless of their seniority. He passed over the committee's second-ranking Democrat, Sam Gibbons of Florida, who had challenged the chairman vociferously and repeatedly during the markup the previous year. He also skipped others, such as his old pal Ed Jenkins of Georgia, who he knew would fight him on some important provisions. Instead, he chose younger committee members, like his Chicago protégé, Marty Russo, and Donald Pease of Ohio, a staunch and hard-working advocate of tax overhaul. Other Democratic conferees included J. J. Pickle of Texas, Fortney "Pete" Stark of California, and Charles Rangel of New York. The Republicans were allowed to choose four conferees—senior Republican John Duncan of Tennessee, Bill Archer of Texas, Guy Vander Jagt of Michigan, and Philip Crane of Illinois—but these members were destined to be irrelevant in the final stages of drafting the bill, just as they had been during the House negotiations.

For Packwood, finding loyal foot soldiers was more difficult. The senators were an independent crowd. Nevertheless, Packwood too decided to lay aside seniority to get members of his committee who were most loyal to his package. He particularly wanted Bradley on board, and also Moynihan, who had supported his efforts in putting together a reform bill. He asked

Long, the ranking Democrat, to include both of these senators among the Democratic conferees. Long, fearing that Bradley and Moynihan might team up to oppose his cherished oil tax breaks, agreed to pick the two, provided Packwood included Republican Malcolm Wallop, an oil-industry supporter, among his conferees. The deal was then set: The conferees would include the core-group senators—Packwood, Chafee, Danforth, Wallop, Moynihan, and Bradley—as well as Long, Dole, William Roth of Delaware, Lloyd Bentsen of Texas, and Spark Matsunaga of Hawaii.

The Senate and House conferees were a study in contrasts. Most of the senators were millionaires, and many had been educated in Ivy League schools. Moynihan was a former Harvard professor and a former ambassador to India and to the United Nations. Chafee was a former governor of Rhode Island and secretary of the Navy during the Nixon administration. Danforth was a Yale-educated lawyer, minister, and heir.

While the members of the House delegation were as knowledgeable as or more knowledgeable than their Senate counterparts about tax law, they were more down-to-earth. Their numbers included Pete Stark of California, a man of great wealth and sophistication; as well as Donald Pease, a soft-spoken, unassuming representative from a battered rust-belt district; and Marty Russo, the tough-talking Chicago arm-twister. The senators sometimes looked down their noses at their House counterparts; one senator noted with a touch of disdain, for instance, that Russo sometimes wore short-sleeved shirts under his sports coat. For their part, the House members thought the senators were haughty and ill-prepared.

On top of these differences in style were differences in substance. The senators thought the House conferees were naïve and feared that the House's heavy-handed corporate reforms could cause serious damage to the economy. The Democratic House members thought the senators had become too caught up in their own "capital formation" rhetoric and that they did not have the stomach for real reform.

Aware of the differences that separated them and their bills, Packwood and Rostenkowski at first acted like two wrestlers on the mat, circling each other, waiting for the other to move first. They were anxious and uncertain about how to approach the opponent.

Then on June 27, three days after the Senate approved its bill, Rostenkowski made the first move. The House chairman recognized the significance of Packwood's surprising legislative rout. Even though the House bill had larger tax cuts for most Americans, the Senate's low 27-percent top rate (32-percent, counting the phantom surtax) had captured the public's imagination. Speaking in Boston on June 27, Rostenkowski said: "If there is a lesson to be learned from the Senate victory, it's the power of low rates. . . . I would be willing to shoot for the Senate's top rate as long as we approach the House's after-tax income distribution."

It was an important concession. Some liberal Democrats, following the lead of Senator Mitchell, were claiming that a 27-percent top rate was too low. It meant a family earning $40,000 a year would fall in the same tax bracket as a family earning $4 million. To liberals, that seemed unfair, but Rostenkowski was forced to accept the fact that the low rate was the magic of the Senate plan. Without it, the senators could not be coaxed into abandoning their special-interest tax breaks. He also knew that the rate was not crucial in determining which income groups got the biggest tax cuts—a central question from his point of view. He came to understand that by eliminating loopholes that benefit the wealthy, a tax system with a top rate of 27 percent could be just as progressive, and show the same distribution of the tax burden among income classes, as his own 38-percent plan.

Rostenkowski also saw political advantage in agreeing to the low top rate. His goal in the conference was to put his mark, and the Democrats' mark, on tax reform. If he accepted the Senate's rates as the starting point for debate, the senators would come under tremendous pressure to accept his bill's corporate reforms. In the Boston speech, Rostenkowski insisted, in effect, that the Senate agree to provide at least as much tax relief to the "middle class" as the House bill did. That was a request that Packwood and the other senators were loathe to reject. But to accomplish it, the senators needed revenue to ensure that the final bill was revenue neutral. If tax rates were not going to be raised to find that money, the only other place to turn was the elimination of corporate tax preferences.

In short, Rostenkowski's speech meant that business tax breaks were on the chopping block—a fact that caused heartburn among the lobbyists on K Street. The conference was going to be their final showdown, their last stand, and many of them were likely to end up losing big. Said Thomas Quinn, a lobbyist for the mutual-fund industry: "Prayer is our number-one strategy. I advise my fellows to go to the church of their choice."

Rostenkowski's concession set the direction of the conference. The House chairman had accepted the Senate's radical low-rate structure for individual taxes; in return, the Senate would have to accept much of the House bill's corporate loophole closing. The negotiations would be tough. In the process, the top tax rate might edge up a bit, but the final bill—if there was a final bill—would have to be more sweeping than either the House or Senate measures in terms of reform. To please both sides, it would have to combine the reforms made in both houses of Congress. The usual dynamic of the congressional tax-writing process had been turned on its head. No longer did the special interests have the upper hand. There was not enough revenue to permit many compromises that would help the lobbyists' clients. Indeed, with a commitment on both sides of the Capitol to dramatically lower tax rates, the general interest would have to prevail, if the conferees were to succeed in getting a bill.

The conference convened publicly on Thursday, July 17, in the cavernous House Ways and Means hearing room. House members, resentful of the acclaim that had been given to Senate tax writers, used the opportunity to complain about the Senate bill's "phantom" 32-percent rate, calling the 27-percent top rate a lie. When Brockway explained that the difference was "in large part a matter of semantics," Representative Archer of Texas shouted back, "No, it's *not* a matter of semantics." And when Deputy Treasury Secretary Darman said that no taxpayer would have an overall effective tax rate greater than 27 percent under the Senate plan, Archer rose and walked out of the hearing room.

But those opening shots were mostly for public display. After the first two days of meetings, the conferees secluded themselves behind closed doors and did not meet again in public until the final night of the conference, three weeks later. Packwood and Rostenkowski both believed that they had to shield the conference from lobbyists, the press, and the public in order to make progress. "Common Cause simply has everything upside down when they advocate 'sunshine' laws," Packwood explained.

When we're in the sunshine, as soon as we vote, every trade association in the country gets out their mailgrams and their phone calls in twelve hours, and complains about the members' votes. But when we're in the back room, the senators can vote their conscience. They vote for what they think is good for the country. Then they can go out to the lobbyists and say: "God, I fought for you. I did everything I could. But Packwood just wouldn't give in, you know. It's so damn horrible."

At first blush, the task of combining the two bills seemed manageable. Packwood's plan raised corporate taxes $100 billion over five years; Rostenkowski's plan raised corporate taxes $140 billion. The Senate conferees thought they would at worst be forced to raise corporate taxes another $20 billion, and then use that money to help middle-class taxpayers. A $20 billion extra hit on business was tolerable, they thought.

Then came the first crisis. On Thursday, July 24, new revenue estimates were unveiled by Brockway and the Joint Tax Committee showing that the Senate bill was not revenue neutral at all. Instead it actually lost $21 billion over five years. The senators had to find ways to make up that money first, before they could even begin serious negotiations with Rostenkowski. In addition, the new estimates showed that the Senate bill raised only $93 billion in new corporate taxes over five years, while the House bill, reestimated using the Senate's effective dates, raised $178 billion in corporate taxes. Suddenly the gulf between the two chambers had widened to $85 billion!

Revenue estimates were a harsh master throughout the tax-writing process, but in the conference they became exceedingly cruel. Everytime a new set of numbers came out of the Joint Tax Committee's computers, they had more bad news for Packwood and his crew. The $21 billion shortfall was a huge new obstacle for the conferees and a serious threat to the bill's success.

The setback was no surprise to the Treasury Department. Months earlier, the Treasury had calculated that the Senate bill lost revenue, but it kept those findings secret. Indeed, the Treasury estimates showed an even bigger deficit than the Joint Tax Committee numbers. The department's calculations found that the bill would add $30 billion to the federal budget deficit over five years. Baker and Darman hid that fact from everyone except Packwood. Their failure to disclose those startling numbers was a serious breach of traditional practice and, arguably, a disservice to the public and the Congress, but Baker and Darman were not willing to do anything that would endanger the chances for reform.

During debates on previous tax bills, the Treasury routinely made its revenue estimates available to the public. Buck Chapoton said that when he was assistant secretary for tax policy during Reagan's first term, he felt it was his duty to release revenue estimates as soon as they were complete. Under Baker and Darman, the Treasury had become a very different place. The two men were clever political operators, and they manipulated everything to suit their ends. They feared that if they revealed the bill's huge revenue loss, the Senate might be less inclined to pass it. So they kept the estimates private and never released them to the public or shared them with senators other than Packwood.

The new Joint Tax Committee numbers, however, publicly confirmed the shortfall and could not be ignored. They increased the pressure on the Senate conferees to clamp down on business tax breaks. Corporate lobbyists became more desperate than ever; they were stuck in a vise, and the new revenue estimates were tightening the grip.

When Packwood learned of the new $21 billion shortfall, he immediately called the Treasury for help. The Treasury and the Finance Committee had worked together closely in fashioning the Senate plan, and Packwood came to rely on Treasury as an auxiliary to his own, relatively inexperienced staff. He and Diefenderfer talked with Darman daily, and they welcomed the Treasury official's many suggestions and judgments.

The Treasury was supposed to make its expertise equally available to both chambers of Congress, but Rostenkowski had no desire to collaborate with the department. His own staff was more skilled than the Finance Committee's was, and he could also rely on Brockway and the Joint Committee for technical expertise. During the Ways and Means markup, he had spurned Darman's advice and had privately called him names like "stone-faced" and other less complimentary terms. Packwood, on the other hand, saw Darman as a clever strategist, and was glad to make him a co-conspirator. As a result, the Treasury became a partisan in the tax-reform battle. It was Packwood, Baker, and Darman working together against Rostenkowski.

Since the days of Stanley Surrey, two and a half decades earlier, the Treasury tax office had been a sort of independent defender of the integrity of the tax code. The assistant secretary for tax policy had always seen it as his duty to stand somewhat above politics, promoting "good" tax policy and opposing "bad" tax policy. At times, the tax office was forced to go against its instincts—such as in 1981, when it was compelled to back Ronald Reagan's campaign promise for a new rapid depreciation write-off scheme; but generally, the office tried to protect the tax code from undue political tinkering.

During the tax-reform debate, however, the role of the Treasury tax office changed dramatically. Baker and Darman were determined to get a tax bill through Congress, and they were not about to let abstract tax-policy concerns get in their way.

Assistant Secretary Pearlman had struggled to maintain the independence of his office, but he left the department at the end of 1985 feeling discouraged and defeated. His successor was a New York lawyer named Roger Mentz, who had a thorough knowledge of the tax system, but who was less insistent on protecting his department's independence.

Mentz was a tall man with a large jaw, and his appearance prompted House staffers to nickname him "Lurch," after the giant-sized butler in the television show *The Addams Family*. He was a proud man, who insisted on calling Packwood and Rostenkowski "Bob" and "Danny" rather than the more respectful appellation of "Mr. Chairman," which even the proud Darman always used. Mentz became indignant whenever anyone suggested that the influence of his office had declined, but the truth was that Mentz knew where his bread was buttered and acted accordingly. Unlike his predecessor, Pearlman, he owed his job to Baker and Darman, and he was a good team player. After he took over the tax office, Darman seized control of tax policy, and the independent influence of the office waned. In the early days of the Reagan administration, Buck Chapoton was always the top official at tax markups. During 1986, however, it was Deputy Secretary Darman who took the lead in tax negotiations. Mentz spoke for the Treasury on technical matters, but it was Darman who cut important deals in private and who was the administration's main spokesman at the most critical public meetings. During the Finance Committee's markup, Mentz sat at a table reserved for Treasury officials while Darman roamed behind the horseshoe podium whispering to senators and their staffs. During the Senate debate, Mentz watched quietly from the visitors' gallery, while Darman negotiated with senators in a room off the Senate floor.

The Treasury tax office remained the city's largest reservoir of talented tax lawyers and economists, and that expertise was frequently called upon to resolve tough technical issues. Skilled tax attorneys like Dennis Ross, Richard D'Avino, Victor Thuronyi, and Linda Carlisle, as well as experienced economists like John Wilkins, contributed immeasurably to the tax-reform effort. The tax office also exerted influence through its close contacts with the professionals on the Joint Tax Committee. But when it came to major problems that could threaten the fate of tax reform, Baker and Darman muzzled the staff. The Senate bill included provisions that the Treasury tax experts privately thought were outrageous: the "phantom" rate, for instance, and the minimum tax on a company's "book" profits. These were proposals that, to tax experts, seemed sheer insanity, but both proposals served political purposes. The phantom rate enabled the senators to claim their top rate was 27 percent even though it was not, and the book-profits provision ensured an end to stories about companies reporting profits to their shareholders but paying no taxes. Baker and Darman refused to allow the Treasury staff to publicly criticize either of the unusual provisions. They did not want their department to do anything that might trip up the progress of the bill. Mentz took the interference philosophically: "That's just the way it goes. You cannot be an idealist and have tax reform enacted."

Packwood met with Treasury officials on Friday, July 25, to discuss ways to close the new $21 billion gap. He asked the Treasury to draw up a list of potential revenue-raisers. Mentz and his staff worked until the early hours of Saturday morning, compiling a hodgepodge of ideas to pick up the revenue, worth a total of $39 billion. The senators then spent most of Saturday reviewing the Treasury's ideas, throwing some out, accepting others. By 3:00 P.M. they had decided on enough to raise $26 billion. That would pay for the revenue shortfall and leave a little money to pay for more benefits to the middle class.

The list was to become the first volley in a long series of offers exchanged between the two sides. The back and forth represented a kind of sparring session that was prelude to the knock-down, drag-out battles that were soon to ensue.

The Treasury proposals were a strange collection, held together only by the faint possibility that they might be politically acceptable. Some of them were Darmanesque tricks: For instance, the senators accepted a cynical proposal that would allow the tax credit for research and development to expire at the end of 1988, one year short of the extension that was included in the Senate bill. Baker, Darman, and the Senate conferees all knew that the popular credit would be extended again before it expired and that the supposed revenue gain was therefore only a charade, but they were perfectly willing to use such tricks if they helped get tax reform enacted.

The Senate's proposals were sent to the House the following Monday, July 28, where they were received coldly. Rostenkowski was incensed at what he considered Treasury's meddling and troublemaking. He was so angry, in fact, that during the conference meeting that day, he asked Packwood to tell Baker and Darman to leave—which they did. Then, Rostenkowski and his House colleagues attacked the senators' Treasury-generated proposals. Russo derided a proposed change in the existing sales-tax deduction tables, which made the savings from repealing the deduction look bigger than before. He called it an insult to his intelligence. Others complained that roughly half of the sixteen proposals went "outside the scope" of the conference. Conferees are only supposed to deal with issues on which the two bills are in disagreement, but the Treasury's money-raising list contained many proposals that were not in either bill. Such forays outside the scope of the conference were not without precedent, but the House members thought it was far too early in the negotiations to resort to such gimmicks, especially when the House bill itself was chock-full of corporate revenue-raising provisions.

The House conferees did accept a few of the senators' revenue-raisers. The proposal to end the research-and-development credit a year early, for example, was adopted. But the senators were sent away from the meeting with instructions to try again. "Our basic position is the Senate came up short," said Representative Donald Pease. "The Senate has to come up with ways to raise the revenue that we find acceptable."

Packwood regrouped and convinced his senators to devise a second plan, this time raising $32.5 billion over five years. This was a more serious effort, drawing on a number of proposals in the House bill. The senators agreed to some cutbacks in depreciation write-offs—although still not nearly as much as in the tough House bill. They also accepted the House provision limiting the bad-debt-reserve deduction for big banks. In a show of good faith, Packwood also agreed to curtail a tax break dear to the timber interests in his state—the preferential treatment of corporate capital gains. These were important concessions, and the outlook for reaching agreement before the Congress left for its August recess began to improve.

Rostenkowski responded to the proposal with a counterproposal that accepted many of the Senate's tax changes for individuals. The House conferees agreed, for instance, to eliminate the preferential treatment of capital gains. That was a blow to a coalition of lobbyists working to preserve that break for investors. Likewise, the House negotiators agreed to the Senate's tough anti–tax-shelter "passive-loss" provision, despite the fact it would severely hurt many of the Democrats' allies in the real estate business. At the insistence of Russo and Rangel, however, the House conferees refused to accept the Senate proposal to eliminate most of the sales-tax deduction. The New York lobby and Governor Mario Cuomo were still fighting hard to save all state and local deductions. Rostenkowski agreed to try and retain the sales-tax deduction for the time being, although, in private, he made it clear to Packwood that the elimination of the popular preference was still a possibility.

While the House conferees accepted many of the senators' proposals on the individual side of the tax code, they continued to hang tough on their corporate provisions. They still insisted on curtailing tax breaks for oil and gas, timber, and military contractors—measures dear to the senators. They also wanted to cut back depreciation allowances by $28 billion, down some from the $38.8 billion cutback in the original House proposal, but still far tougher than the Senate's more modest plan.

When the senators saw the House offer, they were indignant. "It is questionable whether we will have a bill," said Danforth, who insisted the $142 billion increase in corporate taxes included in the new House plan would cause "great damage to our country." Wallop agreed: "I don't consider it a proposal. If ever there was a dead body leaving the morgue, this is it."

Despite the tough talk, the two sides were gradually closing the gap. They had agreed on many important elements of a bill. The House had even made a significant move toward the Senate's controversial proposal to eliminate IRA deductions for people who have pension plans. The House agreed to eliminate the popular savings deduction for families earning more than $50,000 a year and single people earning more than $35,000. Since most IRAs were owned by people in those upper-income groups, it was a significant concession.

Even on the business side, the gap was closing. The Senate offer raised corporate taxes by $115 billion. That was still $27 billion less than the House offer, but the two sides seemed to be within striking range.

Packwood won an important victory on Saturday, August 9, as the senators prepared their response to the House offer. Bentsen still wanted to soften the Senate's tough anti–tax-shelter rule. He had asked Roger Mentz, in conjunction with his own staff, to come up with some proposals to ease the effects on commercial real estate developers, and Mentz complied with his request. Packwood was not happy about the situation; he knew his conferees would find it hard to resist helping the hard-lobbying developers. In addition, House conferees said they would favor passive-loss changes if the senators initiated them. Many of the biggest and richest developers in the nation flew to Washington during this period to meet with lawmakers and members of the administration. But Packwood also thought that any weakening in the passive-loss rule could threaten the entire low-rate structure of his bill.

When Bentsen presented his proposal at the Saturday meeting, sentiment seemed to be evenly split. Five senators supported Bentsen's amendment, and five were opposed. William Roth of Delaware was wavering. He sympathized with Bentsen, but he also was concerned about the proliferation of tax shelters. He asked Mentz to give his view.

Because Mentz had helped draft the Bentsen proposal, Packwood feared the Treasury official might support it, or at least give an equivocal answer. But this time, Mentz was firm. The Bentsen proposal, he said, would be hard to administer. Speaking of the passive-loss rule in the Senate bill, he concluded, "It's quite fair and reasonable the way it is, and I wouldn't change it."

Roth turned to his tax aide, David Raboy, and asked, "What should I do?" Raboy whispered back that the Bentsen amendment had merit and should be adopted, but Roth was moved by Mentz's short speech. (At the same time, John Colvin, Packwood's tax aide, came over to Roth and Raboy to tell them that Packwood had decided to save a tax break dear to an important Roth constituent: Delaware chicken farmer Frank Perdue.) The senator decided to ignore Raboy's advice and vote to preserve the passive-loss rule. The Bentsen amendment was defeated 6–5.

Packwood's troubles, however, were far from over. As the senators completed their counteroffer to the House, a serious blow hit. The Senate plan included a $17 billion revenue-raiser that involved the establishment of a "trust fund" to boost spending by the Internal Revenue Service for its tax-enforcement efforts. It was one of many tricks that Packwood and Darman slipped into the Senate plan. By giving the IRS a bigger budget, the tax writers estimated they could bring in even more money by catching some of the estimated $100 billion that was lost to tax evasion each year. Estimates suggested that every dollar spent on beefed-up IRS enforcement could bring in as much as ten dollars in previously uncollected taxes. The trust-fund proposal was not reform, but it was an easy way to pay for lower rates.

The trust fund stirred complaints from the chairmen of the House and Senate Appropriations committees, whose panels had control over most funding for the government. Creating a trust fund to finance the IRS would remove the agency from the Appropriations committees' control, and that was something that the turf-conscious chairmen were not willing to tolerate. Without a trust fund, however, the Finance Committee could not claim the big revenue increase; there would be no guarantee that the Appropriations panels would provide the funding increase that the tax writers sought.

Eager to keep the big chunk of revenue intact, Packwood and Diefenderfer urged Brockway to find some other way to claim a $17 billion increase in revenue. They suggested that instead of boosting IRS funding, they simply direct the IRS to take money away from other of its functions and put it into enforcement. That prompted a complaint from the new IRS commissioner, Lawrence Gibbs, who told a private meeting of House conferees that the plan could cause serious problems for the agency. The IRS had just gone through a disastrous year in which some people's tax refunds were lost or delayed for months. Shifting funds away from returns processing and taxpayer service and into enforcement would only exacerbate such problems.

On Tuesday, August 12, Baker and Darman dragged a contrite Commissioner Gibbs back up to Capitol Hill to try and salvage the Senate's faltering IRS proposal. With the two Treasury officials at his side, Gibbs's tune changed considerably, and he no longer insisted that the plan was unworkable. Darman, at the same time, told the conferees the plan would indeed work. The House conferees, however, were unmoved. They refused to accept the proposal and insisted the senators find $17 billion elsewhere to make up the difference.

The session was a stormy one. Meeting in private in a hearing room just below the House chamber in the Capitol, the conferees from the Senate and the House grew increasingly irate. They had reached the limits of their patience. The senators felt they had already made major compromises; they could not see their way to raising another $17 billion. Rostenkowski and his House members were adamant; they were not willing to let Packwood and his senators escape from their dilemma using smoke and mirrors. It looked as though the $17 billion problem might cause the conference to break down for good. The conferees were getting weary from the battle, and they were eager to go home for their summer recess. "If that's what this hangs up on, it hangs up on it," Packwood told a press conference. Chafee confessed privately, "For the first time, there has crept into this the view that we may not have a bill."

As the prospects dimmed, Long spoke up. The former chairman was a crafty lawmaker, as skillful and knowledgeable in the dynamics of the legislative process as any member of either body of Congress. He also had a charm that, combined with his quick mind, made him exceptionally influential. When he spoke—waving his hands, slurring words in his strong Louisiana patois, and peppering his speech with endless and wonderful stories about his "Uncle Earl" Long, governor of Louisiana in the 1940s and 1950s—a mysterious spell fell on everyone around him. In conference committees, his power to win concessions from the House was legendary. "The House sees Russell Long coming at it with a freight car full of, let's say, 'shinola'," a House aide once said, "and it gets so terrified it's going to have to eat the whole load that when it's finally presented with just a small brown paper bag full, it gobbles it down gratefully."

Senator William Proxmire of Wisconsin, occasionally a victim of Long's persuasive powers, once characterized Long this way: "If a man murdered a crippled, enfeebled orphan at high noon on the public square in plain view of a thousand people, I am convinced . . . that if the senator from Louisiana represented the guilty murderer, the jury would not only find the murderer innocent, they would award the defendant a million dollars on the ground that the victim had provoked him."

As former chairman, Long had probably done more than any other single person to create the very problems that tax reform was trying to correct. He was no reformer, but he was a politician, and he knew when the winds of popular opinion had changed. Having served thirty-eight years in the Senate, he had risen into the role of a senior statesman and was eager to use that position to give Packwood a hand. Darman explained: "Senator Long is a great respecter of the institution of the chairmanship, having derived enormous benefit from it and having learned that to make the process function you have to be willing to cede some authority to the chairman." In private meetings, when virtually everyone else lapsed into calling Packwood "Bob," Long continued to call him "Mr. Chairman," as a symbol of his regard for the post.

Furthermore, Packwood and Long had developed a close relationship over the years. Even before he came to Congress, Packwood had written a high school essay about the Louisiana senator. "I chose him," Packwood explained later, "because he was new to the Senate so I thought the essay wouldn't have to be long." Packwood later told the *Congressional Quarterly:* "I cannot think of anybody I've learned as much from as Long. There's almost nothing I wouldn't do for him." For his part, Long called Packwood a dear friend. "There was a time in my life when I was taking some lumps," Long explained, "but Packwood helped a lot and helped me to do my job and be an effective chairman."

So when Long saw the conference rapidly disintegrating on that Tuesday, he decided to help out. The room grew quiet as he spoke.

"Well, it doesn't seem to me there's much progress being made here," he said, his eyes looking down as he scratched with a pencil on a piece of paper on the desk before him. "We senators have a lot of confidence in Mr. Packwood, and I suspect you folks do in Mr. Rostenkowski. So I don't see why those chairmen don't get together by themselves and come up with a proposal that we all can then consider."

Long had already suggested the idea to the Senate conferees in a private session, and they had agreed to let the two chairmen work out the problems. Packwood had also told Rostenkowski of Long's idea, and Rostenkowski had responded favorably, but apparently no one had prepared the House members for the proposal. Each of them had their own interests to look after, and they did not want to give up their role in shaping the final package. Nevertheless, Long phrased his suggestion in a way that gave the House members no choice but to agree. If they dissented, they would be demonstrating a lack of confidence in their chairman. Rangel, worried about the sales-tax deduction, said to Rostenkowski, "I want you to know I'll support you all the way," but then quickly added, "as long as I can."

Long's proposal was just what Rostenkowski and Packwood needed. Despite their ill-starred history, the two men had in the past few weeks developed a solid working relationship. They both wanted a bill. Both knew that their reputations would be permanently sullied by defeat. That common desire was enough to overcome their many differences. They seldom got angry at each other. Indeed, at times, they acted like collaborators, negotiating not with each other, but with their respective conferees. When Rostenkowski privately told Packwood his conferees demanded a bigger hit on the oil industry, Packwood urged him to have the House conferees make their case more loudly in their joint meetings, so the Senate conferees would see the House meant business. When Rostenkowski was having trouble with Rangel and others who insisted on keeping the sales-tax deduction, he urged Packwood to get the senators to stress in the group meetings how committed they were to curtailing that deduction.

As a symbol of this new-found friendship, the two chairmen and their staffs went together one evening to Morton's, Rostenkowski's favorite steak house, and spent a long night talking, drinking, and reminiscing. As the alcohol flowed, Packwood asked Rostenkowski's advice about whether he should run for president and pulled out a pen and notebook to scratch down the chairman's response. Rostenkowski, in turn, began to tell stories about the 1968 Democratic presidential convention in Chicago. Both men liked to drink—Rostenkowski had even been arrested and had his license suspended for drunk driving earlier that year—and the food and alcohol served to cement their relationship. Clearly, these two men had put their pasts behind them and were ready to sit down and work out an agreement. Long's suggestion that they go off alone to do just that was the perfect solution, and in the end, would make all the difference for tax reform.

For the next few days, Packwood, Rostenkowski, and their staffs gathered in H 208, Rostenkowski's private hideaway in the Capitol building. It was an impressive room, only a few short steps from the House floor. It contained a long, oval wooden table with brown felt in the middle. A vaulted ceiling soared above the table, and a huge, turn-of-the-century brass chandelier hung from the center. On the walls of the room were prints of former presidents: Madison, Jackson, Tyler, Polk. In the corner was a rolltop desk that hid a television set, and on a windowsill sat a stack of copies of the *Chicago Sun-Times*. The room had been the province of the Ways and Means Committee since 1908, and it was here that Rostenkowski held court. He would meet with the Democratic members of the committee, or with other House members who wished an audience with him. During conference, in fact, it was here that Rostenkowski heard the pleas of both House members and senators who came to him for special favors. It was here that he and Packwood sat down to work out the final details of the tax bill.

The meetings were long, but productive. Rostenkowski usually sat at the head of the table, with Packwood over to his side. Diefenderfer, Colvin, Leonard, Dowley, Brockway, and other members of the staff gathered around on the sides. Some of the issues they discussed were exceedingly trivial and arcane, others were worth billions of dollars. The conversation grew most tense when it turned to oil. Rostenkowski was determined to cut back oil industry tax breaks; he saw it as a test of his strength as chairman. Packwood and Diefenderfer tried to convince him that their tough minimum tax was already a sizable blow to the oil industry, but the chairman was not easily swayed.

Rostenkowski also talked tough when the issue of eliminating the special break for pension payments to federal employees came up. That was the issue that had almost killed his bill on the House floor. The federal-employee lobbyists, working with members from Maryland and other states with large numbers of federal workers, had nearly ruined his bill by scaring up votes against it. The Senate bill delayed this change until January 1, 1988, and Packwood said that Chafee and other senators wanted to give the federal employees a break. But Rostenkowski wanted revenge: He insisted the change take place immediately.

Slowly, the two men began to see a package coming together. Occasionally, they would hit a snag, and Rostenkowski would wave Packwood into the back room, away from the staff. It was a tiny room, dominated by an enormous, round stained-glass window of the seal of the U.S. government. The window was 125 years old and faced out onto the grand stairway that led from the first to the second floor of the Capitol. From the room in Rostenkowski's hideaway, the words *E Pluribus Unum* were displayed in reverse. Sitting on a couch next to this antique window, Rostenkowski and Packwood resolved some of the toughest tax problems they faced. Usually they would compare notes about what different lawmakers had said to each of them separately. Both were being petitioned constantly by their colleagues, but the sob stories they were being given were not always identical. "We sifted out a lot of the blarney," Rostenkowski recalls. There was no shouting or yelling during those sessions, just determined negotiating by two men eager to reach the same end.

From time to time, the two chairmen would leave H 208 and return to their opposite sides of the Capitol to meet with their conferees and report on the status of the negotiations. Then they would return to Rostenkowski's hideaway and begin again. Several times a day, Packwood rushed across the second floor of the Capitol building, under the great rotunda, on his way to meet with Rostenkowski or on his way back to meet with the senators or participate in a Senate vote. Sometimes his staff would be in tow, other times Bradley could be seen at his side, leaning down and whispering advice in his ear. The meetings seemed to go on interminably.

One of the biggest and most difficult issues involved the "stagger." Each tax-reform plan—the president's, the House's, and the Senate's—proposed delaying the cuts in tax rates until the middle of the first year the plan was in place. This so-called stagger was a trick devised to help keep the plans revenue neutral, but as the bill neared completion, politicians began to think more carefully about the political consequences of the stagger. If the rate cuts were delayed until July 1, 1987, but deductions were eliminated as of January 1, many taxpayers would face substantial tax increases the first year of tax reform. Dole, whose ambitions to run for president were well known, noted that taxpayers would be filing their 1987 tax returns in April of 1988—right in the middle of the presidential primaries. If they did not like the first-year results, he said, there might be a backlash against the authors of the bill. Other politicians shared that worry. "This tax bill is going to be a revelation to many people, and it isn't going to be pleasant,"

Representative Tom Downey observed. Joint Tax Committee figures showed that the April surprise would leave millions of middle-income Americans facing tax increases of about seven hundred dollars in 1987.

Darman also worried about the effects of the stagger, fearing it would undermine support for reform. "One of the important reasons for tax reform is to reduce societal resentment and cynicism about government," he said. "If tax reform is ballyhooed and then one hundred million people have their first experience with tax reform and find it a loser, it will only compound cynicism."

The problem was that eliminating the stagger would cost $29 billion over five years. Packwood and Rostenkowski had exhausted their bag of revenue-raising tricks. The senators, Dole and Bradley aside, were willing to tolerate the first-year problem, but the House members, who all had to stand for reelection in 1988, were not. They demanded at least a partial fix, and it seemed that the only way to pay for it was through higher tax rates.

Rostenkowski had thought for some time that the top rate would have to go above 27 percent to pay for the stagger, and he had tried to smooth the way for that change by appealing to the nation's chief proponent of low tax rates: President Reagan. Rostenkowski made his pitch at a meeting with the president and his advisers—including Vice President George Bush, whose ambition was to succeed Reagan in 1988. Rostenkowski recalls saying: "Mr. President, you know this is a great opportunity for us. You've got me hand over fist, you've got the rates you wanted. There's only one thing I'm a little concerned with—and, Mr. President, you know I'm concerned because I think it would be an embarrassment for you. As of April of 1988, seven million people could possibly be paying more taxes rather than getting a tax reduction. You know it would be embarrassing, Mr. President. I mean, people in '88 filling out their income taxes and paying more taxes after you and I said there's a reduction in the rates."

The point was not lost on the president, or on the vice president. They indicated their assent. Baker and Darman also agreed that fixing the stagger was a political necessity. They knew the rate would probably have to creep up to pay for it. The trade-off had been coming for some time, but no one wanted to be responsible for taking the first step toward higher rates. As Packwood and Rostenkowski worked toward completion of their plan, they both knew and agreed that fixing the stagger would be their final move. The stagger would not be eliminated, but its effects would be moderated, particularly for those in middle- and lower-income brackets. To pay for the change, the rate would rise to 28 percent, and the hidden surtax would be reduced to 4 percent from 5 percent to keep the maximum "phantom" rate at 32 percent. It was the last major decision, and Packwood and Rostenkowski seemed ready to put their seal of approval on a tax plan. They had finished in the nick of time. Congress was preparing to leave for its August recess the next day. It looked like Packwood and Rostenkowski would get final approval from the members of the conference before the recess began.

As the two chairmen worked, however, David Brockway watched with a worried look on his face. For almost two weeks, he had been warning both Packwood and Rostenkowski that the Congressional Budget Office was putting out a new economic forecast in mid-August that would probably cause their proposal to fall short of revenue neutrality. He kept hoping the two chairmen would make allowances for this last-minute deficit, which he told them would range between $15 billion and $20 billion, but his words were falling on deaf ears. Packwood, in particular, showed no signs of acknowledging the bad news. He had been plagued by revenue problems long enough, and he did not want to deal with another one. The chairmen continued to tie up the loose ends of the package, expending scarcely a word about Brockway's warning.

Brockway was well known as a mumbler; his sentences sometimes blurred together. Often, he would do this intentionally to help conceal a member's pet tax break. But when it came to the new revenue estimates, he was trying his best to be clear. He knew that his credibility was on the line, and he was getting increasingly worried that no one was paying attention to the impending crisis. On Wednesday afternoon, the day after Long had set the two chairmen off to work out a deal, Brockway finally confronted the chairmen directly. "This is what it looks like," he said, handing over a new set of numbers. Their plan was $17 billion shy of revenue neutrality over five years.

The package that the two chairmen were putting together was supposed to raise corporate taxes in the neighborhood of $124 billion and lower individual taxes by the same amount. Work was not yet finished on that package, but the new estimates showed the increase in corporate taxes was only $114 billion, and the drop in individual taxes was $131 billion. In other words, the lawmakers still had $17 billion to go. It was the third time that the fateful figure $17 billion had plagued the tax process. The Ways and Means Committee had faced a surprise $17 billion shortfall in November of the previous year, and the Senate had raised $17 billion just a few days earlier to make up for the loss of the IRS trust-fund proposal.

"We still have to deal with this problem," Rostenkowski acknowledged.

Packwood, however, was not sympathetic. He was tired of the changing revenue estimates, and he wanted to ignore the new numbers. The estimates indicated the tax writers would have to raise individual taxes by $7 billion and corporate taxes by $10 billion to make the plan work, but Packwood knew his senators would never go along with an extra $10 billion hit on business. Before Brockway delivered the bad news, Packwood and Rostenkowski had been fighting to find an extra one tenth of a billion in revenue. Now, suddenly, they were faced with a shortfall one hundred times that large.

"Let's just not say anything about it," Packwood suggested. He even telephoned Baker and Darman to ask if they would object if the plan was approved with a $17 billion gap. The Treasury officials, still eager to get a bill, said no, they would not object, but Rostenkowski insisted that the problem must be solved. He knew his own conferees would not buy the subterfuge, and he did not want to be blamed for boosting the budget deficit.

The next morning, Brockway prepared some options to solve the new revenue deficit problem, but Diefenderfer quickly told him that Packwood was buying none of them. He wanted to continue to ignore the problem. Rostenkowski, on the other hand, was more insistent than ever. He had consulted with his conferees, and he realized that he could not possibly sell them a plan that reduced revenues by $17 billion over five years.

By Thursday night, Rostenkowski and Packwood had reached the end of their rope. They sat in Rostenkowski's H 208 and talked calmly about the outlook. They were tired, they were $10 billion apart, and they were on the verge of giving up. Rostenkowski and Packwood both considered the possibility of trying again after the August vacation, when Congress returned in September, but they both knew that the consequences of delay could be deadly. During the three-week break, lobbyists would be working full tilt, trying to pressure members of Congress to change the tax bill. Tax reform relied on speedy approval for its success; if left exposed for too long the lobbyists could certainly put together the strength to kill it.

To try to clear the air, the two chairmen left H 208 to take a nocturnal stroll through the darkened corridors of the Capitol. "We have to spend some time talking about this," Packwood said. The two walked toward the Senate chamber. They ambled through the semicircular Statuary Hall, under the great Rotunda, and began to double back through the hall outside the speaker's inner sanctum. The tenor of their talk was mostly frustration. The new numbers presented an obstacle they were not sure they could surmount.

"Son of a bitch, Bob, I wish it was you, I wish it was me, but it's the goddamn numbers," Rostenkowski complained, and Packwood could not help but agree. Packwood, in fact, told Rostenkowski that he had come to believe that the staff was out to get him. Rostenkowski also was angry with the staff, but he knew he could not get away with what Packwood was proposing: pretending the shortfall did not exist.

When the two chairmen returned to H 208, they still had not resolved their differences. They finally broke up their meeting at close to midnight. Reporters who had been waiting outside Rostenkowski's Capitol hideaway could sense the dejection. "I wish it was Packwood's fault or my fault. I wish we could blame somebody other than the numbers," Rostenkowski said as he left H 208. "I'm not saying it's all over, but it's a blow to us to have been so close but yet so far."

"He and I almost cried," Packwood said.

The next morning, when Ways and Means press aide Jim Jaffe went to pick up Rostenkowski at his apartment near the Capitol, the beleaguered chairman appeared with several shirts in his hand. He was not optimistic about the prospects, and was preparing to abandon the negotiations and head for Chicago for the recess. "We're going home today," he told Jaffe dejectedly. Rostenkowski later recalled, "I was ready to sack it."

Jaffe took the chairman to the Capitol, where he was scheduled to meet Packwood at 7:30 A.M. to pose for a possible cover photo for *Time* magazine. It was too early in the morning for both men, and they were discouraged by their failure of the night before. Furthermore, they knew *Time* would use the photo only if they succeeded. The photographer perched the two chairmen next to each other on top of an equipment case and asked them to raise their outside arms to frame the dome of the Capitol. Rostenkowski, who suffered from occasional back problems, was pained by the exercise and quickly grew impatient. When the photo session was finished, the photographer asked both men if they would jump, so he could take a photograph for the famous Time-Life "Jump" series, which includes pictures of famous people going back two decades. Rostenkowski at first thought the request was a joke. When he realized it was serious, he grew angry. "Bullshit," he grumbled. "I'm not going to jump. What do you think this is, a goddamn Toyota commercial?" He stormed back to his office. Packwood stayed and jumped.

At 10:00 A.M., Packwood appeared in the Senate Press Gallery and gave an impromptu news conference. He was still dejected. "I cannot get my fellows to go up again" on corporate taxes, he said. "They will not go up again. Because they know what's going to happen. We'll go up to $124 billion and we'll come back in September, and we'll be $15 billion short again."

The senators had been dogged by revenue estimating problems for too long and were fed up. Packwood told of an incident the previous Saturday when the Senate conferees had voted on Bentsen's amendment to the tax-shelter curbs. Bentsen had been told his amendment would raise $8 billion over five years, but after the vote, Brockway revealed there had been a "sign flip." In fact, the amendment would have *lost* $8 billion. The experience left the senators feeling as though they were working with a chimera that changed each time they turned their heads, Packwood said.

Furthermore, all the mistakes were going against the senators. They had gone into the conference thinking they would have to raise the corporate tax take in their bill by only $20 billion to meet the House halfway. Instead, they had already raised the corporate tax hit by well over $30 billion, and now the House was demanding $10 billion more! "It is frustrating when the damn target keeps moving everytime we are both on the target and we are ready to fire," Packwood complained.

Despite that frustration, Packwood had only kind words to say about Rostenkowski. He called him a "peach," and praised his patience and willingness to negotiate. He directed his venom, instead, at Brockway and the Joint Tax Committee staff. Throughout the televised press conference, Packwood criticized Brockway and the committee for its estimates. "We're getting misinformation, inaccurate information, untrustworthy information," he complained. "We can no longer rely on what we're getting."

It was a hard blow. Usually, legislators refrained from blaming revenue estimators for their problems. Estimating revenues was a difficult business, to be sure, but the staff in charge of the estimates was thorough and conscientious, and they did the best that could be expected with a very inexact science. Legislators had long been careful to shield them from criticism so that politics would not slip into their estimates. As Moynihan put it: "Everyone is entitled to his own opinion, but not his own facts." The revenue estimates, however uncertain, provided a necessary discipline to the tax-writing process.

For the chairman of the Finance Committee to denounce the revenue estimators in a televised press conference was a stark break with tradition. For Packwood in particular to publicly attack Brockway, who had almost singlehandedly saved the chairman from a humiliating defeat in the Finance Committee, was cruel and mindless. Brockway was both angry and hurt. In the frustration of the final negotiations, staff bashing had been taken to astonishing new heights. Packwood never even apologized to Brockway for the harsh words. In fact, when asked about the incident later, Packwood replied, "What did I say about him?"

Still, Packwood and Rostenkowski were not ready to give up. They knew that delaying completion of the bill until after the August recess might spell its death. In a private meeting in Long's hideaway, the Senate conferees urged the chairman to try one more time. Packwood concluded, "It's critical that we get this out so the special-interest lobbyists don't have three weeks to just hit our members over the head and break up the most extraordinary tax-reform package we're ever going to get."

On Friday afternoon, the two determined legislators met again in H 208 to renew their quest for revenue. It was a brutal day, with a lot of tough bargaining. Rostenkowski and Packwood spent much of their time in the back room, away from the staff. Both men had to give, and as a result both stood to lose support of some key conferees. Rostenkowski agreed to raise part of the disputed $10 billion by tightening up on individual taxes, rather than corporate taxes. Packwood sacrificed part of a tax break for military contractors that was dear to John Danforth of Missouri. Danforth had been a loyal backer of Packwood's bill, defending it on the floor of the Senate with passionate zeal, but in the final crunch, something had to give—someone's tax breaks had to be sacrificed to appease the relentless revenue demands. Danforth's pet provision was chosen. It was too large a target to miss.

Packwood and Rostenkowski worked until the early hours of Saturday morning. Finally they emerged, haggard but happy. They had reached an agreement. They were not certain they could sell the package to their conferees, but they were going to go home to get some rest and try to tie up the bill Saturday morning.

Packwood called Secretary Baker early Saturday morning. The chairman knew he was going to have problems getting his rebellious senators to accept the package he had negotiated. "I hope you will be strong in the meeting today," Packwood said.

Baker and Darman left the Treasury to go to Capitol Hill at about 11:30 A.M. in an upbeat mood. They thought the bill was going to be completed that evening and would be chalked up as a triumph for their reign at Treasury. Mentz was supposed to meet the two men at their chauffeured car, but as he walked down the stairs, he saw to his surprise that the car was pulling out without him.

In a moment, the car returned in reverse, with Baker and Darman laughing in the backseat. It had been a schoolboy prank. "Thought we were going to leave you, didn't you?" joked Baker as the bewildered Mentz got into the car.

The Treasury officials arrived at the Senate Dirksen Office Building and went into the Finance Committee's exec room, where they planned to meet with the Senate conferees to review Packwood's plan. Lobbyists and reporters gathered in the hallway, wondering what was going on. For three weeks, they had wandered the corridors, trying to pick up bits of information. Now they knew something was up. In their private meeting, the senators were making one last judgment on the fate of tax overhaul.

"Okay, fellows, you told me to present nothing until I have a package, and I said okay. Now I have a package," Packwood told the group. He passed out an eighty-three-page summary marked "August 16, 1986, 10:30 A.M.," and he proceeded to go over the agreement: It would raise corporate taxes by about $120 billion and cut individual taxes the same amount. Depreciation write-offs would be cut back about $13 billion from the Senate bill; oil and gas write-offs would be cut a slight $850 million from the Senate bill. The stagger would be partly fixed by putting the top rate at 38.5 percent in 1987, and assuring that 80 percent of taxpayers would get a tax cut that year. In subsequent years, the rates would be 15 percent and 28 percent for individuals and 34 percent for corporations. The personal exemption would go up to $1,900 in 1987, $1,950 in 1988, and $2,000 in 1989. The special treatment of capital gains and the sales-tax deduction would be eliminated, and the completed-contract accounting method that benefited military contractors would be cut back by $3.5 billion more than in the Senate bill.

The senators scribbled down the details as Packwood reviewed the important provisions in the bill. Then at the end he noted the Senate and the House would each have about $3 billion more to give out in transition rules, in addition to the transition rules already contained in each bill. Packwood made it clear that those who supported the final conference report would have a better shot at the $3 billion pot than those who did not.

"We've all got a loser or two in this bill," he concluded. "Any one of us would have written it differently. But as a whole, it's a winner for the country." Baker followed with a strong statement of support, and a warning about the dangers of delay.

As soon as Packwood finished, it was clear that his bill was in trouble. A number of the senators believed that the tax bill ought to be put off until September. Danforth, stung by the huge boost in taxes for military contractors and by other changes affecting universities, was the most strident proponent of delay. Wallop and Bentsen had already left Washington to meet commitments at home, but their aides suggested they also would prefer putting it off until after the break. Chafee was worried about the part of the plan increasing the tax burden on property contributed to charities. Only three of the eleven conferees—Packwood, Bradley, and Moynihan—were certain to support the package. Wallop's aide, Pearre Williams, told the lobbyists in the hallway that six senators—a majority—were committed to putting off the final vote on the report until September.

Inside, Danforth spoke up. He had preached in high moral terms on the Senate floor about the importance of tax reform. Now, he was using equally lofty language to urge its defeat. "Nothing's to be gained by signing the conference report before the recess," he argued. "This is a revolutionary change in the law. We need time to reflect." The United States is a democracy, he reminded the other senators, and in a democracy the people should be allowed to at least look at the tax proposal before the conferees make it law.

Packwood noted that the crowds of lobbyists in the hallway were probably the biggest in the history of Congress. "There are more special-interest groups hit by this than any bill ever," he said. To let it sit in the open for three weeks and give those lobbyists a chance to work their will would surely destroy it.

The debate was tense. Danforth had turned against the bill for largely parochial reasons. It would hurt McDonnell Douglas, the biggest employer in his state, and its changes in the treatment of bonds would also hurt Washington University in St. Louis, where Danforth's brother was chancellor. Nevertheless, Danforth couched his opposition in far broader terms. The conference bill was written in secret meetings and no one other than the senators and their aides had seen it, he charged. The "sunlight" of public scrutiny would only help the tax bill, not hurt it.

Packwood and Baker knew that Danforth's priestly rhetoric was a veiled attempt to kill the bill. Baker was especially strong in defending the closed drafting sessions: "It doesn't seem to me you can look at this like you might look at an ordinary tax bill. It has never happened before. It's unique. We saw what happened in this committee when we tried to markup a tax bill in public. If we hadn't gone into back-room sessions, you wouldn't have ever gotten a bill."

Then Moynihan, the historian and scholar of the group, spoke up. The United States is *not* a pure democracy, he said. "We're a representative democracy, and there are times when we as legislators are supposed to make our own judgments as to what is in the best interests of our constituents. If we don't act now, we won't act."

To ease the tension, Packwood suggested the group take a break. As the senators dispersed, the hallway loiterers thought they smelled encouraging signs of dejection. Diefenderfer seemed glum; others were ill-tempered. Rumors began to fly up and down the hall: The senators wanted to reject the compromise; the senators wanted to put the whole thing off until September. When Long emerged from the exec room, he told reporters that Packwood simply did not have the votes. Asked whether the conferees would complete the bill that night, he laughed and said: "I don't know about y'all, but I don't open my presents until Christmas."

On the other side of the Capitol, Rostenkowski also ran into problems. The last-minute fiddling done by the two chairmen had whittled down the tax cuts given to those families earning $50,000 to $100,000 a year, leaving them perilously close to nothing at all. The Joint Tax Committee estimated that the average tax cut for this group would be only about 1 percent in 1988. Referring to these taxpayers as "middle-class," House members insisted on bigger tax cuts for the group, and they proposed raising the top rate to 29 percent to pay for it.

When the senators reconvened in the exec room at 3:30 P.M., Packwood reported the House position. "The distribution isn't satisfactory to the House," he said. "We've got to come up with some way to fix it."

The 29-percent rate did not appeal to the senators in the least, and Baker said the president was strongly opposed to any further rate increases. Moynihan asked the Treasury officials if they would accept a 29-percent top rate if the bill also indexed capital gains to account for inflation. Baker and Darman both said they would be willing to look at that idea. They were disturbed by the sharp increase in the capital-gains tax, which would jump from 20 percent to 28 percent or higher, and they thought an indexing plan would help. Indeed, they had discussed the idea in private with Moynihan and Bradley during the break and had indicated their support.

But the Treasury team had erred in isolating Mentz from their back-room scheming. When asked about the indexing idea, the assistant secretary told the senators he feared that it would be too complicated to administer. With that, indexing faded away.

As the debate continued, the telephone rang. It was Rostenkowski calling Packwood to ask whether his group would accept 29 percent. As the chairman rose to get the phone, Dole quipped, "Twenty-eight and a half." Packwood returned from the conversation and said Rostenkowski had also suggested 28.5 percent—seriously. In the final hours, tax reform was becoming like an auction, with each side trying to find out just how high the bids could go, with billions of tax dollars hanging in the balance. Finally the meeting broke up, and a small group—Packwood, Baker, Darman, Bradley, and Diefenderfer—retired to the main hearing room, where they clustered in a small group of chairs behind the Democratic side of the horseshoe table and tried to come up with a solution.

Baker proposed a political solution that he thought could solve two problems at once. Why not delay any cutbacks in IRAs for two years and then repeal them outright? Roth, who was concerned about the proposed IRA cutbacks, would be more willing to support the bill if Baker's suggestion were accepted, because he knew that in all likelihood Congress would then vote in two years to extend IRAs beyond that expiration date. It was another cynical proposal, an attempt to claim revenue increases that were never going to happen, but Baker was willing to try anything to get the bill through.

Bradley had another idea. Rostenkowski and Packwood had reduced the phantom surtax paid by some upper-income taxpayers to 4 percent from 5 percent. Why not boost it back to 5 percent and use the revenue to give more relief to those earning $50,000 to $100,000. It was a subtle proposal, and Baker and Packwood were slow to understand it. Darman, however, immediately endorsed the idea. "That'll do it," he said. "That's the most efficient way to fix it."

Unable to decide, Packwood, Baker, and Bradley walked together across the Capitol to H 208 where the House chairman was waiting, and they presented him with both ideas. Rostenkowski rejected the IRA proposal immediately, but was willing to listen to the proposal for an increased surtax. Bradley explained that it was the same as getting a one-percentage-point rate increase, without the political disadvantages. Although Democrats had criticized the phantom rate at the beginning of conference, Rostenkowski was now willing not only to accept it, but to increase it. The average tax cuts for those earning $50,000 to $100,000 a year were boosted to about 2 percent, and although it was a small change, the House conferees were willing to say yes.

At 7:30 P.M. the Senate conferees met again. Danforth continued his objections, but the resistance of the others had eased. Packwood had calmed Chafee by providing Rhode Island with an extra $100 million in authority to issue certain types of private-purpose tax-free bonds. Long argued that the conferees should support the chairman—that the oil-state lawmakers should accept their deal on the industry tax breaks before Rostenkowski reneged. When the vote was taken, only two of the senators—Danforth and Wallop—voted to delay the conference agreement until September, while eight supported approving it right away. The final die had been cast, and tax reform was ready to become law. The senators adjourned at about 8:30 P.M.

The conferees agreed to meet for a final session at nine-thirty that evening. The meeting would be open to the public; it would be the first public session since the three-week negotiations began. The conference had been conducted completely in private. The final meeting would be mere pageantry—a chance for the politicians to speak for the cameras.

Baker, Darman, and Mentz left the Senate conferees' meeting pleased with their victory and eager to get some dinner before the final act. As they walked toward the elevator, a White House legislative aide ran up with a copy of a statement that the White House staff had prepared for the president. Darman glanced at the paper, and a look of disgust swept his face. The president was about to win one of the greatest legislative victories of his six years in office, but the White House had once again prepared a mush-mouthed, lukewarm statement, which ended by saying, "We look forward to studying it in detail." Baker immediately asked that the line be deleted. Even without that sentence, the statement was bland. Darman, well-practiced in the art of writing presidential statements, grabbed the paper and scribbled out a new draft. "In my 1984 State of the Union address, I first called for tax reform," he wrote at the opening, and at the end, instead of the equivocating language that was there, he wrote: "This is a triumph for the American people and the American system." Handing the paper back to the White House aide, Darman said: "For goodness sake, get the president into this. He's going to end up supporting this bill, don't let this one pass him by."

As the three men left the building, Mentz imagined that they would go to a nice restaurant and perhaps share a bottle of fine wine to celebrate the occasion. Instead, Baker led the three men to a nearby sandwich shop, where they discussed the events of the day over submarine sandwiches.

As the conferees gathered in the high-ceilinged Ways and Means hearing room, lobbyists poured in to get a seat. By this time the news had spread: The conferees had reached an agreement and the last major step in the tax-reform debate was about to take place. Both the House and the Senate would have to give their approval to the conference report after the August recess, but that would be pro forma. This was the lobbyists' final stand.

Representative Archer used the public meeting to vent the frustrations of the four House Republicans on the conference committee. The men had been completely cut out of the conference. They had made suggestions to Rostenkowski from time to time, but as corporate lobbyist David Franasiak put it, their suggestions "had the half-life of a newt." They were the orphans of the tax-writing process, and complaining in these rare public sessions was their only opportunity to be heard. One bemused Republican staffer wrote a brief poem that epitomized the isolation felt by the GOP conferees:

> Here's to the tax-reform conference,
> Home of low rates and high drama
> Where Rosty speaks only to Packwood
> And Packwood speaks only on camera.

Danforth also used the open session to make one last plea for halting the measure. "It's kind of a scientific experiment," he complained. "When you cross the fair maiden, which is the Senate bill, with a gorilla, which is the House bill, the result is a gorilla."

Once again, the Missouri senator couched his concerns in almost moralistic terms. His voice was filled with emotion as he spoke:

In the back room of the Senate Finance Committee earlier today, I took the same position I'm taking now. I said that this should be ventilated, and there is no reason not to put it out before the public and give us and our staffs a chance to look at it before we sign the conference report. The position that was taken by our chairman, by Secretary Baker, and several other senators who were present was: "Well, we can't do that. We can't put it public, we've got to sign the conference report now." Why? Well the reason given was that if we don't do it now, people are going to find out what we're doing before we do it. And if they find out, they're going to bring pressure on us during the recess. Lobbyists, interest groups, people who have concerns about the bill are going to bring pressure on the Congress, and we can't have that.

Danforth's voice began to rise, and he pounded the table as he warmed to his topic:

Now, Mr. Chairman, I don't understand what's wrong with a little sunshine in government. I understand in drafting a tax bill there are times when you want to go back in a back room, and we have always done it. But this has been to a fault. Nobody has had any knowledge other than what they read in the newspaper or rumors flying about. And I don't see any reason at all why we have to proceed to sign this bill tonight.

As he finished his speech, Danforth's voice grew loud and deliberate:

I don't see any possible argument why we should sign this tonight, and if anybody has an argument as to why we should do it, I would be very pleased to listen to it.

There was a moment's pause, and then the lobbyists who filled the room erupted into loud and spontaneous applause. This was their Little Big Horn, and Danforth's final rousing speech was an acknowledgment of their certain defeat. Rostenkowski, disturbed by the disruption, admonished the crowd and said that no further demonstrations would be tolerated.

"The applause after Danforth's speech was the last gasp of Washington special-interest dominance of the tax plan playing out," said Fred Wertheimer, head of Common Cause and a Bradley ally. "It was quite a dramatic moment, a magic moment. Special-interest Washington was filling the room with noise and basically saying they had lost. It was the perfect symbol of what had just happened."

Before the vote, Rostenkowski turned to Long. He noted that it was Long's last major tax conference before his retirement at the end of the year. "Before he retreats from this chamber, I want to ask my pal and the former chairman of the Finance Committee to say a few words." The room burst into applause again, lasting for a full minute, with all the conferees rising to pay tribute to the legendary Louisianan before he spoke. Bradley called it "the longest standing ovation I've witnessed since Madison Square Garden."

Looking down in his customary fashion, scribbling on a pad, Long said:

As all of you know, my father served in the Congress more than fifty years ago. I was about sixteen years old when my father died. But having observed the Congress, I've always had an ambition to serve here, and I've been watching this Congress for more than fifty years, as one who hoped to serve here and then as one who served thirty-eight years in these halls in Washington.

I've had occasion to watch the revenue bills that were passed. As one who served as chairman of the Finance Committee for fifteen years and served on the Finance Committee for more than thirty years . . .

The Senator paused and looked over toward Rostenkowski.

I didn't feel this way in the beginning but I really feel this way now, Mr. Chairman, that you, Dan Rostenkowski, and Bob Packwood have brought to us what is probably the best, in fact what I believe will be the best, revenue bill in fifty years.

None of us are going to be entirely pleased with it. They'll be some things in this bill that I'm going to have to tell people in Louisiana I'm sorry about. I wish I could have had it otherwise. But there are a great number of things in here I'm going to be bragging about along with many others.

The ambition of my life was to serve in this Congress, and after thirty-eight years, I think I'll find something else to do.

It was a strange swan song for a man who had spent his years in Congress punching the loopholes that tax reform was now going to eliminate, but as always, Russell Long seemed to be speaking from the heart.

Bradley also took the opportunity to speak, his face beaming at his moment of triumph:

You know, this is not just about the economy. It's about something else that each of us senses. Back in 1982, Dan Yankelovich did a poll and he asked the American people a question: "Do you think you'll get ahead if you abide by the rules?" Over 80 percent of those who responded said no.

Well I think that what we're saying tonight is if the question is ever asked again and they say no, they won't be referring to the tax rules. The result of this bill will be greater trust in government and a strengthened democracy. So, Mr. Chairman, I'm pleased to be a part of this. And I must say to *the* Chicago Bear, he did a helluva job. Senator Packwood is a remarkable leader. Thank you.

The conference report was approved by a voice vote, with only Danforth and Representative Archer heard saying nay. Rostenkowski gave the final words, leaning forward on the desk, a proud smile twisted across his broad face:

They said out there that it couldn't be done. Well we've done it. We both compromised at the margin, but clung to our principles. Ladies and gentlemen, the political process worked. The center held. Every economic interest in the country has played a role in shaping this package. Some advocated reforms, and others clung to the status quo. I believe history will show that all were treated fairly.

Tonight we will put our names to a new tax code for America. It brings a sense of justice to the way we tax income, and a new sense of confidence from those who will pay. I am proud of what we have done for the last year. We've had a lot of help around Washington as well, and appreciate it. But we wouldn't have come even halfway without the steady, often silent, faith of the millions of average taxpayers who freely comply and expect better. We're going to give it to them.

Ladies and gentlemen, this conference is adjourned.

Rostenkowski, Packwood, and the rest of the conferees crossed the hall to a room where a late-night party quickly got into full swing. For the photographers, the two chairmen held up glasses of champagne, and Rostenkowski put his arm around Packwood's shoulders. When the photographers finished, Rostenkowski traded his champagne for a beer. One of the photographers offered the Illinois congressman wishes for a good vacation. "Boy, you bet your ass," he replied.

Baker and Darman returned to the deserted Treasury building shortly before midnight. The Treasury secretary reached into his refrigerator and pulled out two cans of Budweiser. There were no glasses, so the two men clinked their cans in congratulations. After finishing the beer, they walked out of the building together, shook hands, and went home.

The next day, President Reagan, who was vacationing in Santa Barbara, California, issued a statement that ended with the line Darman had penned the evening before:

"This is a triumph for the American people and the American system."

Epilogue

The final version of the Tax Reform Act of 1986 sailed through both chambers of Congress with little fuss. The House affirmed the conference report 292–136 on Thursday, September 25. Two days later, in an unusual Saturday session, the Senate gave its approval by a vote of 74–23. It was then sent to the White House for the president's signature.

President Reagan signed the bill on the South Lawn of the White House on Wednesday, October 22. It was a gloriously sunny autumn day, and the Truman Balcony behind him was decorated with rows of bright yellow chrysanthemums. More than fifteen hundred people gathered for the occasion—the largest audience for a bill signing during the Reagan administration. Seated on the podium with the president were many of the key players in the tax-reform drama, including Rostenkowski, Baker, Regan, Long, Dole, and Kemp. Packwood was not there; he decided his time was better spent campaigning for his reelection in Oregon. Bradley, ironically, was also in Oregon, campaigning for Democratic political candidates, and was prevented by fog from flying back to Washington.

For President Reagan, the signing marked a great victory. He had managed to win the most sweeping overhaul of the tax code in the nation's history. He stood before the signing-ceremony audience proud and triumphant:

The journey has been long and many said we'd never make it to the end, but as usual the pessimists left one thing out of their calculations—the American people. They haven't made this the freest country and mightiest economic force on this planet by shrinking from challenges. They never gave up, and after almost three years of commitment and hard work, one headline in *The Washington Post* told the whole story: THE IMPOSSIBLE BECAME THE INEVITABLE and the dream of America's fair share tax plan became a reality.

How did it happen? What created this legislative miracle that defied all the lessons of political science, logic, and history? How could Congress—an essentially conservative institution that most experts thought could only enact major changes at a slow, incremental pace—accomplish such a large, complex, and far-reaching tax overhaul? Why were lawmakers, more beholden than ever before to campaign contributors, willing to vote against such a multitude of special interests? What motivated the bill's unlikely heroes to work together, buck the conventional wisdom, and achieve one of the most impressive legislative victories of recent times?

As the previous chapters have shown, the answer is not a simple one. In part, the deterioration of the tax code had gone so far that something had to be done. The American people were disgusted with the system, and that disgust represented a latent political force waiting to be tapped. Tax revolts, such as the Proposition Thirteen campaign in the 1970s to slash California property taxes, attempted to draw from this reservoir of disenchantment. President Reagan's tax cuts in 1981 also were intended to ease the problem, although the bevy of new tax breaks in that year's bill worked instead to fuel public disillusionment. By the mid-1980s, the loophole-ridden tax system cried out for a fix.

To be sure, public support for the reform proposals debated within the administration and in Congress was never particularly strong. The president's occasional efforts to rouse audiences to the cause almost always fell flat. Opinion polls showed that the public was outraged with the existing system, but had little trust in the government's ability to fashion something better. There was a deep public cynicism, fed by the government's long history of bungled or misguided attempts to fulfill the promise of reform. People doubted that their elected leaders could really achieve such a bold break with the past, and that doubt dampened their interest in the Washington debate.

Smart politicians knew that beneath the apparent public indifference, however, boiled a potential gusher of discontent that could prove to be a fearsome force. Few members of Congress cherished the thought of ending up on the wrong side of the popular president's battle against the special interests. They may not have wanted reform, but they were not about to be seen standing in its way either. As a result, tax reform acquired an extraordinary momentum once it got rolling. "It breathes its own air," said an amazed Illinois Senator Alan Dixon as the bill made its way through the Senate.

Reform was also achieved because it combined goals that were important to both political parties. Ending loopholes for the privileged had long been the desire of some Democrats. But the 1980s also saw the emergence of a new wing of the Republican party that was crucial to tax reform's success—the supply-siders, whose influence grew dramatically after President Reagan's election and who were passionately committed to lowering tax rates. These activist-conservatives had no deep interest in closing loopholes, but if that was the only way to pay for lower rates, they were willing to go along. By combining with the older Democratic reformers, they created an impressive bipartisan coalition.

To be sure, the opponents of reform in both parties initially outnumbered the proponents. Traditional Republican legislators were hesitant to back an effort that would offend so many of their business constituents; many Democrats, as well, had special interests to protect. Some liberal Democrats also disliked the sharp cut in the top individual tax rate, which seemed to help only high-income Americans.

Nevertheless, a pro-reform coalition emerged that was at once strange and impressive. It linked Ronald Reagan, the most conservative president in modern history, with George McGovern, the Democrat's most liberal candidate in decades. It paired Kemp, the conservative darling of the supply-side movement and a driving force behind the 1981 tax bill, with Bradley, a liberal Democrat and a fervent opponent of the 1981 bill. It even united General Motors's chairman, Roger Smith, with his company's long-standing nemesis, consumer activist Ralph Nader.

The most important player in tax reform was Ronald Reagan himself. The president seldom took an active role in the two-year tax debate; when the Finance Committee held its critical vote to approve the bill, for example, he was seven thousand miles away at the summit of industrialized nations in Tokyo. Nevertheless, the conservative president's support for an effort once considered the bastion of liberals carried tremendous symbolic significance. Without his backing, tax reform could never have happened. With it, it became a powerful political juggernaut. Reagan wanted to go down in history as the president who cut the top tax rate at least in half, from 70 percent to 35 percent or lower. If abandoning business tax breaks and raising corporate taxes was the price he had to pay to achieve that goal, so be it. Reagan had been reelected in 1984 in a forty-nine-state landslide and, at that point, was one of the most popular presidents of this century. When he put his full weight and power behind an idea that tapped such a fundamental frustration of the American people, others in Washington could hardly ignore it.

The other major players had their own odd assortment of reasons for backing reform. Don Regan became a reformer in part because he sensed the president's passion for lower rates and was eager to win a prominent place for himself on the president's agenda. James Baker became a reformer because he was a loyal soldier and because his success as Treasury Secretary depended on his ability to achieve the president's top domestic policy goal. Dan Rostenkowski became a reformer because the president's endorsement of reform represented a challenge and a threat to both him and his party: The Republican president was trying to steal the Democratic mantle of "tax fairness," and Rostenkowski vowed not to let that happen. Bob Packwood became a reformer out of desperation: With Reagan and Rostenkowski moving together, he had no choice but to produce a bill or be branded a sellout to special interests; he was sucked into the great maw of reform.

One of the most intriguing questions raised by the two-year tax debate in Congress was why the many powerful interest groups lined up in opposition to reform never joined forces to defeat it. The total firepower of these special interests was potentially fatal to any piece of legislation, yet they never managed to form an effective "killer" coalition. Darman marveled at their fractiousness. "I couldn't help thinking that if I were a lobbyist, I would stand in the hallway with a big sign saying: EVERYONE INTERESTED IN KILLING THIS BILL, PLEASE MEET IN THE NEXT CORRIDOR," he said at one point during the debate. "There would have been an enormous rush, and they would have seen the power of their collective action."

The lobbyists never did that. In part, they, like the politicians they worked with, were afraid to be pinned as opponents of reform. Indeed, most of the groups opposing reform insisted in public that they were for it—they just wanted to make certain it did not hurt them. "They were brought down by the narrowness of their vision," Darman said. "Precisely because they defined themselves as representatives of single special interests, they failed to notice their collective power."

The lobbyists' failure also reflected the difficulty interest groups face in combating "populist" legislation. Even though they had made enormous campaign contributions and had much-vaunted access to important legislators, the anti-reform lobbyists remained outsiders throughout the tax-reform debate. They could find few allies in the highest councils of power. At each step President Reagan threatened to label lobbyists' friends in Congress as toadies to the special interests and enemies of rate cuts for the people, and that was a threat that could not be taken lightly.

Of course, special-interest politics remained strong throughout the tax-reform debate. Some lobbyists, whose clients had only a handful of tax breaks to protect, promoted reform from the beginning, and helped to pass the legislation. Others battled vigorously to retain as many of their tax benefits as possible. Although they failed to halt the bill, anti-reform lobbyists won significant battles: A coalition of labor groups and insurance companies staved off the effort to tax fringe benefits; life insurers succeeded in preserving the tax-favored status of their most lucrative product, cash-value insurance; oil and gas interests kept their pain to a minimum; and hundreds of individual companies won special transition rules.

The special-interest victories, however, were far outweighed by the special-interest defeats. The bill closed loopholes worth roughly $300 billion over five years and replaced them with lower tax rates. It also raised corporate taxes by $120 billion over five years, the largest corporate tax increase in history. Congress was acting in response to larger, broader forces, which, in the end, prevailed.

Tax reform was a uniquely American idea—that somehow the nation could start over and rebuild its entire tax system. "No other country would try anything like this, to go back to the beginning, to be born again," said Aaron Wildavsky, a political scientist at the University of California at Berkeley. "It was quite a radical proposal."

Yet even before President Reagan signed the historic measure, pundits began raising serious questions about its economic and political value. In the long run, few experts doubted that lower tax rates would improve the efficiency of the economy and boost the chances for economic growth, but in the short term, many felt the abrupt repeal of investment incentives would cause some serious dislocations. The economy had become addicted to tax stimulants, and a cold-turkey repeal was certain to cause pain: Investment would probably suffer, real estate construction would decline, and charitable giving stood to take a hit. Such radical tax change, whatever its long-term value, would undoubtedly have some unpleasant side effects.

Likewise, the political value of the effort also came under doubt. To be sure, tax reform helped the careers of a few legislators like Rostenkowski, Bradley, and Packwood, but it clearly did not create the grand national "realignment" of party loyalties that some members of both parties had hoped for. Indeed, in the congressional election campaigns that were underway when the president signed the bill in 1986, it was difficult to find any candidate—other than Packwood—who spent much time talking about tax reform or who was either helped or hurt by it. One reason for this might have been Rostenkowski's ability to make the 1986 tax bill as much a Democratic as a Republican document. Since the legislation was bipartisan, neither side could get credit—or blame.

Whatever its economic and political consequences, tax reform was, without doubt, a landmark piece of social legislation. It took more than four million impoverished working people off the income tax rolls. It also launched a no-holds-barred attack on tax shelters, a growing blight on the American economic landscape. In addition, it ended the ability of large and profitable corporations to escape paying taxes, which, whatever its economic merits or demerits, had become a galling spectacle to the American public. Most important, reform narrowed the enormous inequities that permeated the existing tax system. Although it made no fundamental changes in the distribution of the tax burden among income groups, it did make it more likely that individuals and corporations with similar incomes would pay similar taxes. In that way, it made the tax system more fair.

The legislation also offered the hope of beginning to mend people's faith in government. Over the previous two decades, Americans had lost their confidence in their country's capacity to accomplish great things. The triumph of tax reform was a sign that the tide might be turning. As President Reagan said: "America didn't become great being pessimistic and cynical. America is built on a can-do spirit that sees every obstacle as a challenge, every problem as an opportunity." Tax reform was that challenge and opportunity.

In terms of its substance, the tax bill was an awkward, hodgepodge attempt at reform, not at all like the pure proposals that so frequently came out of academia or Washington think tanks. It attacked tax breaks with an uneven hand—severely paring preferences for real estate developers, for instance, while preserving most of the generous loopholes enjoyed by the oil industry. It had elements of deceit—the advertised top rate of 28 percent belied hidden surtaxes that raised the top marginal tax rate to 33 percent, and in some cases even higher. It certainly was not simple; but then, it probably never could be. Former IRS Commissioner Sheldon Cohen explained it this way:

People think taxation is a terribly mundane subject. But what makes it fascinating is that taxation, in reality, is life. If you know the position a person takes on taxes, you can tell their whole philosophy. The tax code, once you get to know it, embodies all the essence of life: greed, politics, power, goodness, charity. Everything's in there. That's why it's so hard to get a simplified tax code. Life just isn't simple.

Despite its warts and wrinkles, the bill succeeded at the fundamental purpose of reform. To those who had grown accustomed to abusing the tax system and its many chinks and loopholes, it dealt a heavy blow, but to those who paid their taxes each year without taking advantage of the long lists of deductions, exclusions, and credits, the tax plan offered a hefty bonus. It was a heroic effort to address a profound and pervasive social and cultural problem that had been ignored for too long. For all its faults, the Tax Reform Act of 1986 was the rough-hewn triumph of the American democratic system.

Rostenkowski frequently joked during 1985 and 1986 that when the tax bill was completed, he planned to hang a sign on his door that read: GONE FISHIN'. But everyone in Washington knew that the battle was by no means over. Congress had passed a major tax bill roughly every year and a half since the income tax was enacted, and there was no reason to expect that to change. Older legislators remembered that Congress had made a less ambitious attempt at reforming the tax code in 1969, only to find much of its work reversed in the next few years. The investment tax credit, in particular, had been through several deaths and reincarnations. Even before the 1986 tax law was signed, defeated lobbyists were already preparing to launch a campaign to restore their favorite tax breaks as part of the "technical corrections" bill of 1987. Charls Walker noted philosophically that tax sentiment is "cyclical," and he expressed little doubt that the push for investment tax breaks would soon be resumed.

Regardless of the tax changes to come, tax writers realized that it would be a long time before they were back in this sort of spotlight. "We'll never be center stage like we were with tax reform," Rostenkowski said.

The elections in November 1986 brought about some important political changes that raised more questions about the future of reform. The Democrats took majority control of the Senate, forcing Packwood out of his chairmanship of the Finance Committee. The new chairman for the 100th Congress, which convened in January 1987, was Democratic Senator Lloyd Bentsen of Texas, one of the most reluctant reformers on the Finance Committee. Bentsen promised to emphasize trade legislation over taxes, but the lobbyists still had hope. After steering the Senate to triumph on the landmark tax-reform bill and easily winning reelection, Packwood was relegated to head the minority portion of the committee.

Every Finance Committee member who sought reelection in 1986 won, but only one of the three Ways and Means members who wanted to move up to the Senate was elected: Wyche Fowler of Georgia. Henson Moore of Louisiana and James Jones of Oklahoma were defeated in their bids.

Rostenkowski remained in the chair at the Ways and Means Committee, but he served in the 100th Congress under a new speaker, Jim Wright of Texas, who was at times a Rostenkowski rival. Before the tax-reform debate, Rostenkowski had created friction with Wright by expressing interest in usurping Wright's claim to the speakership. Later, Wright angered the Ways and Means chairman by publicly opposing tax reform. After being selected as their speaker by the House Democrats, Wright signaled an attack at the heart of the new law: He proposed freezing the top individual tax rate at the 38.5-percent level the legislation had set as an interim rate for 1987. Though the proposal was roundly criticized, more run-ins between the two leaders seemed inevitable.

Russell Long retired to become a Washington lawyer and elder statesman, but he did not leave Congress without first making his mark on the new tax law. He got the better of Rostenkowski by securing for a Louisiana-based utility company the same kind of favored treatment in the minimum tax that Rostenkowski won for an Illinois utility. The Ways and Means chairman tried to camouflage the recipient of his break by describing the size of the utility's power generator rather than using its name. What Long knew—and what Rostenkowski found out—was that the Louisiana utility had the same size machine and was also eligible for the break. By waiting patiently in the wings until it was too late to turn back, Long secured a $140 million benefit for Middle South Utilities.

In a more far-reaching development, a Russell Long provision in the bill was belatedly discovered to, effectively, all but repeal the estate tax. The senator was trying to bolster tax benefits for employee stock-ownership plans, a cause he had long championed. Instead, he created a $20 billion loophole that would allow wealthy people to convert their bequests into stock, sell them to an employee stock-ownership plan, and in the process, escape estate taxation. Senator Bentsen, in his new role as Finance Committee chairman, promised to close the loophole as soon as he was able.

Only two weeks after the signing of the reform bill, President Reagan became embroiled in the biggest crisis of his two terms in office. Newspaper reports revealed that the administration had shipped arms to the revolutionaries in Iran, bitter enemies of the American people since their seizure of American hostages during the Carter administration. Moreover, some of the proceeds of the secret sale were reportedly diverted to help fund the contras' fight against the Nicaraguan government. The public perception of the president plummeted in opinion polls, and new revelations threatened to prolong the crisis, leaving the White House sinking in a quagmire of scandal and doubt.

The Iranian crisis dragged on for months. The president's inattention to even the most important details of government, which had been evident throughout the tax-reform effort, became the subject of increasing national debate. Chief of Staff Regan was drummed out of office by a torrent of criticism, coming most importantly from the president's wife, Nancy, who had been skeptical of his appointment from the beginning. And in early April, Deputy Treasury Secretary Darman, discouraged by the administration's inability to move on any major policy issues, left to become a managing director at an investment banking firm. Tax reform seemed destined to become the last highpoint of the Reagan presidency.

On a more personal note, Rostenkowski's daughter, Stacy, received a successful kidney transplant at the end of 1985, which has helped her return to good health.

APPENDIXES
AND INDEX

APPENDIX A
The Evolution of Major Provisions Affecting Individuals

Proposal	Individual Tax Rates	Personal Exemption	Standard Deduction (Married Couples)	Mortgage Interest	Consumer Interest	Charitable Contributions	State and Local Taxes
Prior law	14 rates: 11%–50%	$1,080	$3,670	Fully deductible	Fully deductible	Deductible for itemizers and nonitemizers	Fully deductible
Bradley-Gephardt	3 rates: 14%, 26%, 30%	$1,600; $1,000 for dependents[2]	$6,000	Deductible only against 14% rate	Limited to investment income	Deductible only against 14% rate	Deductible only against 14% rate[3]
Kemp-Kasten[4]	25% flat rate; "phantom" rates of 20% and 28%	$2,000	$3,640	Fully deductible	Not deductible	Fully deductible	Property tax only is deductible
Treasury I	3 rates: 15%, 25%, 35%	$2,000	$3,800[5]	Deductible for principal residence	Limited to $5,000 over investment income	Deductible for itemizers if over 2% of AGI	Not deductible
President	3 rates: 15%, 25%, 35%	$2,000	$4,000	Deductible for principal residence	Limited to $5,000 over investment income	Deductible only for itemizers	Not deductible
House	4 rates: 15%, 25%, 35%, 38%	$2,000; $1,500 for itemizers	$4,800	Deductible for first and second homes	Limited to $20,000 over investment income	Deductible for itemizers; for nonitemizers if over $100	Fully deductible
Senate	2 rates: 15%, 27%; "phantom" top marginal rate: 32%	$2,000; phased out for highest incomes	$5,000	Deductible for first and second homes	Not deductible	Deductible only for itemizers	Income and property tax deductible; not sales tax
Final	2 rates: 15%, 28%; "phantom" top marginal rate: 33%[1]	$2,000; phased out for highest incomes	$5,000	Deductible for first and second homes	Not deductible	Deductible only for itemizers	Income and property tax deductible; not sales tax

AGI: ADJUSTED GROSS INCOME

[1] In 1987, a "blended" rate schedule with a top rate of 38.5% will be in effect
[2] Deductible only against the bottom (14%) rate
[3] Income and real property tax only
[4] This chart reflects only the first of several versions of the Kemp-Kasten plan
[5] Kemp-Kasten had a wage deduction that increased the tax-free income level by 25%

Long-term Capital Gains (Top Rate)	IRA Deduction	Medical-Expense Deduction	Two-Earner Deduction	Miscellaneous Deductions	Income Averaging	Fringe Benefits	Life Insurance "Inside Buildup"
20%	$2,000; $250 for spouse	Excess of 5% of AGI	Yes	Fully deductible	Yes	Fully excluded from taxable income	Tax-free
30%	$2,000; $250 for spouse	Excess of 10% of AGI[2]	No	Fully deductible	Repealed	Limited health exclusion; tax all others	Tax-free
25%	$2,000; $250 for spouse	Excess of 10% of AGI	No	Fully deductible	Repealed	Fully excluded	Tax-free
35% Index for inflation	$2,500 for worker and spouse	Excess of 5% of AGI	No	Fully deductible	Cut back	Put cap on health exclusion; life insurance taxed	Taxed
17.5%	$2,000 for worker and spouse	Excess of 5% of AGI	No	Deductible in excess of 1% of AGI	Repealed	Tax part of health insurance; otherwise excluded	Taxed for new policies only
22%	$2,000; $250 for spouse	Excess of 5% of AGI	No	Deductible in excess of 1% of AGI	Repealed	Fully excluded	Tax-free
32%	Only for those with no pension plan	Excess of 9% of AGI	No	Repealed	Repealed	Fully excluded	Tax-free
33%	For those without pension plans, or for married couples with AGI less than $50,000	Excess of 7.5% of AGI	No	Deductible in excess of 2% of AGI	Repealed	Fully excluded	Tax-free

APPENDIX B
The Evolution of Major Provisions Affecting Businesses

Proposal	Corporate Tax Rates	Investment Tax Credit	Depreciation	Business Meals and Entertainment	Oil and Gas	Bank Bad-Debt Reserves
Prior law	48% top rate; 4 lower rates on income up to $100,000	6%–10%	Accelerated write-offs	Deductible	One-year write off for certain IDCs	Deductible
Bradley-Gephardt	30% flat rate	Repealed	Slightly accelerated write-offs	Deductible	IDC write-off repealed	Deduction cut back
Kemp-Kasten	30% top rate; 15% up to $50,000	Repealed	Accelerated write-offs	Deductible	IDC write-off repealed	Deduction cut back
Treasury I	33% flat rate	Repealed	No acceleration	No deduction for entertainment; meals limited	IDC write-off repealed	Deduction repealed
President	33% top rate; 3 lower rates on income up to $75,000	Repealed	Accelerated write-offs	No deduction for entertainment; meals limited	One-year IDC write-off retained	Deduction repealed
House	36% top rate; 2 lower rates on income up to $75,000	Repealed	Slightly accelerated write-offs	80% of meals and entertainment deductible	IDC write-off cut back	Repealed for largest banks
Senate	33% top rate; 2 lower rates on income up to $75,000	Repealed	Accelerated write-offs	80% of meals and entertainment deductible	One-year IDC write-off retained	Deduction retained
Final	34% top rate; 2 lower rates on income up to $75,000	Repealed	Accelerated write-offs	80% of meals and entertainment deductible	IDC write-off cut slightly for big producers	Repealed for largest banks

IDC: INTANGIBLE DRILLING COSTS

Index

AARP (American Association of Retired Persons), 197
Abraham, Jesse, 111
Abrahams, Al, 33
accelerated cost recovery system, 16
accelerated depreciation write-offs, 10, 48–49, 91, 119, 200
accounting, completed-contract, 140
AFL-CIO, 82–83, 184
Agnew, Spiro T., 70
Airlie House, 116, 123, 128
Akers, John, 194
Albert, Carl, 104
Alignpac, 85, 183
Alta Verde Industries, 225
Aluminum Company of America (Alcon), 16
American Association of Retired Persons (AARP), 197
American Association of University Women, 239
American Bankers Association, 161
American Council for Capital Formation, 16
American Electronics Association, 161
American Express, 145
American Frozen Food Institute, 239
American Horse Council, 112
American Revolution, 13
Amway Corporation, 239
Andrews, Kurth, Campbell & Jones, 67
Anthony, Beryl, 140

Appropriations committees, 266
Archer, Bill, 257, 260, 280, 283
Armstrong, William, 200, 202, 230, 239, 242
Aronoff, Marcia, 120
asbestos poisoning, 242
AWACs, 186

bad-debt-reserve deductions, 57, 124
Baker, Howard, 69, 76, 100
Baker, James A., III, 19–21, 39, 46, 62, 65–86, 88–94, 102, 113, 114, 116–17, 124, 128, 132, 135, 141, 143–44, 148–49, 152–57, 165–66, 168–69, 171–75, 189–90, 192, 196, 208–9, 223–24, 226, 231, 233, 238, 260–63, 266, 271–72, 276–80, 283
Baker & Botts, 67
Ballentine, J. Gregory, 87
banking, commercial, 124–25, 178
Barr, Joseph, 14
Barrie, Robert, 179
Basic Industries Coalition, 178
Baucus, Max, 182
Beaufort County, S.C., 112
Belas, Rich, 227
Bell, Jeff, 26, 37–38
Bentsen, Lloyd, 178, 199, 200, 211–12, 221–22, 229, 240, 248, 258, 265–66, 274
Berkeley Springs, W.Va., 191–92
Biden, Joseph, 252

billboard shelters, 10
binding-contract rule, 91, 107
biotechnology, 81
Black Horse Tavern, 23
Blue Earth (Minn.) *Town Crier*, 85
Blueprints for Basic Tax Reform (Simon), 51, 53
Blumenthal, Michael, 15
Bode, Denise, 178
Boggs, Hale, 104, 178
Boggs, Tommy, 178, 179
bonds:
    "builder," 201
    municipal, 137–39
    private-purpose revenue, 112, 137–39, 279–80
    tax-exempt, 136–39, 199–201
Bonior, David, 162
Boren, David, 72, 178, 191–92, 222, 226, 229, 242
Boschwitz, Rudy, 193
boxcar shelters, 10
"bracket creep," 53
Bradley, Bill, 5–6, 19, 23–31, 33–39, 58, 76–77, 100, 110, 119–21, 165, 182, 191–93, 199–200, 202, 207, 210–11, 212, 221, 225, 230, 232–33, 234–35, 238, 251, 257–58, 271, 277, 278, 279, 282
Bradley-Gephardt bill, 31, 33–34, 36, 50, 77, 110, 167, 209–10, 212, 257
Brockway, David, 122, 131–32, 134, 148, 208, 210, 213–19, 222, 225, 260, 266, 272, 274–76
Brooks, Preston, 253
Broomfield, William S., 174
Bryan, William Jennings, 6
Buchanan, Patrick, 135
Buchwald, Art, 56
Budget Committee (House), 11, 186
Budget Committee (Senate), 32–33, 223
"builder bonds," 201
Building cost, depreciation of, 17
Busch, August, III, 197

Bush, George, 39, 40, 67, 68, 94, 271
Business Roundtable, 161
Byrd, Harry, 14
Byrd, Robert, 12, 246

Calhoun, John, 235
Calio, Nick, 151
Campaign Committee (Senate), 186
campaign contributions, 162, 181, 183
"capital formation," 16, 20, 212
capital gains:
    indexing of, for inflation, 54
    low, 10
    preference, 223
capital-gains "carve out," 82
capital-gains tax, 7, 93–94, 119, 221
    on inheritance, 58
    special break on, 20, 54, 227
Caplin, Mortimer, 56
Caplin and Drysdale, 27
Carlisle, Linda, 262
Carlton group, 16, 17–18, 48, 59
Carswell, G. Harrold, 185
Carter, Jimmy, 15–16, 58, 68, 174
Carter administration:
    business-expense deductions under, 56
    deficit under, 19, 31
    tax reform under, 15–16, 20, 53
Caspersen, Finn, 149, 151, 194
cattle-breeding shelters, 54
cattle-feeding shelters, 10, 219, 225
cellular-telephone companies, 178
CEO Tax Group, 161, 194, 238
Chafee, John, 6, 182, 191, 199–201, 210, 212, 219, 221, 225, 230, 240, 242, 258, 279
Chamber of Commerce, U.S., 161
Chapman, Bruce, 55
Chapoton, John "Buck," 44, 47, 78–79, 178, 198, 261–62
charitable contributions, 7, 48, 81, 90, 208
Cheney, Dick, 66, 155, 163, 165
Chew, David, 65

Chicago & North Western, 11
Chicago Sun-Times, 269
Chicago White Sox, 45
child care, 56
Children's Defense Fund, 239
China, Nixon's visit to, 101
Chincoteague Bay penny-oyster shelter, 10
Chlopak, Bob, 114, 115
Christian, Ernest, 200
Christian Science Monitor, 60
Churchill, Winston, 205
Church Women United, 239
Citizens for Tax Justice, 12–13, 138, 197, 238
Clark, William, 68
"close" rules, 161–162
Coalition Against Double Taxation, 114–15
Coalition to Reduce High Effective Tax Rates, 178
Coelho, Tony, 120, 129, 140
Colley, Chad, 80
Colvin, John, 195–196, 218, 266
commercial banks, 124–25
  lobbying for, 178
Common Cause, 180, 181–82, 238, 260
Commonwealth Edison, 147
completed-contract accounting, 140
Conable, Barber, 19, 60
Conference of Mayors, 114
Congress, U.S.:
  "bidding war" in, 18
  PACs in, *see* political action committees
  "rules" in, 161–65
  staff size in, 216–17
  tax breaks as currency in, 13
  tax favors from, 4
Congressional Budget Office, 27–28, 29, 272
Congressional Quarterly, 268
Connally, John, 17, 68
Constitution, U.S., Sixteenth Amendment of, 6–7

consumed-income tax, 51–53
Consumer Federation of America, 197, 239
convention benefits, 242
Cook, Eric, 218
Coolidge, Calvin, 63
corporate taxation:
  decline in, 11–13, 60
  in tax simplification, 59–60, 63, 272
Council for a Secure America, 129
Cox, Archibald, 70
Coyne, William, 138–39
Crane, Philip, 182, 257
Cranston, Alan, 80
Crow, Trammell, 201
Cuomo, Mario, 109, 113–16, 264

Daley, Richard J., 21, 104–5
D'Amato, Alfonse, 109, 113, 241, 244–45, 248, 251
D'Amato-Dodd amendment, 245–46
Danforth, John, 5, 72, 192, 211, 221, 225–26, 228, 249, 258, 275, 277–83
Darman, Richard, 3, 9, 39–40, 67–86, 88–94, 102, 113, 114, 116, 125, 127–28, 131–32, 134–36, 141, 152–57, 159–60, 168, 169, 171–75, 189, 196, 208–9, 213, 217, 220, 223, 225, 227, 231–33, 238, 260–63, 266, 271–72, 276–80, 283
Data Resources Incorporated, 111
Daub, Hal, 146, 174
David and Goliath, Round Two, 85
D'Avino, Richard, 262–63
Dawson, Thomas, 43, 89
DeArment, Roderick, 178
Deaver, Michael, 67, 71
deductions, 9
  bad-debt reserves, 57, 124
  business-expense, 56
  charitable contributions, 7, 48, 81, 90, 208
  in different brackets, 29–30
  dividend, 55–56

deductions (*continued*)
  entertainment-expense, 56
  for excise tax, 196–98, 219
  farming equipment, 7
  for home-mortgage-interest pay-
    ments, 57, 111, 116, 140, 208, 246
  for property tax, 14
  sales-tax, 230, 245–46, 251
  special, 7, 133
  for state and local taxes, 48, 88,
    109, 113–16, 128–32, 134, 142–
    43, 144, 219
  "three-martini-lunch," 15–16
  see also tax breaks
deficit, U.S., 19, 31, 100, 108, 118,
    148, 193–94
Democratic-Farmer-Labor Party, 35
Democratic Study Group (DSG), 118
depreciation write-offs, 10, 48–49, 91,
    119, 200
Despres, Gina, 27–28, 30
Diefenderfer, Bill, 136, 181, 188, 195,
    202, 204–8, 213, 218, 225, 227,
    242, 251, 261, 266, 269, 279
disability payments:
  military, 8
  taxing of, 48, 79–80
Disraeli, Benjamin, 205
dividend deduction, 55–56
Dodd, Christopher, 244–45
Dole, Robert, 5–6, 31–33, 53, 76,
    103, 136, 178, 181, 182, 188, 193–
    94, 197, 216, 220–24, 225–27,
    229, 233, 235, 239, 241, 244, 247,
    258, 270–71, 279
Domenici, Pete, 32, 193
Dorgan, Byron, 140, 149
"double taxation," 52, 55
Douglas, Stephen, 235
Dowley, Joe, 107–8, 118, 123, 128,
    131–32, 134, 138, 149, 151
Downey, Thomas, 109, 125, 271
DSG (Democratic Study Group), 118
Duberstein, Kenneth, 76
DuBose, Gene, 215

Duncan, John, 71, 76–77, 111, 115,
    122, 154–55, 179, 257
Durenberger, David, 182, 192

Economic Recovery Tax Act (ERTA),
    18
Economic Research Associates, 112
education aid, 56
Egger, Roscoe, 8–9, 43, 46, 50–51,
    52, 54, 78
Eisenhower, Dwight D., 63
Eisenhower administration, 14
Emmet, Kathleen, 69
employee stock-ownership programs,
    56, 140
employer-paid legal assistance, 56
employers' contributions, 7
energy tax credits, 57
Enron Corporation, 200
entertainment-expense deductions, 56
entrepreneurial enterprises, 81–82
equipment-leasing shelters, 10, 219
ERTA (Economic Recovery Tax Act),
    18
estate tax, 140
Evans, Daniel, 245–46
Evans, Rowland, Jr., 224
excise tax, 6, 196–98, 219
expense accounts, 10–11
"expensing," 49

Fairmont Sentinel, 85
Fair Tax Act (1982), 31
farmers, 7
Federal Election Commission, 179
federal-employee pensions, 269–70
Feldstein, Martin, 39, 45, 116
Ferguson, James, 81
Ferraro, Geraldine, 94
filibustering, 235–36
Finance Committee (Senate), 3–4, 14,
    19–20, 25, 26, 31–32, 73, 180,
    199, 209–11, 240
Fitzsimmons, Thomas, 115
flat-tax, 26, 39

modified, 61
Flippo, Ronnie, 122, 124–25, 127–28,
133–34, 138–39, 180
Foley, Thomas, 120
Ford, Gerald, 68
Ford, Harold, 133, 140–41, 146
Ford, Wendell, 246
Ford Motor Corporation, 11, 63
Fortune, 15
401(k) pension plans, 109, 201
Fowler, Wyche, 136–37, 145, 181
Franasiak, David, 280
Franks, Thomas, 111, 112–13
Free, James, 179
free market theory, 28
Frenzel, Bill, 109, 116, 141, 160, 182
"fresh-off-the-shelf loophole," 247
Friedman, Milton, 26
fringe benefits:
employer-paid, 7
tax-free, 56, 190
taxing of, 48, 77, 148–50, 255
fundraisers, 179–80

Gainesville, Ga., 108
Gallo, Ernest, 140, 197
Gallo, Julio, 140
Garvin, Clifton, 44
gas industry, 10, 57, 94, 107, 116,
143–44, 199, 230–31
Gekas, George, 172
General Contractors of America, 239
General Electric, 12
General Motors Corporation, 161, 241
Gephardt, Richard, 30–31, 76–77,
110, 257
Gibbons, Sam, 122–23, 128, 140–41,
181, 257
Gibbs, Lawrence, 266–67
Gingrich, Newt, 32, 163
Girdletree, Md., 10
Global Marine, 11
Goldfeder, Howard, 194
Goldwater, Barry, 181
Gooden, Dwight, 145

Gorbachev, Mikhail, 142, 152
Gorton, Slade, 193, 245–46
Gotlieb, Sondra, 69
Gould, Jim, 200
Grace, J. Peter, 12
W. R. Grace & Company, 12, 211
"Grace Report," 211
Gradison, Willis, 108, 125, 141, 171
Gramm, Phil, 245–46
Gramm-Rudman-Hollings law, 110,
145, 237
Grassley, Charles, 180, 181, 182, 192,
226
Greenspan, Alan, 75
Guarini, Frank, 117, 147, 180
Gucci Gulch, origin of term, 4
Gunderson, Steven, 172

Hall, Robert, 39
Hance, Kent, 105
hard money, soft money vs., 181
Hart, Gary, 34
Hatfield, Mark, 184, 254
Haynesworth, Clement, 185
Healey, James, 177–78
health care, 56
health insurance:
national, 190
taxing of, 82
Hecht, Gary, 9
Heckert, Richard, 236
Heftel, Cecil, 150
Heinz, John, 194, 226, 228, 230, 242
Hicks, Chris, 43, 65
high-tech industry, 81
Hilton Hotels, 11
Holt, Marjorie, 172
home-mortgage deduction, 7, 57, 111,
116, 140, 208, 246
horse-breeding tax shelters, 86, 112
House of Representatives, U.S., *see*
specific committees
Houston, Tex., 10
Houston Chronicle, 240
Howell, William, 81

Humphrey, Hubert, 104
Hyde, Henry, 170–71, 174

IBM (International Business Ma-
    chines), 11, 139, 149, 151, 161
income tax:
    capital gains, *see* capital gains tax
    consumption-based tax vs., 51–53
    enaction of, 6
    federal vs. state, 9
    history of, 6–7, 13, 14–16
Independent Petroleum Association of
    America, 239
Individual Retirement Accounts, *see*
    IRAs
industrial development bonds, 138–39
inflation, 7
    "bracket creep" and, 53
    indexing capital gains for, 54
    in 1970s, 9, 54
inheritance, capital-gains tax on, 58
Institute for Research on the Econom-
    ics of Taxation, 112
insurance:
    life, 7, 57, 148–49
    unemployment, 48, 124
interest:
    indexing of, 55, 87–88
    life insurance, 7
    municipal bond, 8
Intergovernmental Relations Advisory
    Committee, 9
Internal Revenue Service (IRS), 26,
    266
International Business Machines
    (IBM), 11, 139, 149, 151, 161
"investment seminars," 11
investment tax credit, 14–15, 48, 140,
    160
Iranian hostage crisis, 74
IRAs (Individual Retirement Ac-
    counts), 58–59, 86–87, 223, 232,
    243–246
Irish Distillers Group, 239
Israel, 186

Jackson, Andrew, 269
Jacobs, Andy, 147
Jacobson, Allen, 81, 194
Jaffe, Jim, 274
Jefferson, Thomas, 205
Jenkins, Edgar, 108, 117, 129, 140,
    257
Johnson, Lyndon, 104, 133
Johnson, Manuel, 43, 45, 46, 49–50,
    78, 79, 87, 91
Johnson, Nancy, 172
Johnson administration, 14
Johnston, Edward, 198
Joint Tax Committee, 3, 7, 27–28, 86–
    87, 131–32, 208, 214, 260, 263,
    271, 275
jojoba bean scam, 10
Jones, James, 122, 128–29, 137, 181,
    182
Jordan, Hamilton, 137
Juliano, Bob, 145

Kasten, Robert, 32, 38–39, 76–77
Kemp, Jack, 17, 36–39, 68, 76–77, 87,
    89, 155, 158, 160, 163, 165, 168,
    170, 173, 174, 207, 224
Kemp-Kasten tax bill, 38–39, 58, 77
Kemp-Roth tax cut, 31, 50, 59, 243
Kennedy, John F., 14, 69, 74, 174,
    184, 253
Kennedy administration, 48
    business-expense deductions under,
    56
Kennelly, Barbara, 112, 122, 182
Kenney, Robert, 12
Kerr, Robert, 84, 178
"kiddie tax," 226
Kies, Ken, 151
Kilpatrick, James J., 12
Kingon, Aldred, 43, 50, 59, 62, 89
Kirkland, Lane, 82
Klaymand, Bob, 27
Kriegel, Jay, 113–16, 130–31
Kristol, Irving, 37
Kuhn, Bowie, 67

Lafayette, Marquis de, 40
Laffer, Arthur, 18
Landow, Nathan, 36
Lawrence of Arabia, 187
Laxalt, Paul, 186, 239
Leahy, Patrick, 217
"Learjet weekend," 18
lease-a-tax-break law, 11
Lehrman, Lewis E., 37–38
Leonard, Rob, 107–8, 131–32, 134,
    146, 149, 217
Leone, Dick, 34
Lerch, Steve, 210, 218
Levin, Carl, 252
Libya, 211
Life, 69
life insurance:
    interest on, 7
    taxing of, 57, 148–49
Life on the Run (Bradley), 25, 26
Lilliston, Bill, 10
limited partnerships, 218–20
Lincoln, Abraham, 250, 253
Lindsay, John, 113
llama-breeding shelters, 10
lobbyists:
    Finance Committee and, 31–32, 209
    hierarchy of, 3–4
    lines of, 178–79
    on Reagan, 4
    real estate, 57
    Senate and, 176–77
    on state and local taxes, 113
    Ways and Means Committee and,
        121–22
"Lobbyists' Relief Act of 1986," 177
local tax, 7
    deduction for, 48, 88, 109, 113–16,
        128–32, 134, 142–43, 147, 219
Loeffler, Tom, 164
Long, Huey, 3, 253
Long, Russell, 3, 5–6, 15, 33, 76–77,
    84, 178, 188, 192, 197, 209, 212–
    13, 227–32, 237, 242, 252, 255,
    258, 267–68, 279–80, 282

Long, "Uncle Earl," 267
loopholes:
    elimination of, 13–14, 21–22, 59, 73,
        198, 206–7
    investment tax credit, 48
    for oil industry, 20–21
    reinstatement of, 14–15
Los Angeles Herald Examiner, 12
Los Angeles Times, 180
Lott, Trent, 105, 155, 163–65, 169–70,
    172
low-income households, 5, 6, 116
Lucas, Jerry, 26
Lugar, Richard, 186
Lutz, Joe, 190

McAuliffe, Mary, 238
McCandless, Al, 172
McCloskey, Frank, 159
McConaghy, Mark, 216
McDonnell Douglas, 277
McEwen, Bob, 159
McGovern, George, 75
McGrath, Raymond, 116, 129, 134,
    138, 141, 147
McIntyre, Richard, 158–59
McIntyre, Robert, 11–13, 88, 138
Mack, Connie, 103
McKinney, Stewart, 29–30
McLure, Charles, 43, 45–54, 57, 59
    61, 62, 72, 78
McNamar, Tim, 43
McPhee, John, 25, 27
Madison, James, 269
Malbin, Michael, 217
Mansfield, Mike, 236
Manville Corporation, 242
"Marriott amendment," 241
Mason, George, 49
Matsui, Robert, 33, 114, 122, 138–39,
    182
Matsunaga, Spark, 72–73, 258
Meese, Ed, 68
Melcher, John, 252
Mellody, Charles, 120

Mellon, Andrew, 42
Mendenhall, John R., 12
Mentz, Roger, 230, 262, 263, 265–66, 278, 280
Menuhin, Yehudi, 150
Merrill Lynch Pierce Fenner & Smith, 45, 147
Metropolitan Transit Authority (MTA), 147
Metzenbaum, Howard, 241–43, 247, 248, 250
Miami Dolphins, 147
Michel, Robert, 155, 159, 163, 168–69, 171, 173, 174
Michelangelo, 222
middle-income households, 9
military benefits, 7
Miller, George, 130
Mills, Wilbur, 18, 106, 146, 174, 257
Minarik, Joe, 27, 29–31
"minimal" tax-reform bill, 135–36
"minimum tax," 88
Minnesota Business Partnerships, 109
Mitchell, George, 192, 198, 212, 225, 227, 230–31, 247, 258–59
Mitchell, John, 227
Mitchell, Martha, 227
"modified closed" rules, 161–62
"modified flat tax," 61
Mondale, Walter, 33–36, 57–58, 63, 94, 101
money, hard vs. soft, 181
Moore, Henson, 85, 128, 137, 138, 150, 181
Morgenthau, Henry, 84
Morse, Wayne, 184–85
mortgage-interest deductions, 7, 57, 111, 116, 140, 208, 246
Morton's, 269
Moynihan, Daniel Patrick, 72, 76, 202, 210–211, 219, 221, 225–27, 257–58, 277–78
MTA (Metropolitan Transit Authority), 147

municipal bonds, 137–39
interest on, 8

Nader, Ralph, 12, 197
National Association of Home Builders, 161
National Association of Manufacturers, 161, 236
National Association of Wholesaler-Distributors, 161
National Black Child Development Institute, 239
National Coalition of American Nuns, 239
National Council of Community Hospitals, 111–12
National Council of LaRaza, 239
National Journal, 159
National Puerto Rican Coalition, 239
Neustadt, Richard, 70
New Republic, 201
Newsweek, 85
New York Mets, 145
New York Times, 19, 24, 74, 247
Niskanen, William, 63
Nixon, Richard, 14, 68, 70, 101, 185
Nixon administration:
Congress under, 216
Watergate scandal, 70, 74, 185
Norris, George, 254
North Star Steel, 242
W. W. Norton & Company, 214
Novak, Robert, 224

Occidental Petroleum, 11
O'Donnell, Kirk, 165
Oglesby, M. B., 152, 155, 157, 171–72
oil depletion allowance, 15
oil-import fee, 192
oil industry, 10, 20–21, 57, 83–84, 94, 107, 116, 143–44, 199, 229–31
O'Neill, Kip, 178
O'Neill, Millie, 168
O'Neill, Thomas P. "Tip," 40, 76, 96,

104, 109–10, 120, 133, 161, 162, 165–69, 172–75, 240, 257
Ooms, Van Doorn, 11
Oregon, financial history of, 187
Oregonian, 234–35

Packwood, Frederick W., 184
Packwood, Georgie, 187
Packwood, Robert, 3, 5–6, 15, 19–20, 72, 76–77, 82–83, 89, 90, 136, 148, 163, 170, 176ff., 217–22, 224–35, 245–49, 251–52, 255–83
Packwood, William H., 184
PACs, *see* political action committees
Panetta, Leon, 130
partnerships:
  limited, 218–20
  oil and gas, 10
  real estate, 10
passive-loss provisions, 218–20, 221, 224–25, 227, 229–31
Patton Boggs & Blow, 178
Paul, Randolph, 13–14
Pearlman, Ronald, 43, 45–49, 51–54, 58–59, 61–63, 74, 78–83, 89, 91–93, 108, 128, 198, 262
Pease, Donald, 257, 258, 264
pension plans, 7
  federal, 269–70
  401(k), 109, 201
People, 85, 188
Pepper, Claude, 146–47
Perdue, Frank, 266
personal exemptions, 30, 48, 55, 119, 168–71, 173, 219–20
Peterson, Geoffrey, 179
"phantom" top marginal tax rate, 220
Philip Morris, 239
Phillips Petroleum, 242
Pickens, T. Boone, 247
Pickle, J. J. "Jake," 10, 243, 257
political action committees (PACs), 18, 19–20, 85, 179–81
  fundraising and, 182–83

Polk, James K., 269
Pollack, Lester, 183
port bonds, 139
poverty level, 55
presidential primaries, 270
press:
  pressure on Congress from, 110
  reform stories in, 61–62
  "Sperling breakfasts," 60–61
Procter & Gamble, 139, 149, 151, 161
"productivity property," 200
"progressive" taxation, 9, 10, 30–31
property tax, 9, 114
Proxmire, William, 267
Pryor, David, 192, 203, 213, 220–21, 228–29, 242–43
Public Citizen, 197
Public Interest, 37

Qaddafi, Muammar, 211
Quinn, Thomas, 259

Raboy, David, 265–66
Rabushka, Alvin, 39
Rahn, Richard, 21, 37–38
Rangel, Charles, 55, 101, 141, 147, 149–50, 151, 257, 264
Rayburn, Sam, 84, 257
Reagan, Nancy, 67
Reagan, Ronald, 17, 26, 68
  address to House, 169–71
  Bitburg visit of, 90
  lobbyists on, 4
  official support for tax reform, 153–75
  reelection of, 42, 43
  Republican support for, 158
  on tax reform, 40–41, 94–95, 118
  as unlikely tax reformer, 21–22
Reagan administration:
  deficit under, 19
  House GOP and, 159
  policy reversal under, 48–51
  tax cuts under, 54–55

Reaganomics, 25
real estate tax shelters, 7, 10, 140, 219
recession (1982), 31
Regan, Donald T., 19–20, 40–41, 42–
    48, 50–51, 53–54, 56–67, 74, 75,
    78, 82, 88–91, 100, 120, 135, 142,
    152–53, 155–56, 159, 168, 171,
    193
research-and-development tax credits,
    10, 140
retroactive tax, 91–92, 108, 118–19
Revenue Act (1954), 84
revenue bonds, 112, 137–39, 229–80
Reynolds, Alan, 37
Ribicoff, Abraham, 105
Richardson, Elliot, 70
Richman, John, 81, 194
Roberts, Paul Craig, 37, 49
Robinson, James, III, 113
Rockefeller, David, 113
Roderick, David, 197
Rolling Stone, 12
Roosevelt, Franklin Delano, 106
Rose, Charlie, 135
Rosenauer, David, 124–25
Rosenberg, Thomas, 36
Ross, Dennis, 262–63
Rostenkowski, Dan, 19, 21, 32, 63–
    64, 76–78, 82, 92, 96–110, 114–
    21, 123–51, 154–64, 175, 179,
    181, 182, 189, 222, 229–30, 237,
    255–64, 267–76, 278–83
Rostenkowski, Joseph, 103
Rostenkowski, Stacy, 144–45, 151,
    291
Rostenkowski plan, 123–26
  corporate opposition to, 160–61
  Kemp on, 170
  Republican opposition to, 158–60
Roth, William, 5, 17, 195, 243–45,
    258, 265–66
Rothstein, Joseph, 97–100
Rudin, Lewis, 13
"rules" in Congress, 161–65
Rules Committee (House), 162, 173

Russo, Marty, 129–31, 145, 148–49,
    150, 257, 258, 264

"safe-harbor lease," 11
St. Louis Cardinals, 192
sales tax, state, 9, 195
sales-tax deduction, 230, 245–46, 251
Salmon, John, 177–78, 240
Sarbanes, Paul, 249
Schneider, Claudine, 174
Schumer, Charles, 130–31
Schweiker, Richard, 85
securities, 7
see-through office buildings, 10
Senate, U.S.:
  honoraria recipients in, 181–82
  see also specific committees
"Senator Death (-and-Taxes)," 185
Sense of Where You Are, A (McPhee),
    25, 27
Shapiro, Bernard "Bob," 216
Sherman, John, 97, 99, 100, 101, 126
Shultz, George, 39
Simon, Paul, 252
Simon, William, 51, 53
Simpson, Alan, 250–51
Sisters of the Humility of Mary, 239
Smale, John, 81, 194
Smith, Howard W., 162
Smith, Roger, 81
socialism, "tax-code," 47
Social Security system, 75–76, 103,
    223
soft money, hard money vs., 181
Solar Energy Industries Association,
    178
solid-waste disposal facilities, 138–39,
    199
Speakes, Larry, 165
special convention benefit, 242
special interest groups, 32
Sperling, Godfrey, 60–61
"Sperling breakfasts," 60–61
Spickard, Steven, 112
Sports Illustrated, 85

Sprinkel, Beryl, 43
stagger, 270–71
Stall, Karen, 227–28
"standby" tax, 40
Stark, Fortney "Pete," 10, 134, 140,
    178–79, 182, 257, 258
Starr, David, 241
State of the Union address (1983), 39
State of the Union address (1984), 40,
    62
State of the Union address (1985), 73
state tax, 7
    deduction for, 48, 88, 109, 113–16,
        128–32, 134, 142–43, 147, 219
"static revenooers," 87
statutory tax rate, 5
steel industry, 201
Steuerle, Eugene, 52–53, 89
Stevens, Ted, 250, 251–52
Stockman, David, 39–40, 45–46, 76
stock-ownership plans, 56, 140
"straddle" tax shelters, 20
Sumner, Charles, 253
Superfund toxic-waste-cleanup pro-
    gram, 128, 255–56
Supreme Court, U.S., 6
Surrey, Stanley, 14, 26, 52–53, 262
Swardson, Anne, 127
Symms, Steve, 72, 181, 192, 232

Taft, Howard, 63
tariffs, 6
tax avoidance, 9
    oil and gas partnerships in, 10
    real estate in, 10
tax bill (1962), 14
tax bill (1963), 14
tax bill (1969), 14–15
tax bill (1981), 11, 48–51, 236
    "indexed" brackets in, 53–54
tax brackets, 9
    "bracket creep," 53
tax breaks:
    accelerated cost recovery, 16
    accumulated effect of, 8

for business, 7, 8
capital-gains, 20, 54
as Congressional currency, 13
for export companies, 15
fairness of, 9
Ribicoff, 105
selling of, 11
special-interest, 4–5, 42, 107, 241
swapping of, 138–40
after World Wars I and II, 7
see also deductions
tax code, U.S., 18, 25–26
    administration of, 46–47
    "indexing" of, 53
    for island possessions, 162
    Rostenkowski on, 145–46
"tax-code socialism," 47
tax credits, 7
    for building rehabilitation, 10, 57
    for campaign contributions, 162
    energy, 57
    foreign, 109
    investment, 14–15, 48, 140, 160
    research-and-development, 10, 140
tax cuts:
    Kemp-Roth, 31
    supply-side, 29
Tax Equity and Fiscal Responsibility
    Act (TEFRA), 31
tax-exempt bonds, 136–39, 199–201
tax incentives, 7
    binding-contract rule and, 91, 107
    as boost to economy, 49
    bunching of, 10
tax reform:
    bank amendment in, 126–27
    "capital formation," 16, 20, 212
    under Carter, 15–16, 20
    Darman on, 159–60
    distributionally neutral, 59, 88–89
    goal of, 13
    intensity of opposition to, 107–8
    under Kennedy, 14
    Long on, 15
    main attraction of, to Senate, 220

tax reform (*continued*)
  under Nixon, 14–15
  O'Neill on, 174
  as "phoenix project," 126–27
  popular interest in, 235
  populist attraction of, 29
  "radical approach" to, 206–8
  Reagan on, 40–41, 94–95, 118
  Reagan's understanding of, 22, 63,
    73
  revenue estimates in, 214, 260–61
  revenue neutral, 26, 29, 59, 90–91,
    116, 123, 148, 259
  in Senate, 176–203
  shifts in support for, 152–75
  splits created by, 160–61
  stagger for, 270–71
  stripped-down approach to, 204–5
  studies on, 111–13
  trade-off in, 13
  transition rules in, 146–47, 220,
    240–43, 247
Tax Reform Action Coalition, 151,
    161, 238, 255
*Tax Reform for Fairness, Simplicity,
    and Economic Growth*, 62
tax shelters, 5, 10
  "builder bonds," 201
  cattle-breeding, 54
  cattle-feeding, 10, 219, 225
  equipment-leasing, 10, 219
  horse-breeding, 86
  passive-loss provisions, 218–20, 221,
    224–25, 227, 229–31
  proliferation of, 50
  real estate, 10, 219
  Senate attack on, 218–20
  "straddles," 20
tax systems:
  disequilibrium in, 8
  distribution problem in, 88–89, 93–
    94
  flat-, 26, 39, 61
  as "industrial policy," 47
  "progressive," 9, 10, 30–31

  public dissatisfaction with, 9
  undermined confidence in, 10–13
TEFRA (Tax Equity and Fiscal Re-
    sponsibility Act), 31
textile industry, 108, 117
Thevenot, Wayne, 236
Thomas, Dennis, 152–53, 155–57, 159,
    167, 169, 171
Thompson, Bruce, 43, 47, 50, 78,
    154–55, 158, 171–72
Thompson, James H. W., 240
"three-martini-lunch" deduction, 15–
    16
Thuronyi, Victor, 262
timber industry, 57, 83, 139–40, 190–
    91, 199, 226
Time, 85, 274
Tisch, Laurence, 113
Toohey, Frank, 124–25
Touche Ross & Company, 153
trade deficit, 71–72, 110
transition rules, 146–47, 220, 240–43,
    247
Trappist monks, 7
Treasury Department, U.S., 3, 10, 42
  lease-a-tax-break-scheme of, 11
Trible, Paul, 247–49, 251
Triumph of Politics, The (Stockman),
    39
Troyer, Tom, 27
Truman, Harry, 84, 99, 118
Ture, Norman, 112
"turkey-buzzard amendment," 243
Tutwiler, Margaret, 69, 78, 81
Twain, Mark, 17
Tyler, John, 269

Ullman, Al, 106, 195
unemployment insurance, 48, 124
Union Oil Company of California
    (Unocal), 247
Union Pacific, 12
"unitary tax," 47
U.S. News & World Report, 85

Vail, Colo., 11
value-added tax (VAT), 52, 128, 136, 195–96
Vander Jagt, Guy, 174, 257
van pooling, 56
Vasquez, Thomas, 86–87
veterans benefits, 79–80
videotape shelters, 10
Vietnam War, 74, 184
Volcker, Paul, 244
"voodoo economics," 39

Walker, Charls E., 16–18, 48, 50, 52, 73, 179, 200, 236
Wallop, Malcolm, 200, 210, 226, 232, 248, 258, 277, 279–80
Wall Street Journal, 9, 37, 61–62, 73 87, 179, 181, 224, 235
Wanniski, Jude, 37
War of 1812, 222
Washington, George, 40, 107
Washington Post, 24, 45, 61, 69, 105, 127, 128, 162, 180, 183, 200
Watergate scandal, 70, 74, 185
Ways and Means Committee (House), 10, 14, 32, 106, 114–18, 121, 141–43
Weaver, James, 206
Webster, Daniel, 235
Weiss, Ari, 120, 166–67, 169

Weiss, Randy, 27, 30, 132, 217–18, 220, 222
Wertheimer, Fred, 177, 282
Wetzler, James, 27–28, 112
Weyerhaeuser Company, 16
Whirlpool, 12
White, Mark, 68
Whitehouse, Alton, 81
"White Whale," 187
Wild Bunch, The, 208
Wilkins, John, 263
Wilkins, William, 217, 227–28
Willard, Frances Elizabeth Caroline, 253
Williams, J. D., 178, 179
Williams, Pearre, 277
Wilson, Pete, 247
windfall recapture tax, 91–92, 108, 118–19
Wirthlin, Richard, 20, 39
Wodell, Page, 240
Woodworth, Larry, 216
World War I, 7
World War II, 7, 56
Wright, Jim, 105, 120, 167, 180–81
Wriston, Walter, 45
write-offs, accelerated depreciation, 10, 48–49, 91, 119, 200
Wyden, Ron, 189

Zeibert, Duke, 56

ABOUT THE AUTHORS

JEFFEREY H. BIRNBAUM, a congressional reporter for *The Wall Street Journal*, covered tax reform's progress through the House and Senate in 1985 and 1986. A graduate of the University of Pennsylvania, he served as a reporter for *The Miami Herald* in 1977 and 1978 before joining *The Wall Street Journal*, for which he has worked in New York and Washington. Mr. Birnbaum lives in Silver Spring, Maryland, with his wife, Deborah, and son, Michael.

ALAN S. MURRAY, an economics reporter for *The Wall Street Journal*, covered the Treasury Department during the tax-reform debate. He was a Morehead Scholar at the University of North Carolina, graduating in 1977, and he earned a master's degree in economics from the London School of Economics. Before joining the *Journal*'s Washington bureau in 1983, he worked for the *Congressional Quarterly* in Washington, the *Japan Economic Journal* in Tokyo, and *The Chattanooga Times*. He lives in Washington with his wife, Lori.